NATIONAL GEOGRAPHIC

TRAVELER

China

NATIONAL GEOGRAPHIC

TRAVELER

China

Damian Harper

National Geographic
Washington, D.C.

軒
Noble House
CHINESE
RESTAURANT
NEW KING TAI
JEWELLERY CO. LTD.
MARY BUILDING
Standard Chartered 渣打銀行
TAX FREE
Financial Centre 私人財務中心
Bank
柏茵花舍
PAK YAN FLORIST
NO: 11 PEKING RD.
JOSEPH KING S
NOBLE HOUSE
滬江大飯店
WU KONG
SHANGHAI RESTAURANT
代客泊車
PARKING SERVICE
16VALVE

Contents

Page 1: Novice Buddhist monk
Pages 2–3: Cormorant fishermen on the Li River
Left: Tsim Sha Tsui, Hong Kong

How to use this guide

See back flap for keys to text and map symbols.

The *National Geographic Traveler* brings you the best of China in text, pictures, and maps. Divided into three main sections, the guide begins with an overview of history and culture. Following are nine regional chapters with featured sites selected by the author for their particular interest. Each chapter opens with its own contents list.

The regions, and sites within them, are arranged geographically. Some regions are further divided into smaller areas. A map introduces each region, highlighting the featured sites. Walks and tours, plotted on their own maps, suggest routes for discovering an area. Features and sidebars give intriguing detail on history, culture, or contemporary life. A More Places to Visit page rounds off the regional chapters.

The final section, Travelwise, lists essential information for the traveler—pre-trip planning, getting around, money matters, emergencies, and a language guide—plus offers a selection of hotels, restaurants, shops, and entertainment.

To the best of our knowledge, all information is accurate as of the press date. However, it's always advisable to call ahead when possible.

83

Color coding

Each region is color coded for easy reference. Find the region you want on the map on the front flap, and look for the color flash at the top of the pages of the relevant chapter. Information in **Travelwise** is also color coded to each region.

Ancient Observatory
55 D3
Jianguomenwai Dajie
Open Tues.–Sun.
$
Jianguomen subway

Visitor information

Practical information for most sites is given in the side column (see key to symbols on back flap). The map reference gives the page number of the map and grid reference. Other details are address, telephone number, days closed, entrance charge in a range from $ (under $4) to $$$$$ (over $25), and nearest subway station for sites in Beijing. Other sites have information in italics and parentheses in the text.

TRAVELWISE

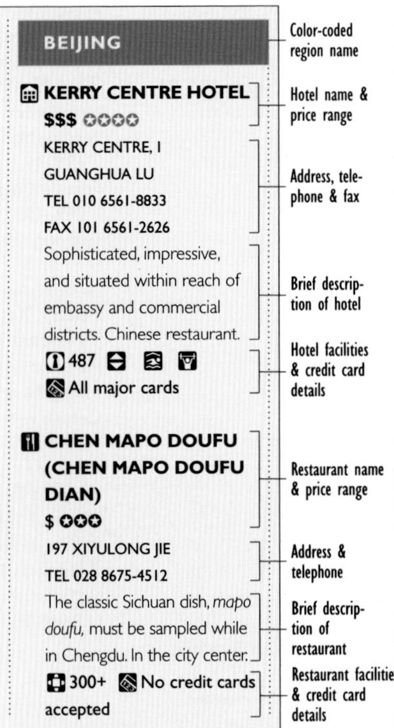

Hotel & restaurant prices

An explanation of the price ranges used in entries is given in the Hotels & Restaurants section (on p. 361).

REGIONAL MAPS

- A locator map accompanies each regional map and shows the location of that region in the country.
- Adjacent regions are shown, each with a page reference.

WALKING/BIKING TOURS

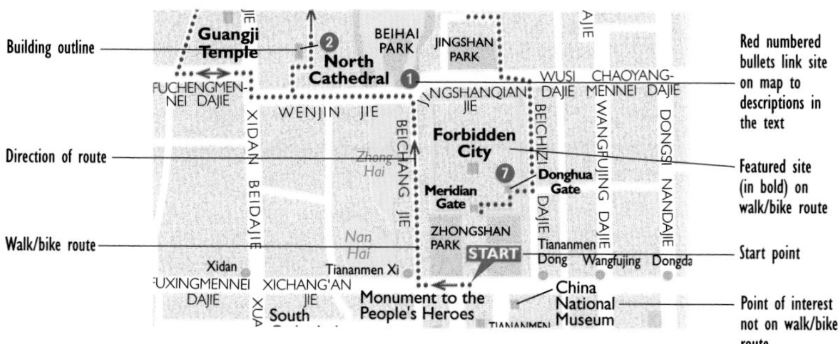

- An information box gives the starting and ending points, time and length of walk/bike tour, and places not to be missed along the route.
- Where alternative walks or rides are marked on the map, the detour route is shown in orange.

BOAT TOURS

- An information box provides details including starting and finishing points, time and length of tour, and places not to be missed along the route.

TRAVELER China

About the author

Educated at Winchester College and with an art history degree and six years of bookselling under his belt, Damian Harper pursued an interest in Chinese martial arts to London's School of Oriental and African Studies, graduating in 1995 with a degree in modern and classical Chinese. The four-year course took him to Beijing for a year where he met his Chinese wife, Dai Min. Damian has lived and worked in Beijing and Hong Kong, has traveled extensively through China and has co-authored several guides on China, Beijing and the Hong Kong region for Lonely Planet. He frequently returns to China with his wife and son.

History & culture

A colorful player in Chinese opera

China today

THE VAST ENIGMA THAT IS CHINA DEMANDS INCREASING ATTENTION. FOR centuries, the country seemed a remote, rarefied realm governed by inscrutable principles. Recent Western inroads explored the peripheries of several of its more familiar aspects: *fengshui, taiji,* Chinese medicine, and an enviable cuisine. Slowly, attitudes became more adventurous. China's numerous dialects were suddenly no longer the exclusive domain of eccentric Western scholars in smoking jackets and missionaries on Christianity's front-line. The distant, mysterious ways of Chinese government suddenly stared business speculators in the face. The Chinese world was rapidly opening up, and the West found itself in a rather unseemly rush to wedge itself in the door.

THE CHINESE

The Chinese are by no means homogeneous. Although Han Chinese account for 93 percent of the population, officially there are 55 other distinct ethnic minorities, from the Muslim Uighurs and Hui to the decorative Dai and Naxi of Yunnan Province.

It is predominantly the Han Chinese, however, who are guardians of the Chinese tradition and its etiquette, language, and culture. A loyal, proud, patriotic, stubborn, quick-witted, resourceful, conservative, and family-oriented group, they are opportunistically building a new China, flaws and all.

The Chinese often note, with resigned stoicism, that one Chinese person can turn a hand to almost anything, but bring a group together and they bungle it. As individuals, the Chinese are hardworking, resourceful, and entrepreneurial. As a group, they often squabble and fight over trifles. Socially, this makes them fun and gregarious; just listen to the noise that emanates from streetside restaurants. This sociability also makes them a lovable people. There is little that is hard-edged and technocratic about the Chinese; they are emotional, haphazard, and unpredictable. Efficiency seems beyond their grasp, but flashes of insight are commonplace. Torn between the poles of compulsion (Taoism) and restraint (Confucianism/ Communism), the Chinese constantly charm and surprise.

Chinese men can often be soft *(wenrou)* and women strong-willed *(jianqiang)*, creating an engaging balance. The hard-and-fast barriers between the sexes that can cause discomfort in countries such as Japan hardly exist here. A deep romantic vein runs through society, finding expression in literature, film, and music (see pp. 49–52).

Despite the push and shove on the streets, the Chinese are a courteous people whose sensibilities are propped up by decorum and

hospitality. This might not be clear as you unwillingly join the chaos ascending the bus in Guangzhou, but remember that this is still nominally a Communist society. All people are born equal so you need those hard-won skills of getting what you want, when you want, in the face of mass opposition. When you meet with politeness in China, however, it is often of the highest and most genuine kind.

MIDDLE KINGDOM

China calls itself the Middle Kingdom (Zhongguo). In ages past, the custodians of the Middle Kingdom savored the certainty that they occupied the space at the center of the world; other cultures simply revolved in barbarian fashion around its perimeter. A sense of destiny lingers temptingly in the name the Chinese still give their land.

The Chinese are also proud of a long, magnificent history and civilization, enjoying the reassurance that their culture has survived the accumulative erosion of millennia.

By the dawn of the 21st century, China had found itself back on the road to glory after the humiliations of the 19th and 20th centuries and the errors of the Communist ideologues. Economic reforms fueled the smoldering business savvy at the heart of the national identity. The opportunity for China to regain its posi-

The changing demographics of Beijing are evident everywhere. Here, a poster for a community in Xuanwu district shows anticipated changes.

tion in the world seemed an achievable reality, and the regeneration of their country is the goal that unites the Chinese. The goal is far less Marxist utopian than pure Capitalist narcissism. The country is designer-conscious, increasingly snobbish (snobbery was one of the first traits to escape the Cultural Revolution alive and kicking), materialistic, and enjoying its new guise.

An acute feeling of disorientation, however, brings a giddiness to today's China. This grand civilization has had its throne snatched by the United States and Japan. There is a feeling that the country has lost its way, for the communism that successfully exiled feudalism to the history books bred its own foibles. And the cunning about-face that allowed capitalism to re-emerge made those selfless sacrifices of previous generations meaningless. The land is as if without a map; it knows what it has departed but is unsure of the destination.

China is naturally curious about the world

Setting its sights far into the 21st century, the Shanghai International Convention Center exemplifies the city's remarkable economic boom.

outside, but Communist blinkering left it unprepared for the country's sudden engagement with the West. The outside *(guowai)* remains a distant universe piped in by television and advertising, where things are very different. The cars are faster, the clothes slicker, the morals softer, and the films better.

This makes certain aspects of China a bizarre pastiche of the West, with Oriental ingredients. Socialist architecture the land over is based on a Western utilitarian model, and the Western suit and tie are worn without a second thought. Shanghai increasingly resembles a city from some future dimension, while the ambition of the rest of the land is to look as much like Shanghai as is possible.

POLITICS & ECONOMY

China is undergoing a painful restructuring, with reform *(gaige)*, the engine of growth. The result is spectacular economic expansion and a dramatic increase in its prestige abroad.

The country is effectively trying to drag itself from the 1940s into the new millennium in half the time; the nation has been revitalized and the ball-and-chain of Marxist dogma jettisoned into history's trash can.

The Communist party is under siege from its reformist agenda, but the student idealism of the Tiananmen Square era (see pp. 41 and 64–5) has seemingly evaporated in the face of undergraduate enthusiasm for work opportunities at home and abroad. Economic advancement has become a personal as well as national goal. China now has a "Me" generation with only a dim notion of the relentless frugality of the Mao era (see pp. 38–41).

The baton of discontent has instead been handed to those not on the gravy train. The

country's losers include the unemployed, workers who slosh in large numbers from city to city in search of work, and peasants robbed of their land by big business and the state.

A healthy forum for political discussion does not exist, the Internet is zealously censored by cyber-police and dissent is ruthlessly quashed. The result is a stagnant political drama whose occasional change of cast is hobbled by an unchanging, drab script.

The behemoth of the Chinese government finds itself stranded on the shores of the new millennium; it must evolve further or perish. The oft-quoted argument that China is too large to be a democracy is debatable. India (population 1.1 billion) has achieved it and it could equally be argued that China is too large for effective Communist governance.

A Hani sorcerer on a water buffalo overlooks terraced slopes; the Hani speak a Tibetan-Burmese language.

TRAVEL IN CHINA

Visitors are making up for lost time in voyaging to China. An appreciation of the range of sights will help in your choice of route through this huge country.

Those on the Imperial China trail will be exploring the drama of the Forbidden City, the stately Imperial Tombs, and the Great Wall in and around Beijing. Further Imperial remnants can be found in Nanjing and Xi'an, and add a splash of grandeur to Shenyang.

China inherited marvelous architectural gems from its unfortunate historical liaison with the West. Guangzhou's Shamian Island is an outdoor museum, but the Bund in Shanghai has the last word. Gulangyu Island in Xiamen is a delight, but don't overlook the mountain retreats of Lushan and Jigongshan. Harbin boasts some extravagant Russian architecture, as does Dalian. Part of Germany has been delightfully re-created in Qingdao, Shandong Province, and Tianjin enjoys a

Although Hong Kong's return to China was celebrated in 1997, tensions still occasionally occur.

cosmopolitan nobility. Hong Kong, the former British colony, is an alluring jumble of modern architecture, Cantonese cooking, and pastoral, verdant islands. A small slice of Catholic Portuguese culture washes up on the south China shoreline with Macau.

China's sacred Taoist and Buddhist mountains lie strewn with traditional temples. Taishan is the country's holiest Taoist mountain, although secular Huangshan is more beautiful. Putuoshan is the only mountain island, suffused with the spirit of the Goddess of Mercy, Guanyin (see p. 178). Shine a light on Buddhist cave art at Dunhuang, Longmen, and Yungang, or gasp at the immensity of the Buddha at Leshan.

Adventurous travelers will be tempted by China's peripheral regions. The capital of

Tibet, Lhasa is an enticing mix of Buddhism, magic, and mystery. Xinjiang fosters an Islamic culture that immigrated via the old Silk Road. Yunnan Province borders Tibet, Myanmar (Burma), Laos, and Vietnam and is home to a quirky patchwork of ethnic communities. The sublime volcanic lake of Tianchi straddles the border with North Korea.

Those who have long been on the China travel circuit rest their feet in Dali and Yangshuo, the two most famous backpacker retreats in the land, with some of China's most magical scenery on all sides, as well as Lijiang.

GEOGRAPHY & CLIMATE

A journey to China throws open to visitors a geographical encyclopedia and a breathtaking exploration of diverse worlds. In the shrinking global village, traveling through China recalls the excitement of being an adventurer.

Geography

China is the world's third largest country, after Russia and Canada. Its most mountainous terrain rises in the west with Tibet and the mighty Himalaya, and in the northwest with the Kunlun, Tianshan, and Pamir mountain ranges. At 29,028 feet (8,847 m), Mount Everest is the world's highest peak. China's lowest point, the Turpan Depression (505 feet/154 m below sea level), is scooped out from the vast northwest. The land increasingly flattens out the farther east you travel.

As the great mountainous highland of west China acted as a huge barrier, Chinese expansion was also resisted by the forbidding deserts, including the Gobi and the parched Taklimakan (see p. 323) that punctuate the great plains of the north.

The vast majority (90 percent) of the population lives along China's coast or in the fertile lands that line the Yangtze River (Chang Jiang), the Yellow River (Huang He), the Pearl River (Zhu Jiang), and the Mekong River (Langcang Jiang). Most of the cultivable land is irrigated by these river systems, which course through China and bring fertility to a place that perennially suffers from cycles of water abundance and shortage. The Three Gorges Dam (see p. 146) on the Yangtze River aims to help reverse this tradition. China's coastline is an affluent bundle of SEZs (Special Economic Zones) and thriving ports. Two-thirds of the land is too mountainous, arid, or otherwise unsuitable for agriculture.

China's provinces & borderlands

China is composed of 22 provinces, four municipalities (Beijing, Tianjin, Chongqing, and Shanghai), five Autonomous Regions, and two Special Administrative Regions or SARs (Hong Kong and Macau). The "renegade province" of Taiwan is being heavily wooed into a reunion.

China's borderlands make for a fascinating cultural tapestry. North Korea, Russia, Mongolia, Tajikistan, Kirgizstan, Kazakstan, Afghanistan, Pakistan, Bhutan, India, Nepal, Myanmar (Burma), Laos, and Vietnam border the country. Many of its most colorful and engaging regions lie on its periphery, a cocktail of different cultures and ethnic minorities.

Chinese maps of China show an unlikely national boundary line lassoing the far-flung Spratly Islands (Nansha) to the south.

Climate

From the arid, desert expanses of the northwest to the humid south and to the ice-clamped winter seizure of the northeast, China has wide disparities of climate.

Winter in China north of the Yangtze River is typically cold, becoming increasingly frigid the farther north you go. The vast northwest alternates between summer's scorching aridity and the blistering chill of the winter months. Heilongjiang (Black Dragon River) Province in the northeast is stupefied by glacial temperatures come December, although enjoying hot summers. Winter in southern Yunnan Province and along China's southern coastline is comfortable, but regions of high elevation (most notably Tibet) can be dangerously cold.

Virtually the land over is hot in summer, with heavy monsoon rainfall (originating over the Pacific) in the south, southeast, and parts of the southwest. The gray skies over Shanghai continuously open, while the warm and heavy August rains in Beijing flush away the desert dust that clogs the roads. Warm, late summer rains in Xishuangbanna fall relentlessly. Summer in Xingjiang's Turpan, China's hottest and lowest spot, is punishing. The season also turns on the "three ovens" of China—

Chongqing, Wuhan, and Nanjing—which sweat under the steam of the Yangtze River.

South Yunnan Province, Guangxi, Guangdong, Hong Kong, Macau, and Hainan Island enjoy a tropical climate. Hong Kong's August humidity relentlessly clings like a warm, wet sheet until a typhoon blows into town. Typhoons can be constant hazards to the southern coastal regions in the summer. Much of Yunnan Province is unexpectedly fresh year-round.

FLORA & FAUNA

China supports a wide diversity of plants and animals reflecting the country's huge geographical disparities. A vast array of species is crowded into the tropical, forested regions of Yunnan Province, among them the snub-nosed monkey, the elephant, and the elusive Indochina tiger *(Panthera tigris corbetti)*. Hainan Island sustains shrinking pockets of tropical rain forest.

At the other extreme, the rugged northeast is a sanctuary of the Manchurian tiger *(Panthera tigris altaica)*, reindeer, bear, and other species suited to Siberian forest conditions. The northwest (former Chinese Turkestan) is a desiccated expanse of desert and hardy, drought-resistant plants, punctuated by green oases and pine-covered mountains. The region supports wild cats, leopards, camels, and hares, among others.

The plants and wildlife of China are suffering serious degradation, however, principally due to the country's rapid economic growth. China could be rushing toward environmental ruin, where acid rain, industrial pollution, and urban toxic palls threaten ecological catastrophe. The outlook is bleak and even officials have warned that China's pollution problems could quadruple by 2020. Hong Kong's harassed pink dolphins *(Sousa chinensis)* battle pollution, overfishing, and collisions with surface vessels. In mainland China, strict new regulations on logging are battling to preserve the country's shrinking forests. There is concern that a shift to a more green consciousness in China will prove to be too little, too late.

Many rivers and lakes steam with pollution, choking life. Industry has scarred the land and the encroachment of agriculture into habitats has further reduced plant and animal numbers. China needs to feed itself and lacks the arable land to do so; wildlife is consequently driven into the forested, mountainous, and desert regions.

The other threat comes from superstition and Chinese medicine. Exotic animals are trapped for their tendons, organs, and skin. Tigers, bears, pangolins, and deer are among the prized specimens.

The endearing panda (its Chinese name means "bearcat") struggles for survival.

Endangered animals include the giant salamander *(wawayu)*, the colossal Manchurian tiger, and the giant panda *(xiongmao)*, whose last refuge is in western Sichuan Province. China's cheerless zoos are generally not worth visiting except for a rare view of the giant panda.

There are a number of sanctuaries that are ideal for bird-watchers and for those in search of wilder destinations, including Hong Kong's Mai Po Marsh, the Zhalong Nature Reserve in Heilongjiang Province, and Qinghai Lake in Qinghai Province (but check on bird flu outbreaks). ■

Food & drink

AN INDISPENSABLE PART OF THE CHINA EXPERIENCE, CHINESE COOKING can be enjoyed in Chinatowns the world over; but if it's the real thing you want, it's mandatory you come to China. A history of famine coupled with a delight in food preparation has produced an obsession with mealtimes. Here eating is not just a necessity but an event.

MEATS

Historically, pork *(zhurou)* was the most popular meat, followed by chicken *(jirou);* beef (*niurou*) and lamb (*yangrou*) are eaten less due to their strong flavor, but Muslim Chinese and Mongolians (from Inner Mongolia) retain a strong affection for them. Fish (*yu*) is also popular.

A host of culinary exotica makes its way onto tables in China, including tortoises, sea snails, snakes, bear paws, cicadas, scorpions, and rats. If you are presented with a menu exclusively in Chinese, one way to avoid these is to look at the prices; exotic food tends to be more expensive. Dog meat *(gourou)* is also eaten, especially in the colder winter months.

OTHER FOODSTUFFS

Vegetables were traditionally served in greater abundance than meat for economic reasons, although this is changing. Popular vegetables include Chinese cabbage *(baicai/qingcai),* spinach *(bocai),* and potatoes *(tudou).* Apples *(pingguo),* oranges and tangerines *(juzi),* bananas *(xiangjiao),* pears *(lizi),* watermelons *(xigua),* and grapes *(putao)* are seasonal.

Tofu *(doufu)* is eaten for its versatility and as a meat substitute. Rice *(baifan)* accompanies most meals, usually in small bowls. Peanuts *(huasheng)* are often served at the start of a meal and feature in a range of dishes. Watermelon seeds *(guazi)* are also widely eaten, and pistachios *(kaixinguo)* and cashew nuts *(yaoguo)* can be found in most shops and supermarkets.

REGIONAL CUISINE

Four groups divide the major atlas of cuisine: northern, southern, eastern, and western.

Beijing *(jingcai)* and Shandong *(lucai)* typify northern cooking, embracing salty flavors and wheat-based staples. Pork-filled dumplings *(jiaozi)*, dipped in soya sauce and rice vinegar, are enormously popular, as are noodles and steamed bread *(mantou)*. The most famous Beijing dish is Peking duck, a rich preparation of oily duck flesh, plum sauce, and onion, which you eat rolled into a wafer-thin pancake.

The Cantonese revel in this flaming type of wok cooking, called *wokhei*.

Stir-frying is the hallmark of southern Cantonese *(yuecai)* cooking, along with boiling and steaming. Lightly fried dim sum snacks and pastries are wheeled around restaurants, served on plates and steamers, and dipped in an array of sauces. Chaozhou cuisine, another southern style, is sweet and based on seafood.

Eastern cooking is typified by Shanghai cuisine, reveling in soups and seafood. Quite oily dishes include "drunken chicken" and *xiaolong bao* (small parcels of meat wrapped in pastry).

Sichuan, the heartland of western Chinese cooking, introduces a galaxy of searing dishes. In Sichuan cooking (*chuancai*), an idiosyncratic herb called *huajiao* numbs the mouth, while the remaining herbs and spices blister the taste buds. Famous Sichuan dishes include *suancai yu*, a pickled vegetable and fish soup, and *shuizhu roupian*, in which slices of pork cook slowly in a sea of chili oil and cabbage leaves. Hunan food *(xiangcai)* and Hubei cuisine are also renowned for their fiery dishes.

DRINK

With meals, the Chinese drink beer *(pijiu)*, wine *(putaojiu)*, or a strong, clear spirit called *baijiu* (literally "white wine"). *Baijiu* is a short sharp shock of a drink, the most famous of which comes from Maotai in Guizhou Province. *Erguotou* (literally "two pot head") is one of the strongest at 65 percent proof.

Tea *(cha)* is drunk everywhere in China, especially at mealtimes. It comes in various guises, including chrysanthemum tea (*juhua cha*), Western tea *(hong cha)*, green tea *(lü cha)*, and the lovely eight treasures tea *(babao cha)*. The latter is a potpourri of flower petals and buds, sweetened with rock sugar.

Coffee *(kafei)* is not a popular drink outside of cafés, and although most restaurants have it on the menu, it is likely to be instant. The Chinese also enjoy drinking boiled, hot water *(baikai shui)*.

Fruit juice *(guozhi)* is widely drunk, and mineral water *(kuangquan shui)* can be found all over the country. ■

History of China

CHINA'S HISTORY IS A CAPTIVATING CHRONICLE THAT REACHES DEEP INTO the past to dim and obscure origins. Exploring the strata of this profound history, an epic tale emerges, peopled by a cast of savage tyrants and shrewd opportunists who steered this huge country to the present.

MYTHS & LEGENDS

Some historians earmark 6000 B.C. as the dawn of Chinese civilization. Ancient legends speak of Pangu who created the world, dividing heaven and Earth. Three divinities successively created humans and brought them animal husbandry, agriculture, and the medicinal properties of plants. The first, Fuxi, formulated the Eight Trigrams of the *I-Ching*, known in English as the *Book of Changes* (an ancient book for predicting the future). They were succeeded by other mythological beings. The Yellow Emperor is accorded the greatest respect as the primeval ancestor. Also regarded as the founder of Taoism (see p. 42), among his many contributions to Chinese civilization, the mythical emperor invented the boat, improved cattle breeding, and introduced bamboo to China. Chinese myth also recalls how the Great Yu harnessed the floods and tamed the Yangtze River, leaving Chang Jie the task of inventing words.

XIA & SHANG DYNASTIES

Archaeological evidence adds credence to the existence of the primordial Xia dynasty (circa 2205–1766 B.C.), although a much larger body of historical evidence relating to the ensuing Shang dynasty (circa 1766–1122 B.C.) survives. Finds reveal an agricultural society whose domain reached along the Yellow River basin from Xi'an to Shandong, buffered by the Yangtze River to the south. This area is the heartland of Chinese civilization.

Shang dynasty society acknowledged a single leader who was also a religious figure. Rulers were both military commanders and leaders of community activities. Succession could be from brother to brother, or from father to son. As this society became increasingly sophisticated, the king delegated more

Smashed terra-cotta heads at Xi'an mark the accomplishment and turbulence of the Middle Kingdom.

China's dynasties

Xia ca 2205–1766 B.C.
Shang ca 1766–1122 B.C.
Zhou
Western ca 1122–771 B.C.
Eastern ca 771–256 B.C.
Qin 221–206 B.C.
Han
Western 206 B.C.–A.D. 9
Xin (Wang Mang) A.D. 9–23
Eastern A.D. 25–220
Three Kingdoms period 220–265
Jin
Western Jin 265–316
Eastern Jin 317–420
Northern
Northern Wei 386–534
Eastern Wei 534–550
Western Wei 535–557
Northern Qi 550–577
Northern Zhou 557–581

Southern
Song 420–479
Qi 479–502
Liang 502–557
Chen 557–589

Sui 581–618

Tang 618–907

Five Dynasties
Later Liang 907–923
Later Tang 923–936
Later Jin 936–947
Later Han 947–950
Later Zhou 951–960

Song
Northern 960–1127
Southern 1127–1279

Yuan 1279–1368

Ming 1368–1644

Qing 1644–1911

Republic of China 1911–1949 (maintained in Taiwan)

People's Republic of China 1949–present

and more tasks to a cadre of officials. Much of the king's authority was derived from his ancestors, who were worshiped and consulted in matters relating to affairs of state. The practice of divination (to gauge the seasons, farming, warfare, etc.) using inscriptions on oracle bones shows that writing had evolved.

Tamed elephants were reportedly used in large building works, indicating advanced techniques in construction. The city of Anyang, in Henan Province, was built on the site of Yin, the last city of the Shang. The dynasty is also synonymous with its fabulous bronze art, notably the ferocious and mysterious animal-like *taotie* designs embellishing vessels (see p. 181). Under the Shang, industry and trade must have flourished; the term "Shang" is still found today in connection with business *(shangren)* and commerce *(shangye)*.

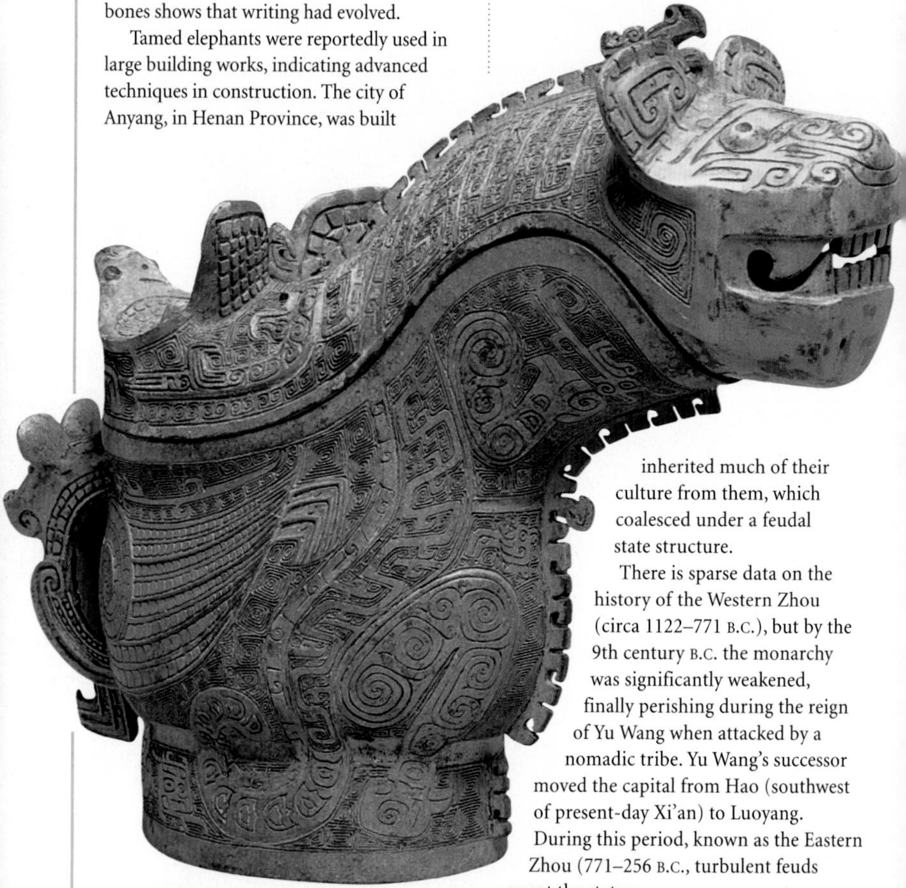

Shang dynasty bronzes are noted for their fantastic and elaborate designs.

ZHOU DYNASTY

The house of Zhou, whose name frequently appears in Shang oracle bone inscriptions, eventually overthrew the Shang. They differed little from their Shang predecessors and inherited much of their culture from them, which coalesced under a feudal state structure.

There is sparse data on the history of the Western Zhou (circa 1122–771 B.C.), but by the 9th century B.C. the monarchy was significantly weakened, finally perishing during the reign of Yu Wang when attacked by a nomadic tribe. Yu Wang's successor moved the capital from Hao (southwest of present-day Xi'an) to Luoyang. During this period, known as the Eastern Zhou (771–256 B.C., turbulent feuds swept the states.

PRE-QIN PHILOSOPHICAL FOUNDATIONS

Historians generally divide the Eastern Zhou into the Spring and Autumn (771–476 B.C.) and the Warring States (476–221 B.C.) periods, a time also termed Pre-Qin. This violent period forged, more than any other epoch, the philosophical culture of China that survives today. Confucius (551–479 B.C.) was a product of his times (see pp. 126–27), with constant war and bloodshed urging him to develop a system of social behavior that would edify and instruct. His model was the *junzi,* or gentleman, who was upright, loyal, and civilized. Confucius's intellectual successor, Mencius (372–289 B.C.) further championed his philosophy, emphasizing the concept of the Mandate of Heaven. This held that Heaven could confiscate the mandate to rule from a corrupt or bad ruler, through rebellion or withdrawal of support by the people.

Incipient Taoism found a mouthpiece during these times with the sage Laozi (circa 580–500 B.C.), whose mystical reflections on the cosmos he distilled into a book of seminal importance, the *Daode Jing (The Classic of the Way and its Power).* His musings were more fancifully presented by the insightful allegories of storyteller-cum-philosopher Zhuangzi (circa 369–286 B.C.). Other philosophical ideas arose, chief among these being those of the Mohists under Mozi (circa 468–376 B.C.), who promulgated a doctrine of universal love—*jian'ai*—despite being keen military strategists. The Legalist school under Han Feizi (circa 280–233 B.C.) also engineered an influential realpolitic philosophy of law fused with statecraft.

QIN DYNASTY

The constant warring between states was halted by the inexorable rise of the state of Qin, which unified China's fragments. Qin was ultimately to lend its name to the foreign word for the Middle Kingdom: China. Qinshi Huangdi was its first, terrible emperor, engineer of mass death and oppression against his countrymen. His short and sharp reign lasted from 221 to his death in 210 B.C. During these years, he instigated a purge of Confucian scholars *(kengru)* and a great burning of the books *(fenshu),* reducing most of China's literature to carbon.

The emperor also led China on a course of territorial expansion, which necessitated the linking up of previously built earthen ramparts into the Great Wall to prevent barbarian incursions. Another lavish building project was the extravagant underground mausoleum of the terra-cotta warriors outside Xi'an. Under Qinshi Huangdi, the Chinese script and weights and measures were standardized.

Provincial rebellion against oppressive Qin power (principally in the hands of Chao Kao) led to a massacre of the Qin army by Xiang Yu, who was in turn defeated by Liu Bang, founder of the Han dynasty.

HAN DYNASTY

The Han preserved much of the state structure instituted by the Qin dynasty before it. The 400-year dynasty did so much to define Chinese culture that the character "Han" is still used to refer to China (e.g., Hanzu: the Chinese race; Hanyu: the Chinese language).

The first emperor of the Qin dynasty was a ruthless tyrant, but he bequeathed China the legacy of the terra-cotta warriors.

The dynasty is divided into the Western Han (206 B.C.–A.D. 9) and the Eastern Han (A.D. 25–220). Separating the two was the short rule of the Xin, who seized power with the usurpation of the throne by minister Wang Mang at a time of growing incompetence in the Han court.

The Western Han had the massive task of rescuing the country from decline and consolidating the state; in its structure, the Han state was closely modeled on that of the Qin.

Confucianism effectively infiltrated the bureaucracy after recovering from the Qin edict outlawing it, adding a veneer of morality to otherwise coercive government.

The Eastern Han was brought to its knees by social discontent, which spawned the Yellow Turban Sect (a secret Taoist group) uprising. In the ensuing chaos, the Han dynasty collapsed under the pressure of feuding warlords. The *Shiji,* or *Records of the Historian,* by Si Maqian (circa 145–85 B.C.) is the most notable literary legacy of the period. The book is an epic record of the rise and fall of the great ruling families of China.

PERIOD OF DIVISION

The disintegration of the Eastern Han marked the end of the centralized state. For almost 400 years the country was mired in incessant war and division. Three states arose from the rubble of the Han—Wei, Shu, and Wu—known as the Three Kingdoms (A.D. 220–

265). They are romantically recalled in the Ming dynasty novel *The Romance of the Three Kingdoms,* while in reality their shared history was stained with blood. Each state considered itself the true successor of the Han dynasty. Wei conquered Shu in 263, which was soon followed by the birth of the Jin dynasty and the conquest of Wu. The country was temporarily reunited, but it soon unraveled again under attack from the "barbarian" Xiongnu and other nomad invaders. The Jin lost

The Great Wall *(wanli changcheng)* was built to protect China from northern invaders. It ultimately failed spectacularly.

control of North China and moved the capital to Nanking, prompting a huge migration south.

In the fifth century, the Tuoba (a Turkic tribe) took control of North China, establishing the Northern Wei (A.D. 386–534) while rapidly adopting the customs and ways of the

Chinese (as the Mongols and Manchus did after them). The country was effectively divided into what is known as the Northern and Southern dynasties, with the Northern Wei and its successors in the north, and the Eastern Jin and the states that succeeded it in the south.

Social disorder split the Northern Wei into Eastern Wei (534–550) and Western Wei (535–557), whose Tuoba rulers soon lost power, hatching the Northern Zhou (557–581) and the Northern Qi (550–577). The two new states indulged in a despicable period of immorality and bad government.

In the south, a succession of generals forged a series of dynasties on the backs of incessant war and death.

Buddhist beginnings

The period of division was manifestly evil and chaotic, but, amazingly, a rich culture flowered from the mess. Taoism responded to a heightened spirituality of the times, while the famous Seven Sages of the Bamboo Grove, a group of intellectuals, got together to discuss Taoist philosophy, write poetry, and drink wine. A more metaphysical mood reigned, bringing a deep and intense searching for meaning in a violent world. Buddhism flourished, as did Buddhist art, including the entrancing Wei Buddhist sculpture. Captured on the faces of bodhisattvas and Buddhas (see p. 72) of this period is a mesmerizing transcendence and divinity; the most famous extant caves with art from this era are at Yungang, Longmen, and Dunhuang. The Taoist poet and hermit Tao Yuanming fashioned beautiful verse.

SUI DYNASTY

The fleeting Sui dynasty (581–618) again unified China when Yang Qian overthrew the ruler of the Northern Zhou in 581 and began reincorporating the states in the south. The dynasty prospered under its first ambitious emperor, Wendi. The second emperor, Yangdi, however, indulged in mammoth building projects that drained the treasury coffers and incensed the peasants. The Grand Canal (see pp. 162–63) was extended with the help of forced labor. Luoyang was extravagantly rebuilt, as were sections of the Great Wall, all at enormous cost. A disastrous war against Korea and a subsequent humiliation by the Eastern Turks further infuriated the luckless peasants, and Yangdi was strangled by a member of his entourage in 618.

TANG DYNASTY

The Chinese consider the Tang (618–907) the most glorious of dynasties. Hatched by an official of the Sui dynasty, Li Yuan, the Tang quickly reasserted Chinese influence over Korea and Central Asia. The civil service developed under the aegis of neo-Confucianism, a philosophy that had been eclipsed by Taoism and Buddhism in preceding dynasties. The Confucian classics-based, conservative examination system (see p. 83) for recruiting civil servants was set in amber.

To avoid the mistakes of earlier dynasties, appeasement of the peasants became policy through a system of land equalization. The early Tang saw impressive economic growth, which encouraged manufacturing and foreign trade. The dynasty also wielded considerable influence over Central Asia and saw growing relations with Tibet. Ample cultural commerce with Japan led to the adoption of the Chinese writing system there.

Fruitful contact with other cultures along the Silk Road (see p. 310) was fostered by a tolerant policy toward foreigners, resulting in a sense of cosmopolitanism. A number of religions, including Nestorianism, Manichaeism, Islam, and Judaism made their way to China, but none of them flourished as successfully as that other main religious import, Buddhism.

China's sole true empress, the notorious Wu Zetian (or Wu Hou) reigned during the Tang. A wicked and deceitful manipulator, she rose from imperial concubine to empress and reigned from 698 to 705, when she was forced to abdicate. Buddhism flourished under her tutelage, largely due to her penchant for Buddhist monks. Her story is fascinating: A soothsayer at the court warned the emperor not to admit any woman with the surname Wu to the palace, for such a woman would destroy the Tang dynasty. Wu Zetian was infuriated by attempts to sideline her and set her sights on the royal throne, which she eventually seized.

No appointment is necessary for dental treatment in Hotan.

WORLD CUP

The reign that followed, under Xuanzong (712–756), is often referred to as the Tang's golden age. However, the dynasty was weakened severely by defeat in battle against the Arabs in 751 (which resulted in a spate of successful incursions by the Tibetans), and the revolt of An Lushan, a Turkish general. The rebellion was eventually crushed, but the state's control was greatly diminished in the process.

The Tang monarchy then came under the sway of the eunuchs, and several emperors were poisoned. The Buddhists encountered a period of repression, the economy nose-dived, and the peasants, exploited to the hilt, rose once more in revolt. The Tang dynasty was leveled by rebellion, and China fell into the hands of warlords.

Tang culture was a high point in China's history, especially during the reign of Xuanzong. Its poetry reached an unsurpassed zenith, with the poets Li Bai and Du Fu poised at the very summit. Han Yu is renowned principally for his marvelous prose writing. Printing in China dates from the Tang dynasty and the world's first known printed book, the *Diamond Sutra,* was found stored away at Dunhuang (see pp. 326-27). Buddhist art also reached its peak in this era, but anti-Buddhist repression destroyed many examples. A selection of the statues at Longmen and Dunhuang survive as a record of this fabulous period. Painting also matured to a form that paved the way for the success of the ensuing Song dynasty.

凡欲讀經先念淨口業真言遍
脩唎 脩唎 摩訶脩唎 脩脩唎 娑婆訶
奉請除災金剛 奉請辟毒金剛 奉請黃隨求金剛
奉請白淨水金剛 奉請赤聲金剛 奉請定除厄金剛
奉請紫賢金剛 奉請大神金剛

The world's oldest printed book—a Tang dynasty copy of the *Diamond Sutra,* excavated from Dunhuang—is now at the British Museum.

FIVE DYNASTIES & THE SONG DYNASTY

Following the Tang dynasty came a period of division, with decentralized power in the hands of a number of states. The ephemeral dynasties in the north of the land charted an oppressive rule alongside ten kingdoms from 907 to 960, a period often called the Five Dynasties.

China was reunited by Zhao Kuangyin, commander of the Imperial Guard of the

Later Zhou (the last of the Five Dynasties), under a new dynasty: the Song (960–1279). This dynasty is generally divided into the Northern Song (960–1127) and the Southern Song (1127–1279).

The administration was rebuilt and the official examination system resurrected (see p. 83); the economy flourished. Paper money was invented and a period of reform (*bianfa*) was instigated by Wang Anshi (1021–1086).

The Song, however, were under constant threat from attacks from the outside. The Jurchen, marauding invaders from the north, forced the northern court south after the capture of the capital, Kaifeng, in 1126. The capital was moved to Linan (present-day Hangzhou), while the Jurchen established the Jin dynasty (1125–1234) in the north. The Jin managed to extract a vast amount of tribute from the Song in return for peace, and the Huai River was deemed the dividing line between the two. The Southern Song still managed to progress, despite the Jurchen presence to the north, and a newfound prosperity emerged in agriculture, foreign commerce, and manufacturing.

This glittering period, however, was soon eclipsed by the Mongol menace. Under Ghenghis Khan, the Mongols devised a fanatical form of scorched-earth warfare that obliterated all in their path. The Jin fell under the Mongols' boot, and the wealth of the Song lay before them. The naive Song had allied with the Mongols against the Jurchen, only to see their new allies turn about and muster on their borders. The Mongols devastated the Song and, in 1279, imposed foreign rule on the whole of China for the first time.

The greatest cultural legacy of the Song lies in its landscape painting, its *ci* poetry, and a thriving neo-Confucian philosophy.

YUAN DYNASTY—THE MONGOLS

The victorious Mongols held sway over a vast domain from Asia to Eastern Europe; their control over China is known historically as the Yuan dynasty (1279–1368). When in China, they made Beijing (Dadu) their capital, while still reserving a capital of their own in Inner Mongolia.

Despite ruling with a determination to exert Mongol control to every corner of China, the foreigners set about administering the empire with a modicum of skill and foresight. The Grand Canal was rebuilt, roads were renovated, and foreign trade began to mushroom. After contact with Europe increased, Venetian traveler Marco Polo visited China and later penned his famous travelogue.

The Mongols imposed their own culture on

The wine-loving poet Li Bai drowned while toasting the moon's reflection in a lake.

the Chinese in the form of an uncompromising and oppressive regime. China was divided into four groups, with the Mongols at the top, their foreign allies below them, the Chinese and other inhabitants of North China further down, with the last rung of the ladder reserved for southern Chinese.

The Mongols used China as a springboard to launch costly attacks on the surrounding regions, including Vietnam and Japan. Again, a rebellious peasantry fired up by agrarian crises overturned the dynasty. Directed by Buddhist secret sects, such as the White Lotus and the Red Turbans, rebellious foment cohered under the leadership of Zhu

Yuanzhang (*R.*1363–67). He overthrew the overlords who were by then squabbling among themselves, and established the Ming—or the Bright—dynasty.

The destruction wrought by the Mongol invasion of China brought huge losses of Chinese art, but despite the upheaval painting continued to refine in technique, especially in landscapes (see pp. 45–48). The dynasty also nurtured the development of Chinese drama and the novel.

MING DYNASTY

Zhu Yuanzhang, ruling under the name of Hongwu, established the capital of the Ming dynasty (1368–1644) at Nanjing (Southern Capital), constructing his palace there and surrounding the city with huge walls.

Hongwu (*R.*1368–1398) effectively ruled China but quickly slid into despotism, displaying a savagery matched only by his severe paranoia. The problem of succession on his death led to civil war, and the throne

ultimately went not to his grandson (his chosen successor) but to the Prince of Yen, who seized power and ruled as the emperor Yongle (*R.*1403–1424). He moved the Ming capital to Beijing and built the Forbidden City (see pp. 56–62).

Europeans, who were later to have a huge effect on the history of the Qing dynasty, began to arrive. The Portuguese captured Macau in Guangdong Province, the English arrived in Canton (Guangzhou), and the Jesuits, led by

Hoping to absorb wisdom, pilgrims crawl beneath stacks of sacred Buddhist texts at Pelkor Chode Monastery in Gyangze.

Matteo Ricci (1557–1610) in the 1580s, tried to graft Catholicism to China's register of religions.

The Mongols continued to harass China on the northern borders, and sections of the Great Wall were rebuilt. The Japanese invasion of Korea (a vassal state) during the reign of Wanli (*R.*1573–1620) prompted a tardy and costly Ming military response.

By the 15th century, the eunuchs were again manipulating the emperors like puppets at the palace. Eunuch domination of state policy often brought the empire close to ruin. Ming authority had degraded in the face of peasant rebellion, and the last Ming emperor hanged himself from a tree on Jingshan Hill in

This Ming Chinese porcelain teapot dates from the 15th-century.

Beijing as rebels swarmed through the capital.

The Ming dynasty's chief cultural advancement was the novel, which was welcomed by a growing audience. *Shuihu Zhuan (The Water Margin)* and the *Sanguo Yanyi (Romance of the Three Kingdoms)* narrated historical stories in an accessible vernacular language, while eroticism found a voice in *Jin Pingmei.* Much admired blue-and-white Ming dynasty porcelains built upon a style fashioned in the Yuan dynasty under Middle East influence.

QING DYNASTY—MANCHUS

A massive famine in Shaanxi Province in 1626 ignited a vast peasant rebellion that coincided with a growing threat to China from their northern neighbors, the Manchus, descendants of the Jin dynasty Jurchen. With the rebels failing to unite against the Manchus, the northern invaders slipped in to establish a new dynasty. From their triumphant entry into Beijing in 1644, the Manchus took four decades to completely wrest power from the disparate Ming elements.

The fragmented Manchus had been united by Nurhachi under a banner system and forged into a formidable fighting force. They first established the Qing (Clear) dynasty in 1636 in northeast China's Manchuria. The banner system *(baqi)*, a military and governmental organization that regimented the upper echelons of society, was maintained; it formed the basis of the state, but many Ming officials were allowed to keep their positions to appease the Chinese. The overlords sought to impose their own stamp on China, however, and top posts were reserved for those of Manchu stock.

Male adult Chinese were forced to wear the *bianzi*, or long braided ponytail, to mark their subservience to the Manchus, while Manchu men were forbidden to marry Chinese women. Manchu women, moreover, never emulated the Chinese custom of binding their feet. With time, however, the Manchus became sinicized.

The early Qing was an auspicious period and an era with some of the most competent rulers China has seen. The Kangxi, Yongzheng, and Qianlong emperors represent a golden age in Chinese history. Under the Kangxi emperor (1661–1722), treaties were made with Russia and the empire was expanded to include Outer Mongolia, Tibet, Nepal, and chunks of Central Asia. Mongol and Tibetan leaders were courted by way of imperial patronage of Tibetan Buddhist temples, such as the Lama Temple in Beijing. The Kangxi emperor oversaw the construction of the Tibetan-style imperial summer retreat at Chengde and encouraged Jesuit tutelage in the sciences, principally mathematics and astronomy (see p. 83).

The reigns of Yongzheng (*R.*1723–1735) and Qianlong (*R.*1736–1795) saw growth in industry and commerce, and healthy patronage of the arts and sciences. Most important, tax reforms and flood control projects pacified the insurgent peasant population. China had become weakened, however, by a series of campaigns in Central Asia and the southwest.

Western encroachment

The greatest challenge to imperial authority arrived in the 19th century, once more from outside the empire. The technologically advanced foreign powers, including Britain, France, and Germany, had become increasingly bewitched by China's great riches and weakness. A rapid encroachment on China became the objective of the West, which sought to establish trade links.

The Qianlong emperor had rebuffed the overtures of the British Lord Macartney and his embassy at Chengde (see p. 116) in the closing years of the 18th century, a precedent that cast them into opposition. The belligerent mood of 19th-century relations with the foreign powers resulted in wars ending in defeat for China, along with equally humiliating treaties.

The result of the first Opium War (1840–42) led to Hong Kong being parceled off to the British with the Treaty of Nanking. The second Opium War (1856–1860) and further treaties saw packets of land slide into the clutches of Britain, Japan, France, and Russia. China was in danger of being carved up like a turkey.

China's woes were manifold. The Middle Kingdom was not equipped to deal with the sophistication of the Western model of warfare. The situation could have been saved by modernization of its military and government institutions, but conservative elements in the Qing court blocked the way. The West was treated by the Chinese court with a mixture of awe and contempt, a neurotic formula that led to insoluble paralysis.

Mutual mistrust and xenophobia led to constant confrontation between China and the West.

Nineteenth-century China was also split by internecine strife. Popular anti-Qing unrest flared up afresh with the hugely damaging proto-Christian Taiping Rebellion of 1850–1864 (see pp. 158–59) that leveled numerous cities and left millions dead. China's plentiful smoking ruins were further turned over by the Nien Rebellion (1853–1868) and a massive Muslim rebellion in the northwest (1862–1873). The Taiping, in particular, almost brought the Manchu dynasty to its knees.

Fall of the Qing

China's stagnation continued further under Empress Dowager Cixi (1835–1908), a former concubine who appropriated power through luck and deceit. Famed for her lengthy, clawlike fingernails, Cixi liked to pose as Guanyin, goddess of mercy, lending her the epithet the "Old Buddha." Behind the divine facade,

A photograph of the Manchu empress Cixi depicts her as a goddess.

however, lay the reality of an inept tyrant. Her nephew, Emperor Guangxu, was nominally sovereign, but in reality Cixi held the reins of power. The catastrophic Sino-Japanese War (1894–95) fueled China's shame. The Reform Movement (1895–98), which tried to shoehorn in modern ideas, failed and led to Cixi imprisoning Emperor Guangxu (who sympathized with the movement) in the Summer Palace.

By the end of the century, the tectonic collisions between Chinese and Western culture erupted in the Boxer Rebellion (see pp. 112–13) in 1900, signaling the last gasp of the old order. Emperor Guangxu and Empress Dowager Cixi died within a day of each other in 1908, leaving the juvenile Emperor Puyi in charge of China at the tender age of two. The dynasty collapse around him in the successful uprising of 1911, which installed the Republic.

MODERN CHINA

The failure of both the Boxer Rebellion to expel the "foreign devils" from China and the fruitless Reform Movement of 1898 signaled a paradigm shift in the Chinese consciousness. It had become increasingly evident to all Chinese that the country must modernize. This grudging awareness, however, came too late.

Among the torch bearing Chinese intellectuals who were committed to reform was Sun Yat-sen (1866–1925), also called Sun Zhongshan, the pioneering father of Chinese republicanism. Sun Yat-sen melded together principles of nationalism, democracy, and the people's livelihood into a formula for his vision of a modern China.

As the Qing dynasty finally crumbled with the 1911 revolution, Sun returned from America, where he was raising funds in Denver, to be elected provisional president of the Republic of China. His position was opportunistically wrested from his grasp by the general Yuan Shikai, a figure who had helped light the bonfire under the failed Reform Movement of 1898.

Yuan set himself up as emperor in 1915 but died in 1916, effectively leaving most of China in the hands of feuding warlords, while Sun Yat-sen retained power in Guangzhou. The subsequent dislocation would survive until the Communist seizure of power in 1949.

ARRIVAL OF COMMUNISM

With China in disarray, the Nationalist Party (Kuomintang or KMT) maintained its republican ethos under the leadership of Sun Yat-sen. On Sun's death in 1925, the mantle of the KMT passed to Chiang Kai-shek (1888–1975), also called Jiang Jieshi. The KMT's goal was to vanquish the warlords in the north of China and unite the land under a Nationalist government.

Republicanism, however, was not the only credo fomenting new ideas. Experimentation with foreign political concepts had encouraged the formation of the Chinese Communist Party in Shanghai in 1921 (see p. 181).

With Soviet encouragement, the Communists decided to unite with the KMT in 1923. But when Chiang Kai-shek replaced Sun Yat-sen, he dissolved the union and blackballed the Communists, seduced by the hope of establishing a capitalist state on his own terms. His northern expedition against the warlords in 1926, which was aided and abetted by Shanghai moneymakers, led to an infamous massacre of Shanghai workers and Communists. Harried, expelled, and radicalized, the Communists undertook to survive and take control by other means.

The northern expedition persisted in its course and installed a government in Beijing, but large swathes of China remained under the control of despotic warlords. Many Communists, led by the young Mao Zedong and Zhu De, retreated to the countryside and mountains in Jiangxi and Hunan Provinces. Mao chose a rural-based revolutionary formula directed at China's peasantry, as opposed to urban-based centers of communism.

THE LONG MARCH

Chiang Kai-shek, whose hatred of the Communists eclipsed that of the warlords, launched a series of punitive campaigns that finally evicted Mao and his combatants from their mountain stronghold. To escape destruction, in October 1934 Mao and his force of 100,000 men and women embarked on the arduous 6,000-mile (9,650 km) Long March. He intended to find a new and more secure base in Shaanxi Province from which to wage his "people's war." A year later, and after massive detours, fewer than 10,000 people struggled into Yan'an and the mountains of Shaanxi Province; the rest had fallen victim to a mixed bag of Nationalist attacks, illness, and desertion. The marchers who had set out from Jiangxi had traversed 11 provinces.

En route, Mao Zedong had won a war of wills over the direction of Communist resistance and had risen to the unchallenged position of Communist leader, asserting his authority at the famous Party Conference of Zunyi in Guizhou Province. The experience also allowed other veterans who would have great influence on the shape of the party—Zhu De, Zhou Enlai, Lin Biao, Liu Shaoqi, and Deng Xiaoping—to assert themselves.

WAR WITH JAPAN

A divided China failed to escape the predatory attentions of Japan, which swiftly occupied Manchuria in 1931. The last Qing emperor, Puyi, was ignobly installed as puppet sovereign of Manchukuo, the renamed kingdom of Manchuria, with Changchun as his capital.

The Japanese, however, were only clearing their throats for a more treasured objective. They invaded China in 1937, in the face of a shaky alliance between the Communists and the KMT. The Japanese advance was swift and successful, swallowing up much of north and east China. Shanghai fell and the citizens of Nanjing were subjected to the horrors of the infamous Rape of Nanjing.

Republican leader Sun Yat-sen's vision of a modern, democratic China sadly failed to materialize.

The KMT fled west, halting temporarily at Wuhan and then going on to Sichuan to establish their new capital at Chongqing. Obsessive hatred of the Communists blunted KMT resistance against the invaders, and an ambivalent, spineless mood reigned. The

Mao Zedong exercised a powerful spell over the hearts of the Chinese people.

Communists, however, grew in strength, organization, and mobility. The great tragedy was China's lack of a firm common front against the forces of the "island kingdom."

A second alliance between Communists and Nationalists failed, and the entry of the United States into World War II after the Japanese attack on Pearl Harbor coalesced American and KMT interests. The United States supported the KMT effort with weapons and money, but the Nationalists, riddled with corruption, still lacked the patriotic resolve to wholeheartedly resist the Japanese. Japan's unqualified surrender in 1945, after the destruction of Hiroshima and Nagasaki, again left China victim to civil war. The Communists made startling gains, using captured KMT equipment (largely supplied by the United States) and defecting troops.

THE PEOPLE'S REPUBLIC

Mao Zedong inaugurated the People's Republic of China from Tiananmen Gate in Beijing on October 1, 1949. The KMT troops were forced to withdraw to Taiwan, where the Nationalists remain to this day (before they left, the Nationalists took China's gold reserves and palace treasures with them).

For the Communists the jubilation of victory was accompanied by the daunting task of national construction, as the country lay in tatters. But land reform, new laws, nationalization, mass projects, and the mobilization of the people led to a rise in optimism during the 1950s. The Korean War (1950–53), however, was a period of uncertainty and nationalism. In industry, the Soviet model of five-year plans *(wunian jihua)* was copied, while a collectivist agenda governed rural production.

HUNDRED FLOWERS MOVEMENT TO THE CULTURAL REVOLUTION

China was a one-party state but moves to restrict intellectual freedom were ambivalent. The confident Mao sanctioned the Hundred Flowers Movement (1957), which encouraged criticism of policy from intellectuals. His dictum "Let a hundred flowers bloom, let a hundred schools contend" opened the floodgates to an outpouring of criticism for which the party was unprepared. Mao instigated an anti-rightist campaign that branded intellectuals as enemies of socialism. Vast numbers had to recant and saw their careers destroyed, while others were deported to labor camps. Chinese Communism was slipping into the tyranny it had tried to eradicate.

Toward the end of the 1950s, the search for

A Nanjing parade in 1974 showcases the political intoxication of the Cultural Revolution.

ideological purity led to society becoming more radicalized. The Mao-dictated Great Leap Forward *(dayuejin)* in 1958 was a victory of economic idealism over common sense, creating divisions in the party and leading China to ruin. An obsession with quotas led to artificial production figures, gross economic imbalance, and mass starvation.

The 1960s saw a damaging Sino-Soviet split (with a freezing of Soviet aid) following Mao's concerns at the apparently revisionist nature of President Nikita Khrushchev's Soviet Union. The possibility of war hung over both countries and air-raid shelters were built.

China sought to reinforce its ideological credentials through the Great Proletarian Cultural Revolution (1966–1976). The Mao-instigated revolution forced itself into every nook and cranny of the nation's consciousness, hunting out the Four Olds: old culture, old customs, old habits, and old ideas. The objective was nothing less than the erasure of traditional, nonsocialist China.

Young Red Guards launched a wave of terror as radical China tore at itself with the sharp tools of self-denunciation and criticism. Confucian standards were inverted as the young criticized their elders, and teachers and intellectuals were herded off to work on farms.

Buddhist, Taoist, and Confucian temples were destroyed or desecrated and their resident monks educated in Maoist doctrine. The monasteries of Tibet suffered in particular. Mao became the object of a personality cult, and his collected quotations or "little red book" became a bible for the young. Liu Shaoqi and Deng Xiaoping were both branded "capitalist roaders" for offering commonsense corrective solutions to the excesses. Liu Shaoqi, banished to Hunnan Province, reportedly died in detention, while Deng Xiaoping eventually went on to become China's leader (see p. 41). The legacy of the Cultural Revolution has still not been properly addressed by either the Communist Party or the Chinese people. A new generation has grown up without hearing any discussion of the issues.

From the mid-1970s, China picked up the pieces. Premier Zhou Enlai (who groomed Deng Xiaoping as his successor) did much to restore balance, and China found a seat in the United Nations in 1971. President Richard Nixon came in 1972, visiting the Great Wall and repairing Sino-U.S. relations.

Within the party, however, a wide rift had developed between reformers and conservatives, with Mao and his chosen successor, Lin Biao, deeply at odds. Lin Biao died in a plane crash while fleeing the consequences of a failed plot to kill Mao (or so the official version went). Zhou Enlai was opposed by Jiang Qing (Mao's wife) and her clique, the Gang of Four (she ended up in prison, where she killed herself).

The death of the hugely popular Zhou Enlai from cancer in January 1976 sparked an outpouring of grief in Tiananmen Square that escalated into a riot. Branded the Tiananmen Incident, it fed from the huge reservoir of desperation and anger at the culmination of the Cultural Revolution. Deng Xiaoping was blamed and removed from his party posts.

Mao died in the same year, a year that was also marked by the massive Tangshan earthquake. A huge mausoleum was built on Tiananmen Square for his body, which still lies there in state.

AFTER MAO

Mao's death saw the blame for the Cultural Revolution being apportioned to the Gang of Four. Deng Xiaoping and his acolytes returned. After a transitional period with Hua Guofeng as leader, Deng found himself in command of China's belated modernization drive.

Ideological concepts were replaced by more pragmatic solutions. In the 1980s Special Economic Zones (SEZs) emerged. Inaugurated by Deng Xiaoping, SEZs enjoyed special economic regimes outside the socialist economy, thus attracting foreign investment. The first ones were Shenzhen, Zhuhai, Shantou, Hainan Island, and Xiamen. China's economy began to flourish in a way undreamed of under Mao, albeit at the price of diluting communist policy; "socialism with Chinese characteristics" was the official parlance.

The future of Hong Kong was decided in the Sino-British agreement of 1984. It guaranteed that Hong Kong's Western economic and legal model would remain for at least 50 years after the return to Chinese sovereignty. Portugal prepared a similar agreement for the 1999 return of Macau.

TIANANMEN

The 1980s ended tellingly with the expression of deep-lying stresses in society. Economic liberalization had not been matched by political reform, and there was endemic corruption in the party. Galloping inflation was further tightening the screw on social harmony.

Beneficiaries of China's unprecedented economic growth toast Hong Kong's return to the mainland in 1997.

The death of the reformer and moderate Hu Yaobang in 1989 prompted a display of mass mourning in Tiananmen Square that escalated into a movement for democracy. Led by student leaders Wang Dan, Chai Ling, and Wu'er Kaixi, the sit-in was brutally crushed by the PLA (People's Liberation Army) on June 3 and 4, with hundreds of innocent deaths. Party Secretary Zhao Ziyang lost his job for sympathizing with the students, and China suffered worldwide condemnation, not least from the citizens of Hong Kong.

TODAY'S CHINA

In economic terms, China's dramatic rise under the leadership of Deng Xiaoping, Jiang Zemin, and Hu Jintao has dazzled the world. A palpable sense that China has advanced in great leaps and bounds is obvious on the streets of Shanghai and Beijing and other large cities, which are awash with smart cars and fizz with commercial energy. The feel-good factor may not infect the whole nation, but it is extending its reach, and many Chinese know they have never had it so good. China has sent a man into space (twice), the Three Gorges Dam was finished ahead of schedule, and the nation is assuming its position on the world stage with an increasingly bold voice.

Behind the impressive economic statistics and hype, however, lurks a confusing picture: The banking sector is in dire need of reform, yawning regional disparities remain, the gap between rich and poor is best described as a chasm, the political system has resisted evolution, restrictions on free speech and access to information are if anything intensifying, rural unrest is on the increase, and the environment is in a state of crisis (the last two being directly linked). The government pays lip service to Marxist-Leninism while knowing that its grip on power may depend purely on economic growth. The consequent gulf between ideology and the reality is an ever present fact.

Taiwan is front page news in Chinese papers almost daily, revealing Beijing's obsession with pressuring the island into unification. The threat of force remains in the growing number of missile batteries along the south coast, while the U.S. pledge of support to Taiwan in the event of a conflict remains a constant thorn in the side of Sino-American relations. ■

Arts & culture

"WHEN I WAS IN CHINA I WAS STRUCK BY THE FACT THAT CULTIVATED Chinese were perhaps more highly civilized than any other human beings that it has been my good fortune to meet," wrote Bertrand Russell in the 1920s.

The Chinese might defer but would privately agree with this accolade from the great British philosopher, for they are proud of the cultural and artistic achievements of their vast country.

Within the dramatic pages of Chinese history is an unbroken and highly idiosyncratic aesthetic. The luxuriant voice of Tang poetry, the splendid contours of Song landscape painting, the classic elegance of Ming porcelain, and even today's lush and highly accomplished cinema emerge from this very same aesthetic. The nobility and sense of propriety that characterize the nation can be seen in China's arts. To understand its language is to fathom the soul of China.

Much traditional Chinese art appeals to Western sensibilities because its aesthetics tend to avoid tension and insist instead on a softness and elegance of touch. The Western preoccupation with forthrightness and realism traditionally never found a home in Chinese art, which instead was more economical, metaphorical, and restrained. This in turn can help explain the popularity of, for example, Chinese landscape painting in the West. Contemplation of landscape art can be liberating and philosophically rewarding, for it reveals a vision of life that is very different from that in the West.

These opposing views resulted in two different philosophies. The West saw itself as more apart from nature and sought to dominate it, while the instinctive involvement of the Chinese in nature denied it the empirical, objective tools with which to dissect it. A more passive acceptance of nature meant that the existential conundrums infusing much of Western art found no place in traditional Chinese aesthetics. In Western culture, God is represented in human form. In Chinese philosophy, the *Tao (dao)*, or "the way," is the closest the Chinese come to expressing an overall deity, yet it is formless. Whether concerning landscape painting or the landscape itself, the Tao permeates without revealing itself.

CHINESE RELIGION & PHILOSOPHY

China is a deeply religious country, with the main faiths being Buddhism, Taoism, and, to a lesser extent, Confucianism (after atheism). Confucianism is not strictly a religion but a philosophy, and Buddhism was imported from India, leaving Taoism as the only truly indigenous faith.

Taoism

Taoism *(daojiao)* is essentially more mystical than religious, although certain strains are presided over by deities (see pp. 72–73). Supposedly founded by Laozi (circa 580–500 B.C.), who wrote the *Daode Jing (The Classic of the Way and its Power)*, Taoism aims to cultivate a philosophical awareness of life. Lacking an anthropomorphic god, it seeks revelation of "the way"—the term used to describe the dynamism of nature and the operating force behind the universe. Taoists believe in achievement through inaction (*wu wei*), allowing things to develop and occur of their own accord. Readers who wish to experience a sensation of "the way" can peruse Laozi's classic, a book that has, as closely as is humanly possible, captured the feeling of the Tao. "The way" is also experientially revealed through the practice of *taiji quan* (see pp. 122–23), a martial art that draws on the Taoist precepts of softness, heightened awareness, and avoidance of conflict.

Buddhism

Most temples in China are Buddhist, pointing to the importance of Buddhism *(fojiao)* among the Chinese. Founded by the Indian prince Siddhartha Gautama (563–483 B.C.), Buddhism migrated to China from the third to the sixth centuries A.D., where it slotted in

Behind the facade of Chinese culture lies a desire for self-expression tempered by both restraint and grace.

alongside Taoism. The faith seeks to cure suffering through the neutralization of desire; following the "eight-fold path" leads to nirvana, a transcendent state of freedom.

The type of Buddhism generally found in China is Mahayana Buddhism (greater vehicle), which differs from Theravada Buddhism (doctrine of the elders) in its belief

Buddhism was brought from India to China and gradually sinicized into a distinctive form with its own religious culture.

that bodhisattvas (see p. 72) should delay Buddhahood in order to help others. The distinctive Tibetan Buddhism (see pp. 304–305) is found in Tibet and Inner Mongolia.

Confucianism

Confucianism *(rujia sixiang)* (see pp. 126–27), named after the sage Confucius, is a paternalistic philosophy of social behavior that teaches the Chinese people their codes, rules, and norms of conduct. Many Chinese consider genuflecting to one's elders as ordained by strict Confucianism a thankless task, yet the philosophy permeated the soul of the nation and was successfully transplanted to Japan, Korea, and Vietnam. Over the millennia, Confucianism has became decorated with religious trappings and institutionalized, despite being a very human philosophy that offers an answer to suffering and bad governance.

Islam

Arab merchants brought Islam *(yisilan jiao)* to China along the Silk Road, and across the sea to the southern coast where they established their mosques. Xinjiang Province in the northwest has a prominent Muslim population in the Uighurs, descendants of these Arab traders. The other large Muslim group, the Hui, live in Gansu, Ningxia, Qinghai, and Xinjiang (see p. 313).

Christianity

The Nestorians (a Syrian Christian sect) arrived in China in the seventh century A.D., followed later by the Jesuits, who helped in the building of the Old Summer Palace in Beijing and gave assistance in the sciences (see p. 83). The 19th-century Taiping Rebellion was led by Hong Xiuquan (see p. 158–59), who believed he was the Son of God. Today, Christianity *(jidu jiao)* is China's fastest growing faith, partly due to associations made between the spirit of capitalism and Protestantism, the spiritual bankruptcy at the heart of society, and the flourishing number of (illegal) house churches, unregistered places of assembly and worship for the swelling number of Christians (who by some estimates now number 100 million).

Judaism

Judaism *(youtai jiao)* in Kaifeng can be traced back to the Tang dynasty, having arrived along the Silk Road. The first synagogue was built in the 12th century but was destroyed twice during floods. After the second flood in the mid-19th century, it was not rebuilt. A large population of non-Chinese Jews settled in Shanghai during its heyday and heavily contributed to the city's prosperity and development.

RELIGION & POLITICS

The Chinese Communist Party has tried to replace religion with devotion to Marxist-Leninism *(makesilieningzhuyi)*, with varying success. Chairman Mao attempted to purge

China of superstition with the Cultural Revolution (1966–1976), but instead turned himself into a demi-god who is still idolized and worshiped in shrines around China. The current bankruptcy of Communist theory has left a spiritual vacuum that has been filled with a medley of religious beliefs. Recent riots involving Chinese Christians point to the growing toehold Christianity has in China and the problems the authorities have in dealing with it. It should not be forgotten that the Christian Taiping came close to overthrowing the Qing dynasty.

The Communist Party reacts with concern to any creed that offers an alternative vision to that bequeathed by Karl Marx. Falun Gong (Art of the Wheel of the Law), a quasi-Buddhist "cult," was banned because of fears that it challenged the primacy of the Communist Party. Despite being marshaled by middle-aged women and the elderly, Falun Gong has managed to worry the Communist Party, whose grip on power is fretful and insecure. Its adherents periodically demonstrated in Tiananmen Square, only to be bundled off to prison. Banning Falun Gong has not solved the problem of spiritual emptiness in China, and may simply have exacerbated it.

CHINESE PAINTING

A number of styles make up Chinese painting, but none is more evocative of the Oriental sensibility than landscapes. A meditation upon the mists, spaces, and mountains brings the Chinese aesthetic, with its grace and composure, into relief. Landscape painting originated in China as early as the fourth century A.D. but did not reach technical maturity until the Tang dynasty. Its apotheosis came in the Song and the Yuan dynasties, where an unsurpassed legacy has been handed down to this day.

The landscape is of actual and symbolic importance to the Chinese for its physical presence in such a huge land and because it reflects the divine. The languorous introspection of Chinese landscapes is passive and inviting. Commotion is absent and a spirit of

"Horses Crossing a River," by Zhao Mengfu, is a sublime example of art celebrating nature.

acceptance governs the waterfalls, pines, and peaks. Technically, the correct depiction of atmosphere and light is paramount. Air is a significant material because it stores *qi*, the energy that inhabits all living things (see p. 122). Blank spaces, washes, contrast, and a temperate use of color create light, while often adding a hazy mood. The use of ink on silk was the preferred medium for artists, which meant that changes could not be made once the ink had been applied.

The landscape must be vital and not just a vapid portrait. This effect is achieved through a suffusion of mood and feeling permeating the scene, rather than through realistic portrayal.

Specific feelings are generally shunned in this style of painting; there is a pervasive mood but no particular message. This lack of focus reflects the Chinese desire to avoid the obvious and the clear-cut. The vaporous mood invites the viewer to enter, and encour-

ages him or her to be quiet, creating an unobtrusive and welcoming atmosphere.

Poetry and painting were enthusiastic bedfellows in China, and the Tang dynasty painter/poet Wang Wei (699–759) probably best personifies this. His frequently snow-filled landscapes embody poetic concepts while his poetry is alive with vivid images of nature. The Song dynasty further nurtured the marriage of the two arts. Ma Yuan (1165–1225) was a master of the technique of leaving large areas of the picture blank, giving the impression of vast space and depth and light.

Paintings such as this powerfully declare the pain of recent Chinese history, in which a society gagged by censorship struggles for expression.

Yuan dynasty landscapes are more personal than their Song dynasty cousins. Attention to brushwork and inking became more important in the Yuan dynasty, with greater emphasis given to experimentation. The union of calligraphy and art was made in the Yuan dynasty and continued from there. In the Ming and Qing dynasties, the search for the subjective led to the romanticism of such artists as Shi Tao (1641–1720) and Zhu Da (1625–1705).

Techniques of traditional landscape painting are still copied today, although the 20th century heralded a revolution in both method and materials. The socialist realist artists of the Mao Zedong era emulated European techniques, forcing a political message onto a protesting landscape. In some ways this signified a change in Chinese consciousness, as the country became more westernized (via Marxist-Leninism, a Western political philosophy). Art became highly subjective and idealistic and, later, more experimental.

Oil on canvas is now a common medium for the artist in China. The successful Ningbo-born artist Chen Yifei painted in oil in a realist vein, largely taken from European schools. Copies of his works, often portraits of musicians, can be found all over China in hotels and street markets.

Buddhist art

Buddha is an object of veneration, and Buddhist sculpture is principally devotional rather than artistic in nature. Nevertheless, Chinese Buddhist sculptures and frescoes, especially those at the famous grottoes at Dunhuang (see pp. 326–27), Longmen (see pp. 118–19), and Yungang (see pp. 108–109), are also fabulous works of art in their own right. Buddhist sculpture evolved with the reinterpretation of Buddhism over the

dynasties. Examples from the Northern Wei (A.D. 386–534) are notable for their slightly smug smiles and divine beauty. They seem remote, metaphysical, and abstruse. Those from the Tang and Song dynasties are more human and of this world.

LITERATURE

The written word in Chinese bears no relation to its equivalent in English. English re-creates sounds alone, which makes listening to English poetry so absorbing. Reading Chinese literature differs because painted on the page is an accompanying portrait of the piece. This is important in the appreciation of classical Chinese poetry, for example, where visual impressions are conveyed by the characters.

Some of China's religious art, including the Dazu grottoes, eluded the ravages of war, purges, and treasure hunters.

Classical poetry

The earliest collection of poems in China is the *Shi Jing (Book of Songs)*, a bundle of verse allegedly compiled by Confucius, who deleted the more licentious entries! Despite being venerably ancient, many of the poems are lively songs bursting with bucolic lyrics and infused with agrarian melody.

An animist China comes to life in the poetry of Qu Yuan (340–278 B.C.). His poems are an often frightening snapshot of a world of witches, demons, and gods, and his most famous poem, *Li Sao (The Lament)* is a fragrant and luminous work, full of passion, primitive belief, and mythical beings. During the Han dynasty, a longer type of prose poem *(fu)* evolved at the royal court.

One of China's most revered poets, Tao Yuanming (365–427), is enjoyed chiefly for the simplicity of his verse and his delightful Taoist pursuit of wine and nature. His most famous work (actually a piece of prose)—*Taohua Yuanji*—magically narrates the discovery of an ancient, forgotten community.

Classical Chinese poetry reached its zenith during the Tang dynasty. The sensitivities of the age are beautifully communicated in poems characterized by a charming economy and balance. The Tang era produced China's two most famous poets, Li Bai (701–762) and Du Fu (712–770). Li Bai was a Taoist eccentric who explored a mystical communion of poetry and wine. Du Fu was a Confucian man of letters whose stoic verses speak of a deep grief juxtaposed by an equally deep sense of grace and charity. Their poems respectively reveal a glimpse of the soul of the nation, a country torn between romanticism and restraint. Other famous poets of the Tang dynasty are Meng Haoran, the poet-painter Wang Wei, Zhang Jiuling, and Li Shangying.

The Tang dynasty ushered in a more regulated poetic form known as *Lü Shi.* These poems are typically eight lines long, with each line of five or seven characters. This established strict rules for tonal patterns and symmetry within the poem. The hard-and-fast rules of the Lü Shi imposed constraints on poetic form but resulted in closer attention to balance and harmony. Language is chosen for its tone so that harmonies of pitch echo throughout the poem.

The end of the Tang dynasty saw the development of the *ci* poem. Sung to music and composed of lines of irregular length, the ci form fully blossomed in the Song dynasty. Famous masters of this style include Su Dongpo (1037–1101) and Ou Yangxiu (1007–1072).

The Shandong actress Gong Li has emerged as an icon of Chinese beauty.

Modern verse is much freer in style and content, influenced by Western innovations in form and theme.

Prose & literature

The abstruse *Yi Jing (I-Ching)* is a very early work, but it is more a book of prediction than a work of literature. Apart from the *Shi Jing (Book of Songs)*, the origins of Chinese literature are marked primarily by philosophical works. These include the *Daode Jing (The Classic of the Way and its Power)* by Laozi (circa 580–500 B.C.), the charming writings of the Taoist sage Zhuangzi (circa 369–286 B.C.), the sayings of Confucius (551–479 B.C.), and the works of Mencius (373–289 B.C.). The *Shi Ji (Records of the Historian)* by the Western Han historian Si Maqian (circa145–85 B.C.) is a monumental and engaging chronicle of Chinese history. The Tang dynasty writer Hanyu (768–824) is notable for his lucid prose and an innovative approach that made classical literature more accommodating to spontaneity. The Song dynasty writers Su Dongpo and Ou Yangxiu excelled in classical writing; drama developed in the Yuan dynasty.

Classical Chinese, with its arcane grammar and characters, was elitist and an impediment to literacy and creativity. The famous Ming and Qing dynasty epic stories, *Shuihu Zhuan (The Water Margin), Xiyou Ji (The Journey to the West)*, and *Honglou Meng (The Dream of the Red Chamber)*, were penned in a semi-classical vernacular that helped pave the way for the future novel.

It wasn't until the appearance in 1918 of *A Madman's Diary* by Lu Xun, however, that colloquial *baihua* (literally "white speech") was adopted for novel writing. Western fiction techniques had considerable influence on 20th-century Chinese writers. The Chinese novel evolved under the patronage of such eminent writers as Lao She (1899–1966), author of *Rickshaw Boy* and *Teahouse,* and Shen Congwen (1903–1988), author of *The Long River.* Both suffered from political coercion at the hands of the Communists, as did a whole generation of writers.

Calligraphy

Accompanying poetry, calligraphy is the oldest of China's arts. Despite being closely governed by structure and form, it ranges from an exacting and pure form (*lishu,* or regular script and *kaishu,* or clerical script) to the more spontaneous and complex (*xingshu,* or cursive and *caoshu,* or grasshand script). The latter is extremely challenging, even for Chinese. Regular and clerical script draw characters of equal size and style, while running script encourages a more cursive rendition. Grasshand script approaches the abstract in the fluid scrawl of its form, where characters may just appear as a line or as a smudge of meaning.

Before tackling the more expressionist cursive and grasshand script, the student of calligraphy has to spend years perfecting regular script. The apparent ease and spontaneity of grasshand script conceals a lengthy apprenticeship. The form of grasshand script emerges from an intuitive understanding of regular technique in much the same way that students of Chinese martial arts deliver inspired performances from a deep knowledge of the basic moves (see p. 123). Intention *(yi)* and technique *(jishu)* must correspond perfectly.

As with poetry, calligraphy reached its peak in the Tang dynasty. The Shanghai Museum is an excellent place to admire some of China's best examples.

Twenty-something Chinese and ex-pats at a rave party in a Beijing bar.

FILM

Modern Chinese film tends to be a sumptuous exploration of texture, color, lighting, and mood, often heavily streaked with tragedy. Unfortunately, unless you can speak Chinese, you will have to settle for the subtitled versions back home.

Despite the straitjacketing of Mainland Chinese cinema by a government fondness for safe subject matter, the results are sometimes impressive. Often lavish, classical period pieces, Mainland Chinese film is an accessible introduction to the Chinese aesthetic. Fifth-generation filmmaking by directors such as Zhang Yimou and Chen Kaige created such fables as *Raise the Red Lantern* (1991), *Farewell My Concubine* (1993), *Red Sorghum* (1987), and *Shanghai Triad* (1995). Gong Li is without doubt the most famous Chinese actress of her generation. The fifth generation was followed by an equally experimental sixth generation.

Hong Kong cinema tends toward the chaotic. Often violent, crass, morbid, given to slapstick, and demented, it has a global cult following. Jackie Chan (*Rumble in the Bronx*, 1995; *Rush Hour*, 1998; et al.) is a household name, and Lamma-Island-born Chou Yun-fat (*Crouching Tiger, Hidden Dragon*, 2000; *The Bullet-proof Monk*, 2002). Jet Li crashed through Tinseltown's back door (*Lethal Weapon 4*, 1998), and director John

Woo has trained his sights on big-budget spectaculars (*Mission Impossible 2,* 1999; *Face/Off,* 1997). Charming crooners Andy Lau and Jackie Cheung long ago discovered hidden acting reserves, put to very good use in a host of films.

There's more to Hong Kong cinema than vampires, ghost stories, and kungfu kicking, however. The city's confused cultural identity, covert romanticism, and violent substrata find expression in excellent art cinema. Wong Kar Wai wonderfully celebrates a sense of longing tinged with brutality in *Chungking Express* (1994) and *Fallen Angels* (1995). *As Tears Go By* (1988) traces the tragic slide into Triad society by two young brothers.

MUSIC

You will most likely encounter traditional Chinese music through Beijing opera (see below). Traditional instruments include the *erhu,* a stringed instrument that makes a mournful wailing sound, the lutelike *pipa,* and the *dizi* (flute). Much traditional music has been lost, having fallen prey to the rapacity of the Cultural Revolution and the banality of socialist art theory. Valiant orchestras such as the Naxi Orchestra in Lijiang have managed to preserve their art.

Chinese popular music tends to seek inspiration from Hong Kong, Taiwan, and Singapore, the distillation of which is Canto-pop. Predominantly sugary, romantic ballads, Canto-pop can be initially repellent, but perseverance pays off. Western music is enjoyed, but real devotion is reserved for homegrown singers. Andy Lau, Jackie Cheung, Wang Fei, and Aaron Kwok all enjoy demi-god status in China. The Convention and Exhibition Centre in Hong Kong is the best venue for foreign bands in China.

Chinese opera

Opera emerged from popular theater, an art form that flourished in the Mongol Yuan dynasty. There are many regional forms of Chinese opera, with their own stories, costumes, makeup, and music. The most famous of the regional opera, the Beijing Opera (Jingju), reached its apex during the Qing dynasty.

Chinese opera has little relation to Western opera. The popular stories are shrilly sung to a clashing of cymbals by heavily made-up performers (usually male). The roles can be very demanding, with leaping, jumping, and other energetic routines that require both flexibility and endurance. In this sense, Beijing Opera is closer to Western ballet, although the choreography is very different.

Characters are identified by their makeup and clothing. The roles are generally divided into male *(sheng),* female *(dan),* warriors and heroes *(jing),* and clowns *(chou).* For Westerners, the language is sadly a major hurdle to comprehension. Shanghai, Beijing, and Hong Kong have the best venues for Chinese opera.

Training for the Beijing Opera is severe, and it was usually reserved for orphans. The movie *Farewell my Concubine* delivers a vivid account of the hardships endured by young opera students. Martial arts supremos Jackie Chan, Samo Hung, and Yuan Biao learned their moves through training in Beijing Opera.

ARCHITECTURE

Traditional Chinese architecture has sadly been given a beating by history. Many wooden buildings were reduced to ash by the fires of war that constantly swept the land. The very point of dynastic succession was regularly marked by wholesale destruction of buildings of importance. The Cultural Revolution attempted to annihilate China's historical fabric, and today's wrecking ball continues in the same way.

Traditional Chinese buildings that survive are exercises in harmony, decorum, and balance. *Fengshui* (see pp. 174–75) was a deciding factor in design and location.

China's great buildings of the past were not the temples but the structures erected for imperial use, such as those in the Forbidden City. Restrained in outline, they occupy the horizontal rather than the vertical plane and tend to be large, interconnected complexes representing a network of form. A sign that China is losing touch with its cultural roots is the contemporary obsession with skyscrapers, where height is the paramount goal. ■

The Forbidden City, Tiananmen Square, the Summer Palace, and the Great Wall—Beijing's hallmark sights—are known to all. But unexpected surprises and hidden worlds await exploration in this intriguing capital.

Beijing

Cap badge, Public Security Guard

Beijing

AT THE CENTER IS THE CAPITAL, BEIJING, THE SEAT OF power in China and a good starting point for your journey in the Middle Kingdom. The Chinese universe orbits Beijing, and political power radiates from here, as do flight connections to just about anywhere in the land.

Imperious seat of political power, proud capital of the Middle Kingdom, and China's showcase to the world, Beijing—Northern Capital—has a powerful allure. The rest of China has at least one eye on this repository of the nation's soul. Wherever you go in China, the city either follows or is waiting for you, in its dialect (Mandarin), its cuisine, and its political (un-)certainties.

Beijing was not always the dynastic capital, but you get the impression it has presided over China's fate since time immemorial. The Forbidden City, Beijing's walled heart, is an arcane yet majestic labyrinth of imperial custom and lore. The plan of this sovereign core extends outward, framing Beijing in a broad grid pattern of wide boulevards and delightful *hutong.*

In its entirety and beyond its showcase commercial areas, the city is a splendid microcosm of today's China. In its breathless race into the 21st century, the city remains a delightful tangle of the old and the new in its hodgepodge of daily life. Skyscrapers rocket into the sky above low-lying districts of crumbling alleyways and shuffling old folk while immaculately-dressed white collar types disappear into a deluge of bicycles, as the streets jostle with the flotsam of itinerant workers, long-haired students, entrepreneurs, and hordes of out-of-towners.

Despite its wholesale modernization, Beijing has no deficit of history. The Forbidden City and the Temple of Heaven are two of the best examples of imperial-era architecture in the land. Both monolithic fence and symbol of a defensive mentality, the Great Wall snakes its way north of the capital, while the extravagance of the Summer Palace makes for an excellent day out.

The mouthy Beijing dialect, bane of students of Mandarin, is best mimicked having just taken a bite from a Big Mac. You'll find that fast food covers the city like a rash. That other institution—Peking Duck—appears at almost every corner; and don't forget: Once bitten, forever smitten. ■

Getting around town

Beijing is a huge entity whose roads are governed by chaos and precision in equal measure. Walking around town is possible but very tiring because the city is so big. You can try your luck with the buses, but expect a long (and crowded) haul on the congested streets. The subway is being rapidly expanded and can be very useful, especially when tied in with taxi trips. For the intrepid, renting a bicycle will thrust you into an exciting world (see pp. 80–82). If you want speed and comfort, jump aboard one of the many cheap taxis cruising the streets or waiting at bus and train stations. ■

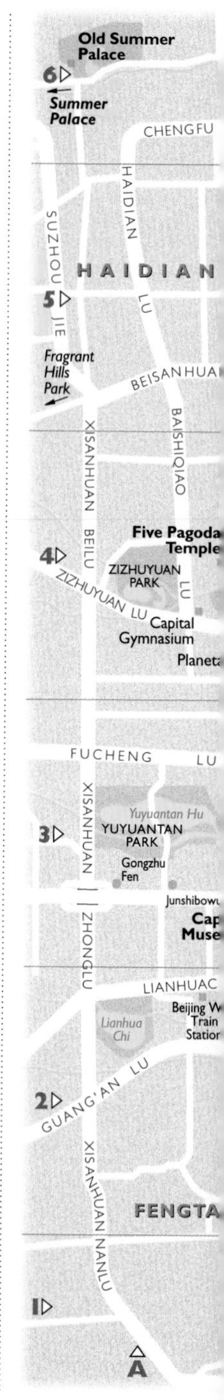

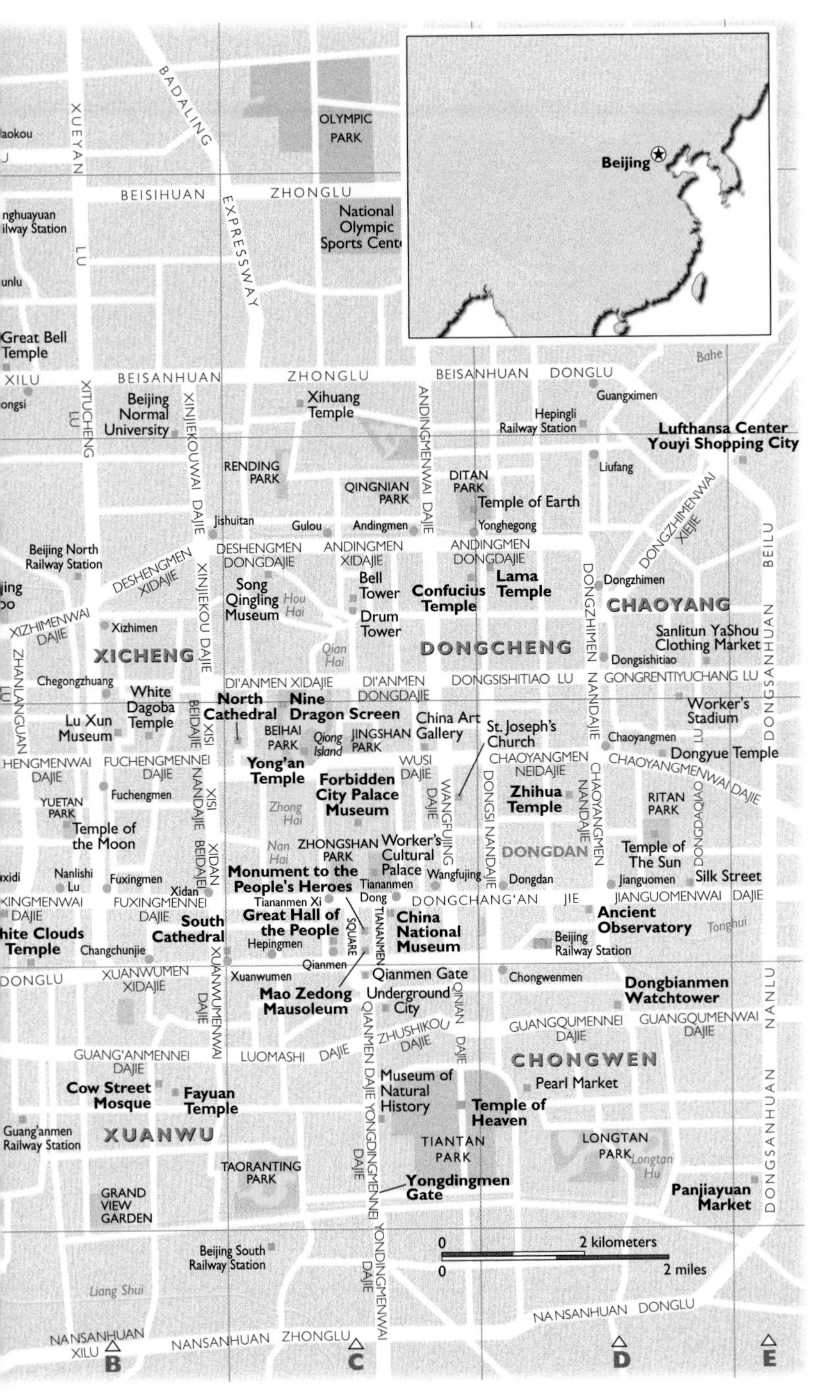
OLYMPIC PARK
National Olympic Sports Cent
Beijing
BEISIHUAN ZHONGLU
BADALING EXPRESSWAY
XUEYAN LU
Great Bell Temple
Beijing Normal University
Xihuang Temple
BEISANHUAN ZHONGLU
BEISANHUAN DONGLU
Guangximen
Hepingli Railway Station
Lufthansa Center Youyi Shopping City
Liufang
RENDING PARK
QINGNIAN PARK
DITAN PARK
Temple of Earth
Yonghegong
Jishuitan
Gulou
Andingmen
DESHENGMEN DONGDAJIE
ANDINGMEN XIDAJIE
ANDINGMEN DONGDAJIE
Beijing North Railway Station
DESHENGMEN XIDAJIE
Song Qingling Museum
Hou Hai
Bell Tower
Drum Tower
Confucius Temple
Lama Temple
Dongzhimen
CHAOYANG
XIZHIMENWAI DAJIE
Xizhimen
XICHENG
Qian Hai
DONGCHENG
Sanlitun YaShou Clothing Market
Dongsishitiao
Chegongzhuang
DI'ANMEN XIDAJIE
DI'ANMEN DONGDAJIE
DONGSISHITIAO LU
GONGRENTIYUCHANG LU
White Dagoba Temple
North Cathedral
Nine Dragon Screen
China Art Gallery
Worker's Stadium
Lu Xun Museum
BEIHAI PARK
Qiong Island
JINGSHAN PARK
St. Joseph's Church
Chaoyangmen
Dongyue Temple
FUCHENGMENNEI DAJIE
Yong'an Temple
WUSI DAJIE
CHAOYANGMEN NEIDAJIE
CHAOYANGMENWAI DAJIE
Forbidden City Palace Museum
Zhihua Temple
RITAN PARK
YUETAN PARK
Fuchengmen
Zhong Hai
Temple of the Moon
Nan Hai
ZHONGSHAN PARK
Worker's Cultural Palace
DONGDAN
Temple of The Sun
Nanlishi Lu
Fuxingmen
Monument to the People's Heroes
Wangfujing
Dongdan
Jianguomen
Silk Street
Xidan
Tiananmen
FUXINGMENNEI DAJIE
Tiananmen Xi
Tiananmen Dong
DONGCHANG'AN JIE
JIANGUOMENWAI DAJIE
Great Hall of the People
China National Museum
Ancient Observatory
South Cathedral
Hepingmen
TIANANMEN SQUARE
Beijing Railway Station
Tonghui
hite Clouds Temple
Changchunjie
Qianmen
Qianmen Gate
Chongwenmen
Dongbianmen Watchtower
XUANWUMEN XIDAJIE
Xuanwumen
Mao Zedong Mausoleum
Underground City
XUANWUMENWAI DAJIE
ZHUSHIKOU DAJIE
GUANGQUMENNEI DAJIE
GUANGQUMENWAI DAJIE
GUANG'ANMENNEI DAJIE
LUOMASHI DAJIE
CHONGWEN
Museum of Natural History
Pearl Market
Cow Street Mosque
Fayuan Temple
Temple of Heaven
Guang'anmen Railway Station
XUANWU
TIANTAN PARK
LONGTAN PARK
Longtan Hu
TAORANTING PARK
Yongdingmen Gate
Panjiayuan Market
GRAND VIEW GARDEN
Beijing South Railway Station
0 2 kilometers
0 2 miles
Liang Shui
NANSANHUAN XILU
NANSANHUAN ZHONGLU
NANSANHUAN DONGLU
DONGSANHUAN BEILU
DONGSANHUAN NANLU
B
C
D
E

Ornate rooftops of the Forbidden City reflect the Chinese tradition of myriad buildings composing palace design.

Forbidden City

THE FORBIDDEN CITY (ZIJIN CHENG), A 78-ACRE (32 HA) pied-à-terre to the emperors of the Ming and Qing dynasties, is one of the most alluring and magnificent Chinese treasures.

When the Yongle emperor (see p. 33) moved the capital to Beijing from Nanjing in 1421, he built the walled Forbidden City near the site of the palace used by the Yuan dynasty emperors. In today's China, the lackluster name of **Gugong,** or **Palace Museum,** describes what was a territory out of bounds to the hoi polloi. The Chinese name translates as Purple Forbidden City, which is not an allusion to the color of the walls but to the Polar Star, at the center of the celestial world and symbolic of the emperor. Purple is also a color associated with royalty.

Considerably restored and embellished since the Ming dynasty (most of the buildings you see today were built during and after the 18th century), the Forbidden City signified the distant and unapproachable emperor. It is also the finest example of Chinese imperial architecture.

Forbidden City

- Map: 55 C3
- Phone: 010 6513-2255
- $: $$; all-inclusive ticket with audio tour $$$. Students half price

The Forbidden City reflects the Ming practice of dividing Beijing into walled sections. This is the heart of China, the nucleus of the Middle Kingdom—a receptacle for the mandate of Heaven and the source from which imperial dictates were issued to even the most far-flung of the country's provinces. The complex is not one stately building as was the Western practice (for example, Versailles or Buckingham Palace), but rather a series of halls and buildings separated by passages, like a small city. It is said that the complex consists of 9,000 rooms in 800 buildings.

The palace was built primarily of wood, so fire was a constant hazard and much was regularly destroyed. The Manchus (who swept down from Manchuria to install the Qing dynasty) put the palace to the torch in the 17th century. The Japanese ransacked it, as did the Kuomintang (the Chinese nationalists who fled to Taiwan in 1949). The whole, labyrinthine complex was almost torn apart during the intoxication of the Cultural Revolution, but it was saved from destruction by the intervention of Premier Zhou Enlai. He interceded more than once to save national treasures from destruction.

China's great buildings were constructed for the use of the emperors. Chinese architecture has preferred to explore the horizontal human plane rather than occupy space vertically. As a result, the palace's buildings are not tall, but the space around them can be breathtaking. China has no equivalent of the West's huge cathedral, a towering structure used to emphasize human smallness (this does not apply to modern Chinese architecture). The interconnected system of the Forbidden City represents a harmonious network of form and allegiance of shape.

Beijing or Peking?

The name of China's capital has changed over the centuries. At one time or another it has been known as Yanjing, Dadu, and Beiping. Indeed you could be forgiven for thinking Peking and Beijing were two different places. Peking is simply the old transliteration of the Chinese pronunciation for "Northern Capital"; Beijing is the officially sanctioned pinyin spelling, based on the Mandarin *(putonghua)* dialect. ■

First built in the Ming dynasty, the huge Gate of Heavenly Peace remains a rostrum from which leaders appear to crowds gathered below.

APPROACHING THE PALACE

Ideally, approach the Forbidden City from the south, which gives you the chance to admire the huge port-red walls that thrust out from either side of the Meridian Gate (Wumen). You can enter from the northern gate, but the cassette tour guides you from the south. The major halls and palaces are set out along a line bisecting the complex, running south to north. All Chinese temples lie along this same axis (see pp. 174–75).

Leaving Tiananmen Square and crossing under Chang'an Dajie by subway brings you to the entrance to the palace. As you traverse the arched marble bridges, you come face to face with the **Gate of Heavenly Peace (Tiananmen)** and its monumental portrait of Mao. The painting was defaced during the democracy protests in 1989, when three workers from Hunan (Mao's home province) flung eggs filled with paint at it. The white characters on the red background to the left of the portrait urge the government mantra "Long Live the People's Republic of China." From this gate Mao proclaimed the founding of the republic in 1949, and it is used today as a spot for watching military parades. For a fee, and a frisking, you can climb up onto the gate for sweeping views over the square.

Walking through the gate brings you into a large courtyard lined by souvenir stalls and restaurants. West of the courtyard is the attractive **Zhongshan Park,** where the emperor used to make sacrifices in spring and autumn to ensure a fruitful harvest. East are the magnificent triple halls of the **Supreme Temple (Taimiao),** more prosaically called the Worker's Cultural Palace. The most sacred Imperial temple after the Temple of Heaven, the complex is often devoid of visitors and entrance is a pittance.

ENTRANCE

Passing through the next gate leads you to the fortresslike **Meridian Gate (Wumen).** This marks the entrance proper to the Forbidden City. The gate was reserved for the sole use of the emperor, with drums and bells sounding his approach to the Hall of Supreme Harmony. The 170-foot-wide (52 m) moat begins its circuit around the walls here. The dwarfing walls, which create colossal silhouettes at twilight, are a massive 28 feet (8.5 m) wide at the base. This is also where you obtain your ticket (and cassette tour guide) from the booths on the left or right.

Through the Meridian Gate you come to a huge paved courtyard with five bridges straddling a central strip of water. The **Gate of Supreme Harmony (Taihemen)** lies beyond. This gate was built in 1420, destroyed by fire in 1888, and rebuilt the following year. The ceiling is a blaze of emerald green and gold. As you walk through the gate, you will see to the east the **Hall of Literary Glory,** which contained the Imperial Library; to the west is the **Hall of Martial Valor** (academic and military functions are often counterposed in Chinese culture).

THREE BIG HALLS

Ahead of you stands the imposing **Hall of Supreme Harmony (Taihedian),** the first of what are known as the Three Big Halls, where the emperor performed state functions. In fact, the emperor used the hall conservatively, reserving it for such events as his birthday and for the announcement of the list of successful imperial examination candidates (see p. 83).

Raised on a three-tiered platform, the hall was for many years the tallest building in Beijing, and a law forbade commoners to construct anything higher. No one could look down upon this most sacred of imperial buildings (there was also the *fengshui* belief that

SYMBOLS

Symbols abound. The dragon denotes the emperor *(huangdi)* and the phoenix represents the empress *(huanghou)*. The two are often depicted together. The image of the dragon chasing the flaming pearl portrays the quest for purity, while the lavish yellow tiling of the roofs denotes the emperor, a color often seen in imperial porcelain. ■

benign spirits flew at a certain altitude, a height that should not be exceeded by buildings). Twin sets of stairs ascend to the hall, divided by a decorated stone slab over which the emperor's sedan chair would be conveyed. Inside sits the imperial throne. The large water drums outside supplied water for fighting fires. Altogether 308 such drums were in the palace.

Tucked away behind is the smaller **Hall of Middle Harmony (Zhonghedian),** where ministers from the Ministry

Above: Until 1911, access to the Forbidden City was denied to all except those with imperial permission. Right: An enormous urn held water for extinguishing fire.

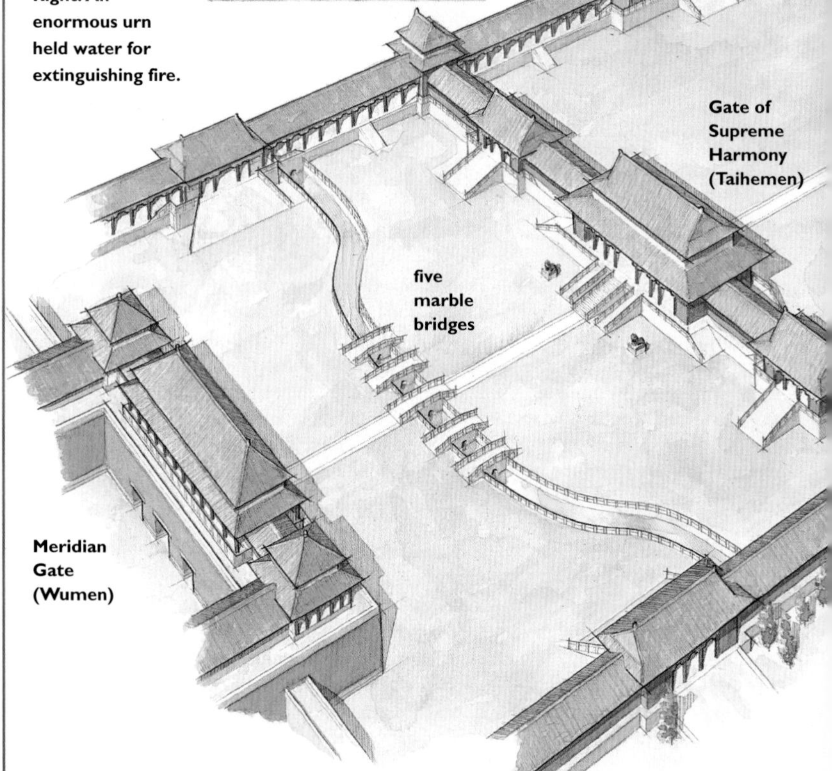

Gate of Supreme Harmony (Taihemen)

five marble bridges

Meridian Gate (Wumen)

of Rites were received. The rectangular **Hall of Preserving Harmony (Baohedian),** where the emperor oversaw the final stages of the civil service examinations, occupies a space just before you reach the **Gate of Heavenly Purity (Qianqingmen).** The carving on the huge marble slab accompanying the stairs shows a dragon flying through the clouds.

THE INNER CITY

The courtyard behind the Gate of Heavenly Purity marks the entrance to the nucleus of the Forbidden City, access to which was only allowed to eunuchs, maids, and

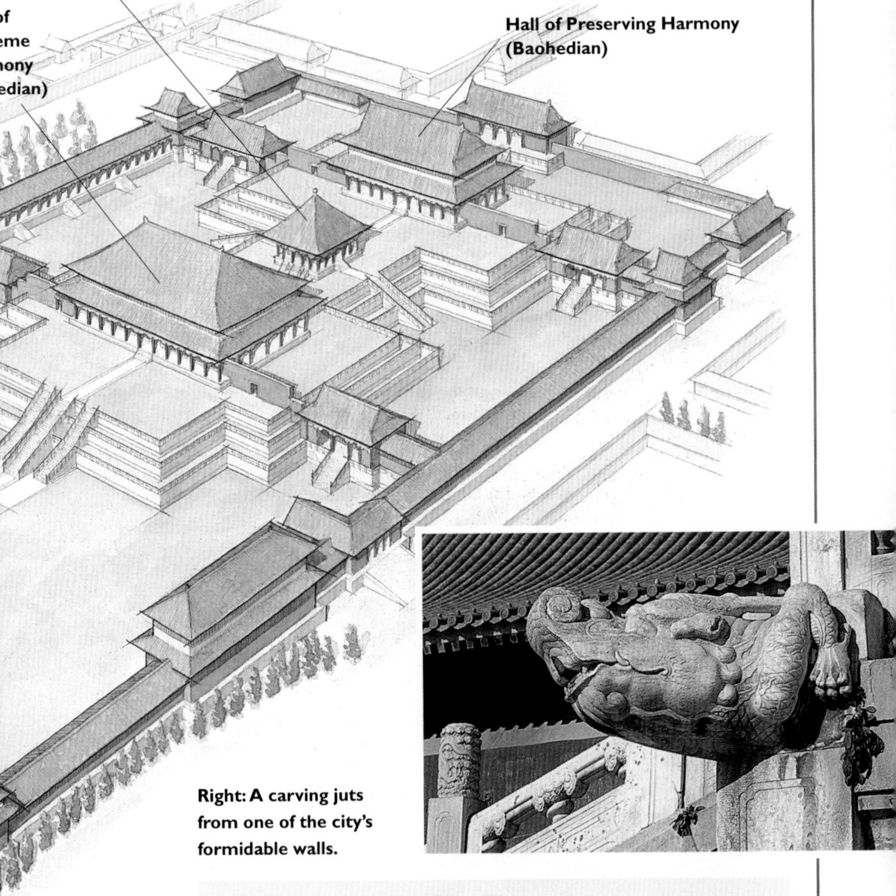

Right: A carving juts from one of the city's formidable walls.

Dragons

You will see the dragon motif carved and painted throughout the Forbidden City. The dragon seems to have had a claw-hold on the Chinese imagination since the earliest times: Fuxi (see p. 22) had a dragon tail. The Chinese believe in several of these serpents: The *long* is the dragon that surges through clouds chasing pearls; the *li* is the dragon of the sea; and the *jiao* is the dragon of marshy land. ■

SEDAN CHAIRS
This genteel means of transport gradually disappeared as road surfaces improved. Until then, sedan chairs were identified by a color code system. The reigning sovereign was carried in a yellow sedan and imperial concubines were given orange chairs. Green sedans identified high-level mandarins, while lesser mandarins were conveyed in blue. ■

imperial relatives. As the republic surrounded this last bastion of the Manchu empire in the early 20th century, it was theatrically presided over by the last Qing emperor, Puyi.

The Gateway of Heavenly Purity leads to what were essentially the residential quarters of the Forbidden City. The first building, the **Palace of Heavenly Purity (Qianqinggong),** served as the emperor's bedchambers. Behind this is the smaller **Hall of Heavenly and Terrestrial Union (Jiaotaidian),** where the empress slept. Other buildings housed the eunuch entourage and advisers to the emperor.

North of this lies the **Palace of Terrestrial Tranquility (Kunninggong),** where Puyi was married in 1922. The palace was the venue of Manchu shaman ritualistic ceremonies, with shaman priests and priestesses overseeing the sacred rites. In the southeast of the Forbidden City a temple known as the Tang Temple, or the Shaman Temple, once stood; its services were later transferred to the Palace of Terrestrial Tranquility. The Qing Manchu court never gave up the shaman belief in nature spirits, and incorporated this primitive faith into their sinicization. Immediately behind is the **Gate of Terrestrial Tranquility,** which leads on to the **Imperial Garden.**

You can leave the Forbidden City at this point if you wish, through the **Gate of Divine Prowess (Shenwumen),** which opens to a bridge over the moat that rings the walled city. Empress Dowager Cixi and Emperor Guangxu fled for Xi'an in August 1900 from a gate in the northern wall, as the foreign powers descended on Beijing for retribution. Several halls in the palace have been converted to exhibition halls, including the magnificent **Clock Exhibition Hall,** where a glittering array of antique timepieces—many of which were gifts to the emperors from abroad—garner rave reviews from travelers. ■

Chinese lion

The Chinese lion, a playful-looking creature with a curly mane, is often seen sitting in pairs outside buildings of note. The female holds her baby under one paw (the Chinese believed that lions could secrete milk through their paws), while the male plays with a ball. Lions are de rigueur in Hong Kong, where you may even see a few Western-style ones (for example, outside the Hong Kong & Shanghai Bank building). ■

The most magnificent examples of the Chinese lion in Beijing can be found in the Forbidden City, the Summer Palace, and the Lama Temple.

Beihai Park

Beihai Park (Beihai Gongyuan), northwest of the Forbidden City, offers a natural balance to the imperial thoroughfares of the palace. The park is a romantic sojourn for young couples who meander from pavilion to pavilion at dusk and look out over the city spread below from the hill on Qiong Island.

The larger part of Beihai Park is a lake, a frozen mass in winter, crisscrossed by children's paddleboats in summer. The Yong'an Bridge straddles the water to **Qiong Island (Qiongdao).** Folklore attributes the scooping out of the lake and its subsequent pile of earth to the great Kublai Khan. He used Beihai as his stomping ground before the Ming dynasty upstaged him with the Forbidden City. The Buddhist **Yong'an Temple** climbs the island's hill in layers.

The dumpy **White Dagoba** crowning the hill is a Lamaist *stupa* inaugurated for a visit by the Dalai Lama in the 17th century. Rattled by earthquakes, the dagoba virtually collapsed in the big Tangshan tremor of 1976. You can ascend a platform behind the dagoba and view a panoramic sweep over Beijing, with the Forbidden City to the east.

The paths snaking down from the summit thread through fanciful pavilions, halls, and rock gardens bordered by pines. On the shore of the lake north of the island is the main tourist destination, the **Nine Dragon Screen (Jiulongbi).** This spirit wall, 88 feet (27 m) long and 16 feet (5 m) high, was designed to deflect bad spirits. Located at the entrance to a temple since destroyed, the screen is a serpentine assortment of more than 400 glazed tiles. ■

Beihai Park
- 55 C3
- Wenjin Jie
- $

The Tibetan-style White Dagoba overlooking the lake in Beihai Park is reached along pleasantly shaded paths on Qiong Island.

Jingshan Park

Jingshan Park (Jingshan Gongyuan), or Scenic Mountain Park, was known as Coal Hill by Western residents in Beijing at the end of the 19th century. The hill was called Meishan (Beautiful Mountain) by the Chinese, and Westerners confused it with the word *mei* meaning "coal" (same pronunciation, but with a different tone). This artificial hill was piled up from the earth scooped out to make the moat ringing the Forbidden City. The park is directly opposite the north exit of the Forbidden City, and the view from the summit over the imperial palace is peerless. ■

Jingshan Park
- 55 C3
- Jingshan Qianjie
- $

Tiananmen Square

55 C3

Tiananmenxi/ Tiananmendong subway

Tiananmen Square

THE SWEEPING SQUARE OF THE GATE OF HEAVENLY Peace—Tiananmen Square—is the soul of China. This vast expanse of paving stones, scene of the 1989 student demonstrations and their gory climax, is an ordered microcosm of the Communist universe and a colossal statement of state power. Chairman Mao is interred here and the monolithic Chinese parliament overlooks the square.

Tiananmen Square literally means "Square of the Gate of Heavenly Peace" and represents a desire for order and harmony in the Chinese universe.

Chairman Mao Mausoleum

Tiananmen Square

Open 8:30–11:30 a.m. Tues.–Sun.; 2:00–4:00 p.m. Tues. & Thurs.; no p.m. hours July & Aug.

The square acts as a huge park, with couples strolling languidly hand in hand, children playing, and enthusiastic kite-flying. On a clear day, toward twilight, the view here can be astonishing. In the early evening, soldiers of the PLA troop out to lower the Chinese flag, attracting an assembly of wide-eyed Chinese (the flag is raised at dawn).

A motley assortment of historical buildings, garish, Soviet-style monuments, and huge museums flank the square. To the north is the **Gate of Heavenly Peace,** viewing stand for military parades, with its huge portrait of Mao. On the north– south axis in the center of the square stands the **Monument to the People's Heroes,** last bastion of the students before their denouement with the People's Liberation Army. The monolith remembers martyrs to the cause of the Communist revolution.

South of this is the **Chairman Mao Mausoleum (Mao Zhuxi Jiniantang),** where the waxen-faced Great Helmsman lies in state. The hall was constructed the year after Mao's death in 1976. A long line of people still files through to pay respect to the ex-chairman, who lies on a slab of black granite from Taishan, one of the five sacred Taoist mountains. The hall is periodically shut for maintenance.

North and south of Mao's mausoleum, socialist realist statues depict a group of idealized workers rallying behind the party line. Such anachronisms pitch a last ditch struggle against the free-market mutiny sweeping China.

The venerable **Qianmen Gate** in the very south is one of the few remaining gates of the old wall of Peking. It was originally constructed during the reign of Yongle (*R.*1403–1423). The wall formerly ringed the old city, and no one was allowed to climb it (the first people allowed to stroll along it were foreigners in 1860). The towers bordering Qianmen were burned down in 1900 by the Boxers as a punishment for selling foreign goods (there used to be a small bazaar running between the gates).

The west side of the square is dominated by the **Great Hall of the People (Renmin Dahuitang),** where China's rubber-stamping parliament meets. You can enter the building when the National People's Congress (NPC) is not in session.

Opposite is the hulking **China National Museum,** with its cheap layout and cheesy waxwork displays, although worth hunting down are the bronzes and ceramics. Captions are largely in Chinese and not all halls are open at the same time, although there are regular temporary exhibitions. Those who take delight in the Marxist thrust will most appreciate the exhibits.

West of Tiananmen Square is the egglike, supermodern titanium and glass **National Grand Theater,** a project that has incited controversy for its out-of-place styling.

Tiananmen Square (Tiananmen Guangchang) was the riotous scene of exultation at the launch of the Cultural Revolution in 1966. Today, it is the backdrop to vast military parades that grind down the northern perimeter of Chang'an Jie (Avenue of Eternal Peace).

Despite the authoritarian design, the square has become a battleground in the lopsided tussle between government and disaffected groups. On April 4, 1976, Beijing residents gathered in hundreds of thousands to mourn the death of Premier Zhou Enlai. Wreaths laid to commemorate his passing vanished, leading to a massive riot (the "Tiananmen Incident"), which was branded a counterrevolutionary plot.

Icon of the present era, Mao Zedong's vast portrait gazes over the square where his body lies.

Democracy protests in the spring of 1989 were similarly molded from public grief (on this occasion, the death of reformer Hu Yaobang). Sadness again smoldered to anger when the authorities rebuffed the people. Bizarrely, the government sent tanks against unarmed workers and students, rather than riot police and tear gas.

More recently, middle-aged followers of a banned spiritual exercise system, Falun Gong (Art of the Wheel of the Law), assembled in the square, only to be arrested and bundled into waiting vans of the Public Security Bureau. The square has become a tempting forum for dissent and is perennially patrolled by plainclothes police. October 1 is China's National Day, and half of Beijing descends on the square to commemorate the event. ■

China National Museum

Open 8:30 a.m.–4:30 p.m.

$

Beijing *hutongs*

Beijing's wide avenues, vast squares, huge palaces, and great distances can leave you feeling rather small. A vanishing labyrinth of charming decay, however, awaits you on a more human scale. It's the unique world of Beijing's *hutongs*—a mesh of narrow lanes that thread across the city. Hutongs (from a Mongolian word for a passageway) often harbor another picturesque world, that of the *siheyuan* (four-walled courtyard).

It is said that there are more hutongs in Beijing than there are hairs on a cow. Today, though, there are certainly less than before; sadly, many have been swept aside to make room for tower blocks and new hotels.

Hutongs are primarily lanes where people live, but they also bustle with markets and commerce of all kinds. They are often charmingly complicated: a tangle of minute passages compressed into a tight area, with sub-hutongs adding to the confusion. Locals navigate their small, private world with ease, while taxi drivers enter a twilight zone, driving in circles and leaning out of the window to ask directions. This is the place to come to really get a sense of community in Beijing.

The thoroughfares are loved by Beijing residents. Bicycles scythe down the narrow passages, bells jingling. Bundles of swaddled schoolchildren race back home from school in the winter air, past glowing brickwork outhouses, chimneys pumping smoke, and the occasional carved doorway laden with snow. Some hutongs are so narrow they pinch; others are broad, breezy thoroughfares, shaded by trees.

Their often fanciful names give an idea of their original function or the people who once lived there. Some names are seemingly plucked from a child's imagination: Rain Lane, Earth Lane, Bright Lane, Luck Lane, Happiness Lane. Others echo the old markets that set up shop there, such as Stir-Fried Bean Lane, Chrysanthemum Lane, Cap Lane, Rice Granary Lane, Aromatic Bait Lane, and Black Sesame Lane. Others have more obscure origins deep in Beijing's history, such as Clean Earth Lane (Buddhist), Three Never Get Old Lane, and Horsetail Cap Lane.

Most of the lanes run east to west in accordance with the dictates of *fengshui* (see pp. 230–31), and the doors and portals face south as they do in Chinese temples (see pp. 174–77). Only occasionally do some hutongs run north to south, linking the major ones.

Hutongs are honeycombed with four-walled courtyards, which for centuries were the standard housing units in the capital. These picturesque nests consist of a communal courtyard, hugged on four sides by a house. Often they are clustered together, or in strings, where whole communities live. Some courtyards are fronted by doorways wonderfully adorned with Chinese characters or religious motifs. In places, the sooty buildings are still decorated by deliciously ornamental tiling; others are more modest. Occasionally, the door to a hutong may be left open so you can peer into the courtyard lying behind. The courtyards are roofless, admitting light and the elements, however fair or foul.

Sidelined by the socialist building programs of the 1960s and 1970s, the courtyards have been further left out in the cold by the slick developments of the last decades. Despite their obvious charm, they lack efficient insulation and central heating, and are inconvenient for car-owning families. Despite this, they are still home to a quarter of Beijing's residents.

You can stumble upon hutongs all over Beijing, but they tend to survive within the second ring road. Rather than leap from one district to another in your quest, navigate the historic grid southeast of the Bell and Drum

Above: Daily life continues along Beijing's many *hutongs,* narrow back streets that date back to the Yuan, Ming, and Qing dynasties.

Left: Beijing's traditionally roofed *siheyuan* courtyards, like temple courtyards, are open to the elements.

Towers (see p. 80). This block of hutongs, surrounded by Gulou Dongdajie, Dongsi Beidajie, and Di'anmen Waidajie and divided by Jiaodaokou Nandajie, is a small township of these charming lanes. Another historical reach is around the nearby Houhai Lake.

Riding a rented bike is the best way to survey this cozy little world, but you can also do it on foot. Tour companies have latched onto the growing tourist fascination: try the Beijing Hutong Tour Co. Ltd. *(tel 010 6615-9097)* or jump aboard one of the small coaches that leave from the pedestrianized southern end of Wangfujing Dajie for short rides past hutong openings.

You can even spend your time in Beijing at your very own siheyuan hotel—the Lüsongyuan Hotel *(tel 010 6404-0436)* at 22 Banchang Hutong, not far from the Drum Tower. This puts you in the heart of hutong territory, and the staff can even arrange bicycle rental for you. ■

Lama Temple

BEIJING'S PREMIER BUDDHIST TEMPLE ATTRACTION, THE Lama Temple was converted from a palace to a temple in 1744 and stood by the old northern wall of the Mongol City. The complex is one of the largest in China.

Fronted by huge *pailou* (decorative arches) to the east of Yonghegong Dajie, the massive Lama Temple is a colorful and exotic Buddhist temple complex that once rose up just within the massive Tartar City Wall that ringed the Manchu sector of Beijing. The wall has disappeared, leveled in the 1950s to ease traffic circulation, but its gates survive in the name of the ring road just to the north—Andingmen Dongdajie (Andingmen being the ghostly name of the gate that stood in the now vanished bastion).

Today, the ebullient Future Buddha greets all, accompanied by the Four Heavenly Kings on either side. Above him is written: "If the heart is bright, the wonderful will appear." Behind him is trusty Weituo, the defender of the faith, holding his staff.

In the next courtyard the **Yonghe Palace** houses two statues of the 18 Luohan (see p. 72) and three golden, robed Buddhas. The decorated ceiling is startlingly beautiful. The **Yongyou Hall** has a statue of the Longevity Buddha.

On the altar of the Qing dynasty **Hall of the Wheel of the Law** stands a statue of Tsongkhapa, the founder of the Yellow Hat Sect of Lamaism (see p. 300). The **Wanfu Pavilion (Wanfuge)** is built around a colossal statue of the Maitreya Buddha. This vertigo-inducing statue (55 feet/17 m high, with an additional 20 feet/6 m below ground) was carved from a single block of sandalwood.

At the rear lies a display of Qing dynasty Tibetan articles and an exhibition on Tibetan Buddhism and the Lama Temple. The collection of Tibetan items includes Dharma wheels (wheels of the law), scepterlike *dorjes* (see p. 305), bells, effigies of Buddha, and a multi-armed statue of Guanyin (see p. 72). This collection is possibly the most fascinating aspect of the temple. There's also an explanation of the gold lots used for the nomination of the next Lama. You can chart the succession of the Panchen and Dalai Lamas (see p. 306) along the walls. English-language guides can be hired at the temple entrance. ■

Tainted in ages past by rumors of diabolical goings-on, today's Lama Temple is a tamer yet equally fascinating spectacle.

Mysteries of the Lama Temple

As a reliquary for the rather frightening spirits and forces of primitive Tibetan Buddhism, the Lama Temple was often associated with strange goings-on. For many years, the secretive temple was out of bounds to Beijing residents. Juliet Bredon's book *Peking* (1922) relates how a Russian bribed his way into the temple with a packet of Huntley & Palmer's biscuits (which he knew the head Lama enjoyed). When he tried to leave, the "fierce monks" shut door after door in his face and asked for payment before opening each in turn. A number of foreigners went missing after visits to the temple, and the rumors of human sacrifices heightened the fear and suspicion. ■

Lama Temple

- Map: 55 D4
- Address: 28 Yonghegong Dajie
- Phone: 010 6404-4499
- Admission: $
- Transit: Yonghegong subway

Confucius Temple

ALONG THE *HUTONG* OPPOSITE THE ENTRANCE TO THE Lama Temple is the Confucius Temple (Kongmiao). Like many temples to Confucius, it is dusty, neglected, and redolent of a disappearing age or a forgotten book. Second in size only to the Confucius Temple in Qufu, this is a tranquil reserve of ancient cypresses, steles (inscribed stone tablets), crumbling buildings, and a forlorn air.

Confucius Temple

- 55 C4
- 13 Guozijian Jie
- $
- Yonghegong subway

Several of the halls sheltering steles on the backs of *bixi* (mythical tortoiselike creatures) are closed. The cypresses claw at the sky, and some have had their branches lopped off to protect nearby roofs. Standing in front of the **Dacheng Hall (Hall of Great Achievement)** is the largest cypress in the compound, planted in the Yuan dynasty by an imperial official. The hall, also from the Yuan dynasty, is where the emperor came to pay homage to Confucius. The mammoth interior swallows up the feeble lighting, but you can pick out a collection of dusty musical instruments, pots, and devotional objects. ■

Cow Street Mosque
55 B2
88 Niu Jie
010 6353-2564
$

Fayuan Temple
55 B2
7 Xuanwai Fayuansi Qianjie
010 6353-3966
$

White Clouds Temple
55 B3
Baiyun Lu
010 6346-3531
Nanlishi Lu subway
$

Other temples in Beijing

BEIJING IS STUDDED WITH AN ECLECTIC ASSORTMENT OF other houses of worship—Muslim, Buddhist, Taoist, and Christian.

COW STREET MOSQUE

Cow Street Mosque (Niu Jie Libaisi) in southwest Beijing is a fascinating little world, inhabiting a small preserve on the east side of Cow Street (Niu Jie). This perfectly preserved, active mosque is in the Chinese style and was originally built during the Song dynasty.

Ancient Muslim worshippers with white beards sit in the shadows reading Islamic texts. Lush vegetation covers the grounds, and pines soar gloriously aloft. Astronomical observations were made from the **Wangyuelou (Moon Observation Tower)** for calculations of the Islamic calendar. The minaret stands in the middle of the courtyard.

Inside the mosque are a **prayer hall** (you can't enter unless you are a Muslim), side halls, a reserve for female Muslims, and vases inscribed with Arabic. Steles on the grounds commemorate the history of the temple, including two inscribed with Arabic at the rear. Dress respectfully.

The area around Cow Street (so named because of the local Muslim predilection for beef) is also notable for its selection of Muslim restaurants.

A monk meditates in the sun at tranquil Fayuan Temple in noisy Beijing.

FAYUAN TEMPLE

Not far from Cow Street Mosque is the large Fayuan Temple (Fayuansi). The complex is extremely quiet but active, so be respectful. Over 100 monks live here, and the most venerable monk has not stepped foot outside this holy domain for over ten years. The Buddhist brothers inhabit a tranquil world apart, a frugal and restrained alternative to the world of today's China. The temple is conservatively decorated, and the grounds are dotted with ancient steles and incense burners.

WHITE CLOUDS TEMPLE

Mainstay of the Quanzhen School of Taoism, the White Clouds Temple (Baiyunguan) off Baiyun Lu is a fascinating multiplex of courtyards and different shrines. Originally founded in the Tang dynasty, it is presided over by Taoist monks, chattering on mobile phones. On the walls of the small **Hall for the Tutelary God (Lingguandian)** are portraits of four famous marshals, including the famous Song dynasty general, Yue Fei. Note the *bagua* prayer mats decorated with trigrams (see p. 288).

There's another temple dedicated to three famous Taoist officials, containing some vivid murals, and the **Hall for the Jade Emperor (Yuhuangdian),** the celestial Taoist God (see p. 73). The walls used to be lined with a set of Taoist statues, which have disappeared. The hall in the fourth courtyard is dedicated to Chang Chun, a famous Taoist monk from Shandong Province, who lived and died at the temple.

Citizens come to worship Karl Marx's nemesis (greed) in the **Hall to the God of Wealth.** They congregate to have their ailments healed at the **Hall of the King of Medicine,** otherwise known as Sun Si Miao (dedicated to a deified doctor of the fifth–sixth century). At the rear of the complex is a temple dedicated to the four celestial emperors.

The **Shrine Hall for the Savior Worthy** has depictions of the Taoist realm of hell (with its apparent shortage of women).

DONGYUE TEMPLE

Dedicated to the God of Taishan, the vibrantly colorful Dongyue Temple *(Dongyue Miao)* is well worth visiting for its numerous spooky "departments," small side halls peopled by fiendish deities and creatures from Taoist myth.

ZHIHUA TEMPLE

Here is one of those rare temples in today's Beijing, largely unrestored and kept in its original state. See the enticing **Ten Thousand Buddhas Hall,** arranged over two floors.

CHURCHES

The baroque **South Cathedral (Nantang),** or the Church of the Immaculate Conception, is a 20th-century replacement for one that was leveled during the 1900 Boxer uprising. This is the focus of Catholic activity in Beijing, with an English mass on Sundays at 10 a.m. Its cousins, **St Joseph's Church** (on Wangfujing Dajie) and **North Cathedral** (see p. 80), survive. ■

Dongyue Temple
- 54 D3
- 141 Chaoyangmenwai Dajie
- Closed Mon.
- 010 6553-2184
- $

Zhihua Temple
- 55 D3
- 5 Lumicang Hutong
- $
- Chaoyangmen subway

South Cathedral
- 55 C3
- 141 Qianmen Xidajie
- Xuanwumen subway

Picturesque Cow Street Mosque is set in a Muslim quarter of Beijing, heavy with the aroma of local foods and the culture of the Hui.

China's gods & goddesses

A host of deities preside over the sacred domain in China. Your visit will be that much more enjoyable if you can lift the lid on the local pantheon and learn to recognize a few of the more popular celestial beings.

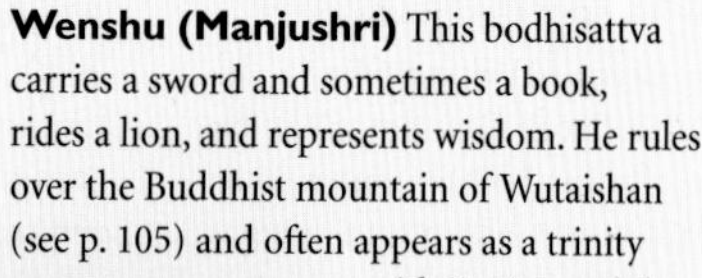

BUDDHAS & BODHISATTVAS

Future Buddha (Milefo or Maitreya) This jovial, golden fellow greets you at the entrance to temples. Buddhists believe there are Buddhas whose time is already in the past, and others who are yet to come. Milefo is a bodhisattva (see below) who will eventually manifest himself on Earth. He is sometimes portrayed with a small group of children. In China, Milefo is a chubby incarnation, based on a real monk called Chang Dingzi.

Historical Buddha (Sakyamuni) The main hall of a temple contains a trinity of golden Buddhas, and the central statue is the Historical Buddha, his hand touching the ground. This deity represents Gautama Siddhartha, founder of Buddhism, in his pre-Nirvana incarnation. He is also represented reclining on a couch, preparing for death.

Bodhisattva The term refers to the Historical Buddha and to those who are capable of becoming Buddhas; in other words, they have attained a pre-Buddha stage of enlightenment. The most prominent bodhisattvas in China are the goddess Guanyin and the Future Buddha, both of whom typify the essentially compassionate mission of the bodhisattva.

Goddess of Mercy (Guanyin or Avalokiteshvara) This ruling deity of the island of Putuoshan (see pp. 178–79) is manifest in the Dalai Lama (see p. 306). In temples, she often faces north at the rear of the main temple; she may also have her own hall.

Wenshu (Manjushri) This bodhisattva carries a sword and sometimes a book, rides a lion, and represents wisdom. He rules over the Buddhist mountain of Wutaishan (see p. 105) and often appears as a trinity with Puxian and the Historical Buddha.

Bodhidharma (Damo) This Indian monk is usually shown with a heavy brow and thick beard. Patron of the Chan (Zen) Buddhist sect, his spiritual home is the Shaolin Monastery (see pp. 124–25), where he left his legacy in the form of *gongfu* (see pp. 122–23).

Luohan (Arhat) The Luohan are perfect humans who have been freed from the cycle of rebirth. There are usually 18 of them, often depicted worshiping Guanyin or ranked in two lines of nine alongside temple walls. Occasionally they appear as a gilded group of 500. They remain in this world until the coming of the next Buddha.

Weituo The defender of the Buddhist faith can be found standing with a staff behind the Future Buddha at the entrance to a temple.

Four Heavenly Kings They are usually present in pairs on either side of the Future Buddha and Weituo. Large and ferocious, they are dressed in armor and carry musical instruments.

TAOIST GODS & GODDESSES

Laozi Born in the seventh century B.C., this founder of philosophical Taoism is often displayed riding an ox and holding a book, his *Daode Jing (Classic of the Way and its Power).*

Eight Immortals This famous group from Taoist legend is often portrayed crossing the sea in a boat.

Jade Emperor (Yuhuang Dadi) This is the supreme god of Taoism, often shown with a black beard, seated on a Dragon Throne.

Three Pure Ones (Sanqing) These are the three large statues grouped together in Taoist temples: Laozi, the Yellow Emperor, and the Jade Emperor.

Queen of Heaven (Tianhou) Reigning principally in southern coastal regions, Tianhou, also known as Niangniang and Mazu, is the protector of seafarers. A large number of temples in Hong Kong are dedicated to her.

God of War (Guandi) This god, typically red-faced, adorned with a black beard, and clad in armor, is also the god of literature and represents both civil and military aspects.

Taoist door gods Taoist temples have similar defenses against evil spirits as Buddhist temples. The Green Dragon and the White Tiger (see p. 230) are Taoist door gods. ■

Above: Two Chinese door gods protect a household from evil spirits.
Below: One of the colorful and unnerving Four Heavenly Kings

The lavish interior of the Hall of Prayer for Good Harvests reveals a circular design that incorporates timeless cosmological principles.

Temple of Heaven

THIS SUPREME EXAMPLE OF MING DYNASTY ARCHITECture is one of Beijing's truly prized landmarks. The temple, a diagram of Chinese cosmology, is both a transmitter to the heavens and an icon of Beijing. On a more mundane note, the Temple of Heaven lends its name to a multitude of commercial products, including the strongest cigarettes on the market.

Set in a vast 660-acre (267 ha) park, a mile south of Qianmen Gate, this sacred plot of land was where the emperor conducted the most significant ceremonies and rites of the year. The rituals performed established the divine link between Heaven (*tian*) and the Son of Heaven (*huangdi*), channeling eternal law to the Earth.

The Temple of Heaven (Tiantan) was a regal domain and out of bounds to the *laobaixing* (common people). In 1918 the temple's former functionaries stepped aside to admit the public, and extensive renovation work has since been carried out. Its sacred geometry retains the cardinal east–west, north–south axis and its celestial metaphors. Buildings are spread through the park, but the principal structures lie along the south–north axis, as with all temples in China.

Temple of Heaven

Map 55 C2

Yongdingmennei Dajie/Tiantan Beilu

$ $

The most striking edifice is the tall, circular **Hall of Prayer for Good Harvests (Qiniandian),** built in 1420 during the reign of Yongle, when Beijing was designated capital. The emperor's geomancers *(fengshui* masters*)* determined this as the exact point where heaven and Earth met. The hall was the focus of sacrificial rituals and prayers for fruitful harvests *(qigu)* in early spring.

It was rebuilt during the reign of Jiajing in 1545 into a triple-eaved structure that glistened with blue, yellow, and green glazed tiles. This chromatic scheme symbolized, in turn, heaven, Earth, and the mortal world. The Qing Emperor Qianlong replaced the tiles with the present azure roofing. During the reign of the feeble Guangxu (*R.*1875–1908), lightning struck the hall, which burned for a day and a night (an unmistakable message from the heavens) and the entire hall was again rebuilt.

The conical roof is a beautiful sight, its roundness symbolizing the extent of heaven. The 120-foot-high (36.5 m) vault was skillfully slotted together without using a single nail. The four inner pillars represent the seasons, and two further sets of 12 columns denote the months and the division of the 24-hour day into two-hour units (their concentric configuration supports the three tiers of the roof). South of the Hall of Prayer for Good Harvests is a raised platform called the **Red Platform Bridge (Danbiqiao),** along which the emperor approached the hall.

The **Imperial Vault of Heaven (Huangqiongyu)** lies south, a round hall tiled in blue and standing on a white platform. The **Echo Wall (Huiyinbi)** ingeniously conveys sound around its circumference, but any personal interface with this technology is usually blotted out by the commotion of tour groups.

The **Circular Altar (Yuanqiu)** to the south resonates with astronomical significance, a cosmic hub that was also the site of the annual winter solstice ceremony. The solemnities involved sacrificial offerings of animals to the accompaniment of music. The altar was also requisitioned during times of natural disasters to entreat heaven.

Built in 1530 of blue stone (later replaced with the present white stone), the mound consists of three tiers that represent Earth, the mortal world, and heaven. Nine steps separate each tier, nine slabs are laid on each tier, and the upper tier is adorned with nine stone rings. The number nine has special significance in Chinese cosmology, for there are nine layers to heaven.

The central feature of the **Fasting Palace (Zhaigong)** near the west gate (Xitianmen) is its large port-red "beamless hall." The neighboring **Living Hall,** surrounded by wilting bamboo, is where the emperor observed abstinence before the sacrificial rites. ■

The meeting point between heaven and Earth, the Hall of Prayer for Good Harvests is a paragon of Ming-style architecture.

VISITING THE TEMPLE OF HEAVEN

The temple park is generally accessed via its west gate from Yongdingmennei Dajie, but gates puncture the wall at all the cardinal points, and the traditional ceremonial route approached the altar through the south gate (Zhaohengmen). ■

Once an imperial retreat, the Summer Palace is a huge domain of halls and temples.

Summer Palace

THE SUMMER PALACE IS A SPRAWLING IMPERIAL ENCAMPment of temples, pavilions, and halls set in a park around the vast Kunming Lake. The imperial family once used this wonderland of noble follies as a summer residence. If the weather is fine, a visit here can make for a memorable day. Expect to stay at least half the day, and pack your camera.

Summer Palace
- 54 A6
- Yiheyuan Lu
- 010 6288-1144
- $$ (some sights have separate tickets); $ (audio guides)

The Summer Palace (Yiheyuan) was conceived in the 12th century, although the buildings here today date from the Qing dynasty. Long before that, the site was a royal garden and retreat, but it was not until the reign of the Qianlong emperor (*R.*1736–1795) that the transformation was made.

From the main entrance east of Kunming Lake you come first to the **Hall of Benevolence and Longevity (Renshoudian).** Here Empress Dowager Cixi (see opposite) sat on her throne during her time of power, hatching her intrigues. The throne is still there, but unfortunately, the hall interior is fenced off and inaccessible to visitors.

The fascinating bronze statues in front of the hall include a *qilin*, a mythical chimera that only appeared on Earth during times of

harmony. The creature can often be seen in Confucian and imperial buildings, a hybrid of dragon, lion, deer, and other animals. To the left of the hall are statues of a dragon and a phoenix, symbols of the emperor and the empress, respectively.

North of the Hall of Benevolence and Longevity lies the **Court of Virtue and Harmony (Deheyuan),** with its impressive theater in which Empress Cixi is said to have dressed up as Guanyin, the goddess of mercy.

On the northern shore of the lake sits the **Hall of Happiness and Longevity (Leshoutang),** where Cixi used to spend the summer months. South of the hall is a pier where she would disembark after crossing the lake.

The Summer Palace's most notable buildings overlook Kunming Lake, with its Seventeen Arch Bridge.

To the south is the **Hall of Jade Billows (Yulantang),** where Emperor Guangxu was kept under lock and key after his involvement in the 1898 Hundred Days of Reform movement (see p. 36).

Follow the shoreline south for sweeping views over the lake. Jutting out from the shore is an island, upon which stands the **Zhichun Pavilion.** Farther along, rows of benches look out over the water. The temple-encrusted hill north of the lake is called **Longevity Hill (Wanshoushan).**

At the southern end of the loop, you will pass a large bronze ox, next to the fabulous **Seventeen Arch Bridge (Shiqikongqiao),** a 492-foot (150 m) span of graceful curves over the water to South Lake Island (Nanhudao). Here resides the **Dragon King Temple (Longwangmiao),** where the empress dowager would come to pray for rain. Alongside the temple is the pier where she would alight from her boat. Inside you can catch a glimpse of the rather ferocious Dragon King. Above the door are characters that translate as "always moist like spring."

From here, jump aboard a tourist boat at the island's northern fringe, and chug over to the other

CIXI—THE OLD BUDDHA

The Qing Empress Cixi (1835–1908), also known in the West as empress dowager, or Old Buddha, began her rise to power when, as a concubine, she had a son by the Xianfeng emperor. The boy became the Tongzhi emperor at the age of five. On his death, Cixi installed her nephew as the Guangxu emperor in contravention of the laws of succession. Throughout her life she dealt in political intrigue and eventually ruled the imperial court with an iron fist. ■

GETTING TO THE SUMMER PALACE

The Summer Palace is 7 miles (11 km) northwest of Beijing's center. It can be reached by bike , taxi, or one of the minibuses that travel between the palace and the city center. In summer, boats run along the canal to the Summer Palace from a jetty north of the Exhibition Centre east of Beijing Zoo. ■

side of the lake. The trip offers some engaging views of the lake: To the north you can make out the stepped arrangement of temples climbing Longevity Hill. The boat ferries you to the decadent **Marble Boat,** a superbly decorated folly, symbolic of the wasteful decline of the Manchu court. The empress dowager paid for its construction with funds earmarked for the Qing naval fleet. To the east extends the Long Corridor (Changlang) with its Pavilion for Listening to Orioles (Tingliguan).

Follow the path to the west to some excellently preserved Qing dynasty roofed docks, where Empress Cixi moored her boats.

The Marble Boat, extravagant plaything of a Manchu court in irreversible decline, remains permanently moored on the shores of Kunming Lake.

If you want to see inside, hire a paddleboat from the dockside and take a torch.

From here, take the path through the trees up Longevity Hill and work your way east to the **Sea of Wisdom Temple (Zhihuihai)** on the crest. This temple is covered with small glazed-tile Buddhas, many of which have had their heads smashed off (especially on the lower tiers) by French and British troops who swarmed through the Summer Palace in 1860, during the Second Opium War. The foreign troops returned in 1900 after the Boxer Rebellion for a repeat performance.

Work your way downhill to the octagonal structure of the **Pagoda of Buddhist Fragrance (Foxiangge).** The descent takes you through a network of steep steps and corridors. **Cloud Dispelling Hall (Paiyundian)** was used by the empress dowager for holding grand ceremonies. In front are bronze phoenixes marked with the reign of Guangxu.

At the base is the **Cloud Dispelling Gate (Paiyunmen),** in front of which sit a pair of noble Chinese lions (see p. 62). From here, you can enter the **Long Corridor,** which runs along the northern shore of Kunming Lake and links the Marble Boat with the Hall of Happiness and Longevity (Leshoutang). Originally built in 1750, the corridor is decorated with thousands of detailed paintings from Chinese myth and legend, including views of Hangzhou's **West Lake** (see pp. 169–70). It was torched by Anglo-French troops in 1860 and reconstructed in 1888. The corridor swarms perennially with visitors.

Over the hill to the north, a string of lakes leads from west to east, culminating in the **Garden of Harmonious Interest (Xiequyuan),** a copy of a Wuxi garden (see p. 168). The area called Suzhou Creek, near the North Palace Gate, has been restored and comes replete with "Olde China" teashops.

The summer climate is refreshingly cooler here than in Beijing, but in winter Kunming Lake is gripped in the clutches of ice, skating is popular then.

If you really want to get in the mood before a visit, read either Stirling Seagrave or Marina Warner's biography of Cixi, the empress dowager. ■

Old Summer Palace

The ruins of the Old Summer Palace symbolize the humiliation of China at the hands of foreign powers.

THE MAGNIFICENT RUINS OF THE OLD SUMMER PALACE, torched and plundered by Anglo-French troops in 1860, are scattered through a huge park in northwest Beijing. The vast grounds of the park are a tremendous sprawl of lakes and ponds surrounded, in summer, by the somnolent figures of fishermen.

The walks here are enchanting—past ponds thick with lilies, along shaded paths, and away from the grinding snarl of Beijing's traffic. The perfect antidote to the mayhem of the metropolis, the Old Summer Palace (Yuanmingyuan) attracts couples seeking a romantic retreat, especially at twilight.

The main attraction is the sublime tangle of marble pillars, column bases, and stone slabs that once formed the European-style palace. The remains are scattered in the **Eternal Spring Garden (Changchunyuan).** If they are not crawling with visitors posing for photos, something of their silent beauty can be enjoyed. The original palace was a colossal estate, with over 200 buildings and a circumference of 4.5 miles (7 km). A few remaining photographs capture its magnificence. A giant reproduction ancient bronze vessel has been added, presumably to give some local flavor. Looting troops filled their knapsacks with treasures, which still pass through auction houses and private collections in Europe and the United States.

Apart from the palace structures, a huge number of ruins dot the park. Some appear to have been moved to create the proper mood, and a stone pavilion set in a maze has been built for the benefit of visitors.

Rumors circulate that the Old Summer Palace will be renovated. This would serve the dual purpose of restoring a national treasure and pumping up visitor figures, but such work would rob the park of its unique ambience. ■

Old Summer Palace

54 A6

Yuanmingyuan Donglu

$

Beijing bike ride

Flat as a Peking duck pancake, the capital's wide avenues and vast distances are awash with a sea of cyclists. Bicycles get their own (broad) lanes, where they jockey for position through sheer number and lobby successfully for control at junctions. It looks terrifying, but this is one of the best ways to bring this huge city to heel. Go with the flow.

Set out from Chang'an Jie, north of Tiananmen Square (see pp. 64–65), and head up Beichang Jie, the road running just to the west of the Forbidden City (see pp. 56–62). To the west is Zhongnanhai, the political nerve center of Beijing, named for the two lakes of Zhong Hai (Middle Sea) and Nan Hai (South Sea). Beijing's leaders control the destiny of the land from here, hidden away behind the wall on your left.

Ahead is **Beihai Park** ❶ (see p. 63), the stomping ground of the Yuan dynasty emperors. Strike out west along Wenjin Jie and, if you are feeling energetic, continue west to Fuchengmennei Dajie and the **Guangji Temple** (see p. 92) and the **White Dagoba Temple** (see p. 92). If not, turn north onto Xishiku Dajie where you will see the twin spires of the Gothic **North Cathedral (Bei Tang) ❷,** with its rather gaudy gray and white paintwork. This monument to Christianity in Beijing is the third of this name to have been built. It was unsuccessfully besieged by the Boxers in a gripping chapter of the 1900 uprising and then served as a school during the Cultural Revolution and later as a warehouse. Now it is once more an active place of worship. The church's Jesuit sisters, the baroque South Cathedral (see p. 71) and the marvelous St Joseph's Church on Wangfujing Dajie, both endured repeated destruction.

Keep going north up to Di'anmen Xidajie and turn right. After about half a mile, turn left up Longtoujing Jie opposite the north of Beihai Park and continue up Liuyin Jie after the junction with Qianhai Xijie.

At No. 14 is the marvelous **Mansion of Prince Gong (Gongwangfu) ❸,** originally the home of a high-ranking Manchu official *(Liuyin Jie 14, $)*. This abode is considered to be the inspiration behind the great house in *Dream of the Red Mansions* (also called *Story of the Stone*), written by Cao Xueqin circa 1715–1763. The book is considered one of the greatest Chinese novels, written in a semiclassical vernacular. The mansion consists of a series of elegant courtyards enclosed by rocky arrangements and walls and gardens threaded with restful walking paths.

Backtrack to the crossroads. Turn east along Qianhai Xijie to the fringes of the Shicha Qian Hai Lake and cross the bridge.

Turn left and run along the bar-littered edge of Hou Hai Lake, which freezes over in winter, attracting ice skaters. The small **Guanghua Temple** ❹ is tucked away down Ya'er Hutong to your right; cycling at will around this area will turn up a pleasant mix of lake views and old traditional *hutong*. Alternatively, loop back and head east along Yandai Xiejie, a charming and fun bar and café-lined street that takes you to Dianmenwai Dajie where you can cycle directly north up to the **Drum Tower** *(Gulou Dongdajie, $)*, which stands on the remains of the original 13th-century structure. A drum used to beat out the hours of the day and night from here, with the night divided into five two-hour periods.

To the north of the Drum Tower, the **Bell Tower (Zhonglou)** *($)* ❺ was first erected during the Mongol era in the 13th century, but rebuilt by both the Ming and the Qing. The huge bell rang as the city gates closed at night. You can climb up the steep steps for long views over to the nearby Drum Tower and beyond. There is a small fee for both.

Heading south takes you to the edge of the block of ***hutongs*** described on pages 66–67. Explore it if you have the energy, and take your time just navigating through this quiet world of narrow lanes.

Inside this complex of thoroughfares lies the **Former Residence of Mao Dun**

The bold Christian edifice of the North Cathedral miraculously survived the Cultural Revolution.

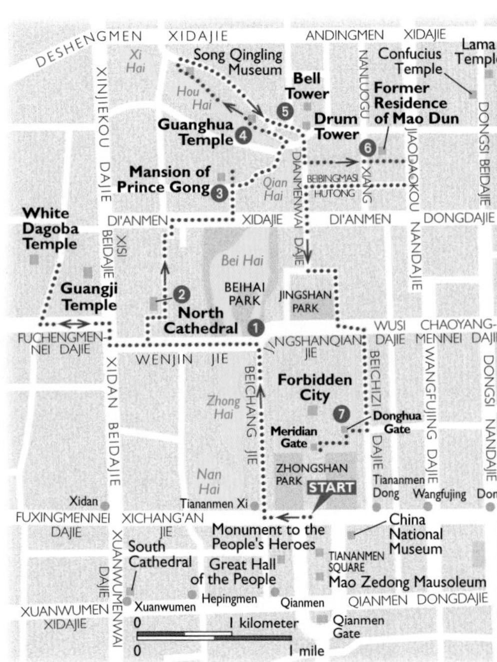

The Five-Dragon Pavillion, once the emperors private domain, now accomodates visitors.

- See city map page 55
- Tiananmen Square
- 9 miles (14.5 km)
- Half day; whole day (including *hutong* trip & Lama Temple)
- Tiananmen Square

NOT TO BE MISSED

- Beihai Park
- Mansion of Prince Gong
- Bell Tower

(Mao Dun Guju) 6. The name Mao Dun sounds exactly like the word "contradiction" in Chinese, and it was the nom de plume of Shen Yanbing (1896–1981), one of China's most famous modern novelists. The building is a modest but charming *siheyuan* (four-walled courtyard), replete with the author's effects (*Closed Sun., Mon., Wed., & Fri., $*).

The small **Wenchengxiang Temple (Wenchengxiangci)** can be found just to the east on Wenchengxiang Hutong. The truly energetic should continue along through the hutongs and head north along Dongsi Beidajie to the Buddhist **Lama Temple** (see p. 68) and the **Confucius Temple** (see p. 69).

Otherwise, turn right along Dongsi Beidajie and right again at the crossroads into Di'anmen Dongdajie. On your right you will pass the attractively fronted **Princess Hejing Palace (Hejing Gongzhufu)** and the **Former Occasional Residence of Sun Zhongshan** 7 (*13 Houyuanensi Hutong*). Continue along Di'anmen Dongdajie and turn left onto Di'anmennei Dajie; then follow it down to the left of Jingshan Park (see p. 63), east of Beihai Park. The view from the peak of Jingshan Park offers an excellent sweep over the Forbidden City.

From here head south along Beichizi Dajie, which runs east of the Forbidden City, taking you back to Tiananmen Square. ■

Ancient Observatory

SURROUNDED TODAY BY A ROAR OF TRAFFIC, THE ANCIENT Observatory (Guguanxiangtai), built on the remains of the old city walls, allowed the Middle Kingdom access to the stars.

Beijing's first observatory was Kublai Khan's, an astronomical wooden tower designed to aid astrological predictions; the Mongols were keen sky-watchers. Construction of the present building began in 1437 and its role included astronomy, astrology, and seafaring navigation. At one time run by Muslims, it was later under the control of the Jesuits.

The Chinese originally thought that the Earth was the center of the universe, orbited by the celestial spheres. In the 17th century the Jesuits arrived with astrolabes, heavenly mathematics, and other devices to set the record straight.

Chinese astronomers were generally (but not always) successful, as Juliet Bredon notes in her book *Peking* (1922). Under the tutelage of Father Verbiest the Belgian Jesuit priest who came to China in 1659 and was made president of the Board of Works, they learned how to predict eclipses accurately; on eclipse day, members of the official board would appear, beating drums to scare away the dragon about to swallow the moon or sun (the Chinese word for eclipse is still *shi*, to eat).

The observatory houses a museum dedicated to Chinese astronomy. Displayed on the roof are pieces designed by the Jesuits in 1674 on the orders of Emperor Kangxi. These include an ecliptic armilla, a theodolite, a sextant, and a dragon quadrant. The large azimuth was a present from Louis XIV to the emperor. Fantastic Chinese designs adorn the instruments. The Jesuits encouraged the Chinese to construct these instruments to replace the old Mongol versions that had been used for centuries. Most survive, despite being stolen by Germans during the Boxer Rebellion; they were returned after World War I.

Near the observatory were the Imperial Granaries and the Examination Halls (Gongyuan), both of which have long disappeared. The Examination Halls housed the candidates for the imperial examinations, a highly conservative selection method that was reformed out of existence by Empress Cixi. ■

Star-gazing device at the Ancient Observatory

Ancient Observatory

- 55 D3
- Jianguomenwai Dajie
- Open Tues.–Sun. 9:00–11:30 a.m. & 1:00–4:30 p.m.
- $
- Jianguomen subway

Imperial examinations

Passing the imperial examinations was an essential step up the ladder of the official elite. The exams tested candidates' verbatim knowledge of huge tracts of Confucian classics, spread over three days and two nights, in solitary confinement. Each cell in the hall had a board for a seat and a small table. Before entering their cells, examinees *(juren)* had to change clothes to prevent cheating. The corridors between the cells were patrolled by vigilant overseers. To further prevent cheating, once a cell door was sealed, it could not be opened again until the exam was over, even in the case of death (when a hole would be cut in the wall and the body removed). ■

Around Beijing

The region around Beijing is where you will find that eternal symbol of China, the Great Wall, the solemn grandeur of the Imperial Tomb, and a crop of temples in the surrounding hills.

WESTERN HILLS

The Western Hills (Xishan) stretch out 12 miles (19 km) west of Beijing, not far from the Summer Palace (see pp. 76–78). Excellent hiking options lie in the hills, most easily accessed through **Fragrant Hills Park** in the eastern section. Temples once dotted the park, but many were damaged by the French and British in 1860 and later during the Boxer Rebellion (see pp. 112–13).

You can reach **Incense Burner Peak (Xianghufeng),** the summit of Fragrant Mountain, either by cable car or by clambering up its slopes, beyond which sprawl the remainder of the Western Hills.

Not far from the park's North Gate is the **Azure Clouds Temple (Biyunsi),** distinguished by its unusual Indian-style, 110-foot-high (33.5 m) **Diamond Throne Pagoda.** Before finally being laid to rest in Nanjing, Dr. Sun Yat-sen's body remained in the pagoda for four years. Five hundred carved, lacquered Luohan figures (see p. 72) congregate in the Luohan Hall.

To the south of the Western Hills is the area known as **Badachu (Eight Great Sites),** celebrated for its eight nunneries and temples. Temples here include the Ming dynasty **Changan Temple,** the **Lingyuan Temple,** which houses a tooth belonging to Buddha, and the **Xiangjie Temple.** To reach Badachu, take the subway to the last stop west at Pingguoyuan, then a taxi.

OTHER TEMPLES

About 28 miles (45 km) west from Beijing is the **Tanzhe Temple,** on the slopes of Tanzheshan (Pool and Mulberry Mountain). The temple's history goes back to the third century A.D. (predating Beijing).

Below: Some of the 500 Luohan at the Azure Clouds Temple (right)

Jietai Temple, or Ordination Terrace Temple, 5 miles (8 km) southeast of Tanzhe Temple, is a Tang dynasty house of worship, although most of the surviving buildings are of later construction. The chief features of the temple are a 10-foot-high (3 m) terrace, which was built in the Liao dynasty (907–1125), and its community of pine trees in the courtyard. ■

The Great Wall

COLOSSAL ENDEAVOR, BRAVE FOLLY, FUTILE CONTRIVANCE, or splendid achievement, the Great Wall of China inspires awe. Sections of it have been restored outside Beijing, but for the larger part, it staggers fitfully over North China.

CITS visitor information

✉ 28 Jianguomenwai Dajie

☎ 010 6515-8587 or 24-hour Beijing Tourism Hotline: 010 6513-0828 (for complaints)

WEST TO EAST

Not so much one wall as an articulation of ramparts, the punctuated Great Wall (Wanli Changcheng) straddles China from the sea in the east to its crumbling finale beyond Jiayuguan in the Gobi desert of Gansu. In its entirety, the wall is almost 4,000 miles (6,430 km) long. Schoolboys love to quip that it is the only man-made structure observable on Earth from the moon, but the wall is far too slender and disconnected to be visible.

HISTORY

The wall is not the work of one dynasty. Begun as early as the seventh century B.C., it only took on its gargantuan character under the first emperor of the Qin dynasty that unified China, Qinshi Huangdi (*R.*221–210 B.C.). Qinshi Huangdi, whose other lasting legacy was the terra-cotta warriors (see pp. 101–103), threaded together the existing ramparts, erected watchtowers, and constructed beacons on the fortification to alert the capital (near present-day Xi'an) of attack.

The wall advanced with the Han dynasty, which further extended Qinshi Huangdi's fine efforts into the Gobi desert, but was chiefly dormant during the flourishing Tang and Song dynasties. The Jin and the Ming dynasties heralded a spate of enthusiastic construction. The Ming, in particular, encased sections of the wall (constructed principally of rammed earth) in brick. Slaving at the wall was a motley assortment of disaffected farmers, soldiers, and prisoners, many of whom died of exhaustion or malnutrition.

The purpose of the defense was to keep the hostile tribesmen of the north out of China. The wall failed spectacularly, most notably with the incursions that established the dynasties of the Jin (Jurchen), Yuan (Mongols), and Qing (Manchu). Perhaps that's why the Qing spent so little time on the wall. Ultimately, the wall was superseded by technology and circumvented by forces that emptied into China from other directions: the Western powers that mustered along the coastline, and the Japanese.

Like other symbols of division (the Berlin Wall, the Iron Curtain, and the Bamboo Curtain), walls are out of fashion these days, and the Great Wall serves only to attract visitors (in huge numbers).

THE WALL TODAY

The wall is impressive for its magnitude. The sections you can realistically visit have been rebuilt and cosmetically touched up for the benefit of visitors; this gives a false impression of the condition of the wall (in large measure derelict). The fortresslike segments viewable around Beijing quickly peter out.

You don't have to go to Beijing to visit the Great Wall; trips can be made at Shanhaiguan (see p. 138), where the wall meets the sea, and Jiayuguan (see p. 328), in the far west of Gansu, among other points.

Badaling

Most people visit the Great Wall from Beijing, as day-trips from the capital. Badaling, 43 miles (70 km)

Opposite: Undulating across North China, the Great Wall is a monument to the country's historic sense of vulnerability.

Following the contours of the hills, some stretches of the Great Wall are strenuous climbs and plunging descents.

northwest of Beijing, heads the thrust of the local tourist industry.

The wall here snakes dramatically over undulations in the land, punctuated occasionally by watchtowers and gates. The Ming sections, clad in stone, surround a core of rubble and earth. Parts of the wall at Badaling can be steep to the point of being mountainous, so take shoes with good grip. To the west, this stretch of wall eventually dissolves into ruins.

Badaling is generally besieged by tour buses and full-on commercialization (the authorities still need to fine-tune profit with preservation), so don't expect a romantic sojourn with just you and the wall. Unless, of course, you go in midwinter. This is actually a good idea, for you will be rewarded with peace and quiet and a wonderfully frosted landscape. In addition, you won't be surrounded by a crowd of hawkers proffering bundles of "I climbed the Great Wall" T-shirts. If you do go in the glacial Beijing winter, be sure to wrap up well.

Most of the hotels that cater to foreign visitors can arrange tours to Badaling. If you go independently, tour buses depart from the Beijing Sightseeing Bus Center *(tel 8353-1111)* west of Tiananmen Square between 6:30 and 10 a.m.

Badaling Great Wall
89
Badaling
$

Mutianyu

Another fragment of wall was rescued from oblivion at Mutianyu, 56 miles (90 km) northeast of the capital. This part was restored in an attempt to divert the crowds from Badaling. The section of wall here is

just a mile long, however, and has also succumbed to the commercial onslaught; a siege mentality reigns. Tours to Mutianyu are easily arranged through your hotel. Also, tour bus No. 6 runs on weekend mornings from the South Cathedral.

Simatai

Among the official tourist sections, the most secluded and genuine part of the Great Wall can be found at Simatai. At 68 miles (110 km) northeast of Beijing, it is farther away than either Badaling or Mutianyu. This distance has protected it from overexposure to tour groups but, equally, has made it harder to reach.

Only partially restored, the wall here offers a more authentic stretch of ruins. The powerful landscape backdrop makes for marvelous hiking along the crumbling remains, but the wall can be dangerously steep in parts and occasionally comes to an abrupt halt over a drop.

The wall here begins at the minute **Simatai Village.** One option for getting here is by private car or taxi, but many travelers arrive on early morning tours run by hotels and youth hostels in Beijing, so it's worth phoning around. Less conveniently, buses from the Dongzhimen bus station run to Miyun, from where minibuses run to Simatai. ■

Mutianyu Great Wall

89
Mutianyu
$$ (including cable car)

Simatai Great Wall

89
Simatai
$

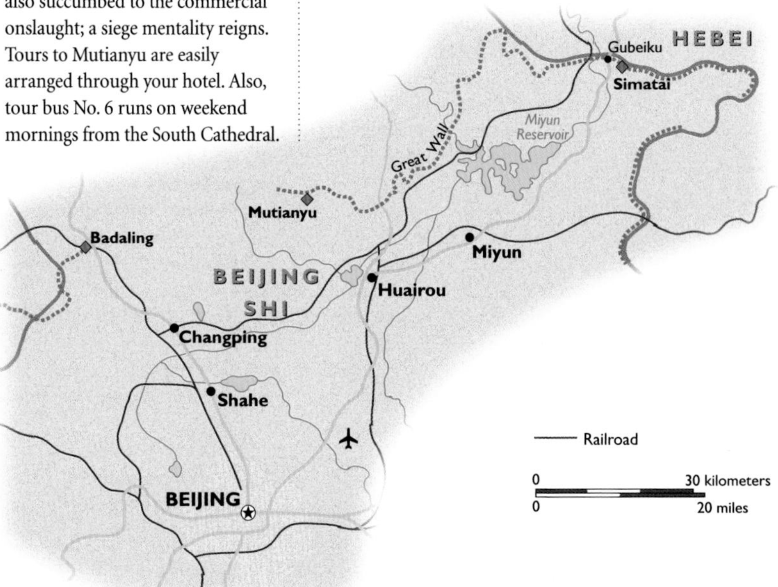

Statues along the Sacred Way to the Ming Tombs

Imperial Tombs

THE TOMBS OF MING AND QING EMPERORS LIE TO THE north, south, and east of Beijing. Grandiose and solemn, the tombs display some of the finest of Beijing's carved stone and the majesty of centuries of imperial lineage.

Ming Tombs
$ (charge per tomb)

MING TOMBS

The Ming Tombs (Shisanling) or 13 Tombs, located 30 miles (48 km) northwest of Beijing, constitute one of the city's major historical sites. They can be disappointing, however, unless you have a knowledge or appreciation of imperial history.

The founder of the Ming dynasty, Hongwu (*R.*1368–1398), is buried in Nanjing, but there are 13 Ming emperors interred here, including Xuande (*R.*1426–1435), Jiajing (*R.*1522–1566), and Wanli (*R.*1573–1620). In all, three tombs have been opened to the public—Changling, Dingling, and Zhaoling.

The tombs are reached under a five-arched gateway (*pailou*), behind which stands a further three-arched brick gateway (*da gongmen*). Through the gates stands the **Stele Pavilion (Beilou),** which holds a large engraved stele eulogizing the Ming emperors.

Beyond lies the long **Spirit Way (Shendao),** lined with statues of animals (some mythological, including a *qilin,* see p. 176) and officials. The emperor's coffin would have been conveyed along this route and through the **Dragon and Phoenix Gate (Longfengmen)** to his tomb.

To reach the tombs, the avenue crosses a seven-arched bridge over water before fanning out to the individual crypts (avoiding straight lines prohibited by *fengshui*).

Changling, the first tomb ahead, is the resting place of Emperor Yongle (*R.*1403–1423). The tomb complex contains an impressively large hall whose roof is supported by 32 huge cedarwood pillars.

Dingling, the tomb of the rather hopeless Wanli, was opened in the late 1950s. You can visit the underground passageways and chambers (Dixia Gongdian).

The last tomb open to visitors is **Zhaoling,** where Emperor Longqing (*R.*1567–1572) was buried. The rest of the tombs at this site await excavation.

Travelers generally tie in visits to the Ming Tombs with the Great Wall. Line A buses from the Beijing Sightseeing Bus Center, west of Qianmen (Tiananmen Square) take in both the Great Wall at Badaling and the Ming Tombs, with buses leaving between 6:30 and 10 a.m. Also ask at your hotel for details of other buses.

Right: The Ming Tombs are laid out on a strict geomantic scheme according to the immutable laws of *fengshui*.

EASTERN QING TOMBS

Entombed 78 miles (125 km) east of Beijing are five Qing emperors, including the Kangxi emperor, the Qianlong emperor, the Xianfeng emperor, and a multitude of empresses. The layout echoes that of the Ming Tombs, with a series of stone gates funneling a Spirit Way to the tombs. **Empress Cixi's tomb (Dingdongling)** is an extravagant feat of self-congratulation. The carved ramp leading to her sacrificial hall depicts the phoenix (representing the empress) above the dragon (the emperor).

The tomb of the Qianlong emperor was a costly money pit from which the Qing dynasty had to extricate itself. The chamber is notable for its Buddhist images, usually absent in imperial tombs.

WESTERN QING TOMBS

If you want to pay further homage to the Qing dynasty, you can do so at the Western Tombs of the Qing emperors. Seventy miles (112 km) southwest of Beijing are the final resting places of the Yongzheng, Jiaqing, Daoguang, and Guangxu emperors. ■

Eastern Qing Tombs
$ $

Western Qing Tombs
$ $

Tomb architecture

When the imperial tombs were originally sealed, they contained a horde of gold, silver, lacquer, porcelain, and other riches to accompany the departed emperor; these were later plundered by thieves. Tombs often designed during the emperor's lifetime would consist of either one chamber or an interconnected cluster. Geomancers would faithfully determine the superlative site for the tomb, paying strict attention to the surrounding *fengshui* of hills and rivers. The south-facing complex typically consisted of a crypt covered in a mound of earth, fronted by altars and halls, and a strip of water (to deflect bad spirits). It should be noted that the governing aesthetic is imperial and Confucian, rather than Buddhist or Taoist. ■

More places to visit in & around Beijing

SHOPPING

The place to come for souvenirs, ersatz imperial porcelain, and mementos of your stay in China is **Liulichang,** also a sight in its own right. The "Olde Beijing"-style teahouses, antiques stores, and art galleries join forces to preserve something of the flavor of China's pre-Communist era.

Littered along Liulichang, southwest of Qianmen are testaments to this country's troubled, yet glorious, past. Busts of Chairman Mao smile beatifically from behind lacquer screens. Walls of alarm clocks from the Cultural Revolution tick furiously under the ineffable gaze of Guanyin, the goddess of mercy. Antique books jostle with Ming and Qing furniture, and crude wooden carvings sit alongside Buddhist carvings, while silk screens, piles of antique lacquer, cloisonné, and fake ceramics complete the picture. Venture in with a critical eye and get the bargaining gloves off. You could easily spend half a day here panning through the detritus for the occasional nugget.

Nearby **Dazhalan,** running west off Qianmen Dajie (not far from Liulichang), is a chaotic lane stuffed full of silk shops, herbal medicine stores, and theaters, as well as food and clothing specialists.

Silk Street, on the corner of Jianguomen Dajie and Dongdaqiao Lu, is floor after floor of silk, clothing, shoes, jewelry, and more, all managed by garrulous vendors. Haggle hard.

Another full and fun hands-on shopping experience for cheap clothing and nice silk can be had at the five-floor **Sanlitun Yashou Clothing Market** *(58 Gongrentiyuchang Beilu)*. The **Pearl Market** *(16 Hongqiao Lu)* is a vast compendium of goods ranging from pearls to silks and arts and crafts, with a great toy store to the rear.

The premier Chinese shopping street in Beijing, the long **Wangfujing** is a pedestrian-only, north–south street to the east of the Beijing Hotel (*33 Dongchang'an Jie*). Called Morrison Street in the old days, it reemerged with a new name after liberation in 1949 and is now in the hands of the slap-it-on-credit generation.

Beijing's most absorbing curio market is **Panjiayuan,** located on the south side of Panjiayuan Lu in the southeast of town. The market is a fascinating sprawl of antiques and collectables, at its liveliest from 6 a.m. to mid-afternoon on Saturdays and Sundays.

For further information on shopping in Beijing, and China in general, see page 386.

TEMPLES & MOSQUES

The **Great Bell Temple (Dazhongsi)** *(M 55 B5, $)*, on Beisanhuan Xilu in north Beijing, is a Qing dynasty complex housing a stout Ming dynasty bell. The bell, cast in 1406, is over 22 feet (6.5 m) high, 8 inches (20 cm) thick at its widest point, and weighs 46.5 tons. Further-more, it is adorned with Buddhist sutras. It was one of six cast, designed to be hung at the six corners of the old city walls.

The **White Dagoba Temple (Baitasi)** *(M 55 B3, $)*, off Fuchengmennei Dajie, is topped with a 13th-century bottle-shaped dagoba that originally housed Buddhist relics. The temple's highlight, however, is its riveting display of Tibetan Buddhist statues.

AROUND BEIJING

The **Peking Man Site (Sinanthropus Pekinensis Zhoukoudian)** *($)*, 30 miles (48 km) southwest of the city, features caves where this primitive man lived. Anthropologists and archaeologists will find the site interesting, while the museum may have some general appeal. The exhibits include the remains unearthed at the site: flint tools, bone needles, animal parts, all with English explanations.

Students of the Japanese invasion of China in the 1930s may like to pilgrimage to the **Marco Polo Bridge (Lugouqiao)** *($)*, 10 miles (16 km) southwest of Beijing. The Japanese were searching for a *casus belli* and the bridge obliged, being the scene of the July 7, 1937 skirmish that finally ignited the war between Japan and China. The marvelous bridge, dating from 1189 and decorated with carved lions capping its balustrades, was described by the great Venetian writer in his travels, a book certain scholars declare to be a work of fiction. ■

From the dynastic capitals of Xi'an, Datong, Luoyang, and Kaifeng to the Shaolin Temple, Taishan, and a coastline harboring a medley of Western treaty port architecture, the North is a fascinating journey through Chinese history.

The North

Guardian deity, Luoyang

The North

THE NORTH IS THE HISTORIC HEARTLAND OF CHINA. CHINESE CIVILIZATION first blossomed along the lower reaches of the muddy Yellow River (Huanghe), charting its colossal course through this historic domain.

The provinces of Shaanxi and Shanxi are stained with the yellow earth *(huangtudi)* that dyes the Yellow River ocher and with which the Chinese mythically associate themselves. As China's cradle *(fayuandi)*, the North is unequivocally Han in custom and folklore, possessing a cultural continuity missing in the minority-rich border regions.

Southern Chinese see their northern counterparts as unsophisticated, simple, and honest *(pushi)* folk. In today's competitive China, this may seem demeaning, but there is brotherly respect for the region's historical legitimacy. Northern Chinese may only be taking up the rear of China's economic drive, but all Chinese traditions flow from this northern fountainhead.

Chinese from the south furthermore vaunt their "many mountains, rivers, and saints" *(duo shan, duo shui, duo shengren)*. Those from the solitary northern province of Shandong curtly reply they have the cream of the crop, "one mountain (Taishan), one river (the Yellow River), and one saint (Confucius)" *(yi shan, yi shui, yi shengren)*. Unassuming Shandong, where the Yellow River leaves China for the Bo Hai Sea, also sports Qingdao, one of China's most attractive port cities, host city of the 2008 Olympics sailing events.

China was first united by the northern state of Qin, whose capital was at Xianyang, outside of Xi'an, itself capital to 11 dynasties. The vast ranks of the terra-cotta warriors assemble outside of Xi'an, guardians of an imperial birthright that belongs to North China.

Other past and present dynastic capitals—Anyang, Luoyang and Kaifeng (all in Henan Province), and Beijing itself—endow the North with a pageant and heritage envied by the rest of the land.

The West's 19th-century colonial imprint barely reaches inland, but foreign architecture of the period has left an indelible mark on the eastern coastal outposts of Tianjin, Yantai, and Qingdao.

Sacred monuments dot the North. Temples cluster at the imperial resort of Chengde and cling to the slopes of Huashan, Taishan, Wutaishan, Songshan, and Laoshan. Buddhist carvings at Longmen and Yungang pay homage to this religion, further evidenced by the legendary monastic order of Shaolin. ■

Known as China's Sorrow for its frequent flooding, the Yellow River flows through North China to meet the sea in Shandong Province.

The Bell Tower sits at the city's axis where the main streets meet. During the Tang dyansty, Xi'an was the world's most prosperous city.

Xi'an

THE VENERABLE AND ETERNAL CITY OF XI'AN, ONE OF China's most important monuments, sprang from almost mythological beginnings. Some Chinese scholars attest to a flourishing town coexisting with the dawn of Chinese civilization. The affluent Silk Road began here, and incoming foreign emissaries brought with them an Islamic flavor that lingers today.

Xi'an
Map 94 B1 & 97

CITS visitor information
Map 97
48 Chang'an Lu Xi'an
029 8524-1864

Ming City Walls
Map 97
$ $

Great Mosque
Map 97
$ $

The city was apocryphally the Yellow Emperor's capital, and some Chinese believed that Xi'an was thriving when the god Fuxi was born, although he appears in the earliest pages of Chinese myth (see p. 22). What is certain is that the capital of the Zhou dynasty existed near here. Xi'an grew considerably under the first emperor of the Qin, Qinshi, who instigated his infamous mass book burning in 213 B.C. not far from the city. Often sacked and rebuilt (even being taken by invading Tibetans in A.D. 763), the city has been the national capital of 11 dynasties; its apogee was reached in Tang dynasty China, when it was called Chang'an.

Numerous religions entered Xi'an along the Silk Road (see p. 310). Islam found a toehold here, and Christianity arrived when the Nestorians established an outpost in Xi'an, while Buddhism crept in from India.

THE CITY TODAY

Xi'an is the capital of Shaanxi Province. The Tang grid pattern of old Chang'an survives in Xi'an today (making navigation straightforward), as does a considerable quantity of historic architecture. The Ming city walls encompass downtown Xi'an, itself divided into sections by its major avenues and streets. Running north–south from the Bell Tower are streets called Bei Dajie and Nan Dajie; east–west of it are Dong Dajie and Xi Dajie. Try to pick up a copy of the easy-to-use

Xi'an Tourist Map from the visitor information center.

A host of historic attractions lie beyond the city walls, including the Big Wild Goose Pagoda, the Small Wild Goose Pagoda, the Shaanxi Museum of History, the Eight Immortals Temple, and, farther afield, the Army of the Terra-Cotta Warriors, Banpo Neolithic Village, the imperial tombs that ring Xi'an, and Famen Temple.

WITHIN THE WALLS

The imposing defensive walls, 8.5 miles (14 km) long, 40 feet (12 m) high, and 50 to 60 feet (15–18 m) thick at the base, were built by the founder of the Ming dynasty, Hongwu. Each flank has a gate at the cardinal point and a chain of watchtowers. Add to that almost 6,000 battlements and a wide moat. From the ramparts, the walls give an enduring sense of impregnability. Like most city walls in China, these have been restored.

You can access the battlements from a number of points, mainly the southern reaches. The walls are not high enough to offer a bird's-eye view over the city, and the ramparts have attracted a swarm of substandard amusement attractions, but you get a good idea of the grand scale of the undertaking. Rubber-wheeled buses are on hand to ferry around those who prefer not to walk.

Xi'an's sizable Islamic population converges on the **Great Mosque (Da Qingzhensi)** in the Muslim quarter, the area to the northwest of the Bell Tower (see pp. 97–98). The mosque has been styled with a Chinese temple handbook and built with several courtyards. The prayer hall is barred to non-Muslims. Elsewhere this engaging corner of the city has a fascinating Islamic complexion.

The **Drum Tower** is similarly rooted in the Muslim quarter, set in a seemingly distant land of Islamic aromas and motifs. This is an excellent area to find a good Muslim restaurant. The **Bell Tower** sits on Xi'an's north–south axis, at a point

MARKETS

The road leading up to the Temple of the Eight Immortals has a flourishing market of relics and fakes, operating on Wednesdays and Sundays. Take a close look at what's on offer. Antique Chinese round eyeglasses in their pouches and ceramic busts of Chairman Mao nestle up against heads of Buddha. The latter are clearly forgeries, but they look as if they have been hacked from the Longmen cliff face. Scattered piles of old Chinese coins with a heavy (and fake) patina heap up against fossils (they look carved), suspicious-looking ceramics (but you never know), jade jewelry, faded photos of Empress Cixi, Taoist volumes on alchemy, old pipes, and magic funeral paper. ■

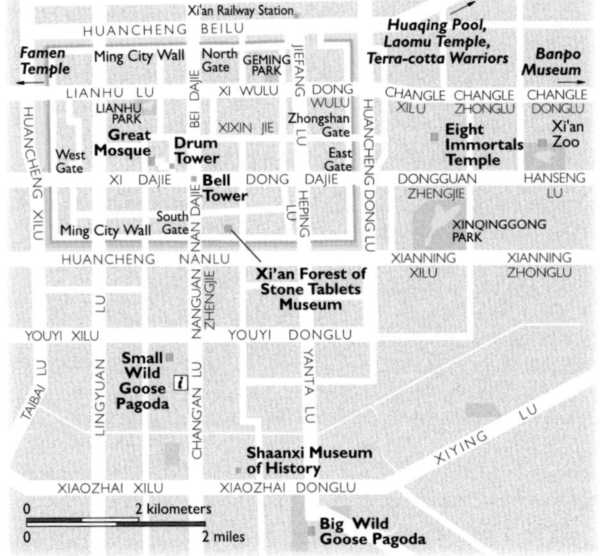

Xi'an contains a large Muslim *(hui)* community, descendants of the merchants that ferried the religion into China along the ancient Silk Road.

Bell Tower
- Map 97
- Nan Dajie
- $

Xi'an Forest of Stone Tablets Museum
- Map 97
- 15 Sanxue Jie
- $$

Eight Immortals Temple
- Map 97
- Off Wudaoshizi Dongjie
- $

upon which the main thoroughfares converge.

The **Xi'an Forest of Stone Tablets Museum (Beilin Bowuguan)** near the city wall in the south was originally a Confucian temple, as can be discerned from the two characters on the main wall outside *(kong miao)* and above the secondary entrance *(wen miao);* both mean "Confucian temple."

Many of the steles celebrate such Confucian virtues as filial piety, and they are inscribed with the complete text of ancient classics, documents, and historical records.

Among the texts carved on stone here are the *Book of Songs* (the first collection of Chinese poems), the *Book of Rites,* and the *I-Ching* (*Book of Changes*). To prevent copying errors, the classics were inscribed on stone and kept in Chang'an (Xi'an) during the Tang dynasty. Students of classical Chinese will find the collection fascinating, but it may prove inaccessible to most foreign visitors.

An intriguing item kept here is the **Nestorian Tablet.** The Nestorians were Christians from Syria who argued that Christ's human and divine natures were separate. Another tablet is an imperial announcement made during the Boxer Rebellion, and it concerns an uprising against Christian missionaries in Luohe Town, Shaanxi Province.

BEYOND THE WALLS

The **Eight Immortals Temple (Baxiangong)** lies east beyond Zhongshan Gate and the city walls. The eight immortals are central characters in Chinese Taoist mythology. You can find images of them in the **Hall of the Eight Immortals** inside the temple complex. At the rear is a temple dedicated to Doumu, the Taoist goddess of the twelve stars and goddess of all the stars in heaven.

The **Hall of Master Qiu** at the rear on the left is where Empress Dowager Cixi and Emperor Guangxu lived after fleeing to Xi'an following the Boxer uprising in 1900 (see pp. 112–13). The plaque in front of the hall is signed in red by the empress and dated the 30th year, the 8th month, and the 21st day of the reign of Emperor Guangxu.

On the corridor to the left of the main courtyard are a number of fascinating black plaques, including one of Confucius. One rare item pictorially describes a diagram of the internal classic, the *Neijing* (a book treasured by Taoists for its lessons on correct breathing and the cultivation of *qi,* essential for the quest for immortality). Another plaque celebrates the five Taoist mountains of China and represents them with five Taoist symbols. Other plaques describe the principles of Taoist spiritual alchemy.

There is little to see at the **Small Wild Goose Pagoda (Xiaoyanta),** on Youyi Xilu, just south of the city walls. Founded in the 8th century, the pagoda was originally 15 stories high, but earthquake damage reduced it to 13 and left a jagged top to the elegant building. You can climb to the top for a view over the city, but be warned: The pagoda is over 130 feet (40 m) high.

Big Wild Goose Pagoda (Dayanta) was originally built by Emperor Gao Zong in A.D. 648 in honor of his mother Empress Wende. This was the most famous temple in Chang'an (the former name of Xi'an) during the Tang dynasty (seventh to tenth centuries). In the main temple, three statues of Buddha are flanked by the 18 Arhats or Luohan (see p. 72).

Xuan Zang (602–664), the famous Buddhist emissary who collected scriptures from India, managed the temple. The Big Goose Pagoda was built to store the hundreds of volumes that he brought back. It was rebuilt as a square, brick pagoda in Tang-dynasty fashion during the reign of Empress Wu Zetian (see p. 28).

The **Shaanxi Museum of History (Shaanxi Lishi Bowuguan),** northwest of the Big Wild Goose Pagoda, allows visitors to get up close to a couple of the life-size terra-cotta warriors from the army of Qinshi Huangdi (see p. 100). Their facial expressions are worth studying in detail; of the thousands of warriors found, no two faces are alike. A pottery horse from the same tomb shows exceptional skill and artistry. The warriors and horse indicate a technical expertise that was rarely repeated in later dynasties.

The collection includes a range of pottery figures from other dynasties. The Han dynasty pieces exhibit the brute vitality and dynamism very typical of this forceful people; however, ceramics from the less interesting earlier dynasties far outnumber those made during the more skillful Yuan, Ming, and Qing dynasties.

A stunning collection of Shang dynasty bronzes reveals how advanced early metalwork was in China, but the lighting in the museum could be better. ■

Small Wild Goose Pagoda

- Map 97
- Youyi Xilu
- $

Big Wild Goose Pagoda

- Map 97
- Yanta Nanlu
- $

Shaanxi Museum of History

- Map 97
- 91 Xiaozhai Donglu
- $

The Shaanxi Museum of History has an important collection of relics.

Around Xi'an

Banpo Museum
94 B1 & 97
Banpo Lu
$

Famen Temple
94 B2 & 97
Fufeng County
$

Huaqing Pool
94 B1 & 97

FRAGMENTS OF IMPERIAL HISTORY AS WELL AS PRIMITIVE remains dot the environs of Xi'an. The most arresting of all is the awe-inspiring army of the terra-cotta warriors, crafted with expert skill and dedicated to the vanity of a supreme emperor.

BANPO MUSEUM

This site just east of town celebrates the Banpo period (4800–3600 B.C.) of the neolithic and matriarchal Yangshao culture that itself lasted from around 5000–2800 B.C. This culture saw the dawn of China's painted pottery tradition (see pp. 202–203). **Banpo Neolithic Village (Banpo Bowuguan),** as the museum is otherwise known, was excavated in 1953. The remains of the village (huts, pottery kilns, and storage cellars) and its cemetery are open to the public, accompanied by the more interesting pottery pieces. Viewing the ancient remains is a rather dry experience, although current renovations aim to inject more attraction for the average traveler.

HUAQING POOL

The hot springs at Huaqing close to the army of the terra-cotta warriors first became popular in the Tang dynasty when emperors visited a complex of bathing houses and pools. You can still bathe in the 123° F (43°C) mineral water.

TOMBS

Emperor Qinshi Huangdi's burial mound is yet to be excavated. For the present, it remains a pile of earth and is not worth a visit unless you wish to pay homage to the despotic monarch. You can glean much more from the nearby terracotta warriors. It is likely that grave robbers have ransacked the interior, but if they never broke into its vaults, a veritable treasure trove awaits. Other imperial tombs near Xi'an are testament to the city's importance as a dynastic capital. They are difficult to reach except on a tour that covers Xi'an's environs.

FAMEN TEMPLE

Situated 73 miles (117 km) northwest of Xi'an, **Famen Temple** has a history that dates back to the Eastern Han (A.D. 25–220). The temple's **pagoda (Zhenshen Baota)** is one of a legendary total of 84,000 built to accommodate relics of the body of Sakyamuni (Buddha), making Famen a significant place of pilgrimage. ■

Army of the Terra-cotta Warriors

STUMBLED UPON BY PEASANTS DIGGING A WELL IN 1974, the 2,000-year-old army of the terra-cotta warriors (Bingmayong) is a fascinating record of artistic achievement and a grandiose expression of imperial power.

CITS visitor information
www.bmy.com.cn
97
48 Chang'an Lu, Xi'an
029 8524-1864

Emperor Qinshi Huangdi united China for the first time under the Qin (see p. 25) and embarked on a series of huge construction projects including the Great Wall. The best preserved of these undertakings is probably the army of terra-cotta warriors, interred within the outer wall of the emperor's mausoleum (which was built during his lifetime) as his eternal imperial guard.

The thousands of pottery warriors stand inside three vaults. These were originally covered with wooden roofs, under a layer of earth. Remarkably, no historical records acknowledged the existence of this army, so they were lost to time.

The tallest warrior stands over 6 feet (1.8 m), and all were equipped with still-sharp bronze weapons—swords, spears, crossbows, and longbows (the weapons have been removed and are not on view). Soldiers and horses were modeled from yellow clay and painted after

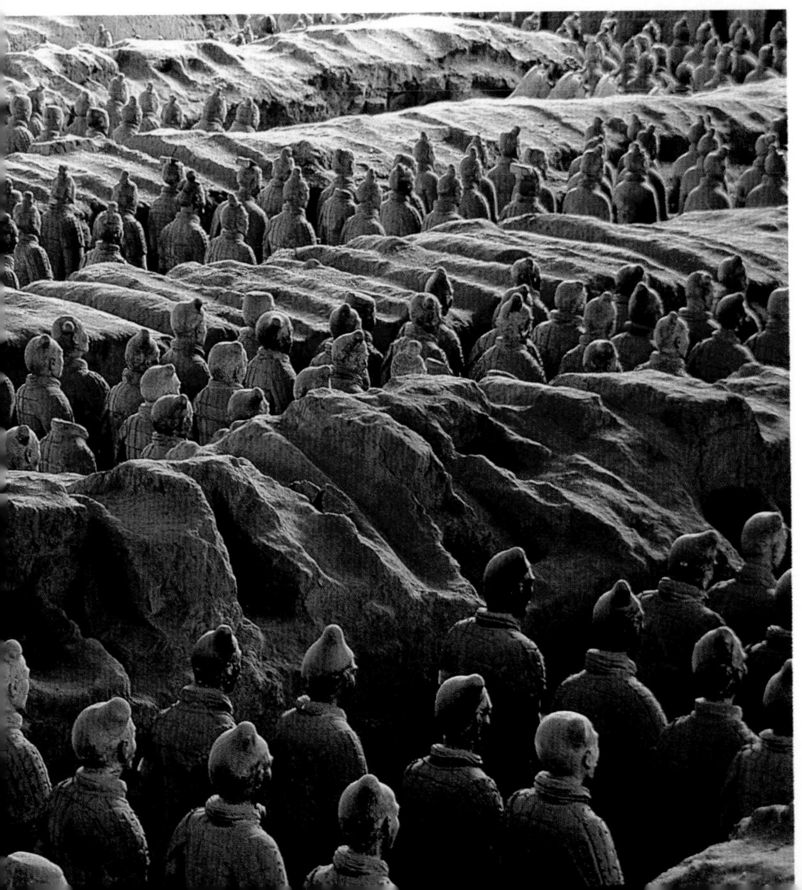

Each terra-cotta warrior represents an individual man.

firing, but the paintwork, which must originally have been vivid and colorful, has faded almost completely.

PIT NO. 1

The main army stands in Pit No. 1; 6,000 of the 8,000 soldiers and horses are here. As you enter, the silent ranks of the terra-cotta warriors stare fixedly back through the millennia. The rows of figures are separated by walls roughly 8 feet (2.5 m) wide; high-level walkways lead between the rows so that you look down on the warriors. (Photography is not permitted). The ranks of soldiers face east, away from the emperor's tomb. A group of terra-cotta horses wore harnesses with brass fittings and perhaps drew chariots, which must have been wooden and are long-since gone. Toward the rear of the vault you can see a pile of collapsed warriors with smashed heads; in fact, a number of the statues at the front are headless. Archaeologists are trying to reassemble whole figures from this jigsaw puzzle of shattered fragments.

The scale of the endeavor is awe-inspiring, and the image of warriors (many toppled by earthquakes) solemn and moving. Close examination reveals the superlative skill that has given each figure a unique expression. The figures are hollow from the legs up; hands and heads must have been modeled separately and then connected to the bodies.

The find propelled Xi'an into the tourist age when the first vault was opened to a clamoring public in 1980. Rivaling China's other premier attractions—the Great Wall and the Forbidden City in Beijing—the terra-cotta warriors were just one part of the enormous imperial necropolis planned by Emperor Qinshi Huangdi.

PIT NO. 2

This pit was discovered in 1976 and opened in 1994. More recently excavated, buried here were chariots, cavalry, and statues of infantrymen, terra-cotta effigies that numbered 1300 in all. On view are several figures, including archers, an officer, a horseback soldier, and further soldiers, all modeled with an exacting eye to detail and craftsmanship.

PIT NO. 3

Of the three chambers in this small vault, one is still unexcavated. The two others have been opened and their contents look to be reasonably intact. They contain 68 soldiers and a war chariot; the figures appear to be high-ranking officers because

VISITOR TIPS

Recorded tours and guides are available on site. Running the gauntlet of hawkers outside the museum can be trying.

Most hotels can arrange trips to see the terra-cotta warriors, 18 miles (29 km) east of Xi'an, taking in other sights en route. Getting there yourself by bus is simple; just take bus No. 306 or 307 from Xi'an train station, both of which terminate at the museum. The trip takes one hour. ■

Below: A terra-cotta warrior as excavated
Left: A painted model shows how a warrior may have looked when first buried.

Terra-cotta Warriors
$$
Minibuses run from the train station

Qin Warrior Museum
$

they are dressed in more elaborate costumes than the infantrymen in vault No. 1; was this the command center for the ghostly army? Photographs taken during the original excavations carried out in the 1970s line the walls.

QIN WARRIOR MUSEUM

This small museum (Tongchema Chenlieshi), near the warriors' site, contains a pair of highly detailed bronze chariots unearthed 65 feet (20 m) west of Emperor Qinshi Huangdi's tomb (see p. 100). ■

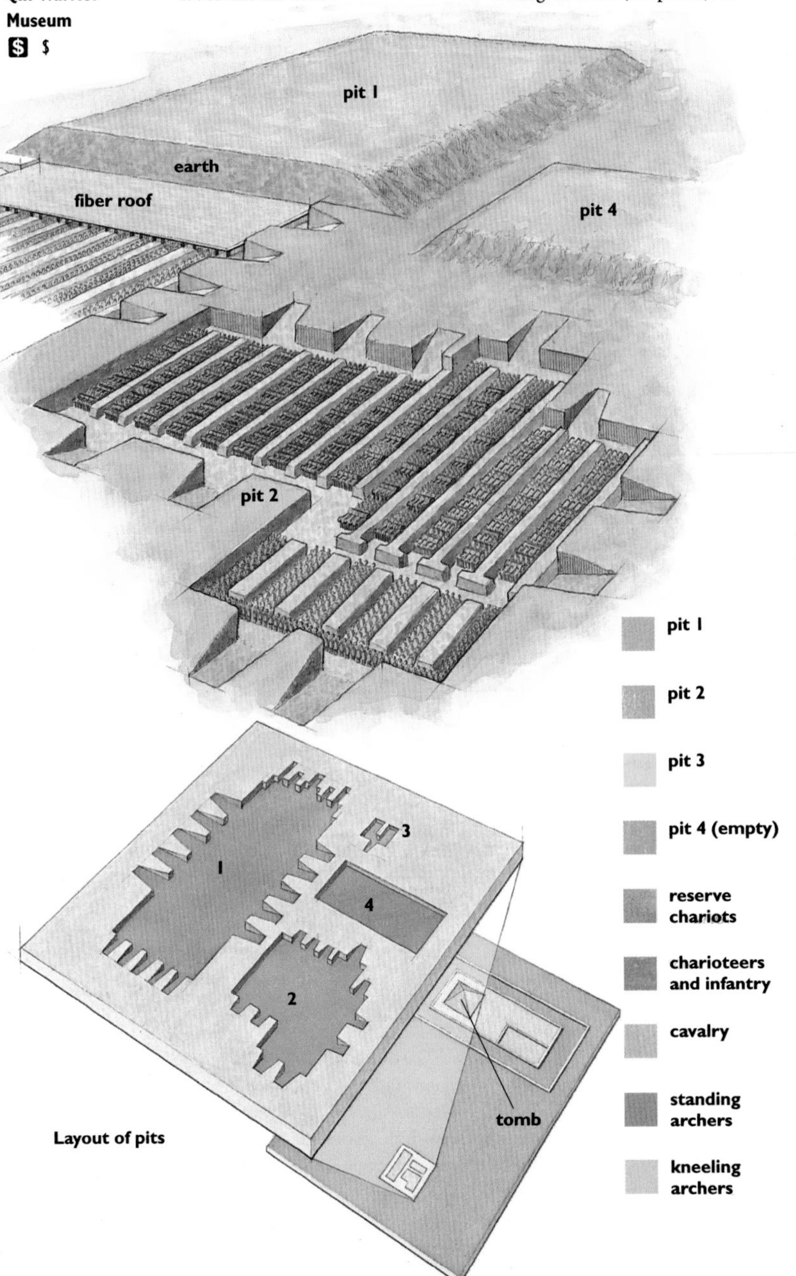

Layout of pits

Huashan

HUASHAN IS THE WESTERN PEAK OF THE FIVE HOLY TAOIST mountains. In ages past, the mountain, which overlooks the lower Shaanxi plain 75 miles (120 km) east of Xi'an, swarmed with cave-dwelling Taoist hermits reputedly endowed with magical powers.

A horizontal ascent for this traveler on Huashan makes the precipitous climb less heart-stopping.

Huashan
94 B2

CITS visitor information
48 Chang'an Lu, Xi'an
029 8524-1864
$$$

Legend says that a white fungus growing on the mountain will, once consumed, transform you into an immortal. More prosaically, the mountain was the scene of a great victory for a group of Communist forces during the civil war.

The mountain has five peaks: East, South, West, North, and Central. Among the peaks lies a valley, with waterfalls cascading down its sides. The sight of Huashan in the mist is a most beguiling spectacle.

The climb to the first peak—North Peak—from Huashan Village, at the foot of the mountain, is comfortable to begin with, but after a few miles it becomes increasingly strenuous. The path clings to the mountainside, rising through the **Huashan Gate** near the **Jade Spring Monastery (Yuquanyuan).**

Huashan has a reputation for being a dangerous climb, as some terrifying sections consist of little more than incisions in the perpendicular rock (a few fatalities occur every year). The ascent is about 9 miles (14 km), so you will need a day for the round-trip. Another option is a cable car that ferries you from the eastern base to the **North Peak,** from where you can access the other summits.

Cratering the mountain rock surface are caves bedecked with carved statues, silent companions to the hermits who sought sanctuary here. Many of the caves suffered violence at the hands of Red Guards during the Cultural Revolution. Some hermits still live on the mountain, but the ground-swell of tourism has made such an ascetic life difficult. The hermits are served by a sprinkling of Taoist temples. Although Huashan is a Taoist mountain, there's also a temple dedicated to Guanyin, the Buddhist goddess of mercy.

A footpath winds up to the summit of **South Peak,** the highest point (7,085 feet/2,160 m). Here lies the **Laozi Cave,** dedicated to Taoism's enigmatic founder, also called Laojun.

As with Taishan (see pp. 129–31) and Emeishan (see pp. 292–93), sun watchers make the ascent to see the dawn sun, and there are accommodations on the summits (such as North Peak Hotel; *tel 029 430-0062*). Spring and autumn are the best seasons for climbing Huashan. ■

Wutaishan & Taihuai

THE SLOPES OF WUTAISHAN, THE NORTHERNMOST OF China's four sacred Buddhist mountains, are scattered with a profusion of temples set against a marvelous alpine backdrop. Wutaistan's peaks group around the charming hamlet of Taihuai.

In fact, Wutaishan (10,000 feet/ 3,058 m) is a parking lot of temples. Not long ago, 200 temples congregated around the mountain, but the ravages of war and revolution have reduced the figure to about 40 (Chinese guides say there are 58). The peaks are presided over by Wenshu (Manjushri) (see p. 72), the Buddhist god of wisdom.

Wutaishan (Five Terraces) is around 4 to 5 hours by bus from either Taiyuan (see p. 138) or Datong (see pp. 106-107). The highest part of the mountain is the **Northern Peak (Beitaiding),** at over 10,000 feet (3,050 m).

Taihuai village nestles between the "terraces" of Wutaishan (north, south, east, west, and central). Swamped by visitors in summer, but relaxed in winter, it is a cornucopia of temple architecture, much of which displays Tibetan and Mongolian Lamaist features. The most distinctive example of this is the white Tibetan-style dagoba of the **Tayuan Temple** to the south of the village. The dagoba stands over 150 feet (45 m) tall and is hung with 250 tinkling bells.

Behind lies the **Xiantong Temple,** whose origins stretch back to the Eastern Han (A.D. 58–75), much further than the multitude of Ming and Qing dynasty halls that survive. The **Bronze Pavilion** is an enticing tiny hall made entirely out of metal. Just to the east, the **Luohou Temple** contains a wooden lotus flower with eight movable petals, on each of which sits a Buddha figure. When the flower rotates, the petals open to reveal the figures. Next to it stands the small **Guangren Temple,** run by Tibetan and Mongolian monks.

The yellow-roofed temple of **Bodhisattva Peak (Pusading)** is 108 steps up Central Terrace, 108 being a significant number in Buddhist numerology. On either side of Taihuai village, you can trek to several other temples overlooking the valley.

The large complex of the Yuan-dynasty **Nanshan Temple** is 1.5 miles (2.5 km) south of Taihuai, on the Southern Terrace. Other temples around the terraces of Wutaishan include the **Shuxiang Temple,** the **Longquan Temple,** and the **Cifu Temple.** Basic accommodation is available in Taihuai village. ■

Nestling in an alpine valley, the *dagoba*-capped Tayuan Temple draws travelers and worshipers to the monastic village of Taihuai.

Wutaishan & Taihuai

Map 95 C3

CITS visitor information

✉ Shijuliangcheng Gonglu

☎ 0350 654-3210

Supported by pillars, the Hanging Monastery clings to its perpendicular perch on the Taoist mount of Hengshan.

Datong

THE WALLED CITY OF DATONG WAS THE IMPERIAL capital under the Northern Wei (A.D. 386–494) before Luoyang took its place, but today it wears an industrial face. For the most part, travelers pilgrimage west of the city to the splendid Buddhist caves at Yungang. Digging deeper beneath the city's dirty countenance exposes a rich vein of temples. Across the desolate wastelands to the south, the vertiginous Hanging Monastery miraculously suspends itself over a dizzying void.

Datong
95 C3

CITS visitor information
Datong Train Station
0352 502-1601
or
Yungang Hotel
21 Yingbin Donglu
0352 712-4882

Datong sits in Shanxi Province, with Inner Mongolia's wide sweeping plains sprawling just to the north, a contrast to this grimy city surrounded by China's leading coalfield. But Datong has several points of interest in its ancient center.

In the western part of the old walled city off Da Xijie is the **Huayan Monastery** *(Huayansi Jie, $)*, whose roots reach back to the northern dynasty of the Liao (907–1125), though it was largely built by the nomadic Jin (1125–1234). The monastery houses the marvelous **Mahavira Hall,** at 16,785 square feet (1,560 sq. m) one of China's largest temple buildings. Its scale is a pronouncement of the city's former importance. Inside are 31 lifelike, colored clay figures from the Liao period representing the Buddha and bodhisattvas.

About half a mile to the east along Da Dongjie (the eastern extension of Da Xijie) you will find the **Nine Dragon Screen (Jiulongbi).** This 150-foot-long (45 m) tiled "spirit wall" *(Da Dongjie, $)*, built in 1392, protected a former palace. Spirit walls are *fengshui* defenses for deflecting demon spirits (see pp. 230-31), although the palace itself burned down!

Shanhua Temple *(Nansi Jie, $)*, abutting the old Ming city walls in the south (themselves accessed at a few points), also contains a small dragon screen. Datong's city walls are being slowly restored.

From a distance, the **Hanging Monastery (Xuankongsi),** 47 miles (75 km) to the southeast, is seemingly wallpapered to the cliff face. This eccentric achievement dates back more than 1,400 years and is a spectacular sight. The temple buildings *($$)* are linked together by boardwalks and bridges laid over piles rammed into the rock. Caves along the temple length are decorated with sculptures, one of which depicts the three faiths of Taoism, Buddhism, and Confucianism.

The **Wooden Pagoda (Muta),** in Yingxian 43 miles (70 km) south of town, is one of the oldest wooden structures in China. Built in A.D. 1056 in the Liao dynasty, the pagoda *($$)* has miraculously survived earthquakes and war to struggle through to the present. ■

Yungang Caves

THE CAVES AT YUNGANG ARE BOTH A MAJOR LANDMARK of Buddhist art and a place of veneration and worship. An army of some 40,000 workmen, under the direction of devout Buddhist artists, carved the caves and statues from the sandstone rock. Protected from inquisitive eyes for centuries, the remaining artifacts have survived plunder, weathering, and industrial pollution.

These entrancing Buddhist cave-temples in the Wuzhou Mountains of Shanxi, 10 miles (16 km) west of Datong, were largely completed during the Northern Wei dynasty. One of the earliest chronicles of Buddhist art in China (and the earliest grottoes containing stone carvings), the major caves were hollowed out between 460 and 494, when Datong was the dynastic capital. The capital later moved to Luoyang, and the sculptors followed with their tools to continue carving at Longmen (see pp. 118–19). The imperial art direction was carried out in the first instance by the Buddhist monk Tan Hao.

CONSERVATION

The caves were carved from a sandstone cliff by a massed workforce of 40,000, and they have survived better than many of the wooden temples of the early dynasties. For centuries, they were appreciated only by devout Buddhists, and this endowed them with an anonymity and purely religious value.

This precious protection was traded for recognition in the early part of the 20th century when statues were stolen by archaeologists and antique collectors. Valuable artifacts from Yungang found their way into collections in Japan and the West, where they remain. Conservation efforts today extend to protecting the Yungang statuary from the combined effects of rock fractures, groundwater, weathering, and pollution (from nearby industrial Datong), and, despite successes, many unsheltered statues have been irretrievably scoured away by wind and rain.

FOREIGN INFLUENCE

These carvings show the many artistic influences that affected Buddhist artists. Hellenistic themes had made their way to Gandhara in north India, gathering Persian elements on the way, and a fused aesthetic had emerged. From here, Buddhism was exported along the Silk Road to China, passing through the lands of Central Asia, acquiring their flavor.

BUDDHIST THEMES

Fifty-three caves remain, housing a gathering of 51,000 statues. Stylistically, some of the caves are simply capsules containing colossal statues of Buddha (the tallest is 55 feet/17 m high). Others are designed as temples, enclosed behind wooden galleries and decorated with numerous carved murals and effigies.

Recurring themes focus on Buddha himself or recount Buddhist stories and legends from India. Buddhism found a comfortable niche in China during the Northern and Southern dynasties (386–586), possibly as an antidote to the incessant wars and relentless human suffering of the period.

Buddhist parables, or *jataka*, adorn the walls, including the tales of the man who gave his own flesh to save a dove and the 500 bandits

Yungang Caves
Map 95 C3

CITS visitor information
Datong Train Station
0352 502-1601
$$

who had their eyes gouged out. Sakyamuni (the historical Buddha) is pictured having strips of flesh cut from his legs to feed a hungry eagle preparing to feast on a dove; this was a test of faith designed by the gods. The scenes are animated by the lively facial expressions of the statues.

THE CAVES

The south-facing caves stretch for about a kilometer and are more accessible than those at Dunhuang. They are grouped in three clusters. Of the four caves in the eastern section (1–4), the largest is **Cave 3,** which once contained a temple and now houses a seated Buddha and two bodhisattvas. The caves in the central section (5–13) are magnificent. They are shielded by a much later, Qing dynasty temple, other examples of which have not survived. **Cave 5** shelters a colossal 55-foot (17 m) Buddha. The walls of **Cave 6** revel in stunning detail (relating Buddhist stories) and revolve around an intricately carved central pillar. **Cave 8** is peopled by Indian gods and goddesses, including Vishnu and Shiva, while the remaining caves in this central section teem with Buddhas.

Many of the western section caves (14–53), the largest group, are badly eroded, though there are a few surprises. **Cave 19** reveals another 55-foot (17 m) Buddha, and **Cave 21** is wrapped around a central pagoda. The statue of Buddha in **Cave 20** shows Central Asian influence in its wide features, cloth folds, and broad chest. ■

The majority of work on the Yungang Caves ended when the Northern Wei moved their capital to Luoyang in A.D. 494.

Tianjin

Tianjin
95 D3

AT FIRST GLANCE, TIANJIN IS AN UNINVITING INDUSTRIAL sprawl, much like other Chinese cities. A closer look at the center of town, however, reveals a patchwork of European, Russian, and Japanese architecture in this former foreign concession city.

Pedestrian street in the former concession city of Tianjin

CITS visitor information
22 Youyi Lu
022 2810-9988

Great Compassion Monastery
40 Tianwei Lu
Open daily
$

Wanghailou Cathedral
Shizilin Dajie
Closed Mon.–Sat.

The municipality of Tianjin (Tientsin) has a long history as a trading center. Its proximity to the sea and to Beijing, and its siting at the northern reaches of the Grand Canal (see pp. 162–63), made it the economic hub of North China by the time of the early Qing dynasty. The Treaty of Tientsin (1858) opened the city to British and French concessions, followed in due course by others. Foreign troops shelled and occupied the city during the Boxer Rebellion and destroyed its old walls. It was badly rocked by the notorious Tangshan earthquake of 1976.

Tianjin has a variety of places of worship that survived the great earthquake and symbolize the city's cosmopolitan history. The **Great Mosque (Qingzhensi)** in the northwest of the city near Xibeijiao subway station has a Chinese look, but it remains an active place of worship (non-Muslims may not enter).

Great Compassion Monastery (Dabeiyuansi), also in the northwest of the city, is Tianjin's most impressive Buddhist temple. The Tangshan earthquake gave the temple a bad shake, but it has been restored.

Bordering the river not far to the south of the Dabeiyuan Monastery is the **Wanghailou Cathedral (Wanghailou Jiaotang).** Outside this solemn, dust-choked Gothic church, a plaque (in Chinese) commemorates an incident in 1870 when the cathedral and the French Consulate were burned down by an irate mob. The notice relates that some 20 missionaries were killed after rumors circulated accusing the European Christian community of kidnap-ping children for nefarious purposes, including human sacrifice (in fact, the infants were orphans). The cathedral was later rebuilt, torched again during the Boxer uprising, and rebuilt again. It suffered further during the Tangshan earthquake and also at the hands of the Red Guards who gave the church a battering during the Cultural Revolution.

Poking out from the bric-à-brac of Ancient Culture Street (see opposite) is the fabulous little **Tianhou Temple (Tianhougong),** dedicated to Tianhou, goddess of seafarers. Those who have been to Hong Kong will probably be familiar with this deity; temples to her are a feature of that city. The restored frescoes in the main temple show exploits from the life of Tianhou (also known as Niangniang or Mazu). Here, too, are models of Ming and Qing dynasty sailing ships from the provinces of Fujian and Zhejiang (where Tianhou is most actively worshiped). Fierce-looking weapons displayed on either side in the temple are there to protect her. At the rear, is a small temple to Guanyin, goddess of mercy.

A block west stands the **Confucius Temple (Wenmiao),** a rather dry and mothballed monument to the sage. Confucius sits on his altar, surrounded in perpetuity by dust and ancient musical instruments. The temple sits toward the eastern edge of the old—formerly walled—town of Tianjin, marked at its center by the Drum Tower.

The massive **Xi Kai Cathedral (Xikai Jiaotang)** was originally dedicated to St. Vincent de Paul and was managed by missionary priests from the order he founded. Its towers sport green domes, the whole edifice being a copy of Notre Dame de la Garde in Marseilles.

MARKETS

You can hunt for souvenirs and relics at the massively revamped **Ancient Culture Street,** near the Confucius Temple. Meant to re-create an ancient Chinese street, the buildings here have carved balconies, red- and green-painted shops, and curling tiled roofs. It's worth exploring, for surfacing on the stalls are occasional rarities, such as documents from the Cultural Revolution era (including 1960s pamphlets screaming "Down with Deng Xiaoping!").

Tianjin's bustling **Antique Market** can be found on Shenyang Dao, south of Heping Lu. It operates every day of the week, but is at its busiest and most fascinating on Sundays.

The Astor Hotel, a home-away-from-home for British concession holders

CONCESSION ARCHITECTURE

South of the Hai River were the European and Japanese concession areas. Tianjin's Western-style buildings show a dogged determination to bring your home style with you wherever you went. Typical French buildings grace the French concession (Jiefang Lu). Farther down this road the British concession reveals grand Edwardian establishments that would not be out of place in London. The **New World Astor Hotel** is worth a look (see p. 365). Nearby were the offices of great British commercial houses, such as Jardine & Matheson. Across the river lay the Russian concession. ■

Confucius Temple
✉ 1 Dongmennei Dajie

Xi Kai Cathedral
✉ Binjiang Dao
🕒 Closed Mon.–Sat.
🚌 Yingkou Dao subway

New World Astor Hotel
✉ 33 Taierzhuang Lu
☎ 022 2331-1112

Boxer Rebellion

The 19th century was a long chapter of mutual frustration for China and the West. The empirical West tried constantly to open China to trade (as it still tries today). The Chinese saw the Westerners as barbarians.

This was a clashing of diametrically opposed cultures. China, the Middle Kingdom, was padlocked in a complex, parochial culture, while the West was out restlessly exploring the world. Chinese misgivings about Western culture were bolstered by the conviction that China needed nothing from the West. Western diplomatic overtures were rebuffed (see p. 35).

By the end of the 19th century, anti-West indignation was uncontainable. Suspicions abounded, from the fear that Western missionaries were kidnapping Chinese orphans (see p. 110), to anger at the new, Western-introduced railroads crossing over ancestral graves and violating the sacred principles of *fengshui.* The rapid encirclement of China by the Western powers and the unequal treaties foisted on the Qing government (such as the Treaty of Nanking, whose terms were dictated by the British), stoked tensions. Qingdao, Hong Kong, and other areas of China had drifted into foreign hands. A collective xenophobia against the "hairy ones" was growing.

Magical charms

As a patriotic movement, the Boxers (The Group of Righteous Harmony) were a last spluttering of old China. Originally spawned from anti-Manchu (Qing) elements and secret societies, the Boxers performed breathing exercises closely related to martial arts, or *quanfa* (see pp. 122–23). They imagined their charms and calisthenics would confer invulnerability. Their resentment was not matched by military competence, however, for they lacked the hardware and organization of the West. Armed with broad swords, headbands, and magical spells, the Boxers were driven by a naive faith forged from superstition and magic. With their ranks swollen by refugees from poverty and natural disasters, the Boxers rose in 1899 and began to massacre Christians and attack Western interests.

Siege

Sensing an chance to rid China of Westerners, the Qing (Manshu) court at first decided to collude with the Boxers, spurring rebel activity in North China. The Boxers dropped their anti-Qing agenda and united behind the court to evict the *yang guizi,* or foreign devils.

Bands of Boxers were roving through the streets of Peking by May 1900. On June 20, they killed the German minister to China, Baron Von Ketteler (his death is still remembered by a memorial in Zhongshan Park southwest of the Forbidden City).

This signaled the start of a 50-day siege of the Foreign Legations in Peking, as the foreigners in the capital held out against a

determined army of besiegers. The Foreign Legation Quarter (the center of the foreign community in Peking) lay south of the Grand Hotel Beijing; much of it was devastated during the rampage of the besieging Boxers.

Relief

An international relief expedition consisting of Japanese, Russians, British, Americans, French, Austrians, and Italians was rapidly assembled and dispatched. After some setbacks, they entered Peking at the eleventh hour to relieve the trapped foreigners.

Empress Dowager Cixi fled with the emperor via a gate in the northern wall of the Forbidden City to Xi'an on a "tour of inspection." She stayed for a period at the Eight Immortals Temple there (see p. 98). The foreign soldiers then embarked on an orgy of looting and vandalism, sacking the Summer Palace and cavorting among the riches of China. The foreign powers furthermore foisted a punishing indemnity on the Qing court known as the Boxer Protocol, which took years to repay.

Consequences

The bitter lessons of the Boxer Rebellion forced China to make an unpalatable decision: If China was to survive, it had to copy the West. China overturned the Qing dynasty soon afterward, flirted with Republicanism, and finally embraced Communism, one of the West's most enduring legacies to China. ■

Western armed forces confronted the Boxers in the Battle of Tientsin.

Chengde's temples and monuments have been restored, including these buildings on Gold Mountain.

Chengde

CALLED JEHOL (WARM RIVER) BY THE MANCHUS, THE IMPERial resort of Chengde was established during the reign of the Kangxi emperor (*R.*1662–1722) in the early 18th century. The spectacular complex, set on a sheltered river plain, was known as Bishu Shanzhuang, or "mountain hamlet for escaping the heat." Today it is called Chengde after the adjacent town.

Chengde
95 D4

CITS visitor information
3 Wulie Lu
0314 202-4816

The mountain-fringed resort, 159 miles (255 km) northeast of Beijing, was much expanded during the reign of the Kangxi emperor's grandson, the Qianlong emperor (*R.*1736–1795). Work continued during the reign of Jiaqing (*R.*1796–1820), but his death from a fire at the resort (ignited by a bolt of lightning, rumors said) tarnished Chengde's standing. The kiss of death came with the demise of the Xianfeng emperor here in suspicious circumstances in 1861. Chengde never recovered from its reputation for misfortune, and even the feeble last emperor, Puyi (see p. 36), refused to visit the resort, although he had nowhere to go as he fled from Beijing.

Chengde is a sprawl of palaces, pavilions, temples, and monasteries (the latter two are called the Eight Outer Temples). Though a number

of buildings are in ruins, much survives and forms an impressive architectural museum.

Originally, a 6-mile (10 km) wall enclosed the resort. The chief entrance is called Lizheng Men; another entrance (Dehui Men) pierces the wall to the east. Through the Lizheng Men you come to the **Main Palace (Zhenggong),** with its nine courtyards (nine being the number of heaven) set amid pines and rocks. It houses a museum of imperial memorabilia: furniture, costumes, and weapons of the period.

Leaving the palace by the north gate brings you to the main park, threaded by lakes. From here, you can see the wooded area to the west. The plain stretching to the north was the site of imperial hunting parties and archery competitions, and the lake to the east (divided into Ideal Lake and Clear Lake) is studded with temples and pavilions. The **Hall of Mist and Rain (Yanyulou)** sits on a small island hill in the north of the lake; it was once an imperial study.

On the eastern shore of the lake is **Gold Mountain (Jinshan),** a small hill topped by the elegant hexagonal pagoda and temple, the **Building of God (Shangdilou),** built for the Kangxi emperor in imitation of the Jinshan Temple in Zhenjiang (see p. 161). Also on the lake, and erected as one of the Qianlong emperor's 36 beauty spots of the resort, are the **Water's Heart Pavilions (Shuixinxie).**

North of the lakes and visible from afar is the tall **Yongyousi Pagoda,** rising from the grounds of its vanished, namesake temple (destroyed by the Japanese).

EIGHT OUTER TEMPLES

The **Eight Outer Temples (Waibamiao)** lie a couple of miles from the imperial garden

Built to impress the Buddhist lamas of Tibet and Mongolia, the great red walls of Putuozongsheng Temple rise powerfully from the hills.

(catch a bus from the garden's front gate). Of the original 12 temples, 8 remain today, built mainly during the reign of the Qianlong emperor. Most were designed in non-Han style to impress visiting Tibetan and Mongol envoys.

The temples have suffered the ravages of time: Some were damaged during the civil war of the 1930s and 1940s, and some were marred by the war with Japan, while others fell victim to the iconoclastic Cultural Revolution. This neglect is being slowly reversed, but you may find that some temples are closed or parts are off-limits. Sadly, all have been ransacked of their former treasures.

Largest is **Putuozongsheng Temple** in the hills to the north of the imperial complex, built in 1771—a miniature facsimile of the Dalai Lama's Potala Palace in Lhasa. It was built by the very religious Qianlong emperor in the hope that the Dalai Lama would visit Chengde (he didn't). The dagoba-topped temple is the largest in Chengde, containing 60 halls. Inscriptions in Tibetan, Mongolian, Manchurian, and Chinese illustrate the link with Potala Palace.

To the east of the Putuozongsheng Temple, the **Temple of Sumeru Happiness and Longevity (Xumifushouzhimiao)** was built in honor of a visit from the sixth Panchen Lama in 1779. It imitated his Tibetan monastery in Shigatse. High outer walls with many windows surround the magnificent temple, adorned with a huge, dragon-encrusted roof.

Tibetan motifs also dominate the **Temple of Universal Tranquility (Puningsi)** to the northeast, likewise styled after a Tibetan monastery. Inside stands a colossal and magnificent 42-armed statue of Guanyin, the goddess of mercy.

The **Anyuan Temple (Anyuanmiao),** east of the Wulie River (Wulie He), is a copy of a temple in northwest China, unusually topped with a black-tiled roof. The huge, quadrilateral exterior houses decayed Buddhist frescoes.

Just to the south is the circular, two-tiered roof of the **Temple of Universal Happiness (Pulesi),** which resembles Beijing's Hall of Prayer for Good Harvests at the Temple of Heaven (see p. 75). Other temples include the **Puren Temple,** the **Shuxiang Temple,** and in Chengde itself, the recently restored and fascinating Taoist **Guandi Temple,** west of Lizheng Men, the main gate to the imperial resort. ■

Culture clash

In 1793, Lord Macartney and his embassy from Britain arrived at Chengde for an audience with the Qianlong emperor. Macartney's brief was to make diplomatic overtures and secure trade links with the Middle Kingdom.

The audience went awkwardly. Lord Macartney would only kowtow to the Chinese emperor if courtiers would likewise bow in front of a portrait of the English sovereign, George III. This request was refused. Despite the extravagant gifts presented to the emperor, his final message was, "We possess all things. I set no value on objects strange or ingenious, and have no use for your country's manufactures." This marked the beginning of a war of wills that saw Britain try to force trade on China. Ultimately, China would reluctantly buckle and accept things foreign. ■

Worshipers light *xiang*—incense—from a brazier at the White Horse Temple, established in the first century A.D.

Luoyang

THE ANCIENT CITY OF LUOYANG, SOUTH OF THE YELLOW River on its sweep through Henan Province, was capital to ten dynasties. China's first Buddhist temple opened its doors here, and the awesome endeavor of the Longmen Caves lies outside town.

Luoyang's eminence ended with its sacking by Jurchen invaders during the Northern Song dynasty and the fleeing of the court to Kaifeng (see p. 120). Communist-era industrial development has transformed the little town to a city of more than a million people. Artifacts and artwork, including some stunning jade pieces, in the **Luoyang Museum (Luoyang Bowuguan)** guide you through local history.

The enchanting **White Horse Temple (Baimasi),** 6 miles (10 km) east of Luoyang, is considered China's first Buddhist temple.

A colorful legend lies behind its inception. When Luoyang was capital of the later Han dynasty, in A.D. 64, Emperor Ming had a dream. In his vision, a golden deity flew in front of his palace. Asking his advisors for an interpretation of this symbol, one replied that it was Buddha. The king promptly dispatched men to India to bring back scriptures. After several years, they returned on two white horses with sutras (scriptures of Buddhism). These were ostensibly the first Buddhist writings to come to China. A temple, named for the two horses, was built in which to house the manuscripts. The story is probably apocryphal: Buddhism was already finding a tentative toehold in China along trade routes, although the faith was not to flourish for several centuries.

The present buildings date from a later time, but the temple has a recorded history traceable to the first century A.D. Inside the temple are two tombs, the final resting place of two Buddhist Afghan missionaries. ■

Luoyang
Map 95 C2

CITS visitor information
✉ Changjiang Lu
☎ 0379 432-3212

Luoyang Museum
✉ 298 Zhongzhou Zhonglu
$ $

Longmen Caves

THE LONGMEN STATUARY OUTSIDE LUOYANG IN HENAN Province is an exhilarating legacy from master Buddhist sculptors. Like Dunhuang and Yungang, Longmen is an important reliquary of Buddhist cave art.

Longmen Caves

Map 95 C2

CITS visitor information

✉ Changjiang Lu

☎ 0379 432-3212

The statues were created by devout carvers over a 600-year period, beginning in A.D. 493, but the majority of the statues took shape between 473 and 755. The colossal endeavor began when the capital of the Northern Wei moved from Datong to Luoyang (see pp. 108–109). The hard rock of the cliffs along the Yi River, 9 miles (14.5 km) from Luoyang, provided an ideal site for further carving.

From the entrance at the north end of the site, you walk along the west bank of the river just below the caves. The Binyang caves you reach first are among the oldest, begun under the Northern Wei.

The size of the larger Buddha statues, especially in the Ancestor Worshipping Cave, reveals the diligent efforts of the Longmen sculptors. The fascinating sideshow of a set of large, unfinished Buddhas (the sculptors downed their tools at this point) reveals the deities emerging unformed from the rock, suggesting the Buddhist themes of

Legend tells how the cliffs at Longmen appeared miraculously from the ground, adorned with a pantheon of Buddhist statues.

metamorphosis, transcendence, and eternal change.

Scars of history

A sense of loss and defilement may accompany your admiration of the carvings. The large number of headless Buddhas and bodhisattvas is a depressing statistic. Many were plundered by antiques collectors, but a number appear to have just had their faces smashed off, possibly by anti-Buddhist forces. Years of neglect have also taken their toll on the statues, and for a period the caves were requisitioned by farmers who lit fires in them. This damage creates a powerful sense of sacrilege, but there is an equally strong sense of immortality in their remains, partly due to the toughness of the rock they are chiseled from and partly from the sheer magnitude of the undertaking. Altogether, there are nearly 1,400 caves, 2,800 inscriptions, and 100,000 statues (the smallest about an inch high). Among the scars of repeated vandalism and the onslaught of the elements, flakes of paintwork still gleam from ceilings and walls, and the larger Buddhas are largely still whole.

THE CAVES

Among the Buddhas and bodhisattvas recorded in stone are Guanyin, Amitabha, Sakyamuni, Maitreya, and other celestial beings (see pp. 72–73). The figures range principally from the Northern Wei to the Tang dynasty. Buddhas from the Northern Wei are ethereal and subtle, divine and idealistic, while those from the Tang appear more mundane. Also reflected in the carvings is a maturing of technique that accompanied successive dynasties. The Tang dynasty Empress Wu Zetian (*R.*698–705), a famous patron of Buddhism (see p. 28), commissioned a number of pieces.

Many of the grottoes are high up, but these are accessed by steps and walkways. It is difficult to get a good view of the statues, though, as fences keep you at a distance and the English translations of the informative signs are hard to read. A trip to Dongshan on the other side of the Yi River (cross by the bridge to the south) puts the undertaking into colossal relief. Dongshan contains a further network of caves, but they are often inaccessible.

Longmen's caves are clustered together, generally reflecting the period in which they appeared. The three **Bingyang Caves,** near the entrance, are some of the earliest carvings here, dating mainly from the Northern Wei.

Farther along is the spectacular **Cave of the Ten Thousand Buddhas (Wanfodong),** dating from the late 7th century. The cave is crammed with a universe of small Buddha figures and a large central statue.

In the **Lotus Flower Cave (Lianhuadong),** whose ceiling is decorated with a lotus flower, stands a headless Buddha that was carved in 527.

The Tang dynasty **Ancestor Worshipping Cave** is the most impressive sight at Longmen. The central statue is 55 feet (16.5 m) tall and flanked by bodhisattvas and a ferocious guardian figure. The face of the central figure supposedly captured the visage of Empress Wu Zetian.

The **Medical Prescription Cave (Yaofangdong)** is carved with small medical prescriptions; the ancient Guyang Cave was first carved in 495. The **Shiku Cave (Shikudong),** decorated with ceremonial figures, was carved during the Northern Wei.

The Longmen caves lie 9 miles (14.5 km) south from Luoyang; they are easily reached by bus. ■

The Iron Pagoda was built during the Northern Song when Kaifeng was at its zenith.

Kaifeng

THE FLOOD-PRONE WALLED CITY OF KAIFENG HAS SERVED as capital to seven dynasties, including a glorious period during the Northern Song (960–1127). Prosperous and cosmopolitan, the city even boasted a far-flung community of Israelites, whose faith had entered China along the magnificent Silk Road.

Kaifeng
95 C2

CITS visitor information
98 Yingbin Lu
0378 393-4702

Kaifeng is an attractive city still decorated with a smattering of traditional architecture, and a concerted effort has been made to restore the buildings that reveal its imperial heritage.

Most of its sites of historical interest lie within the city walls. **Xiangguo Temple** on Zi Lu was originally founded in A.D. 555. During Kaifeng's heyday as capital of the Northern Song it was China's foremost temple. Xiangguo was washed away in 1642 when the Yellow River was deliberately allowed to flood the city in a botched attempt to halt the invading Manchu army. Rebuilt by the Manchu victors, the temple resumed its position as the focal point of the city. Dine at the temple vegetarian restaurant for a taste of China's Buddhist cuisine.

The temple's bell tower contains a vast bronze bell and an umbrella that belonged to Cixi, empress dowager. The 1,000-armed figure of Guanyin, goddess of mercy, in the octagonal pavilion at the rear was carved from a single piece of ginkgo wood.

About half a mile directly to the west on Dazhifang Jie is the tiny Taoist **Yanqing Temple,** badly damaged by the floodwaters of the Yellow River. The **Pavilion of the Jade Emperor** (supreme god of Taoism) remains.

In the northeast of the city, just within the old city walls, is Kaifeng's **Iron Pagoda (Tieta).** The slender brick tower is wrapped in metallic-looking tiles, imparting an ironlike sheen. The tiles on the lower flanks of this octagonal

pagoda display damaged Buddhist images. The temple that was attached has vanished. You can climb to the top of the pagoda for unobstructed views over the city.

The Qing dynasty **Dragon Pavilion** stands within Longting Park in the northwest. The park can be reached by walking along the reconstructed **Imperial Way (Songdu Zhengjie),** the Song capital's main thoroughfare.

Kaifeng's Jewish community used to worship at the **Synagogue (Youtai Jiaotang),** of which nothing remains except three stelae on show in Kaifeng Museum *(Yingbin Lu)*. The synagogue stood near or under the No. 4 People's Hospital on Beixing Tujie. ■

Right: The Iron Pagoda rises up near the old defensive city walls, which can be climbed at several points.

Songshan

Songshan, the mountainous home of the legendary fighting monks of the Chan (Zen) Buddhist Shaolin Temple, is also the central mountain of the five sacred Taoist peaks and site of possibly China's oldest Taoist shrine—Zhongyue Temple.

The area's ugly duckling is the town of Dengfeng at the foot of the mountains; it is the usual point of departure for tours of Songshan.

A mile (1.6 km) to the northeast of Dengfeng is the **Songyang Academy (Songyang Shuyuan),** founded in the Song dynasty (960–1279) and one of the four great Confucian academies (it was previously both a Buddhist and a Taoist monastery). The other academies are in the provinces of Hunan and Jiangxi. Despite being a major Confucian monument, Songyang offers little to see, apart from two (originally three) old twisted cypresses. These trees were promoted to the rank of general by the Han emperor Wudi, when he ascended the mountain in 110 B.C.

Three miles (5 km) farther to the northwest is the pagoda of the **Songyue Temple.** The pagoda and the temple, which date from the 6th century A.D., are sadly crumbling away. Empress Wu Zetian (see p. 28) was a guest during the Tang dynasty, when she came to Songshan to offer sacrifices.

Heading northeast from the Songyang Academy, you will reach **Central Peak,** the highest of Songshan's mountains at 4,893 feet (1,490 m). To the east of Dengfeng is the start of another route to the summit. Here you will find the Taoist **Zhongyue Temple (Zhongyuemiao).** It claims a venerable ancestry, reaching back to 215 B.C., although all the present buildings are of a later date. The two carved pillars south of the main temple were erected in the second century A.D.

A cable car from the Shaolin Temple (see pp. 124–25) takes you into the Songshan range to the west for walks among cliffs and woods. ■

Songshan

Map 95 C2

CITS visitor information

Beihuan Lu (Dengfeng)

Tel. 0371 6288-3442

Gongfu

Whether it is esoteric or athletic, *quanfa* (Chinese boxing) is a mysterious and captivating art. The enticing path to *gongfu* (which you may know as kung fu) is a strenuous one for its disciples, fraught with hardship and littered with failure. For the spectator, it is a colorful and dazzling performance that offers a glimpse of transcendent skill.

Skill

Gongfu simply means "skill." This can mean perfection in calligraphy, painting, martial arts, or any other endeavor. It has, however, become irretrievably embedded in the notion of the fearless and exceedingly skilled fighter.

The concept has been warped by its cinematic variant: the high-kicking, wrathful, and fearless hero. This perception swamps *gwoon* (Chinese kung fu schools, *guan* in Mandarin) the world over with suspect personalities.

The high-kicking and elastic fighter of the movies could not be further from real gongfu. True gongfu stresses not awesome flexibility, but more the ability to change quickly from ethereal to solid. It is an internal ability, rather than an external piece of equipment. Flashy displays often belong to those who have lost their way on the road to mastery. The Chinese call those who make a lot of noise "half a bottle of vinegar," for the insubstantial sloshing sound it makes. True skill in gongfu can be elusive and difficult to retain, once discovered.

Ren—patience

Gongfu stresses depth, rather than what is "up in the air." "Pretty flowers, but no roots" is another Chinese saying, describing what is visually impressive but lacks solidity. This is perhaps best demonstrated by the emphasis paid to standing, for long periods, in fixed postures. It develops the "root" of the student and the circulation of *qi* or "energy" within the body, and it also instills an essential ingredient into the student; only through patience and endurance can gongfu be attained.

The rewards of gongfu appear in equal measure to the amount of work put in. Even students of the "soft" or "internal" arts of *taiji quan* (supreme ultimate boxing, also known as Tai Chi) and *bagua zhang* (Eight Trigram Palm), an esoteric Taoist martial art that employs the palm as a striking weapon, rather than the fist, have to invest pain in pursuit of their art.

Students who attain true gongfu are very different from the disciples who first set foot on the path to skill. The change is both physical and mental. Not only are the students more aware of their body and its capabilities, but they have endured a long and punishing voyage where the virtues of perseverance and reward are understood. Furthermore, they are no longer necessarily aware that they have skill for it feels inherent. Humility results from this.

Hard & soft schools

Fighting tactics tend to fall into two groups, the "soft" or "internal" school and the "hard" or "external" school. Taiji quan, with its slow moves and ethereal lightness typifies the former, while *baimei quan* (white eyebrow boxing), characterized by ferocious and rapid strikes and grabs, belongs to the latter.

In its purest form, softness in boxing equals nothingness and is a Taoist pursuit (see p. 42). The soft arts of taiji quan, bagua zhang, and *xingyi quan* (body-mind boxing) all take Taoism as their guiding creed. The hard arts such as *laohu quan* (tiger boxing) and white eyebrow boxing are Buddhist in inspiration.

Softness may seem like a recipe for defeat, but the aim is to approximate a vacuum at one moment and solidify the next, so an attacker is led into nothingness and then repelled by an

attack. In the soft armory, taiji is the most weightless, while bagua zhang is weightier and xingyi quan is the most aggressive.

In practice, many schools are mixed bags of hard and soft moves, and *wing chun* is an example. Invented in the 18th century by a nun called Ngmui from the Shaolin Temple, the art combines evasiveness and yielding with hard and fast, snappy punches. Wing chun is what Bruce Lee studied, and it is one of the more successful arts for the beginner who seeks a speedy acquisition of skills.

Zui quan (drunken boxing) also mixes hard and soft moves. The student moves as if drunk, a state of mind that relaxes the body and deceives the aggressor, who is lured into a trap. A high degree of flexibility is necessary for this style. Other styles include praying mantis boxing, five ancestors boxing, red sand palm, wuji, white crane boxing, monkey boxing, and long boxing.

If you wish to observe students training, or to find a teacher, the best place is at dawn in city parks throughout the land. ■

Chinese boxing runs to scores of different styles, all of which enhance spiritual awareness and demand physical strength.

The Forest of Dagobas commemorates famous monks of the Shaolin Temple.

Shaolin Temple

THE WARRIOR MONKS OF THE SHAOLIN TEMPLE ARE synonymous with Chinese *gongfu* (see pp. 122–23). Buddhism and martial arts are the dawn-to-dusk staples that nourish the Shaolin monk throughout his day. Theme of countless films and schoolboy make-believe, Shaolin's mystery emanates from the very real religious fraternity that worships here.

Shaolin Temple
- 95 C2
- Songshan, Henan Province
- $

CITS visitor information
- Beihuan Lu (Dengfeng)
- 0371 6288-3442

The Shaolin Temple, on the slopes of Songshan between Luoyang and Zhengzhou, was founded in the fifth century A.D. by a monk named Ba Tuo, a martial arts exponent. One of his two disciples, Seng Chou, could vault onto rooftops with a single leap.

Bodhidharma, the Indian sage who founded the Chan (Zen) Sect of Buddhism, a tolerant strain of the religion, visited in A.D. 527. He developed a series of physical exercises for the monks to perform after their long periods of seated meditation. The seeds for the great flourishing of *wushu* (martial arts) at the temple had been sown. Unlike karate, taekwondo, or kick boxing, the Shaolin martial arts foster a religious sense and a way of life.

The temple welcomed artistic and idiosyncratic monks who were refused by other monasteries. It

also became a refuge for hundreds of soldiers, militiamen, and bandits, who were often skilled in the fighting arts. These regular arrivals helped protect the temple against the threat of outside attack, while growing imperial patronage added to its fortunes.

The monks of Shaolin were sometimes called upon to fight for the court, and a standing army of monk-soldiers was formed. By the time of the Ming dynasty, the monks were at their zenith, only to face a decline during the Qing dynasty. The temple has suffered numerous sackings and torchings in its history, including a visit from Red Guards in the 1960s.

Today, thousands of would-be Shaolin monks come to the temple, often for what amounts to a crash course in self-defense. The temple's accountants long ago noted there was a yuan or two to be made out of opening up to the masses, and many a bodyguard has studied the arts of instant death here. Martial arts schools have sprung up around the temple and you may see their students practicing in the precincts. Many foreigners also enroll in the hope of becoming tomorrow's David Carradine, star of the TV series *Kung Fu,* but some sadly get fleeced and return disconsolate.

Thousands of gongfu enthusiasts make the pilgrimage to Shaolin every year. Some pay their respects to the spirit of Bodhidharma; others are inspired by Bruce Lee or Jet Lee; some are just plain curious. Behind the flashing cameras and souvenir stalls they find a great monument. The Shaolin Temple is still the home of all the Eastern fighting arts.

THE TEMPLE

The main courtyard bristles with a series of commemorative steles, some from as far away as fighting clubs in England. This testifies to Shaolin's powerful sway over the global imagination. Three golden Buddhas and an effigy of Damo are displayed in the main temple. Damo stands, slightly obscured by a velvet curtain to the right-hand side, and can be identified by his beard and Indian countenance.

Toward the rear of the temple is **Standing Snow Pavilion,** where a monk named Huihe cut off his arm while standing in the snow to commune closely with the substance of Chan (Zen) Buddhism. Adjacent **Wenshu Hall** houses a stone whose surface has captured the likeness of a bodhisattva.

The deep impressions on the floor of the **Pilu Pavilion** behind, whose walls are covered with murals, were made by the stances and footwork of legions of fighting monks. The **Guanyin Temple** to the right displays the famous frescoes of Shaolin monks fighting. These pictures are reproduced in numerous books on gongfu.

Chuipu Hall displays large ceramic figures depicting gongfu and meditational postures. A number of different forms of Shaolin boxing are represented, including Luohan fist, a vigorous style named after the famous Luohan of Buddhist mythology (see p. 72).

Tragically, a number of the "monks" have taken up begging, although the rest continue their ascetic, disciplined fighting existence, despite the flurry of commerce around them.

The famous **Forest of Dagobas** lies 650 feet (200 m) up from the main temple, but it is not difficult to locate (follow the map on your ticket). Each of the hundreds of small dagobas commemorates a notable monk.

The weekends see the temple at its commercial worst, so plan to visit on a weekday if possible. ■

Confucianism

The influences of China's greatest social philosopher, Confucius, upon Chinese values and political doctrine have been colossal. Furthermore, his teachings found fertile ground in other Far Eastern countries. The Chinese characteristics of frugality, diligence, and veneration of the family structure owe much to the Confucian vision.

Confucius (551–479 B.C.), whose name comes from the Chinese pronunciation of his name, Kong Fuzi, or Master Kung, was born into poverty in the state of Lu (in present-day Shandong). He lived during the pre-Qin era, a period of great division when China was assailed by immoral government, internecine strife, and oppression (see p. 24). Despair prompted Confucius to seek a code of ethics that would encourage rulers to govern fairly and win the hearts of the people.

Confucius is seen as an official in a Western engraving of Master Kung.

There was little of the metaphysical about his philosophy, which hoped to offer rational solutions to the problems of the age. Central to his beliefs was respect for the past and for authority, whether the elders of the family or leaders of the social hierarchy. Confucius stressed the importance of education and the study of classical texts and rites, his teachings formed the basis of the grueling civil service examinations all the way up to the 20th century.

Permeating his teachings was a strong sense of humanity and sympathy that heralded an escape from primitive belief in superstition and magic. The emphasis on respect for your elders and the political hierarchy, however, encouraged the static nature of Chinese society. Confucius never lived to see the practical application of his theories (he failed to assume an official position of significant influence) and only achieved fame in the centuries after his death. Even so, he attracted around him a group of disciples to whom he conveyed his body of thought. Confucius encouraged his disciples to better themselves through the study of poetry, music, history, and the rites *(li)* or ceremonies that formulated the etiquette of the period. His hope was that his converts would fashion a society governed by principles of uprightness and honesty.

After his death, his teachings were brought together by his disciples into a volume called *Lunyu (The Analects)*. Later Confucianism was championed by the philosopher Mencius (372–289 B.C.) and also by Xunzi (circa 313–238 B.C.).

Confucianism is often contrasted with Taoism (see p. 42): The former embraces the human world, while the latter seeks to escape it. Taoism is nature-bound and spontaneous, while Confucius's goal was a utilitarian philosophy; they represent the two sides of the human mind, one cognitive, the other emotional. The balance between both systems creates a satisfying order.

Confucianism through history

Confucius has ridden a roller coaster of praise and condemnation through successive dynasties. The Qin, who unified China, condemned his works to the bonfire, but the Han dragged them out of the embers. The Wei Jin era (A.D. 220–420) was an indulgent period of metaphysical flights of fancy and Confucius was outclassed. The 19th-century Taiping (see p. 35) were zealously anti-Confucian, as were the Red Guards in the next century, while today the sage is tolerated. The cycle of condemnation and worship points to the ambivalence in Chinese society regarding Confucius. Although a rationalist philosophy, Confucianism failed to evolve. Its patriarchal nature, coupled with the respect accorded to long-deceased ancestors, led to its gradual but steady ossification.

Confucianism today

The position of Confucianism remains ambiguous today. Though it is an anachronistic impediment to China's drive to adapt to Western science and technology, as well as a potential critic of the Communist Party's autocratic governance, Confucianism is also lauded as a corrective to the spiraling greed and crime that is overtaking China's towns and cities. A fundamentalist reading of Confucius has an uncomfortable position in the modern age. It can be argued that the prejudices of Confucianism, with its praise of earlier epochs, and a golden age when harmony reigned, help explain the inflexibility of Chinese politics and the ease with which, even in the 21st century, power falls into a few, aged hands. Confucianism belongs within the culture of the Far East and is less a global philosophy than a civilization indicator.

There are a number of Confucian temples scattered through China, but it is at Qufu (see p. 128), Confucius's birthplace, that the finest example can be found. This is a place of sacred pilgrimage not just for millions of Chinese, but for devoted bands of Japanese and Koreans who also flock here. ■

Dacheng Hall, Confucius Temple, Qufu—an exercise in balance and harmony

Direct descendants of Confucius can still be buried in the Confucian Forest.

Qufu

QUFU, THE HOMETOWN OF CONFUCIUS AND HIS FAMILY and capital of the state of Lu during the Zhou and Han dynasties, is a pilgrimage site for Chinese, Japanese, and Korean visitors, with some of China's finest examples of Confucian temple architecture.

Qufu
95 D2

CITS visitor information
36 Hongdao Lu
0537 449-1492

Confucius Temple
$

Confucius Mansions
$

Confucian Forest
$

The importance of Confucius (see pp. 126–27) to the cultures of the Far East is inestimable, but the philosophical resonances require a Confucian upbringing to appreciate fully. What can be enjoyed, however, are the architecture and the sense of history permeating the place. The Chinese rank the town alongside the Forbidden City and Chengde in the importance of its buildings.

The **Confucius Temple (Kongmiao)** has grown considerably since its humble inception as a memorial hall, with the complex now covering a large part of central Qufu. Inside you will find twisted and gnarled cypress trees and more than a thousand steles, both hallmarks of Confucian temples (see pp. 175–76). Also rooted in the grounds is a juniper tree planted by Confucius himself; the pavilion from which he taught his students is here, too. His words were collected by his disciples into a volume called *Lunyu (The Analects)*, copies of which can be bought in small editions. The impressive **Dacheng Hall (Dachengdian)** is the hub of the complex and the site of Confucian rites and festivals celebrating the philosopher.

The **Confucius Mansions (Kongfu),** just to the east of the temple, was the abode of the aristocratic Kong class, who apparently lived in great luxury, protected by their own laws and imperial favor. Just over a mile to the north of Qufu lies the **Confucian Forest (Konglin),** the burial place of Confucius and his family and heirs, thick with pines and cypresses. You can either walk there or take the No. 1 bus. ■

A climb up Taishan

Taishan's Welcoming Pine greets pilgrims near the summit.

MOUNT TAI IN SHANDONG PROVINCE IS THE HOLIEST OF China's revered Taoist mountains. The twisting climb to its summit is the *dao* or "way," a voyage and a metaphor for life, making the ascent a spiritual journey.

The mountain is a place of creation. It was commonly believed that the sun began its daily trek from Taishan, and many pilgrims stay overnight at one of the guesthouses on the summit to catch the famed dawn. The souls of the dead also flee to Taishan. Much of the allegory and legend associated with Mount Tai predates Taoism, rooted in a deeper, more primordial ancestry.

The Chinese take climbing Taishan (5,000 feet/1,524 m) seriously. Streaming up its slopes are the old and decrepit, businessmen from Taiwan, Hong Kong accountants, peasants, soldiers, and tourists. Pilgrims flow past sinewy porters making more routine assaults with bottled drinks, food, and building materials. In ages past, devout climbers would knock their heads *(kowtow)* on the stone steps during their ascent.

At least one climb is a mandatory pilgrimage for Taoists. Shandong (East of the Mountains) Chinese are justifiably proud of Taishan, and they look down on China's other sacred peaks.

The mount, being in the eastern realm, is further governed by the Green Dragon of *fengshui* lore (see p. 230), lord of springs and streams. The emperor would come to Taishan to offer sacrifices to the god of Taishan and seek his blessing in times of crisis or lack of rain.

The ravines, gullies, twisted outcrops, trees, and temples of Taishan are also infused with the spirit of the Princess of the Azure Clouds, a Taoist deity (and daughter of the god of Taishan) worshiped in this region.

Taishan

Map 95 D2

$ $

CITS visitor information

✉ Puzhao Hotel, Puzhaosi Lu

☎ 0538 820-7797

A gate near the summit is inscribed with these characters: the place where one becomes immortal.

CLIMBING TAISHAN

The ideal seasons are spring and autumn; summer is packed out and very sticky, and winter can be bitingly cold, especially at the summit. Even in summer, temperatures can drop; taking waterproofs is advisable. Food and drink on the trail is pricey, so stock up before. You will need at least eight hours up and down in total. You can also climb the route at night, when the way is lit by lamps, or cheat by taking the minibus or the cable car. ■

THE ROUTE

It's not Everest and you won't need ropes, but the 6,660 steps will knock the stuffing out of the unfit. If you feel weak-kneed, glance at the bright-eyed, aged wayfarers and the one-legged hopping up alongside you. The Pan Lu, or Pilgrim's Road, is marked with inscriptions and calligraphy.

You have a choice of two paths up Mount Tai: the Central or the Western route. The **Central route** is the most popular, littered as it is with places of historical interest; along this path the emperor sauntered on horseback. The **Western route** is longer, more circuitous, and with fewer historical sites, but it is scenically pleasant.

Regardless of the route you take, you should start your journey from the **Dai Temple** in Tai'an, at the foot of the mount. The temple, a huge, walled complex of halls, cypresses, and steles, has a history reaching back 2,000 years. The main temple is the **Palace of Heavenly Blessing,** dedicated to the god of Taishan. It contains a retouched Song dynasty fresco depicting the journeying god in the form of an emperor.

Leave the temple to start your ascent of the Central Route and pass Daizong archway along Hongmen Lu. The **Pool to the Cloud Mother (The Queen Mother of the West)** is marked by a small nunnery. Ahead, the archway of **Yitianmen (First Gate of Heaven)** precedes this inscription: "the place where Kongzi (Confucius) began to climb."

The temple of **Red Gate Palace (Hongmen)** pays homage to the Princess of the Azure Clouds. Past the tower of the **Building of 10,000 Immortals (Wanxianlou)** rises a revolutionary monument, a jarring effigy of socialist China (Mao climbed Taishan). Beyond that lies **Doumu Hall (Doumugong),** the Nunnery of the Bushel Mother, the Taoist equivalent of Guanyin (goddess of mercy). A path twists down to your east, leading to a carving of the Buddhist Diamond Sutra on the mountainside, unusual considering this is principally a Taoist mountain.

Horse Turn Ridge marks the point where the horse of Emperor Zhen Zong (*R.*998–1023) died. Pilgrims drag themselves up to **Zhongtianmen (Middle Gate of Heaven),** where a cable car awaits those gasping for breath. This is a major resting post and the climb's mid point. Zhongtianmen is a bit of a circus, like much of Taishan, but try to look beyond the cola vendors and hawkers.

Continuing up, cross over **Cloud Step Bridge** and ahead is the **Five Pines Pavilion (Wusongting),** marking the spot where Emperor Qinshi Huangdi, invoking the blessings of the mountain, instead ran into a tremendous thunderstorm. He sheltered under pines and promptly promoted them to the rank of ministers of the fifth degree. You may need divine inter-

vention to scale the steep **Path of Eighteen Bends,** which ends with the temptingly close but ever-distant **Nantianmen (South Gate of Heaven).**

You still have a short way to go to get to the summit, where the small **Azure Clouds Temple (Bixiaci)** finally awaits the triumphant pilgrims. The **Jade Emperor Temple (Yuhuangding)** stands at the highest point of Taishan. Below is the **Wordless Stele,** whose writing has long been worn away by inquisitive hands.

If you are planning to see the sun rise, the assembly point is the **Gongbei Rock.** In times past, devout pilgrims would throw themselves off the edge of the peak in a religious trance. ■

The tranquil South Gate of Heaven caps the punishing haul up the Path of Eighteen Bends.

Qingdao's *hongwa lüshu* (red tiles, green trees) make a splendid panorama.

Qingdao

QINGDAO (GREEN ISLAND), ON THE SHANDONG PENINSULA, is a refreshing town by the Yellow Sea. It is dotted with parks, caressed by ocean breezes, and heavy with the aroma of the sea and kebabs (the local delicacy). China's fourth port is also home to its world-famous namesake—Qingdao (Tsingtao) beer. Qingdao's European heritage—the town was once a German concession—has branded it "China's Switzerland." Architectural enthusiasts will admire its jumbled fabric of styles. The seafood *(haixian)* is excellent, and you can either walk off your meal along some fine sandy beaches or tackle mountainous Laoshan to the east.

Qingdao
95 E2

Visitor information
Tourist Service Center, Qingdao Train Station
0532 296-8663

CITS visitor information
73 Xianggang Xilu
0532 8389-2065

Sleepy Qingdao had a rude awakening at the end of the 19th century, when it became the focus of foreign ambitions. As China was sliced apart by the Western powers, the Germans joined the land-grabbing game in 1897 and occupied the port after the murder of two German missionaries. Qingdao woke to find its streets cobbled, the town electrified, a university in place, and the famous brewery installed. A railroad snaked to the provincial capital, Jinan, and authoritarian Bavarian architecture followed wholesale.

The Japanese took delight at the prospect of a modernized port on the Shandong Peninsula, and they successfully wrested Qingdao from German clutches at the end of World War I. Qingdao slipped back into Chinese hands in 1922, returning to the Japanese between 1938 and 1945 during the war with Japan. Since 1950 Qingdao has developed rapidly, and today the city is a wealthy enclave that makes Shandong one of the most dynamic provinces in China. The walk that follows (pp. 133–35) offers the best way to enjoy the sights. ■

A walk around Qingdao

Qingdao is not a large town, and the most interesting sights can be enjoyed while ambling through its pleasant streets rather than by racing between points. The walk will take you through the picturesque reaches of Qingdao and its historic German area.

Start by strolling up Zhanqiao—the pier reaching out into Qingdao Bay—to the **Huilan Pavilion** ❶ at its tip. Look out over the bay to the southeast and you can see the **Little Green Isle (Xiao Qingdao),** which lends its name to the town. The pavilion is the symbol of Qingdao and graces the label of Tsingtao beer brewed in the town. In summer you will see vendors advertising speedboat trips around the bay and beyond.

Just west of Zhanqiao is **No. 6 Bathing Beach,** a stretch of beach active in the early hours with locals exercising and children playing.

Heading north up Zhongshan Lu (opposite the pier), you will pass a number of kebab sellers serving up their irresistible snacks. Go for the ones with the crowds out front: Try the lamb *(yangrouchuan),* pork *(zhurouchuan),* or squid *(diankao youyu);* grab a stool, a drink, and enjoy. This is an inexpensive and appetizing way to dine.

Continue up **Zhongshan Lu**—once a premier shopping street until all the money went east to the new commercial area of Qingdao—and take Feicheng Lu to your right,

Also see area map p. 95
➤ Zhanqiao
3.5 miles (5.5 km)
4 hours
➤ Huashilou

NOT TO BE MISSED

- St. Michael's Catholic Church
- Qingdao Ying Binguan
- Protestant Christ Church
- Xiaoyushan
- Huashilou

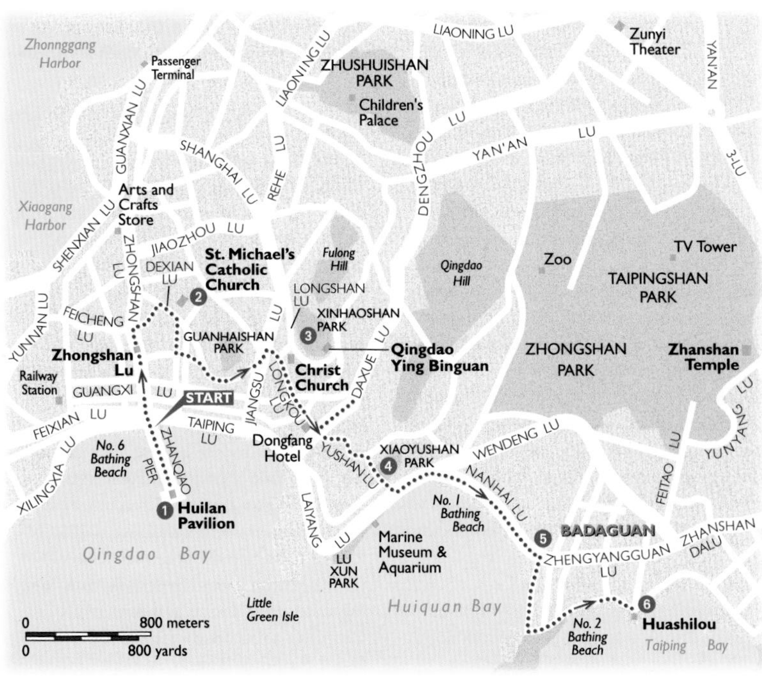

A covered market in Qingdao, Shandong Province's premier economic success story

which leads uphill to **St. Michael's Catholic Church (Tianzhu Jiaotang)** ❷. This twin-spired church *($)* dominates the town, and it still holds regular Sunday services. A couple of Red Guards fell to their deaths while trying to knock the crosses off the steeples during the Cultural Revolution; the crosses were later hidden by locals in the hills around Qingdao. Next to the church is a convent. A daily fish market sets up nearby, among the German concession architecture.

From St. Michael's, walk south down Zhejiang Lu, over Qufu Lu (named after Confucius's birthplace), and turn left (east) onto Hubei Lu. The road twists south and becomes Yishui Lu. There is a charming diversion not far from here up to the top of the minute **Guanhaishan Park (Guanhaishan Gongyuan),** where you are rewarded with an expansive view over the red-tiled rooftops of Qingdao and out to sea. A plaque (in Chinese) states that the park was originally used as a golf course by the Germans. The park is not easy to find. From Hubei Lu, roads corkscrew up to the small summit; turn left into Guanhai Lu, which twists around the hilly park (you will find steps leading up to the park).

Keep going along Yishui Lu to Jiangsu Lu; then take Longkou Lu (Dragon's Mouth Road) south, which runs south of **Xinhaoshan Park (Xinhaoshan Gongyuan)** ❸. In the eastern section of the park is the former hotel known as the **Qingdao Ying Binguan** *($)*, Qingdao's most prized chunk of German architecture that is now a museum. Originally built for the German governor, the ex-hotel once hosted Mao Zedong as a guest. The interior is a snapshot of the early 20th century, replete with dark wood paneling and a German grand piano made in 1876. The building's exterior is constructed from blocklike stone, similar to many other Teutonic vestiges visible around the west of town.

Opposite the park you will see the patina-green towered Protestant **Christ Church (Jidu Jiaotang)** with its fine, white clockface. Sledgehammer-wielding Red Guards smashed the stained glass of this Evangelical church, built in 1910, during the Cultural Revolution. The interior is typically austere and Lutheran, but the outside is impressively well kept. The church is generally accessible and you can climb the clock tower for views out over the sea.

Continuing south down Longkou Lu, you will pass the **Dongfang Hotel** on your right. It is worth taking a short diversion up Daxue Lu (University Road), similarly notable for its historic architecture, including the German buildings of the Haiyang Daxue (Ocean University).

Backtrack to the continuation of Longkou Lu on the south side of Daxue Lu. This is the rather steep Yushan Lu, which takes you to the picturesque small park of **Xiaoyushan (Little Fish Mountain)** ❹. The peak is graced by a three-tiered pagoda (Lanchaoge), which once served as an observation tower. From the peak you can see all around the *hongwa lüshu* (literally "red tiles, green trees") that give Qingdao its charming picture-postcard appeal.

Yushan Lu leads to Laiyang Lu, running east along the waterfront. **Lu Xun Park (Lu Xun Gongyuan),** named after China's most famous modern writer (see p. 173), is to your right. Speedboat rental agents will try to coax you aboard their dangerous-looking vessels (you decide, at your peril). Carrying on east brings you shortly to **No. 1 Bathing Beach,** and just beyond

The German-built St. Michael's Catholic Church reopened to worshipers in the early 1980s.

that the smart **Badaguan** 5 area, a shady, tree-lined haven of sanatoriums and quiet guest houses. This sheltered area of villa-lined streets is worth strolling around. Overlooking Taiping Bay is **No. 2 Bathing Beach,** a quieter and more secluded beach than the others. At the easternmost end of it stands the magnificent castle-like **Huashilou** 6**,** otherwise known by locals as the **Chiang Kai-shek Building** (the Kuomintang leader stayed here in 1947). This was the former German governor's residence, modeled on a German palace. You can visit the grounds and rooms of this marvelously Teutonic and brave folly. The bird's-eye view out to sea from the roof is excellent.

The building stands on the rise up to **Zhongshan Park (Zhongshan Gongyuan),** previously called Mount Diederich by Qingdao's German colonials. To the northeast of Zhongshan Park is **Taipingshan Park (Taipingshan Gongyuan),** where you will find the **zoo (Dongwuyuan),** the **Zhanshan Temple,** and the **TV Tower (Dianshita),** capped by a revolving restaurant. ■

Around Qingdao

TWENTY-FIVE MILES (40 KM) TO THE EAST OF QINGDAO IS Laoshan, a mountain infused with Taoist mystery and legend. It is associated with the Eight Taoist Immortals and the popular Taoist fairy tale about the Laoshan Daoshi (a monk), who perfected his transcendental technique of walking through walls on Laoshan. Rumor has it that the first emperor of the Qin dynasty visited Laoshan in search of the pill of immortality. The magic no doubt still permeates the local water, for Laoshan is famed far and wide for the springs that put the crispness into Qingdao beer.

Right: German colonial buildings in Qingdao
Opposite: Laoshan's mountainous terrain is bordered by the Yellow Sea, where the energetic, local fishing community finds its livelihood.

Laoshan
95 E2
$$

Most travelers visit a few temples (there were once 72 Taoist temples on Laoshan) and only scratch the surface of this dramatic area; the farther you penetrate Laoshan, the more you will unearth wild hiking opportunities.

The principle shrine is the Song dynasty **Taiqing Palace,** a Taoist monastery. The main temple is the **Hall of the Three Pure Ones,** where three large statues represent Laozi, the Yellow Emperor, and the Jade Emperor (see p. 73). To the left is the **Three Emperors Hall** and to the right the **Three Officials Hall.** The temple also contains a proclamation from Genghis Khan calling for the protection of Taoism.

From the temple, a cable car climbs up the side of the neighboring peak. Clinging precariously to the mountainside is the **Songqing Palace,** while below plunges the **Dragon Pool Waterfall (Longtanpu).** The highest peak is Jufeng, at 3,700 feet (1,127 m). Beyond lies a huge swath of undulating territory, drilled with caves and washed by waterfalls.

To the north, steep rock formations punctuate **Beijiushui,** a wild area laced by rivers, streams, and cascading waterfalls.

Qingdao's best beach is in a more remote location a boat ride from town to the west (boats leave from the ferry terminal west of the train station). **Huangdao (Yellow Island)** is fringed by **Golden Sand Beach (Jinshatan),** a lovely expanse of sand free of the mobs that often besiege Qingdao's other beaches (except on weekends). ■

More places to visit in the North

ANYANG

Anyang, in Henan Province, is built on the ruins of Yin, the last capital of the primeval Shang dynasty (circa 1766–1122 B.C.). Fragments from the old city can be found in the **Yin Ruins Museum (Yinxu Bowuguan)** in the west of town. Anyang's other historical landmark is the **Tomb of Yuan Shikai (Yuan Shikai Mu),** the self-proclaimed emperor who tried to restore imperial authority in 1915 (see p. 36). The old quarter of town is an attractive retreat of traditional housing.

Trips can be made to the **Red Flag Canal,** west of Anyang. This 900-mile (1,450 km) irrigation canal was cut through a mountain with bare hands and a utopian vision during the days of the Cultural Revolution (1966–1976).

95 C2 **Yin Ruins Museum** Yinxu Lu $

BEIDAIHE & SHANHAIGUAN

When the Beijing summer gets too dry and dusty, beat a retreat to the popular beach resort of Beidaihe on the Hebei coast, established at the end of the 19th century by foreigners living in the Beijing legations and the Tianjin concession areas.

A short train or bus trip east along the coast is Shanhaiguan, where the Great Wall meets the sea. The name means "the pass between the mountains and the sea," and the former garrison town is surrounded by a wall and cut by charming *hutong*. At the time of writing the old town was undergoing considerable redevelopment, but it remains a pleasant place to visit or even to overnight.

Ascend the towering **First Pass Under Heaven** (and visit the nearby Great Wall Museum on the same ticket), or visit the more dramatic backbone of wall at **Jiaoshan,** just north of town. Restored **Laolongtou** (Old Dragon Head) south of town marks the wall's conclusion at the sea.

95 D3 & 95 E3 **First Pass Under Heaven** Dongda Jie 0335 505-2894

PENGLAI

The ancient castle of Penglai, 40 miles (64 km) west of Yantai, is carved from myth. Legend has it that the eight immortals of Chinese Taoism (see p. 42) set out for their sea crossing from Penglai. The place is a fascinating tangle of temples, creepers, ivy, pavilions, and crenellated walls. Weekends see marauding tour groups laying siege to the fortress, so go during the week. A cable car connects the castle to the cliffs opposite.

95 E3

PINGYAO

The delightful, historic Shanxi town of Pingyao is a UNESCO World Heritage site. Rising to prominence as a banking center in the Ming dynasty, the old town is enclosed within an intact city wall complete with wooden gates and cast-iron cannons for protection. The town's charms lie in its historic Ming and Qing dynasty architecture, easily perused on foot along its gridlike streets. Pingyao is well served by hotels and can be reached by train from either Taiyuan or Beijing.

95 C2

TAIYUAN

Taiyuan, capital of Shanxi Province, was lauded by Marco Polo, and despite today's industrial scars, it is still blessed with a few temples. The **Chongshan Temple,** off Shangma Jie, stands near the center of the city and was once the largest Buddhist monastery in China. The **Jinci Temple,** 15 miles (24 km) southwest of Taiyuan, is noted for its collection of Song dynasty clay figures.

95 C3 **CITS visitor information** 282 Yingze Dajie 0351 406-3562

ZHENGDING

The **Longxing Temple (Dafo Si)** in the Hebei temple town of Zhengding is notable for its awesome bronze, multi-armed, 70-foot (21 m) statue of Guanyin, dating from the Song dyansty. Within the town are preserved several other notable pagodas, including a Tang dynasty pagoda at **Kaiyuan Temple (Kaiyuansi)** and the **Lingxiao Pagoda,** also dating from the Tang period.

95 C3 ■

Gushing through Chongqing, the Three Gorges, Wuhan, and Nanjing, the Yangtze exhausts itself in the sea by Shanghai. The eastern coastal provinces are a watery world of canal towns and the Grand Canal terminus of Hangzhou.

The Yangtze region

Temple dragon motif, Shanghai

The Yangtze region

TUMBLING FROM THE TIBETAN Plateau, the Yangtze River nourishes the fertile valleys below but also subjects settlements on either flank to catastrophic flooding. Some of China's great cities cluster around this major artery of communication and irrigation. The river pumps through Chongqing, cuts Wuhan in two, and is later straddled by Nanjing's great bridge. It leaves the waterlogged province of Jiangsu, emptying into the East China Sea just north of that mightiest of Chinese cities—Shanghai.

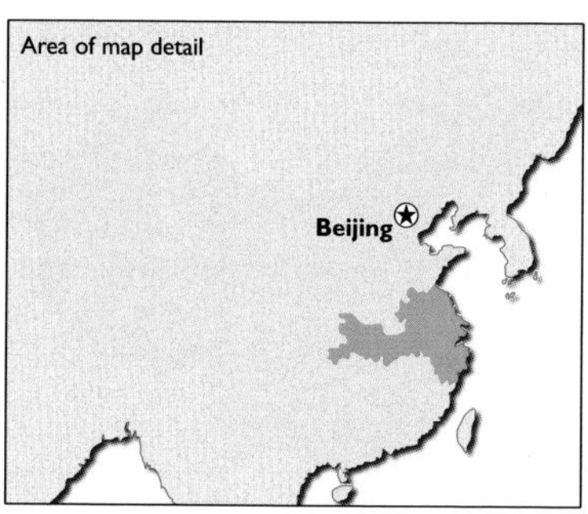

The great Yangtze River conveniently cleaves China into North and South on the map. Life (and death) in the Yangtze region traditionally revolved around the river—its rapids extolled by poets and dreaded by oarsmen, its floods feared by everyone. The river has long linked eastern and western China, providing a transport route that was as dangerous as it was essential. Trains, planes, and automobiles may have robbed the river of its former importance, but its allure remains.

For enthusiasts, the Yangtze can be navigated all the way from Chongqing to Shanghai, but most settle for the splendor of the Three Gorges. Temples, historic walled towns, and eccentric rock formations stud the dramatic route. The massive Three Gorges Dam has already begun to alter the geography of the region, however, submerging towns and monuments and transforming the Three Gorges.

The river slices through poor Anhui Province to the east, anonymous perhaps but for China's most famous peak, Huangshan. Farther east, the river flushes through its last province, Jiangsu, known as the land of fish and rice. Here, the Grand Canal feeds in from the north, leaving the watery province awash with lakes and charming, canalled towns. Historic Nanjing, the provincial capital, deserves eager exploration.

Glittering Shanghai, that eternal byword for modernity and decadence, sits south of the river's final plunge into the sea. Fiercely independent and inherently rebellious, Shanghai is China's torchbearer to the rubber stamp political conservatism of Beijing. The city is simultaneously a museum of European antiquities and a showcase of newfangled architecture.

The famous city of Suzhou is a graceful vignette of bridges and gardens. Lake Taihu, Yixing, and picturesque Yangzhou further stock the province of Jiangsu with sights.

The Grand Canal feeds farther south to northern Zhejiang Province and Hangzhou, one of China's premier tourist destinations. South again, more reserved Shaoxing is cut by pleasant canals. Off the coast lies a string of islands, including the sacred Putuoshan, home of China's goddess of mercy, Guanyin. ■

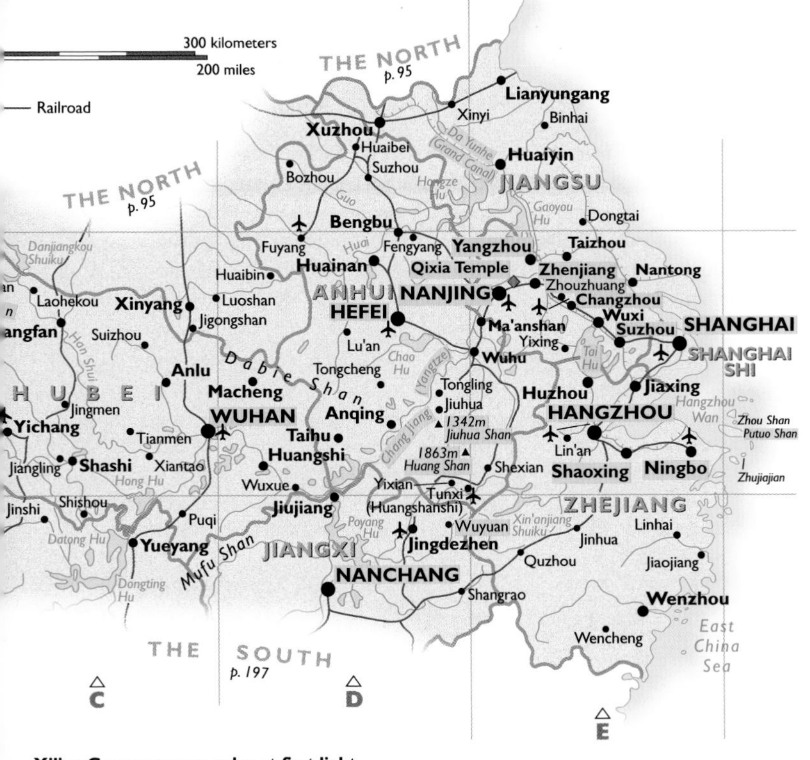

Xiling Gorge appears calm at first light.

A cruise through the Three Gorges

Called the Yangtze Kiang, the Yangtze River, or the Chang Jiang (literally "long river"), this vast body of water casts a powerful spell and offers a dramatic cruise. The river is China's longest, starting out as a trickle in the Tanggulashan Mountains in Qinghai, swelling through the Tibetan highlands, then plummeting into Yunnan Province and surging through the Sichuan Basin. It courses 3,500 miles (5,630 km) through a string of provinces and finally disgorges its waters into the East China Sea above Shanghai.

The Yangtze basin is a highly fertile valley, but a dangerous one: Floods occur during the seasonal summer rains and are made worse by the deep silting up of the riverbed. The floods frequently cause disasters. The worst recorded by history was a double flood that also involved the Yellow River, in 2297 B.C. It is said to have covered virtually the entire North China plain. Every 50 years or so the Yangtze basin sees a disastrous flood, although the

Also see area map p. 141
- Chongqing
- 840 miles (1,350 km)
- 4 days
- Wuhan

NOT TO BE MISSED
- Fengdu
- Qutang Gorge
- Wu Gorge
- Peaks of Wushan
- Little Three Gorges

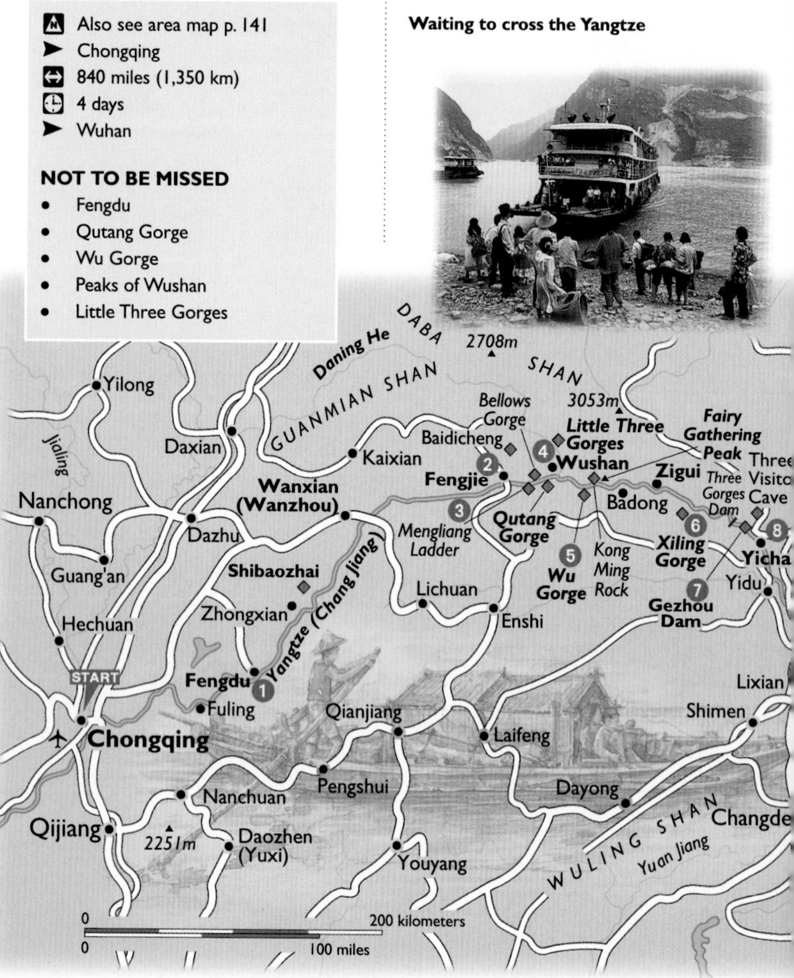

Waiting to cross the Yangtze

Three Gorges Dam was designed to lessen the chance of serious flooding. Completed in 2006, the Three Gorges Dam has already visibly reduced the grandeur of the Three Gorges, but even when the waters have reached their full height, the gorges will remain spectacular and far from overwhelmed by the rising river.

THE ROUTE

This cruise, starting at Chongqing in Sichuan (see p. 146), funnels you past dramatic rock formations, vast, hanging curtains of stone, mist-shrouded peaks, the fragments of ancient settlements, and swirling eddies. Rocks, eroded by the elements or split by water, adopt fanciful forms that resemble a legion of abstract shapes long ago given whimsical names by the Chinese who traveled the river.

It is still possible to journey all the way from Chongqing to Shanghai, although most tours just cover the stretch between Chongqing and Yichang. This tour terminates in Wuhan in Hubei Province (see p. 147). The most celebrated and interesting section lies between Fengjie and Yichang—the famous and dramatic Three Gorges. Boats stop at towns and historical sights along the route, allowing you time to ponder the dramatic story as it unfolds. The cruise can be done in the other direction (i.e., Wuhan or Yichang to Chongqing). It is also possible to jump on a hydrofoil from Chongqing (or Wanxian) for an 11-hour high-speed trip through the gorges; you get to see the gorges, but vessels do not stop at the sights.

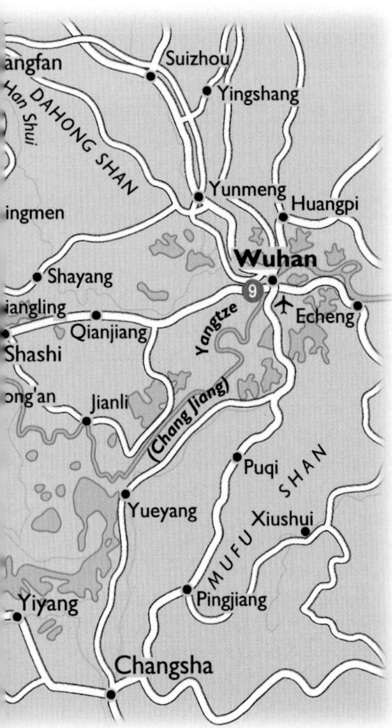

From mighty **Chongqing,** the boat initially travels past a long belt of uninspiring scenery. The haunted "Ghost City" of **Fengdu** ❶ has literally become a ghost town, as most of its residents have been relocated due to the rising river level. A spooky crop of temples and statues of Yinwang, god of the netherworld, survive on the mount of Mingshan overlooking Fengdu. Boats used to moor midstream in case of attack by phantoms!

The boat drifts past **Shibaozhai (Stone Treasure Storehouse),** a 100-foot (30 m) rock resembling a seal-chop (a type of small, cylindrical marble seal). A towering, crimson temple, dating from the Qing dynasty and shaped like a pagoda, crowns the peak.

Perched above the river, the functional town of **Wanxian (Wanzhou)**—its lower slopes deserted to the rising waters—provides an overnight berth for many boats. If time is tight, you can take a three-hour bus ride from Chongqing to Wanxian and then board the hydrofoil here for rapid seven-hour trips to Yichang through the Three Gorges. Further downstream beyond Wanxian, the 2,000-year old town of **Fengjie** ❷ marks the western entrance to Qutang Gorge (Qutangxia), first of the Three Gorges. The two great poets of the Tang dynasty, Li Bai and Du Fu, lived here and captured the great river in song. Li Bai wrote the following verse entitled "Departing early from Baidicheng":

In the morning, I leave Baidi between colorful clouds,
A thousand miles of river and land, to return the next day.
On each bank the gibbons scream without pause
My boat has already drifted past endless hills.

The **Baidicheng (White King Town)** in

the poem, at the entrance to Qutang Gorge, was christened by a king of the Western Han who saw a well emitting a white vapor "like a white dragon." He promptly called himself White King and named White King Town his fief. The town is rife with folklore from the time of the Three Kingdoms period (A.D. 220–265, see pp. 26–27), most notably in the White King Temple.

The splendid **Three Gorges (Sanxia)** start at this point with **Qutang Gorge,** the shortest of them at 5 miles (8 km) long. The water flows rapidly through the gorge, pinched between the cliffs that narrow at points to 328 feet (100 m). The effect is thrilling and many say that this is the most amazing of the gorges. The geological oddity of the Monk Hung Upside Down certainly resembles a suspended figure.

At the eastern entrance to the gorge, the **Mengliang Ladder** ❸ is a series of holes made in the rock; these originally supported piles driven into the rock face, upon which a pathway was laid for travelers. The other type of pathway that lined the gorges was cut out of the rock, and this can be seen from the boat on the northern face of Qutang Gorge. The furrows for the ropes that hauled boats up against the current of the river also remain.

On the opposite bank to the Mengliang Ladder is a set of crevices high in the rock face called the **Bellows Gorge.** These were the final repository for coffins of an ancient tribe called the Ba. For centuries, the boxes positioned there were believed by wayfarers on boats to contain the bellows of a blacksmith or carpenter called Lu Ban, who helped the mythical Yu the Great cleave the Yangtze gorges and dredge the river.

Travelers can explore the **Daning River (Daninghe),** and boats wait for them to transfer from the larger tour vessels. This stretch is called **Little Three Gorges,** a narrower and fiercer section than the larger gorges, and a thrilling ride. A coffin can be seen high on the rockface in Iron Coffin Gorge, the second gorge. The round-trip takes around five hours.

The ancient walled town of **Wushan** ❹ may make for an overnight berth, at the point where the Yangtze and the Daning Rivers meet. The town has 12 streets named after the

mountain peaks in the next gorge.

Bewitching **Wu Gorge (Wuxia)** ❺—the Gorge of the Witches—towers ahead with its supernatural peaks and frequently misty cliffs. It starts in Golden Helmet and Silver Armor Gorge, pleated and fractured shafts of rock resembling a warrior's battle dress.

The 12 cloudy peaks of Wushan (Witch Mountain) lie ahead: Fairy Peak, Immortals Gathering Peak, Clean Altar Peak, Climbing Dragon Peak, Holy Spring Peak, Emerald Green Screen Peak, Flying Phoenix Peak, and others rise up on both sides.

The spirit of Yaoji—the daughter of the Queen of Western Heaven, who came to earth to assist Yu the Great in his labors— is believed to occupy Fairy Peak. Yaoji chased away wild animals and helped farmers grow crops, while tending magical herbs to cure the sick.

Kong Ming Rock, on the side of **Immortals Gathering Peak,** is supposedly carved with an inscription by Zhuge Liang, the master military strategist from the Three Kingdoms period.

Xiling Gorge—longest and most treacherous—is the last of the Three Gorges as you head east.

At the port of **Badong,** you can take a rowboat along the tributary of Shennongxi, past caverns to an attractive beach by the river

Farther ahead the Fragrant Stream (Xiangxi) empties into the Yangtze River, and **Xiling Gorge (Xilingxia)** 6—the longest and perhaps least spectacular—begins. At 50 miles (80 km), it's a marathon stretch, but it's still impressive. The Sword and Military Strategy Book Gorge is associated with Zhuge Liang, and the eccentrically named Ox's Liver and Horse's Lung Gorge may impress you if you actually know what a horse's lung looks like. There's also Shadowplay Gorge.

Xiling Gorge was historically the most hazardous of the gorges for vessels plying the river, but it was long ago tamed by dredging and the rising waters. A particularly nasty stone, wonderfully called Here it Comes, sent many a boat to a watery grave until it was blown up by soldiers.

Beyond, the river widens, announcing the locks of the **Gezhou Dam** 7. Farther ahead and shortly before boats pull in at **Yichang** 8, the gargantuan Three Gorges Dam rears into view. Some boats stop here for trips to the dam, and hydrofoils also berth at the terminal; otherwise you can visit by bus from Yichang *(CITS visitor information, Yunji Lu, tel 0717 625-3088)*, the next town downstream. The voyage through the Three Gorges can also be done in reverse from Yichang to Chongqing. After Yichang lies **Wuhan** 9 (see pp. 147–48) and the end of this cruise. From here on, towns begin to blur into a gray stream of industrial buildings.

What largely remains on the river from this point are cargo vessels shipping coal and cement to Shanghai. Some passenger boats still struggle on despite the competition from far faster routes to the east of China, but if you continue, you will pass through **Nanjing** and terminate at the mouth of the Yangtze River just north of **Shanghai.** ■

The People's Liberation Monument is perched in the center of Chongqing.

Chongqing

THE HUGE CITY OF CHONGQING WILL FIND ITSELF ON THE banks of the largest artificial lake in the world with the completion of the Three Gorges Dam. Traditionally, it's the point of arrival or departure along the Yangtze and home to fiery Sichuan cuisine.

Chongqing
140 A1

CITS visitor information
151 Zourong Guangchang
023 6903-7560

Chongqing Museum
Pipashan Zhengjie
$

The largest city in the world (by some estimates), rapidly-developing Chongqing is also one of China's "three ovens" come summer.

Glinting from the smog of central Chongqing is the **Luohan Temple.** The Luohan (see p. 72) are usually only fashioned in numbers of 18, but 500 lifelike Luohan effigies reside here. On the wall behind the huge Buddha effigy, look for the likeness of Siddhartha Gautama cutting his hair to renounce the world.

Pipashan Park (Pipashan Gongyuan) presides over Chongqing on a hill that rises some 1,100 feet (335 m); at the summit is **Hongxing Pavilion,** a teahouse with long views over the city.

Chongqing Museum, on the south side of Pipashan, is one of the few remnants of history, but it's rather a disappointment. ■

Three Gorges Dam

The controversial construction of the Three Gorges Dam, which aims to control flooding on the Yangtze River while generating vast amounts of hydroelectric power, was completed ahead of schedule in 2006. When fully functioning, the reservoir built up behind the dam at Sandouping will have submerged entire towns and villages. The Three Gorges (see pp. 143–45) will have been reduced in stature and over a million people relocated. ■

Wuhan

Hubei Provincial Museum possess many treasures including 2,500 year old chimes.

WUHAN, CAPITAL OF HUBEI PROVINCE, IS AN AMALGAM OF the three cities of Wuchang, Hankou, and Hanyang, which cluster around the Yangtze River. Wuchang was a former capital of the state of Wu during the Three Kingdoms period (A.D. 220–265) and served as an anti-Qing center during the Taiping Rebellion. Hankou became a treaty port in 1861, with a complement of French, Japanese, British, Russian, and German concessions. Hanyang, the smallest of the three, became heavily industrialized during the 20th century.

GUIYUAN TEMPLE

Inside the courtyard of this temple in Hanyang is a sizable pool with two large, carved lotus flowers in the water. The Maitreya Buddha (see p. 72) welcomes all in the initial temple, and behind him is Weituo, standing with natural poise and grace on a splendidly carved altar.

The **main temple (Daxiong Baodian)** contains a magnificent altar with a central golden effigy of Guanyin, goddess of mercy, surrounded by a host of other colorfully painted deities.

The hall at the rear on the right is where the Buddhist scriptures were stored. There is also a fascinating hall containing 500 almost life-size Luohan and seated monks. Each one displays its own individual temperament. In front is a black statue of Guanyin dressed in a robe, surrounded by a constellation of pottery figures. Signs in Chinese warn worshipers away from the hordes of fortune-tellers outside.

HUBEI PROVINCIAL MUSEUM

Over the Yangtze River in Wuchang, Hubei Provincial Museum (Hubeisheng Bowuguan) has an absorbing collection of relics from the state of Zeng, a small Zhou dynasty kingdom (1100–221 B.C.)

Wuhan
Map 141 C2

CITS visitor information
✉ Zhongshan Dadao
☎ 027 5151-5955

Guiyuan Temple
✉ Cuiweiheng Lu, Hanyang
$ $

in the middle of the Yangtze region. Of particular note are grave relics from the tomb of the Marquis of Zeng, who was buried in Zeng in 433 B.C. Ritual vessels, chariot fittings, musical instruments, weapons, gold, jade, and lacquerware make for a fascinating display. The bronzes are particularly interesting. The crane piece with deer antlers is arresting, but the main attraction is the Marquis's magnificent coffin. Consisting of an inner and outer coffin, it is covered with early Zhou designs and motifs. You will see a reproduction of the coffin chamber as you enter.

Visitors pause for thought at Wuhan's sacred Guiyuan Temple in Hanyang.

Hubei Provincial Museum
- ✉ Next to East Lake (donghu), Wuchang
- 🕒 Closed 11:30 a.m.–1:30 p.m.
- $ $

Villa of Mao Zedong
- ✉ Donghu Lu
- $ $

Yellow Crane Pavilion
- ✉ Snake Hill (She Shan) Wulou Lu, Wuchang
- $ $

Twenty-two sacrificial coffins were also found at the site—mainly containing women. Other bronzes that accompanied the coffins in the tomb show an evolved stage of craftsmanship. Pieces include bronze picks, ladles, a wine cooler, *ding* and *zun* (types of vessels), filters, and an exquisitely detailed bronze weight. There is also a vast bronze for serving wine at important ceremonies, inscribed with these words: "For the permanent use of the Marquis of Zeng."

Also unearthed was a huge set of bronze bells; the amount of bronze alloy controls the note of each bell. Along with the bells was a large set of chimes, both commonly seen in Confucius temples across China (see p. 175).

HISTORIC ARCHITECTURE

For a taste of Wuhan's foreign concession past, wander around Hankou, which contains several buildings from concession days, when the city was a major center of trade (and missionary activity). Wander along the premier shopping street of **Jianghan Lu** and note its sporadic historic architecture. Pop into the **Xuangong Hotel** *(57 Jianghan Yilu)* just west of Jianghan Lu; built in 1931, the building is typical of the old-world charms of the area. Also note the imposing historic building that houses the **Bank of China** where Jianghan Lu meets Zhongshan Dadao. Yanjiang Dadao runs along the Yangtze River in Hankou, punctuated with pompous old architecture, including the **National City Bank of New York** building, at No. 142. Also worth a look is the former **Hankou Railway Station** building, built by the French and still sitting at the northern end of Chezhan Lu. The impressive **Former Headquarters of the Wuchang Uprising** in Wuchang is now a museum, while the **Villa of Mao Zedong** on Donghu Lu is a weary remnant from Mao's itinerant past. The villa itself is more like a dreary two-star budget hotel, but you see his swimming pool, bathrobe, and other scattered objects from his life.

OTHER SIGHTS

Yellow Crane Pavilion, by the Yangtze River on Snake Hill, is a much restored tower lauded by the Tang dynasty poet Cui Hao. ■

Yixian & Shexian

YIXIAN COUNTY, A SHORT BUS TRIP WEST OF TUNXI (Huangshanshi)—a city that usefully doubles as the main hopping off point for trips to Huangshan (see pp. 150–52)—is a delightfully pastoral region of southern Anhui Province, also known as Wannan, with scenic towns.

The area is characterized by its elegant Huizhou villages and traditional Huizhou culture and architecture, which coalesced around the wealthy merchant families that prospered in this region during Ming and Qing times. Little authentic traditional village character of this kind survives in modern China, and visits here are highly recommended, especially if you are en route to nearby Huangshan. Note that visits to Yixian County require a travel permit (Y50), available on the spot from the Public Security Bureau *(108 Changgan Lu, tel 0559 231-8768)* in Tunxi. Travel permits are not required for visits to Shexian.

Yixian's two most famous villages are the gorgeous **Xidi** and **Hongcun,** both easily reached by bus from Yixian town itself, 30 miles (47 km) west of Tunxi. Both Unesco World Heritage Sites, each village is typified by picturesque and distinctive Huizou buildings, typically painted creamy-white, topped by black tiles and bookended by the lovely horse-head gables you see throughout this region. The building's interiors reveal further hallmarks of the Huizhou style, including the use of oblong light wells (openings in the roof), courtyards, and upper galleries.

Introduced by way of a splendid *paifang* (decorative arch), Xidi's charming tangle of streets are flanked by delightful Huizhou architecture. Numerous halls and former residences are open to the public, so you can wander in and absorb the charms of their interior arrangements. Once you have finished exploring the village, opportunities exist for short treks into the surrounding countryside.

Nearby **Hongcun** has a different, and altogether more unique, aspect. Reputedly designed to resemble an ox (when looked at from above), the village is centered on the pond of Yuezhao at its heart, linked to the lake bordering the south of Hongcun by small water channels that run along the sides of the small alleys that fragment the settlement. Follow the signs around the village for a tour of its highlight halls and residences. Other villages in the Yixian area can also be explored (with a travel permit), although reaching them can be inconvenient. Technically, foreigners are barred from spending the night in Yixian County, so you will have to reapply for a visitor permit to visit the next day, or squeeze it all into one day.

The town of **Shexian,** less than an hour by bus from Tunxi, was the former capital of the Huizhou region. In exploring the old town, seek out the magnificent and richly decorated **Xuguo Archway**—one of China's most elaborate paifang. Nearby, the Huizhou residential architecture of **Doushan Jie** can be explored alongside Chinese guides, otherwise just meander the charming streets with your camera. A few kilometers west of Shexian, a sequence of seven paifang called the **Tangyue Decorative Arches** stand alone in a field. ■

Yixian
Map 141 E2

Xidi
$ $$$

Hongcun
$ $$$

Shexian
Map 141 E2

Xuguo Archway
$ $

Doushan Jie
$ $

Tangyue Decorative Arches
$ $$

Huangshan

ADORNING PILES OF COFFEE-TABLE BOOKS ON CHINA IS stunning, pine tree-clad Huangshan in south Anhui Province, China's most famous, probably most beautiful, mountain.

Huangshan
141 D2
$$

CITS visitor information
6 Xizhen Jie, Tunxi
0559 252-6184

The 160-mile-long (257 km) Huangshan range is a dramatic panorama of 72 peaks, capped by Lotus Flower Peak (Lianhuafeng).

During the Qin dynasty, the mountain was called Qianshan, but it was rechristened Huangshan in A.D. 747, in honor of the Yellow Emperor (Huangdi).

The mount was later the hideaway of Chan Buddhist recluses, who foraged for inspiration among the pines, waterfalls, and hot springs. If you slip away from any tour-group trail, you could well find what it was that hermits, poets, and artists of old came here to discover.

On the summit, Xihai (West Sea) and Beihai (North Sea) are famed for their jaw-dropping misty panoramas. The main loci of interest on Beihai are **Lion Peak (Shizifeng), Monkey which looks out over the Sea (Houzi Guanhai),** and an old, twisted pine tree charmingly labeled **Flowers Springing from a Dreaming Writing Brush (Mengbi Shenghua).** Come sunrise, bleary-eyed

One of China's most legendary panoramas—over Huangshan's sea of clouds and fairy-tale archipelago of lofty peaks

wayfarers muster in padded coats on **Refreshing Terrace (Qingliangtai)** along the slopes of Lion Peak. If you have the time, spend the night on the summit at one of the hotels, and be sure to polish up the lens of your camera, because the view can be astonishing. From **Cloud-Dispelling Pavilion (Paiyunting)** on Xihai, the view reaches out over layers of small peaks prodding through the clouds and mist.

CLIMBING HUANGSHAN

The first hurdle is the rather steep entrance charge. Ahead lie various routes, the easiest being the eastern one. The less energetic visitors ride up on the cable car, pursuing the eastern route from the **Yungu Temple,** which marks the start of the trail. This is an option if you just can't face the walk, but your patience can wear thin after hours of waiting in line. Sedan chairs await the truly decadent.

The eastern ascent is a 5-mile (8 km) stretch, and this should take you about three hours to finish. There's less to see than on the western route but the climb is far easier and it's pleasantly shaded.

The western ascent is a gut-wrenching 10 miles (16 km); around every corner waits a further flight of steps, mocking your stamina and testing your endurance. Along the western trail are the **Merciful Light Pavilion (Ciguangge)** and, farther up, the **Halfway Mountain Temple (Banshansi),** now a hotel and restaurant. The dwarfing granite

Opposite: Huangshan's grueling climb is rewarded by breathtaking, if somewhat breathless, views.

pinnacle of **Tiandu Peak** rises south of Jade Screen Tower Hotel (Yupinglou Binguan), with its spectacular vista. The path then winds around **Lotus Flower Peak** before grinding on to **Bright Summit Peak (Guangmingding)** and the summit proper.

An ascent by the eastern route and descent by the western trail is a popular strategy. Guides are available for tours to the summit, but they only speak *putonghua* (Mandarin). The best weather occurs when the peaks are shrouded in mist (which is much of the time), and the Chinese insist on climbing to the very top for the breathtaking views over the **Sea of Clouds (Yunhai)**.

The thermometer can dip, so take warm, waterproof clothes and extra layers. Summer sees Huangshan infested with climbers, and is best avoided, if possible.

The nearest town is **Tunxi (Huangshan Shi)** served by an airport from where buses reach Huangshan. Alternatively, stay in the the pleasant village of Tangkou at the foot of Huangshan and climb early the next day. ■

Jiuhuashan

Jiuhuashan
141 D2
$$

CTS visitor information
135 Baima Xinchen
0566 501-1588

Easily climbed in a day, Jiuhuashan makes a practical alternative to the more rigorous ascent of nearby Huangshan.

The divinity ruling Jiuhuashan (Nine Flower Mountain) in southern Anhui Province is Dizang, a salvationary god of the dead and the underworld, called Ksitigarbha in Sanskrit, to whom pilgrims flock to pray for the souls of the departed. Dizang has apparently manifested himself on the mountain more than once in human form. A Korean monk named Kim Kiao Kak came to Jiuhuashan in the eighth century to dedicate a temple to the god. As with other Buddhist mountains in China, Jiuhuashan was occupied by Taoist recluses before being converted wholesale to Buddhism. The enigmatic Tang poet Li Bai wrote a devotional poem to Jiuhuashan after living on its slopes, lending the mountain its name.

The lofty peak of **Tiantaishan** lies a staggering 5 miles (8 km) of steps up in the clouds from **Jiuhua** village, itself about halfway up the mountain from Wuxi Town below. Many temples, shrines, and nunneries still decorate the slopes, despite a spate of desecration and torching during the Taiping Rebellion (see p. 158–59) as troops surged through Anhui Province.

In the village of Jiuhua you will find the Ming dynasty **Zhiyuan Temple,** the largest of the local monasteries. On the ridge behind stands the **Baisui Temple,** which contains the remains of a wandering monk who came to the temple in the 1600s. When he died at the age of 126, his body refused to decay, and it remains, seated and embalmed by his faith (and a coating of gold).

A cable car whisks those with little time or energy to the peak. Near the summit are two nunneries, before the path trails up to the **Ten Thousand Buddhas Temple** on the peak.

Spring and autumn are the most refreshing seasons for the climb; summer is hot and humid. Daily buses arrive at Jiuhuashan from Huangshan (see pp. 150–52), and services also run from Nanjing and Hangzhou. ■

Stone statues stand sentinel on the Spirit Way to the tomb of Hongwu.

Nanjing

NANJING IS AN ATTRACTIVE CITY WITH WIDE BOULEVARDS and an enduring sense of history; it was frequently the capital of regional empires and twice the capital of China.

Nanjing
Map 141 E2 & 155

CITS visitor information
Map 155
Address: 202 Zhongshan Beilu
Phone: 025 8342-1125

Ming City Wall
Map 155
Address: Zhonghua Gate, Zhonghua Lu. Alternative access via Jiming Temple or Zhongshan Gate
Admission: $

The provincial capital of Jiangsu, Nanjing lies on the Yangtze River's southern bank. It is probably best remembered in the West for the devastation brought on it by the invading Japanese army in 1937.

The treaty ending the First Opium War was penned in this former Ming capital in 1842. Eleven years later the city found itself capital of the terrestrial heaven of the remarkable Taiping (see p. 158–59). They demolished the city's famous Ming imperial palace, only to have their replacement structures leveled by the Qing. The city later served as the Kuomintang capital (see pp. 36).

There's a palpable sense of confidence among Nanjing citizens, despite their traumatic past. Getting around is easy; taxis are cheap and plentiful and a new metro system shuttles passengers through the center of the city.

MING LEGACY

Nanjing retains much of its Ming heritage. The most stunning example is the **Ming City Wall (Chengqiang)** that encircles Nanjing; at over 20 miles (32 km), it is the longest city wall in the world. It was too long to defend adequately against the Taiping, but although some of the fortifications were demolished during their occupation, a good portion stands.

Interestingly, the wall avoids the standard square layout and instead follows the contours of the land, creating a fluid shape. Some of its gates survive, most notably **Zhonghua Gate** to the south and **Zhongshan Gate** to the east. Zhonghua Gate, an elaborate barrier of tiered portals and vaults, was used to house troops. Follow the steps to the overgrown ramparts and fine views over the city.

If visiting **Zijinshan** (see p. 157), take bus No. 20W back to the city, which gives dramatic views of the city wall, terminating at **Jiming Temple.** Here you can ascend the ramparts and a section of wall that runs south of Xuanwu Lake Park. The north exit of the temple crosses a bridge to the wall. You can also walk along a 0.75-mile (1.2 km) length of wall to the east, with excellent views over the lake and hillside pagodas. It's very overgrown in parts, but easily passable.

Wuchaomen Park sits on the ruins of the former **Ming Imperial Palace (Ming Gugong),** built by the first Ming emperor, Hongwu (*R.*1368–1398). The buildings, which were the model for the Forbidden City in Beijing (see pp. 56–62), were alternately sacked by the Manchus and destroyed during the anti-Manchu Taiping rebellion in the mid-19th century. All that remains are some strewn fragments—enchanting nonetheless—and the park is sublimely attractive. The ruins of the Gate of Heavenly Worship consist of stone pedestals overlooked by cypresses.

Five old Ming bridges cross a moat, behind which stands a stele carved in the 40th year of the reign of the Wanli emperor (*R.*1573–1620). Also still standing is the ancient wall of **Wumen,** overgrown with creepers and topped with the symbol of the current dynasty, the PRC (People's Republic of China) flag. The **Drum Tower** and the **Bell Tower** standing on either side of Zhongshan Lu were both originally constructed during the Ming dynasty.

MUSEUMS

The **Taiping Museum (Taiping Tianguo Lishi Bowuguan),** on Zhonghua Lu, is essential viewing for anyone interested in the troubled history of Christianity in China. The Taiping was one of the bloodiest rebellions in Chinese history, led by the obsessed Hong Xiuquan (see pp. 158–59). Much to the chagrin of historians (and the Taiping faithful), Hong's palace in Nanjing was razed and only a few documents and tablets remain to record their whirlwind social experiments.

As you enter the museum gate, you pass a bronze bust of Hong

Wuchaomen Park

- Map: 155
- Address: Zhongshan Donglu
- Price: $

Taiping Museum

- Map: 155
- Address: 128 Zhanyuan Lu
- Price: $

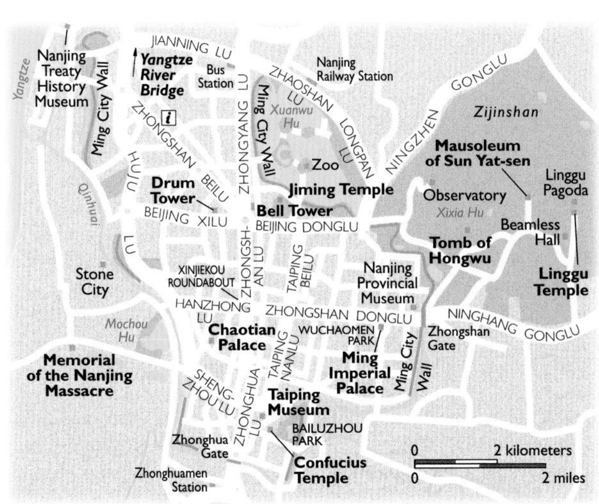

The Mausoleum of Sun Yat-sen on Zijinshan is a colossal monument to the father of Chinese Republicanism.

Xiuquan and a row of cannon used during the rebellion. Some of them are stamped with the characters *Tianguo*, or Heavenly Kingdom. You will also find a diagram of Hong Xiuquan's palace, and intriguing documents, including a treatise called *The New Guide to Government.* The treatise written by Hong Rengan reveals considerable borrowing from Western political models. The jade seal of the Heavenly King, called the great seal of the Taiping, is a square seal (chop) composed of Chinese characters.

The daring exploits of the Taiping are recorded in murals in chronological order and some weapons are displayed.

The **Memorial of the Nanjing Massacre (Datusha Jinianguan),** outside the city walls to the west, remembers the appalling barbarity of the invading Japanese army in December 1937. A hideous but necessary memorial to those who suffered, it makes for fascinating (though nauseating) viewing.

The museum resembles a colossal tomb, emblazoned on the facade with the number 300,000 (the upper estimate of those killed).

A visit is essential viewing for those wanting to comprehend why Sino-Japanese relations remain fraught, and why China insists on a full apology from Japan for the war.

Memorial of the Nanjing Massacre
- Map: 155
- Address: 418 Shui Ximen Dajie
- Price: $

Confucius Temple
- Map: 155
- Address: Gongyuan Jie
- Price: $

TEMPLES

A stone's throw from the Taiping Museum is the **Confucius Temple (Fuzimiao).** This Song dynasty temple has been continuously added to after repeated damage and most of the structures you see today are from the late Qing dynasty. The cells where students prepared for the official civil service examinations (see p. 83) are displayed.

Inside an expansive hall is a vast portrait of Confucius overseeing a set of bells, chimes, and musical instruments, and along the wall are some rather gaudy bas-reliefs in colored glass, which relate stories from Confucius's life. One parable tells of a *qilin* (mythical chimera) slaughtered in a world without ethics. The *qilin* only appeared during times of morality; in such an immoral world, the animal was doomed. The hall at the very rear offers classical Chinese music and performances by singers and dancers in period costumes. The area around the temple is a lively shopping/restaurant district.

The focal point of the **Chaotian Palace** on Mochou Lu is a Confucius Temple. In front of the palace is a statue of Confucius, clasping his hands. Inside the

Dacheng Hall is a fascinating exhibition of pottery and model ships illustrating life during the period of the Southern dynasties.

ZIJINSHAN

East of Nanjing lies Zijinshan, a wooded hill hosting a collection of historical sights. The overblown **Mausoleum of Sun Yat-sen (Zhongshanling),** founder of Republican China, is approached along a long avenue bordered with pines. The roof is grandly tiled in blue. Through the main gate stands a large stele emblazoned with gold characters declaring that the Kuomintang (Nationalists) buried Sun Zhongshan (Sun Yat-sen) here. Sun swore to make Nanjing the Nationalist capital, and Chiang Kai-shek made it so in 1928. In the mausoleum itself, a seated statue of Sun sits beneath a huge mosaic on the ceiling of a white sun on a blue background—the Kuomintang (Taiwan) flag. The design reappears in the vaulted tomb. Signs in Chinese remind visitors to salute.

Nearby are the remains of the **Tomb of Hongwu (Mingxiaoling),** the first Ming emperor. The tomb suffered devastation at the hands of the Taiping, but the Spirit Way (Shendao) survives, set at an angle to the tomb and lined with statues of animals, including elephants and camels.

The main approach takes you to the Military and Civil Gate, a large construction with bright red doors. Behind that is a stele inscribed by the Kangxi emperor and a Ming bridge that takes you to the Soul Tower. The original yellow-glazed tiles and double-eaved roof of the tower, behind which is the mound of the emperor's tomb, were all damaged during the Taiping Rebellion. Also leveled during the rebellion was the Xiaoling Palace, but you can make out the original foundations.

On the slopes of Zijinshan is the small **Zixia Lake (Zixiahu)** and **Linggu Temple.** Near the temple stands the **Beamless Hall,** a simple but impressive construction. It is now a museum celebrating the life of Sun Zhongshan (Yat-sen) and highlights the foreign menace of the Opium Wars. There are no English captions. Tall pines grow in the courtyard of the quiet, gracious **Linggu Temple.** The nine-story Linggu Pagoda, designed in 1929 by the American architect Henry Killam Murphy, rises behind. In the area, there are pavilions, amusement parks, and museums.

YANGTZE RIVER BRIDGE

An engineering feat of considerable importance straddles the Yangtze to the north of Nanjing. The Yangtze River Bridge opened at the height of the Cultural Revolution in 1968, at the same time as the Confucius Temple was being daubed with Maoist graffiti. Until it opened, trains crossed the river by ferry, a two-hour trip. The hefty Bolshevik lines and monumental scale will appeal to students of socialist iconography. You can get a good view if you are taking a day train to or from Beijing. ■

Chaotian Palace
- Map: 155
- Address: Mochou Lu
- Closed 10:30 a.m.–2 p.m.

Mausoleum of Sun Yat-sen
- Map: 155
- Address: Zijinshan
- Admission: $

Tomb of Hongwu
- Map: 155
- Address: Mingling Lu, Zijinshan
- Admission: $

Linggu Temple
- Map: 155
- Address: Linggusi Lu, Zijinshan
- Admission: $

The robust Military and Civil Gate ushers visitors to the tomb of the first Ming emperor.

Taiping Rebellion

The bloody Taiping Rebellion (1850–1864) caused the deaths of an estimated 20 million Chinese during the middle of the 19th century. While the violence was indescribable, the Taiping doctrine was transfixing. The movement's founder, the Hakka Hong Xiuquan (1814–1864), believed he was the Son of God and brother of Jesus.

Fired by feverish Christian visions (inspired by his dealings with missionaries in Guangzhou), and harboring a grudge after failing the civil service examinations, Hong Xiuquan embarked on his religious quest to conquer China. In 1851 he proclaimed the founding of the Taiping Tianguo (Heavenly Kingdom of Great Peace), encouraged by a multitude of disaffected peasants. His ambition was to rid the world of the Qing dynasty and to establish a radically new society. The Manchus were biblically seen as devils fit for destruction.

The Taiping devised an innovative form of Christian communism where property was shared, a common treasury was established, and the sexes were separated. Women were led by their own battle-hardened veterans, and homosexuality was forbidden on pain of death. Prostitution, opium smoking, and foot binding were similarly outlawed.

The egalitarian promise of the rebellion cemented together a devout assortment of anti-Qing faithful, and a disciplined fighting force a million strong was built. After an unsuccessful 33-day siege of Guilin (see pp. 276–77), the Taiping erupted out of south China and swept along the fertile Yangtze Valley via Wuchang to storm the great walled city of Nanjing on March 9, 1853; the city's entire Manchu population was put to the sword.

En route, the Taiping besieged the capital of Hunan Province, Changsha, but failed to take the city; in their wake, the provinces of Hunan and Hubei lay devastated. Nanjing became their capital and was renamed Tianjing—the Heavenly Capital. Hong Xiuquan conferred upon himself the absolutist title of Heavenly King.

From Nanjing the Taiping struck out at the rest of China, with Hangzhou suffering great devastation and falling to the rebels in 1861. The hard-won advantage began to slip from the rebels' grasp, however. Although the capture of Nanjing was a dramatic success, it signaled the start of a decline for the Taiping.

Conquered domains fell back into Qing control, and the 1853 northern expedition to take Beijing failed, as did the later western expedition to occupy Shanghai. Hong Xiuquan sought a powerful alliance with the Christian Western powers, but they shunned his heretical brew. If the West had accepted Hong's Christianity, the Qing dynasty would almost certainly have been overthrown.

Fearing usurpation, Hong eliminated a number of influential high-ranking rebels, encouraging desertions from the Taiping ranks. Power was shared by Hong's hopeless relatives, and a creeping malaise set in. By the end of 1863, many of the gains in eastern China had been lost and the disastrous expe-

dition to seize Shanghai was repelled by a Western-trained Manchu army known as the Ever Victorious Army, which eventually besieged the Heavenly Capital of Nanjing. Hong Xiuquan died during the city's encirclement. The city capitulated on July 19, 1864, after a mammoth siege, with the Taiping fighting to the last man or taking their own lives. The rest of the rebels, scattered through south China, were rooted out and ruthlessly eliminated.

The Taiping system is unique in Chinese history and is seen by many as a progenitor of Chinese communism. Defying Chinese traditional beliefs, fiercely anti-Confucian and radically experimental, the Taiping creed stressed brotherhood, equality, and common ownership. Some of the Taiping furthermore promoted democratic principles and incubated inventive plans for economic transformation. The whole edifice of Taiping social planning was glued together by the dictates of the Christian gospels. The Communist Party remembers them as champions of the people and dresses them up suitably for public consumption. The Taiping Museum in Nanjing (see p. 155) is a fascinating chronicle of the period.

If the Taiping had succeeded in their ambitions, China would have become the most populous Christian domain in the world. The apostasy of its Christianity, however, would have ultimately led to a clash with the rest of Christendom. ■

Below: Engraving of the Franco-Chinese Treaty of 1858. Right: The ill-treatment of Europeans in the Taiping Rebellion depicted by W. Dickes, circa 1860

Yangzhou

Yangzhou
141 E2

ENRICHED BY THE BURGEONING TRADE OF THE GRAND Canal (see p. 162–63) yet devastated in the 19th century by Taiping rebels, Yangzhou in Jiangsu Province is a pleasant city noted for its picturesque grid of waterways, bridges, parks, and gardens.

Five Pavilion Bridge, Shouxi Lake Park

Daming Temple
Pingshantang Lu

He Garden
Xuningmen Lu

Ge Garden
Yanfu Lu

Tomb of Puhaddin
Jiefang Nanlu
$ (temple & gardens)

Many of Yangzhou's sights are settled on the periphery of town, and taking a taxi is the best way to reach them. The **Daming Temple,** to the northwest, was originally established in the Southern dynasty of the Liu Song (A.D. 420–479). It was rebuilt in the late Qing dynasty after being torched by the Taiping, who established their Heavenly Capital in nearby Nanjing. It is celebrated for its Jianzhen Hall, dedicated to a pioneering Tang dynasty monk who, after many failed attempts, succeeded in reaching Japan to further the cause of Buddhism there. The temple is not far from the remains of the Tang city wall. The nearby Pingshan Hall belonged to the Song dynasty writer Ou Yangxiu (see p. 50).

Shouxi Lake Park (Shouxihu Gongyuan) is a Tang dynasty lake historically exalted by visiting wordsmiths and forever seething with tour groups, so weekends are best avoided. The elaborate **Five-Pavilion Bridge (Wutingqiao)** spans the lake, and nearby stands a white **dagoba (baita),** based on the example in Beijing's Beihai Park (see p. 63).

Yangzhou is famous for its gardens, bequeathed by merchants who made their fortune in salt. **He Garden (Heyuan),** not far from the hook of the moat in the southeast, between Nantong Donglu and Guangling Lu, is surrounded by pavilions, while the **Ge Garden (Geyuan)** on Yanfu Lu is a Chinese classical contrivance of bamboo and rockeries.

To the east of the Ge Garden, across the Grand Canal, is a Muslim monument called the **Tomb of Puhaddin (Puhading Muyuan).** Puhaddin was a wayfaring Yuan dynasty Islamic missionary. The tomb shelters the remains of other Muslims and is devoted to the history of Muslim contacts with China.

The city also preserves a small Catholic church and a Baptist church in the center of town. A reminder of the once sizable Protestant population in Yangzhou, the Baptist church still functions, and contains a baptismal pool. ■

Zhenjiang

Zhenjiang
141 E2

CITS visitor information
92 Zhongshan Xilu
0511 523-7538

ZHENJIANG IS ANOTHER JIANGSU CITY WHOSE RICHES came with the building of the Grand Canal. Although it is now busy and industrialized, its hilly parks are attractively dotted with temples and there are enduring shades of treaty port architecture.

Jinshan Temple lies on the slopes of **Jinshan (Golden Mountain) Park** in the northwest of town. This active temple is a layered sequence of halls and steps that mount the hill (formerly an island in the Yangtze River). Don't miss the three golden, seated Buddhas in the main hall.

The **Cishou (Benevolence and Longevity) Pagoda** above was supposedly built to celebrate the 65th birthday of Empress Dowager Cixi in 1900. Caves punctuate the hills, and the "First Spring Under Heaven" is celebrated for the quality of its water.

To the east, also abutting the Yangtze River, lies **Beigushan Park,** with the intoxicatingly named **Sweet Dew Temple (Ganlusi).** The temple has suffered much attrition through the ages, but most features date from the Qing dynasty. Not far away is a rather peculiar and weather-beaten **iron pagoda,** sitting on the site of the original Tang dynasty version that was destroyed.

On a street north of the railway station stands an intriguing monument to American Pearl S. Buck, author of *The Good Earth.* The **Pearl S. Buck House,** where the novelist lived, is a well-preserved testament to Buck, who wrote so vividly about China and its people.

The exhibits of the hilltop **museum (Bowuguan),** housed in the former British consulate, are rather dull. The attractive building, set in the grounds of Boxian Park, is a reminder that Zhenjiang was a foreign treaty port. The area around the museum forms the historic core of the city, with its picturesque cobbled streets and river-port views.

Jiaoshan (Burnt Hill), a delightful park, lies beside the river in the northeast of town. The views over the river are excellent. There are pavilions galore, venerable pine trees, and the **Dinghui Temple,** whose current buildings replace previous incarnations that failed to weather the tempest of Chinese history. ■

Yuan dynasty pagoda, Zhenjiang

Jinshan Temple
Xinhe Lu
$

Sweet Dew Temple
Zhenjiao Lu
$

Pearl S. Buck House
6 Runzhoushan Lu

Museum
85 Boxian Lu
$

Grand Canal

The Grand Canal, like that other mammoth engineering endeavor—the Great Wall—has sadly decayed through old age, neglect, and the dawn of new technologies. The remnants of this network of watercourses, however, constitute the longest man-made waterway in the world, cutting a 1,000-mile (1,610 km) route from Hangzhou to Beijing.

Segments of the canal system date back almost 2,500 years, but the first concerted effort to enmesh north China and the Yangtze River basin in a web of waterways came during the reign of a megalomaniac emperor. The second emperor of the Sui dynasty, Yangdi (*R.*604–618), was a man of extreme vision. His designs included the rebuilding of the capital Luoyang and the Great Wall. There was method to his imperial madness, however, and the logic behind the titanic canal scheme was to afford a transport link between the fertile Yangtze region and Luoyang. This would allow the smooth and efficient transport of both grain and soldiers in times of unrest.

In keeping with the tradition of great construction projects in China, forced labor made up most of the muscle (any surplus manpower was dispatched to the Great Wall). Up to 5.5 million workers slaved on the project, overseen by a colossal and brutal police force.

The new waterways were, in many places, carved out from the shells of existing canals cut during the Han dynasty. Upon its completion, Yangdi made a number of ostentatious outings along the canal until he was hanged in Yangzhou by justifiably mutinous members of his entourage.

Later dynasties made full use of the waterways. The Tang dynasty availed itself of the Grand Canal, while the Song dynasty grafted its capital Hangzhou onto the system. It was further extended during the Yuan dynasty to transport food to the new capital in Beijing; thus appeared the canal in its present route.

The emperors in Beijing relied upon the canal to bring north the produce of the fecund southern regions, which included rice, silk, and tea. Much of the brick and other material that made up the Ming dynasty Forbidden City and the Temple of Heaven in Peking were ferried up the Grand Canal.

The canal maintained its structure (which was not one canal but a linked chain of waterways) until the 19th century, when catastrophic flooding of the Yellow River caused major damage to both the waterways and vessels. The Taiping, who established their capital in Nanjing, further jeopardized the canal industry with their constant assaults on north China, and the canal's northern reaches gradually fell into disuse and disrepair.

The 20th century saw a host of rival transport options emerging to challenge the

redundant technology of the Grand Canal. Railways and, more recently, air travel have led to further stagnation along the reaches of Yangdi's great enterprise.

The canal today

Dredging of the canal has not saved it. The Beijing–Tianjin section is silted up and other reaches are unnavigable. South of the Yangtze the picture is generally more optimistic, and the section between the famed silk capital of Hangzhou, Suzhou (with its wonderful gardens and temples), and Wuxi remains open. It teems with flat-bottomed vessels, making for an interesting overnight journey.

Don't go expecting the Grand Canal of Venice though. For centuries the waterway served as a conveyor belt of produce and was a functional, rather than an aesthetic, masterpiece. This has resulted in grubby boats plying the route and sooty factories scarring some of the shoreline. Nevertheless, if you are planning to travel between Suzhou and Hangzhou, this is an alternative to taking the train.

Boats depart Suzhou and Wuxi wharfs daily at 5:30 p.m. for the overnight chug to Hangzhou (taking 13 to 14 hours), arriving the next morning. Tickets can be bought at the jetty or at CITS in either Suzhou, Wuxi, or Hangzhou for either direction. ■

Boatmen ferry hay past crumbling houses along the Grand Canal, once a major conduit between Hangzhou and Beijing.

Suzhou's gardens

Suzhou
141 E2 & 167

CITS visitor information
Next to Lexiang Hotel, 18 Dajing Xiang
0512 6520-9362 or 0512 6522-3783

Note: All gardens have individual $ fee

Master of the Nets Garden
Off Shiquan Jie

Blue Wave Pavilion
Off Renmin Lu

Cultural events are held nightly in the Master of the Nets Garden.

SUZHOU IS ONE OF CHINA'S PREMIER ATTRACTIONS, FABLED for its picturesque canals and traditional gardens. Chinese gardens aim to inspire a meditative mood, so there's no need to rush from one to another in a bid to see them all in one day.

Suzhou's gardens are not beautiful in the idyllic sense, and they depend heavily on the weather for mood. They are microcosms of nature and bring elements of *shan-shui,* or mountains and rivers, to the city. As such, the weather is as much a part of the garden as its physical features. Depending on the season and the weather, Suzhou's gardens can be golden with autumn colors and frosty, clear, and bright, or grey and downcast. This interplay of the elements (wind, rain, snow, frost, sunlight) with the garden is critical. On a colorless day, the gardens can look limp and washed out; in the right light conditions, however, an inspirational mood reigns. Some contain teahouses, where you can rest and enjoy the view over a steaming cup.

MASTER OF THE NETS GARDEN (WANGSHIYUAN)

The arrangement of pavilions, halls, music rooms, winsome bamboo groves, and waterside perches is an exercise in natural harmony. The hub of the garden, surreptitiously tucked down an alleyway, is a large pool surrounded by ribbons of walkways and pavilions reflected in the water. Visit the gardens early in the morning to escape foraging tour groups blotting out the view. When approaching a garden such as this, aim to sit down and find peace within its natural setting.

BLUE WAVE PAVILION (CANGLANGTING)

The best feature of this garden is its charming canalside setting. The rustling of wind in the bamboo leaves creates a tranquil mood, and stone recesses offer shelter from sudden showers. The rising and dipping contours create a hilly dimension, distinguishing the pavilion from the flatland of other Suzhou gardens.

GARDEN OF HAPPINESS (YIYUAN)

The Garden of Happiness is one of Suzhou's more relaxing gardens—not too large and a real pleasure to explore. The rock garden within is an intricate network of narrow stairways.

HUMBLE ADMINISTRATOR'S GARDEN (ZHUOZHENGYUAN)

Considered one of Suzhou's finest, this is a harmony of water, stone, pavilions, bamboo groves, islets, and bridges in the north of town. Designed in the 16th century, it is the largest garden in Suzhou and is divided into two balanced sections.

COUPLES GARDEN (OUYUAN)

A pleasantly designed space near the moat in the eastern part of Suzhou, the Couples Garden offers an unruffled escape, a quiet retreat of birdsong, and slowly sauntering couples rather than hordes of vacationing Chinese. The attractively named **Moon-viewing Pavilion** overlooks the water. The small figures on the plaque outside the **Zaijiu Tang** have had their heads smashed off—possibly the work of Taiping rebels.

East Garden (Dongyuan), north of Couples Garden, is more of a modern sprawl, offering noisy animal shows and lions riding on horseback when the fair's in town.

LION GROVE (SHIZILIN)

The origin of this garden's name is rather a mystery, though some say the shapes of lions can be discerned in its stones. Most popular with Chinese tour groups, it is easy to get completely lost in the cave-filled rock garden here, so take note. The garden was once attached to a monastery; it was also tended by the architect I.M. Pei. Because the garden is constantly overrun, it's not an enclave of peace and quiet.

GARDEN FOR LINGERING IN (LIUYUAN)

This is probably the least successful of Suzhou's gardens, with a contrived mystique and a rather tired feel to the gardens. ■

Garden of Happiness
☒ Off Renmin Lu

Humble Administrator's Garden
☒ Dongbei Jie

Couples Garden
☒ Off Cang Jie

Lion Grove
☒ Yuanlin Lu

Garden for Lingering In
☒ Liuyuan Lu

A romantic retreat, the Couples Garden is quietly set aside from the main tourist route.

A bike ride around Suzhou

From the Panmen Scenic Area near the city moat, this bike ride takes you along Suzhou's pretty streets past famous gardens, canals, and noteworthy temples. Bicycles can be rented from many places around town, including a number of hotels and opposite the train station.

The delightful arch of Wumen Bridge in Suzhou's Panmen Scenic Area

Before you set out at the start of the tour from the Panmen Scenic Area—an attractive, historic place in Suzhou's southwestern corner—leave your bike and clamber up this section of the old city wall. Below is the Wuxiang Temple (Wuxiangci), included in the price of your ticket to Panmen.

Cycle north to Xinshi Lu, passing the restored **Ruiguang Pagoda (Ruiguangta).** Follow Xinshi Lu and then go left along Renmin Lu to the double-eaved, 11th-century **Confucius Temple (Kongmiao)** ❶, presiding over a collection of ancient steles. Take your bike up the path along the canal opposite the **Blue Wave Pavilion** (see p. 164).

Around the corner along Shiquan Jie, the **Master of the Nets Garden** ❷ (see p. 164) is tucked down an alleyway.

Return to Shiquan Lu. Take the first right north up Fenghuang Jie (Phoenix Street) past the 10th-century **Twin Pagodas (Shuangta)** ❸ on your right. The temple that accompanied them was torched by the Taiping in 1860.

Cross the canal and continue heading north along Lindun Lu. At the next major intersection is Guanqian Jie, a pedestrian-only street (you may have to leave your bike behind) marked by the **Xuanmiao Temple (Xuanmiaoguan)** ❹. This Taoist temple, originally built in A.D. 276, was formerly called the Zhen Qing Temple. In the Sanqing Hall are the Three Pure Ones (see p. 73), accompanied by images of the 12 Heavenly Generals. At the rear of the temple stands a constellation of golden Taoist figures; a separate temple holds an effigy of eight-armed Doulao, the goddess who governs the Big Dipper constellation.

Continue north along Lindun Lu, turn right on Baita Donglu, and then go left into Yuanlin Lu, where you will find the **Lion Grove** (see p. 165). North again is the **Humble Administrator's Garden** ❺ (see p. 165) on Dongbei Jie.

The road becomes Xibei Jie as you cycle west, above which rises the **North Pagoda (Beita)** ❻. Although the upper floors are covered in graffiti, the climb offers a decent view over Suzhou. The wind at the top is chill and refreshing in summer.

Cycle south on Renmin Lu, then west along Dongzhongshi, which follows the canal, and turn right and then left into Liuyuan Lu. You will pass the **Garden for Lingering In** (see p. 165), but far more interesting is the **West Garden Temple (Xiyuansi)** ❼ ahead.

The main temple houses imposing statues of Buddha, and behind, a colossal statue of Guanyin, is draped in a robe and standing on the head of a fish. Clustering around her are the supplicant Luohan (see p. 72) in acts of benediction. The miniature palace to her on the far left is called the Crystal Palace.

A truly mesmerizing sight here is the Arhat

(Luohan) Hall, first built in the Ming dynasty (and later burned down and rebuilt). The Guanyin facing you as you enter literally has 1,000 arms. There are 500 gilt clay Luohan in small corridors here, surrounding the four sacred Buddhist mountains sculptured in the center.

The figures are breathtaking for their quality of detail and the uniqueness of every statue. Each one has a different facial expression. Some are joyous, others sagacious, this one at peace with himself, another vehement, some devotional, others pensive; you'll see laughter, sadness, and everything in between. Each stands encapsulated in a glass box, but some break out of their cages. The arms of one Luohan shoot out through holes in the glass, and others have staffs that pierce the ceilings. Models of children clamber over other Luohan. The Luohan with the completely mad expression is the Jigong monk.

Farther east on Fengqiao Lu stands the **Hanshan (Cold Mountain) Temple.** It's not worth making an expedition to the temple unless you want to explore what inspired the Tang dynasty poet Zhang Ji to write his famous nocturnal poem "Night Mooring by Maple Bridge":

The moon lowers, crows call and the whole world is frost
Facing the riverside maples and the fisherman's torch light I feel troubled in my sleep
In the middle of the night, the sound of the bell reaches my boat
From the Hanshan Temple outside the city of Gusu. ■

Also see area map p. 141
Panmen Scenic Area
6.5 miles (10.5 km) to West Garden Temple
Whole day, including time spent in gardens
West Garden Temple or Hanshan Temple

NOT TO BE MISSED

- Master of the Nets Garden
- Xuanmiao Temple
- West Garden Temple

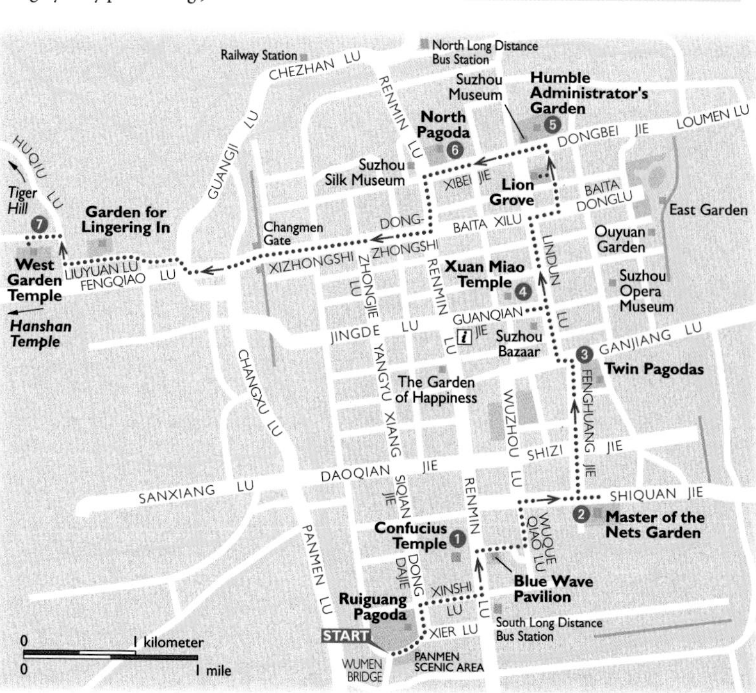

Lake Taihu
141 E2

CITS visitor information
18 Zhongshan Lu
0510 270-5369

CTS visitor information
88 Chezhan Lu
0510 868-9888

Xihui Park
Huihe Lu
$

Li Garden
Hubin Lu
$

Locals say that they can make tea in an old Yixing teapot by just filling it with boiling water.

Lake Taihu & around

NOT FAR FROM SUZHOU IN JIANGSU PROVINCE IS CHINA'S third largest freshwater lake, Taihu. Studded with islands, it lies next to the port city of Wuxi on the Grand Canal, and Yixing town, home of its famous namesake pottery.

The city of Wuxi has buried its long history under a modern face, and the lake is the main attraction. **Xihui Park (Xihui Gongyuan),** pushing up against the Grand Canal in the west of town, has some items of note. From the **Longguang Pagoda** adorning the hill you can cast long looks over Taihu. **Jichang Garden (Jichangyuan)** is an echo of Suzhou's famous gardens. An artificial lake, a zoo, and the **Huishan Temple** complete the park. **Li Garden (Liyuan)** adjoins the lake in the south of town, attracting tour groups.

The frequently misty lake is the real reason to come here. It remains more popular with the Chinese, for around Taihu lie vestiges of two ancient kingdoms, Wu and Yue.

The most famous sights cluster on the lake's northern edge. The peninsula sticking out into the lake southwest of Wuxi, **Turtle Head Island (Yuantouzhu),** offers a vantage point over the water. At the south end of the island is a collection of amusement parks.

Ferries travel routes from the peninsula to islands in the lake.The trip to the 5-acre (2 ha) **Three Hills Isles** (also called the Fairy Islands) is a short hop and a popular excursion. The island supports a population of wild monkeys, and the views are excellent; overblown classical Chinese structures, however, seem rather contrived. Speedboats also cross the lake for two-hour trips.

Dingshan, in Yixing County on the western shore of Lake Taihu, is where the purple sand (*zisha*) Yixing teapots are produced. These teapots, which can be found all over China, appear in a range of dark colors through brown, green, and purple and have a porosity that best augments the color and fragrance of tea. The **Ceramics Exhibition Hall (Taoci Zhanlanguan)** features pots from Yixing over the ages.

Yixing County is also riddled with limestone caves. The recesses of **Shanjuan Cave (Shanjuandong)** can be navigated by boat along an underground river, and **Zhanggong Cave (Zhanggongdong)** is honeycombed with a network of smaller caves. ■

Hangzhou's West Lake evokes classic Chinese beauty.

Hangzhou

FAMED THROUGHOUT CHINA FOR ITS SILK AND THE IDEalized West Lake, Hangzhou has had a checkered history. It prospered as capital of the southern Song, but was destroyed by the Taiping between 1860 and 1862. The city today is only a faint shadow of its former self, but it remains one of China's premier holiday destinations.

Hangzhou's origins lie in the Qin dynasty (221–206 B.C.), though it was not until its connection to the Grand Canal (see p. 162–63) in the seventh century that it flourished. The southern Song fled here from Kaifeng to establish their capital (then called Linan), further promoting its development. Marco Polo, Odoric of Pordenone, and other Western travelers eulogized Hangzhou, as did many Chinese emperors. The visitation of the Taiping saw the fiery destruction of most of Hangzhou's temples and buildings of note, prompting a reversal of fortunes.

WEST LAKE

The Chinese consider West Lake to be a heavenly, archetypal lake, the model for others. As such, it is stormed by tour groups, stampeding from one sight to another and crowding out the view. A visit to Hangzhou is obligatory for all Chinese, so it's often preferable to slip away to less visited sights.

West Lake may be commercialized, but the area has enjoyed considerable prettification over recent years. If you want to complete a circuit of the lake, you will need about half a day—longer if you want to ponder some of the sights.

The **Temple of Yue Fei (Yuefeimu)** on the northwestern shore tells the story of the heroic Song dynasty general who is buried here. Master strategist, loyal patriot, and inventor of a popular Chinese martial art (see p. 122) linked with *taiji quan* (*xingyi quan*), Yue Fei was imprisoned and executed despite his successful incursions against the northern Jurchen invaders. He was posthumously exonerated and later elevated to the status of hero and demigod. He is also feted by the Communists, who admire his patriotic example.

In the temple grounds are kneeling statues of the perfidious Qin Hui (the man who betrayed Yue Fei), his wife, and two treacherous generals.

To the west are the **Hangzhou Botanical Gardens (Hangzhou Zhiwuyuan),** and spanning south over West Lake is

Hangzhou
Map: 141 E2 & 170

Hangzhou Tourist Center
Address: 1st Floor, Huanglong Stadium, 3 Huanglong Lu
Phone: 0571 8796-8560

Temple of Yue Fei
Address: Beishan Lu
Price: $

the Su Causeway, named after the Song dynasty poet Su Dongpo, who was also governor of Hangzhou for a period. The causeway stretches past **Huagang Garden** near the southern shore, famed for its goldfish.

Across the causeway, to the east, lies the **Island of Small Oceans,** with its four lotus-choked ponds. South of the island a cluster of small pagodas rises from **Three Pools Reflecting the Moon.** Candles are placed in each pagoda on nights of the full moon, the yellow light piercing out from five small holes.

Lingyin Temple
170
Lingyin Lu
$

Solitary Hill (Gushan) is the largest island in the lake; it is attached to the north shore by the Baidi Causeway and Xiling Bridge. Dotted with small pavilions and pagodas, the island is home to **Zhejiang Provincial Museum,** where you can find **Zhongshan Park** and exhibits relating to Hangzhou and Zhejiang Province.

The slender **Baochu Pagoda** overlooks the lake from the hills to the north. At a height of 125 feet (38 m) and originally built in 968, it has been repeatedly restored.

Hangzhou was also a center of Christian missionary activity, a remnant of which survives in the simple but intriguing church (*104 Jiefang Lu*) east of West Lake. An active house of worship, the unusual church has upturned eaves and Chinese tiling.

LINGYIN TEMPLE

To the west is Hangzhou's most celebrated sacred site, Lingyin Temple. In the fourth century A.D. an Indian Buddhist Huili noted that nearby rocks resembled a holy peak in India and suggested they had flown to China from there. The rocks were consequently named **Feilai Feng** or the Peak that Flew From Afar. Huili's remains were supposedly laid to rest in a nearby stupa.

Lingyin Temple was promptly built on the spot, which has endured a roller-coaster ride of successive

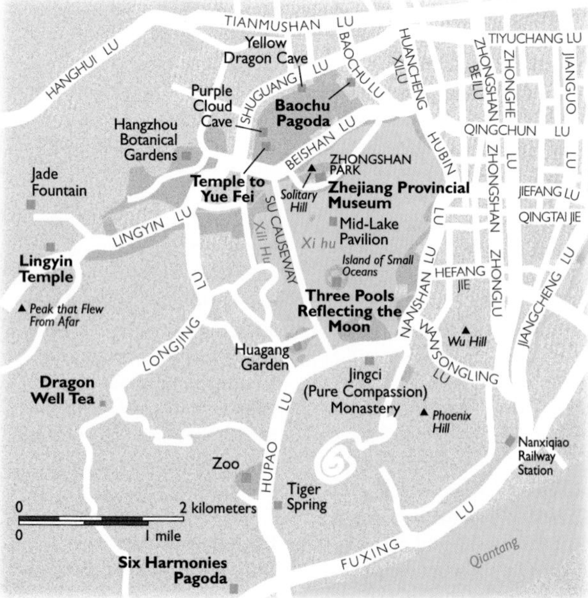

destruction and restoration. Destroyed and rebuilt at least 16 times, it miraculously survived the menace of the Cultural Revolution.

The chubby Qing dynasty Future Buddha (supposedly based on a real Chinese man who loved children) greets all with his welcoming laugh, while Weituo (see p. 72) stands behind him. The Four Heavenly Kings stand on either flank.

The Great Hall behind presents its magnificent 65-foot-tall (20 m) statue of Sakyamuni (see p. 72), carved from camphor wood. The hall was constructed in the 20th century to accommodate the statue, which was completed in 1956. On either side of the Great Hall stands a stone pagoda.

PEAK THAT FLEW FROM AFAR

A network of caves and Buddhist statues in the Peak that Flew From Afar, opposite the Lingyin Temple, makes for an interesting tour. The statues date from as early as the Five Dynasties (A.D. 906–960), and many are from the Song and Yuan dynasties. The most popular is a statue of the corpulent laughing Buddha. Most Buddhist art grottoes of note belong to north China, and this is one of the few in the south.

DRAGON WELL TEA

The town of Dragon Well (Longjing), southwest of West Lake, is celebrated throughout for its distinctively flavored tea. Coming out here may not be every one's idea of fun, for the whole enterprise has been overdeveloped for the tourist dollar; however, the scenery is attractive, if you can shake off the hawkers.

SIX HARMONIES PAGODA

Farther to the southwest, nudging up against the Qiantang River, is the Six Harmonies Pagoda (Liuhe Ta). Situated on a hill, the octagonal structure served as a lighthouse and was thought to exert an esoteric influence over the annual tidal bore that swamped Hangzhou. It is named after the Six Codes of Buddhism. The hillside above the pagoda offers pleasing walks among statues and shrines. ■

During the Cultural Revolution, Premier Zhou Enlai saved Hangzhou's Lingyin Temple from destruction.

Six Harmonies Pagoda

- Map: 170
- Address: Zhijiang Lu
- Price: $

Shaoxing

Shaoxing
141 E2

CITS visitor information
341 Fushan Xilu
0575 515-5669

Former Home of Lu Xun
208 Lu Xun Zhonglu
$

Ancestral Home of Zhou Enlai
369 Laodong Lu
$

THE CHINESE CELEBRATE THE PRETTY TOWN OF SHAOXING for its charming canal scenes and the picturesque decay of its waterside houses. It is also the birthplace of the iconoclastic writer Lu Xun, one of China's greatest modern novelists. Shaoxing wine, a strongly flavored culinary wine, has been fermented here since the sixth century; it has since found its way to kitchens throughout the land.

The old city of Shaoxing, capital of the state of Yue in the seventh century, lies in the middle of a heavily irrigated region of Zhejiang Province. One of the best ways to enjoy this town is to amble along its waterways and narrow, quaint streets.

The **Former Home of Lu Xun (Lu Xun Guju)** is where the writer lived before studying in Japan and moving to Shanghai. A reading of *Diary of a Madman* (see opposite) before visiting this site could help you empathize with this radical writer. Not far from his home is the **Lu Xun Memorial Hall (Lu Xun Jinianguan),** which documents his life and works, and the school where he studied.

The area around the memorial hall is an attractive part of Shaoxing and is well worth exploring for its canal textures and enchanting arched bridges. At the western tip of Lu Xun Zhonglu is Lu Xun Cultural Square, which marks an intersection of waterways.

Shaoxing's other darling son was the much loved Zhou Enlai, China's premier who died in 1976. He was an effective counterbalance to Mao Zedong's bad judgment and a sane voice in a time of madness. He never actually lived in Shaoxing, but his family came from here. Zhou's **Ancestral Home (Zhou Enlai Zuju),** which houses a museum dedicated to the man, can be found on Laodong Lu. Leave here, head east along Changqiao Zhijie (Longbridge Straight Street), and turn south when you meet Guangningqiao Zhijie (Extensive Peace Bridge Straight Street). This will take you across the canal and down to the **Eight Character Bridge (Baziqiao),** one of Shaoxing's oldest, having been built in the Jin dynasty.

The hexagonal and much restored **Dashan Pagoda (Dashanta)** rises on Guangming Lu southwest of the intersection of Jiefang Lu and Shengli Lu. Shaoxing's other pagoda, **Yingtian Pagoda (Yingtianta),** is in the south of town. It was rebuilt after a visit by the Taiping in the mid-19th century.

The Great Yu, China's famous water worker and mythical founder of the Xia dynasty (see p. 22), has an unlikely grave outside town. The **Tomb of the Great Yu (Yuling),** 2.5 miles (4 km) southeast of Shaoxing, is marked with a statue of the man, pavilions, cypresses, steles, and memorial halls, and it may only be of interest to those preoccupied with Chinese legends and deities (take the No. 2 bus that runs along Jiefang Lu).

Orchid Pavilion (Lanting), much touted by CITS, appeals most to Shaoxing's Chinese visitors. The pavilions are famous for their association with the famous fourth-century calligrapher Wang Xizhi. His most famous piece is the *Lanting Xu* or *Preface to the Orchid Pavilion,* which marks a literary feast held there in A.D. 353. ■

Shaoxing's canals add charm to Zhejiang Province's waterlogged north.

Lu Xun

China's first great modern novelist, Lu Xun (Lu Hsun, 1881–1936) was born in Shaoxing and originally studied medicine in Japan before turning his attention to fiction. He became involved with the nascent Chinese May 4th literary movement, which aimed to replace the use of classical Chinese in literature with the spoken form of Chinese; in 1918 his best work, *Diary of a Madman,* was published. This was the first short story to eschew classical Chinese, the establishment language that had exercised a stranglehold on literary creativity. The sinister and discomforting tale depicts a lunatic who feels enveloped by a man-eating society. The story is a thinly veiled critique of the self-consuming nature of Confucian society.

Lu Xun's anti-conservatism found free reign in *The Story of Ah Q* (1921), probably his most famous work, and *Medicine,* a short story that dealt with the messy world of superstition in Chinese society.

The writer also excelled at prose writing, penning *A Brief History of Chinese Fiction* and translating a large body of literature from other languages. He lived his last years in Shanghai, increasingly sympathizing with the Communist cause, which he saw as offering salvation to China. His tomb is in Shanghai. ■

Chinese temples

If you can interpret the sacred symbols of the temples you visit you will be well rewarded. The divine architecture of Chinese temples is a world governed by the sacred science of *fengshui* and other mysterious forces. This short guide aims to ease open the door to that rich domain and help you to understand it more fully.

Fengshui

Regardless of faith, Chinese temples are principally laid out on the advice of a fengshui (geomancy) expert (see p. 230). The axis runs north–south, with temple gates and doors facing south. Temples are often perched on mountainsides, not only because mountains are sometimes infused with Taoist or Buddhist myth but also because the Green Dragon and White Tiger (see p. 230) follow mountain ranges and imbue hilly land with *qi* or "cosmic energy."

Water guards against attack from evil spirits, hence the common positioning of pools and canals in temples. Evil spirits cannot travel over water, so the body of water acts as a repellent. Most temples are also protected by

menacing door gods, including the Four Heavenly Kings (see p. 72), who act as a further line of defense.

The five elements of fengshui (metal, water, wood, fire, and earth) are important aspects of temple design, interwoven into the structural fabric of the buildings and statuary. The Wong Tai Sin Temple in Kowloon, Hong Kong, is an example of this (see p. 240).

Confucian temples

The primary courtyard of Confucian temples is typically a small grove of steles inscribed with the names of dignified local scholars. The steles are frequently supported on the backs of vast *bixi* (mythical tortoise-like animals), themselves occasionally housed in individual pavilions. A statue of Confucius with clasped hands often welcomes visitors, although the statue is generally a recent carving.

The main hall surrounds an effigy of the sage flanked by two rows of disciples, including a statue of the Confucian philosopher Mencius. Also on show is an assortment of musical instruments, a set of bells, and stone chimes. The chimes are an important part of the Confucian canon, for they were apparently tuned in accordance with the *Tao,* or Way; a

In temples such as this one at Emeishan, you will find the ancient custom and lore of traditional China.

fluctuation in pitch indicated earthly imbalance and consequent implications for the imperial sphere. Statues or effigies of the *qilin*, a mythical chimera, are often found at these temples (see pp. 90 & 128). The animal sometimes appears in Confucian literature, signifying earthly harmony.

Temples dedicated to Confucius are few in number. The significance of religious Confucianism dwindled with the emergence of Communism, and many temples sank into a state of untended neglect. Dry and dusty, the ones that survived the Cultural Revolution (Confucius was especially singled out for his conservatism) seem lifeless and crumbling, like a set of decaying books.

Confucian temples are called *wenmiao* (cultural temple) or *kongmiao* (Confucius temple). Famous examples can be found in Qufu (the largest of them all), Beijing (the eponymous Confucius Temple), Yixing, Harbin, and Jilin.

A common pigment in Chinese temples, red represents good fortune and signifies fire in fengshui.

Buddhist temples

As loci of spiritual power, Chinese Buddhist temples hum with sacred energy. Balls of incense smoke rise from braziers, cross-legged monks sit reading sutras, and worshipers divine their futures with bamboo slips *(qian)* and prayers. Often you will find temples hidden among the cool pines of a forest or clinging to a mountainside.

Entering, you are traditionally greeted by a golden Milefo, the plump and jovial Buddha of the future. Standing back to back with him is Weituo (see p. 72), carrying his staff. On either side are the colossal Four Heavenly Kings (see p. 72), who protect the temple from evil spirits.

The jovial bodhisattva is located here to remind Buddhists that the future awaits those who believe. Two strips of calligraphy on either side of him generally tell of his toleration of what is unendurable and his hilarity at life's comedy. Milefo often sits within a hall called the Hall of Heavenly Kings.

Behind Milefo lies the first courtyard of several. Large bronze incense burners, often fantastically decorated, send up smoke in vast plumes. On either flank stand the bell and drum tower, which sound to alert the faithful to prayer. Ahead is a succession of temples.

The main hall, the Daxiong Baodian, or Great Heroic Treasure Hall, is first. Here you will encounter a trinity of bodhisattvas. Guanyin, the goddess of mercy, is often present, generally facing north at the rear.

The second hall is not usually notable, but the third generally contains the salvationary Amitabha Buddha or Wenshu. The 18 Luohan line the sides in rows of nine (see p. 72). There may be a fourth hall, which will contain a group of male and female bodhisattvas.

Some temples retain pagodas (such as Guangzhou's Temple of the Six Banyan Trees), but many pagodas survive without companion temples. The pagoda was used for storing sacred sutras and translations from India. Surviving spirit walls, often decorated with dragons, were designed to deflect bad spirits. Buddhist temples also feature a further number of small side halls and temples.

Buddhist temples are called *simiao* (temple) or *chansi* (Zen temple). They are found all over China in greater numbers than their Confucian and Taoist peers. Famous examples include Nan Putuo Temple in Xiamen, the Lama Temple in Beijing, the Jade Buddha Temple in Shanghai, and the Jokhang Temple

Above: A Tibetan pilgrim crawls in a display of veneration. Left: Incense is an important element in Chinese worship.

in Lhasa. The four sacred Buddhist mountains of China, such as Emeishan or Wutaishan, are dotted with them.

Taoist temples

Taoist monks (*daoshi*) differ in appearance from their yellow-robed, shaven-headed Buddhist brethren (*hesheng*). Their hair is long and twisted up in a knot, and they wear small, squarish jackets and straight trousers.

The sequence of temples also diverges from the Buddhist pattern. The main hall holds the Three Pure Ones (see p. 73), who are three representations of the *Tao,* or Way. This hall is often surrounded on either side by clusters of lesser halls.

Other deities who have their own halls include the Eight Immortals, the Jade emperor, Laozi (author of the classic *Daode Jing*), the goddess of seafarers Tianhou (otherwise called Mazu, or Niangniang), and the Queen of the West. The temple guardians are represented by the fearsome combination of the Green Dragon and the White Tiger.

Laozi can often be found seated in an octagonal pavilion whose design echoes the arrangement of the *bagua,* or the eight trigrams of the *I-Ching* or *Yi Jing* (see p. 50).

There is a relaxed atmosphere in Taoist temples, which reflects the passive doctrine of *wuwei,* or inaction. Taoism is less concerned with salvation and more preoccupied with the manifestation of the Way and living in accordance with its rhythm. The internal martial art of *taiji quan* (see p. 122) is a Taoist practice that attempts to move with the Way.

Taoist monasteries are called *guan,* or *gong* (palace), although the latter are occasionally Buddhist. Famous temples include the Qingyang Palace in Chengdu; the temples that dot Qingchengshan, also near Chengdu; Taiqing Palace on Laoshan; the Eight Immortals Temple in Xi'an; and the White Cloud Temple in Beijing. ■

Putuoshan

PUTUOSHAN, ONE OF THE FOUR SACRED BUDDHIST mountains, lies off the coast of Zhejiang Province in the East China Sea. Its sympathetic goddess, Guanyin, presides over her maritime dominion of caves, pavilions, and monasteries.

Putuoshan
141 F2
$$$

CITS visitor information
117 Meicen Lu
0580 609-1414

GETTING TO PUTUOSHAN

The only way to reach Putuoshan is by boat. Regular fast ferries leave daily for the island from Ningbo (two hours) and Shanghai (four hours); there is also the alternative of the 12-hour overnight ferry to Shanghai, leaving Putuoshan at around 4:40 p.m. ■

"Putuo" is the Chinese approximation of the Sanskrit Potala, or Potalaka—the mountain home of the deity. The Potala Palace in Lhasa (see pp. 302–303) is inhabited by the very same bodhisattva.

Putuoshan was originally a Taoist preserve (a few Taoist shrines still remain). Its appropriation by Buddhist folklore was assured, however, when a vision of Guanyin appeared on the island, quickly succeeded by further sightings. A spate of temple building generously sprinkled the island with shrines. At one time they numbered over 200, but a combined assault by pirates and Red Guard fanaticism destroyed the majority.

Putuoshan is only 3.5 miles (5.5 km) long and 2 miles (3 km) wide. If you have the time, it is better to walk around, but minibuses also travel the routes between the major sights. Sadly, the island's secluded charm is threatened by large numbers of tour buses and encroaching modernization.

Pleasant beaches border Putuoshan's eastern shore. Both **One Hundred Step Beach (Baibusha)** and **One Thousand Step Beach (Qianbusha)** are attractive and clean, but they can be crowded in summer. Lonely **Houao Beach** looks out to sea on the island's northern fringe. The fantastically named, though small, **Roaring Tiger Beach (Xiaohusha)** lies on the northeast shore next to Lotus Sea.

PUJI MONASTERY

Upon arrival at the ferry terminal, take the road leading left through the trees north to the Puji Monastery, also known as the Front Temple (Qiansi). This area also the island's hub—a knot of small hotels, shops, and restaurants. The

Guanyin

Guanyin is the ruling deity on Putuoshan. She is a salvationary goddess who emanates a powerful sense of compassion, not unlike the Virgin Mary.

Guanyin is a bodhisattva or future buddha, who is worshiped over the length and breadth of China. Women in particular show keen devotion to her, especially if they are praying for a child. A Songzi (literally "offering son") Guanyin is shown holding a child, but she appears in many other manifestations. The thousand-armed Guanyin (Qianshou Guanyin) is also common, as is the Dripping Water Guanyin (Dishui Guanyin); she is also portrayed holding a lotus flower or a cup of nectar.

There is a question as to the true sex of Guanyin. Some argue that the deity is without gender, and some statues attest to this ambiguity. It appears that Guanyin was originally male and then endowed with female characteristics. Certainly, early representations—of Guanyin exhibit a distinctly masculine appearance. ■

temple, which was begun in the northern Song dynasty, is fronted by a lotus pond, its main hall filled with manifestations of Guanyin on either side of the principal effigy. To the southeast of the temple lies **Many Treasures Pagoda (Duobaota),** a Yuan dynasty structure adorned with Buddhist images.

BUDDHA'S SUMMIT PEAK

At the far end of One Thousand Step Beach, on the east flank of Putuoshan, is **Law Rain Monastery (Fayu Chansi).** Also known as Rear Temple (Hou Si) it clings in layers to the slope of Buddha's Summit Peak (Foding Shan), and safeguards a huge statue of the merciful bodhisattva.

A path leads up the northern hill—Buddha's Summit Peak—where you'll find the island's second major temple, **Huiji Monastery (Huiji Chansi),** amid the trees. As with most of Putuoshan's temples, this monastery has mushroomed over the centuries from its humble beginnings as a solitary structure to become a cluster of halls and pavilions.

OTHER TEMPLES & CAVES

A vestige of Putuoshan's Taoist past can be unearthed at the **Meifu Nunnery (Meifuan)** west of Puji Monastery. The temple was built where a Taoist recluse, Wei Meifu, came during the Han dynasty to smelt cinnabar and achieve immortality (cinnabar was a major ingredient in the Taoist elixir of life). Farther along the road to the south is the nunnery of **Guanyin Cave,** overshadowed by a large camphor tree.

South of One Hundred Step Beach, on a promontory of land, is the **Hall of the Unwilling to Depart Guanyin (Bukenqu Guanyinyuan).** Legend records that a Japanese monk called Hui'e was returning home from Wutaishan in 916 with a statue of Guanyin. As he passed Putuoshan, his boat was unable to continue; the monk intuitively took this to mean that Guanyin wished to remain on the island. The hall celebrates the beginning of the worship of Guanyin on Putuoshan.

Farther south along the shoreline is **Sound of the Tides Cave (Chaoyindong),** where the foaming waves are funneled with a crash into hollows in the cliff.

A number of other caves pockmark Putuoshan. **Buddhist Tidings Cave (Fanyindong),** with its small Guanyin temple, is carved from the promontory of land reaching out east. There is a thrilling view down to the roaring waves. **Morning Sun Cave (Zhaoyangdong)** lies sandwiched between One Hundred Step Beach and One Thousand Step Beach.

ZHUJIAJIAN

South of Putuoshan is the larger and less visited island of Zhujiajian with its crop of temples. ■

Incense sticks burn in Puji temple.

THE SOUTHSEA GUANYIN

Visible from many parts of the island, the Southsea Guanyin (Nanhai Guanyin) is a giant golden effigy of the goddess of mercy. A moving sight at sunrise and sunset, the huge goddess at the southern tip of the island stands above exhibition space dedicated to effigies of Guanyin and her relationship with the island. ■

Shanghai

Stylish Shanghai, metaphor for decadence, class division, spectacular riches, corruption, nepotism, sophistication, and snobbery, is also a stylish byword for today's China and the glittering offspring of an enticing engagement between the East and the West.

Challenging orthodoxy and leading the country on its exciting journey to riches or ruin, Shanghai has often shunned decency and temperance in favor of a wilder agenda. It is here to make history and not to follow it.

The great Yangtze River empties into the Yellow Sea just north of Shanghai, as if sapping the country's ingenuity and depositing it on the shores of this great city. Many locals admit the wherewithal comes from its peculiar hybrid culture of Occident and Orient—a potent formula that leaves the rest of the country fumbling for the switch to success.

Unlike Shenzhen or Zhuhai, where beneath the veneer you will quickly discover that they were recently mere specks on the map, Shanghai (literally "on the sea") gives the impression of having been great once, and is arguably great once more.

In earlier centuries, the town of Shanghai earned its living through cotton and silk production. By the mid-18th century a huge task force of 20,000 was engaged in the cotton industry.

The British established their first concession here after the treaty of Nanking,

Shanghai is a sparkling appendix to the revolutionary chronicle of 20th-century China.

which ended the first Opium War in 1842 (see p. 35). They were followed quickly by other powers busy nibbling away at China's rump. The French, Americans, and Japanese all took a slice, and the city was divided into settlements with their own jurisdiction. With the foreign powers in charge of an unrestricted trading base, Shanghai quickly emerged as China's greatest port while Hong Kong was still a rural backwater. Along with the inflow of money came the big Western names of commerce and banking, bringing a measure of nobility and some dashing architecture.

Built on the back of the opium trade, the city was from the very start a lawless endeavor where the rules were different. It was administered by greed and exploitation, becoming a very rich but insurgent domain of brothels, gambling, and opium dens.

By the early 20th century, Shanghai had added an industrial base to complement its trading success. With half of the city dandified and the other half in rags, however, the stifling inequality rapidly incubated protesting sentiments. The Chinese Communist Party was born here in 1921, with its creed of justifiable outrage and accurate sense of destiny.

The Communists liberated the city in 1949, filled the yawning gaps of inequality, eradicated child labor and prostitution, and restored respect to the poor. A by-product of this was a stalling of the city's drive, followed by a creeping passivity.

Since the 1980s, however, Shanghai has been exploring the outer fringes of capitalist permissibility; with friends in high places, its status is assured. China's highest salaries and property prices are to be found here, as well as the nation's tallest buildings.

Its dubious history has equipped it with all the tools of success: confidence, panache, money, and a brain up top. Here you will find not just socialism with Chinese characteristics, but capitalism with textbook characteristics. ■

The clock-towered Customs House overlooks the Bund.

A walk along the Bund

The embankment known as the Bund, with its elegant sweep of European architecture and landmark hotels lining the low bow of the Huangpu River, is perfectly evocative of old Shanghai. Stoically facing the monumental construction project that is giving Pudong its irreversible facelift, the Bund is a proud and gentrified chapter of history, housing, as it did, the many makers and shakers of this rich city.

The Bund (an Anglo-Indian term for a muddy embankment) was the financial motor behind Shanghai's success and Europe's corporate perch in China. It was rechristened Revolution Boulevard during the heady Cultural Revolution, but as Shanghai reemerged as a city of huge financial importance, its original significance was reestablished.

The waves of visitors that surge up and down the Bund (Waitan in Chinese) do so in amazement. Other cities (such as Qingdao) have their colonial stamp, but nowhere, apart from Hong Kong, is this statement so loud and so bold.

The most romantic way to take in the Bund is from the decks of the Huangpu River cruise (see p. 191). The night ferry from Putuoshan, which chugs into Shanghai at dawn along the curve of the river, sees the Bund warming under the yellow light of the rising sun.

A slow walk along the Bund itself will, however, equally immerse you in the location's history and unique character. Shanghai's first hotel, the **Pujiang Hotel** (see p. 371), is a good place to start, north of Suzhou Creek; it was formerly called Richard's Hotel and, in later years, the Astor House Hotel, a name that is being reassumed by the hotel once again.

Pop into the reception area to gauge the scale of the place, and clamber up to the galleries for a sense of its history. This is a museum of old, varnished floorboards, high ceilings, faded photos, and wooden rafters. Follow the corridors around numerous

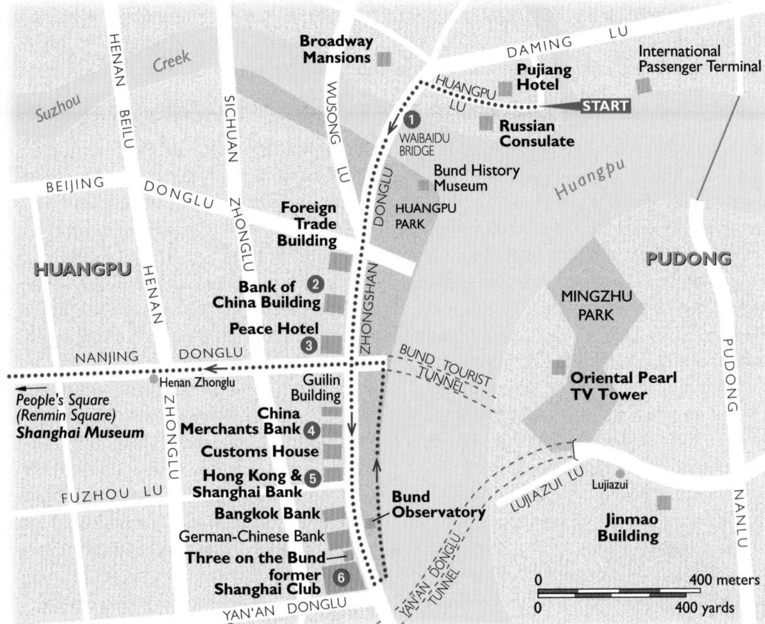

Also see area maps on pp. 141 & 181
Pujiang Hotel
1.2 miles (2 km)
0.5 to 1 hours
Nanjing Donglu

NOT TO BE MISSED

- Pujiang Hotel
- Peace Hotel
- Hong Kong and Shanghai Bank

musty twists and turns. Everywhere is the pervasive aroma of the 1920s. Albert Einstein and Charlie Chaplin both stayed here.

Opposite the Pujiang Hotel, on the bank of the Huangpu River at 20 Huangpu Lu, stands the **Russian Consulate,** built in 1917.

The brick 1935 **Broadway Mansions**—a hotel with good views of the Bund—looms up to your right as you head south to **Waibaidu Bridge** ①, looking out over Suzhou Creek. Cross Waibaidu Bridge (originally known as Garden Bridge), with its excellent view out east to the glittering buildings of **Pudong** (see p. 186). Setting foot on the Bund itself, note the ornate building hidden away behind the garden and foliage at No. 33 Zhongshan Dongyilu; it was formerly the British Consulate. Unfortunately, you are not allowed to enter.

Flush with the banks of the Huangpu River is Huangpu Park (formerly called the British Public Gardens), site of the absorbing collection of the Bund History Museum.

A long stretch of neoclassic grandeur starts at No. 29, the old address of the French Bank de Indochine. The edifice at No. 28 was originally the Glen Line building, and the heavyweight, chunky, and grandiose affair at No. 27 was owned by the venerable Jardine & Matheson trading company that built its fortune from opium. The Corinthian pillars say it all. Now it's the **Foreign Trade Building.**

Number 24 was originally the Yokohama Bank, built in 1924. Number 23—the **Bank of China Building** ②—interrupts the occidental theme with its accent on traditional Chinese architecture, including a smattering of modern elements. It was jointly designed by Palmer & Turner and a Chinese architect (hence the traditional Chinese roof). The building was the highest in Shanghai when completed in 1937.

Sitting on the eastern extremity of Nanjing Donglu, the art deco **Peace Hotel** ❸ *(20 Nanjing Donglu, tel 6321-6888),* formerly the Cathay, was built in 1926 and opened in 1929. The Chinese outpost of wealthy businessman Victor Sassoon's empire, it was the place to stay on a visit to Shanghai attracting such types as Noel Coward, who penned *Private Lives* here. The hotel is very redolent of the past; peek at the interior, and especially the marvelous lobby and the stained glass. It's a bit scuffed but still a grand slice of Shanghai's past. Discerning guests check into one of the nine-nation deluxe suites, furnished in period Spanish, Chinese, German, American, British, French, Italian, Japanese, and Indian style. In the basement, the hotel has an elderly jazz band that has been strumming to tourists since time immemorial.

The Peace Hotel extends to No. 19 on the next block—the red-and-white brick building called the Peace Palace Hotel. No. 18 is a boastful affair—previously the Chartered Bank of India, Australia, and China building—and now the very smart Bund 18, a constellation of chic bars, restaurants, and shops. The building at No. 17 was once the offices of the *North China Daily News* and was known as the Guilin Building. Slip in through the side entrance and take in the gold mosaics on the ceiling.

On the next block down, No. 16—the **China Merchants Bank,** again overdone in classical style with huge pillars—was the old address of the Bank of Taiwan.

Number 14 is an arresting 1940s construction, sharp-edged with vertical lines and a then futurist agenda. Note the brass doorway, and inside, '40s handrails and balustrades.

Number 13, the **Customs House** ❹**,** was built in 1927. It was home to the "People's Peace Preservation Corps," who operated from room 410. A huge plaque on the wall outside commemorates this and shows the citizens of Shanghai waving banners that read: "Welcome, People's Liberation Army" and "10,000 years for the Chinese Communist Party." Inside are some period deco features and mosaics. The Customs House is crowned by Big Ching, a clock that chimed every quarter hour. The bell was silenced during the Cultural Revolution and substituted with propaganda broadcasts and the Mao anthem "The East is Red."

At No. 12 you'll find the extravagant former headquarters of the **Hong Kong and Shanghai Bank** ❺. Along with the Peace Hotel, this is probably the most famous building on the Bund. A plaque reveals that it was opened by Sir Ronald Macleay, minister to China, on June 23, 1923. It was designed by the architectural firm Palmer & Turner. The original mosaic floor remains intact, and a stunning octagonal ceiling with panels depicts Tokyo, New York, London, Paris, Calcutta, Bangkok, Hong Kong, and Shanghai. Classical figures (Probitas, Historia, Fides, Sapientia, Veritas, etc.) ring the walls. This is one of the most alluring interiors in the whole of the city. The pair of bronze lions that guarded the door were removed during the Cultural Revolution; one of them can be seen in the Shanghai Municipal History Museum (see p. 186). The red star on a pole hoisted above the building finishes the picture and the building is currently occupied by the Pudong Development Bank. The Bonomi Café upstairs is an ideal place for a restorative coffee and a snack.

In the next block, on the corner with Fuzhou Lu, No. 9 is an interesting building partially overgrown with ivy and surrounded with hedges. It was constructed in 1912. The **Bangkok Bank** at No. 7 was the China Mercantile Bank in a previous incarnation.

The Gothic windows and arches of No. 6 belong to the former German-Chinese Bank. On the other side of Guangdong Lu, Three on the Bund is one of Shanghai's most celebrated addresses, converted to house an assortment of luxurious restaurants, bars, shops, and the Shanghai Gallery of Art.

Farther down, No. 2 was the former address of the **Shanghai Club** ❻. Built in 1910, the club was the site of the world's longest bar and the venue of the most exclusive colonial coterie in town. In more recent years it served as the Tung Feng Hotel, but is now closed and inaccessible.

From the former Shanghai Club, you can cross over Zhongshan Donglu to the promenade overlooking the Huangpu River and walk back up the Bund, savoring the views. The **Bund Observatory** tower contains a small

In Shanghai, the interior of the Peace Hotel (top) still captivates. Along the Bund pedestrians view venerable monuments (above).

display of exhibits related to the Bund. Turn left at the Peace Hotel into the shopping strip of **Nanjing Donglu** to taste Shanghai's commercial fever. You can either walk along Nanjing Donglu (or take the metro from Middle Henan Road station) to Renmin Square and the magnificent **Shanghai Museum** (see pp. 187–88).

While sauntering down the Bund, steal a glance at Pudong opposite. The Pudong New Area is larger that Shanghai itself. It's a huge economic zone fronted by some daring architecture, including the spectacular edifice of the **Jinmao Dasha** and the bizarre, but arresting, **Oriental Pearl Tower,** resembling a 1950s monument to the atomic age. ■

Oriental Pearl TV tower's circular base and the Shangai convention center's globe highlight Pudong's modern architecture.

Pudong

WHEN CHINA DEALS WITH THE OUTSIDE WORLD, PUDONG is at the top of its CV. Lujiazui, its finance center visible from the Bund, is a Brave New World of high-rises, luxury hotels, and financial institutions—socialism with Chinese characteristics, as they say here.

Pudong
181

TRANSPORT
Pudong is easily reached by taking the metro line No. 2 to Lujiazui station. Alternatively, take the Bund Sightseeing Tunnel from the Bund to the far side of the river; or take a taxi. To ride the astonishing 267 mph (430 km/h) Maglev train to Pudong International Airport, take the metro to Longyang Rd. station. ■

Pudong, Shanghai's newfangled face, challenges the antiquated arrogance of the Bund. To understand what the Chinese want China to look like, come to Pudong, a shrine to international finance, a concrete expression of vanity, and the very symbol of the Chinese reform drive.

Paving its way through its heart is 2.8-mile (4.5 km) **Century Avenue (Shiji Dadao)**. Splitting the Pudong New Area, it is a grand gesture of the new zeitgeist.

China's tallest buildings have been earmarked for Pudong since 1990, when the wrapping came off the blueprints. Rocketing into the clouds are dynamic examples. The crystalline **Jinmao Dasha** is a bold testament to China's newfound confidence, a searing 1,379 feet (420 m) high. It was China's tallest, and the world's third tallest, building. This is the lofty perch of the world's highest hotel above ground level, the **Grand Hyatt Shanghai,** a hotel in the clouds with an observation platform on the 88th floor.

Pudong's other eye-catching edifice is the concrete tripod **Oriental Pearl TV Tower,** with excellent views over town and home to the highly informative **Shanghai Municipal History Museum** in the basement. Within walking distance, the **China Sex Culture Museum** is a riveting exploration of Chinese sexual mores, detailed by fascinating exhibits.

Most Western visitors come to see old China, not an American derivative. Pudong is growing, however, with a flourishing retail and restaurant scene and a sightseeing tunnel linking it to the Bund. ■

Shanghai Museum

OCCUPYING A PRIME PIECE OF REAL ESTATE IN RENMIN Square in the heart of Shanghai, the Shanghai Museum (Shanghai Bowuguan) is a unique and inspiring piece of architecture hoarding a magnificent collection of Chinese art and antiquities. If you only have time for one museum in China, make sure it is this one—a stylish and welcome fixture on the visitor circuit. It's easy to spend the whole day here, and many visitors come back for more.

Shanghai Museum
Map 181
201 Renmin Ave.
021 0372-3500
$. Audio guide avail.
People's Square Underground Station

China Sex Culture Museum
Map 181
2789 Riverside Ave.
$

Shanghai Municipal History Museum
Map 181
Oriental Pearl TV Tower
$$

Built in 1994 and in many ways the symbol of a new China, the museum is a transformation of its original incarnation on South Henan Nanlu Road. The entrance fee is a bargain, but you may wish to avoid the expensive coffees in the Yen Yu Yun Pavilion teahouse upstairs. The bright interior, lit by an impressive atrium, is exciting, as is the ascending floor plan, accessed by a sweeping staircase. And the galleries are intelligently laid out, with utmost consideration to the visitor. Gone is the stuffy, monotonous, and somnolent atmosphere of socialist museums of old.

The millennia of Chinese history are beautifully illustrated via the stories of each individual gallery. Whether you are interested in Chinese bronzes, sculptures, calligraphy, paintings, seals, jade, Ming and Qing dynasty furniture, or the flawless perfection of the ceramic pieces on view in the Zande Lou Gallery, the museum is an education. These are some of the best pieces left in China.

FIRST FLOOR

The **Gallery of Ancient Chinese Bronzes** takes you on a dazzling journey through the millennia of early bronze design from its earliest days to its subsequent apogee. Observe the ferocious *taotie* designs on the Shang dynasty bronzes, which point to an animist creed. The exhibition then continues to chart the development of this art form through the successive dynasties of the Zhou (1122–256 B.C.) and the Spring and Autumn period (770–476 B.C.).

Exploring the **Ancient Chinese Sculpture Gallery,** also on the first floor, is like nosing through the cave sculptures of Dunhuang, Longmen, or Yungang, without the rattling bus ride. The stone and wooden Buddhas, bodhisattvas, and other figures have been gathered from the four corners of China, and range from the Warring States period (475–221 B.C.)

Right: China's premier Shanghai Museum, inventively designed and housing a range of imaginatively laid out artifacts, is a must see.

to the Ming dynasty (1368–1644). Coming together under one roof, they give you the excellent opportunity to compare how the countenance of Buddhist images has changed over the dynasties.

The shop on this floor stocks an impressive range of books covering the arts of China and including general literature on Chinese culture. There is also an excellent selection of postcards and souvenir items.

SECOND FLOOR

For many, the highlight of a visit to the museum is the **Ancient Chinese Ceramics Gallery,** which feeds chronologically into the **Zande Lou Ceramics Gallery.** This wonderful collection of Chinese ceramics ranges from the neolithic era to the late Qing dynasty. There's a medley of colors from brightly glazed Tang horses to the cool jade of celadon bowls, from playful *doucai* stem cups to the fragile crackle of Song Ge ware and overblown Qing famille-rose. Crowning them all are the exquisite underglaze cobalt blue-and-white pieces known as *qinghua* (see p. 202). The earliest blue-and-white pieces appeared in the Yuan dynasty but reached their apogee in the Ming and Qing.

Exquisite pieces represent the zenith of Chinese art at the Shanghai Museum.

THIRD FLOOR

The superb layout of the **Chinese Painting Gallery** is intelligently illuminated and inviting. Paintings are lit as you approach them, in an effort to preserve their ancient colors. Primarily landscapes, they range from the Tang through the Song, Yuan, Ming, and Qing dynasties.

The **Chinese Calligraphy Gallery** is on the same floor as the paintings, because they are considered by the Chinese to be parallel arts. The major calligraphic styles are all displayed here, from the formal and exacting *kaishu* (regular) to the dynamic and exciting *caoshu* (grasshand). It is difficult to fully appreciate Chinese calligraphy unless you can read the language, but it is nevertheless still mesmerizing.

The **Chinese Seal Gallery** displays over 500 pieces from the Zhou to the Qing dynasty.

FOURTH FLOOR

Jade occupies a prime position in Chinese culture, and the **Ancient Chinese Jade Gallery** presents excellent specimens. The exhibition has mustered together prize examples of jade carvings from the Shang dynasty and earlier cultures through to later dynasties.

The **Ming and Qing Furniture Gallery** guides you through the functional beauty of classical Chinese furniture. The pieces range from the more restrained, yet voluptuous Ming examples to their elaborate and overblown Manchu equivalents.

The vivid cultural traditions of China's ethnic minorities are represented in the **Minority Nationalities' Art Gallery,** while the **Chinese Coin Gallery** paints the story of China's currency. ■

Old Chinese City

A relaxing pot of Chinese tea awaits guests at the Huxinting Teahouse.

SOUTHWEST OF THE BUND LIES THE OLD CHINESE QUARter, an echo of historic Shanghai. Many of the city's old buildings remain, along with labyrinthine Yu Gardens and the Yuyuan Bazaar, a busy, commercial tangle of souvenir and antique shops.

The **Yuyuan Gardens** are a pleasant side step off the city's busy streets. They were designed by a rich Ming dynasty family of officials, the Pan clan. Altogether, the gardens were destroyed three times, once being carpet-shelled during the First Opium War (a museum in the gardens chronicles the disasters). The French also destroyed the place during the Taiping Rebellion in the mid-19th century. Later restored, the gardens are now made up of inner and outer sections and are comparable to Suzhou's (see pp. 164–65). Paths wind under rocky outcrops, past pools thick with goldfish, and through caves and rockeries. Avoid the gardens on weekends, when crowds of visitors annihilate the last remaining shred of tranquility, and try to get here in the morning.

At the Yuyuan Bazaar and the shops along **Fangbang Zhonglu** you can hunt through a mound of bric-à-brac, fake antiques, and the occasional gem. The whole setting is ersatz-period China with a themeland feel, but it is an ideal hunting ground for souvenirs and gifts. For some of Shanghai's mouth-watering steamed dumplings (*xiaolong bao*), try the **Nanxiang Steamed Bun Restaurant** (85 Yuyuan Lu, see p. 371). The crabmeat versions (*xiefen xiaolong*) are scrumptious.

In the middle of the lake, China's famous **Huxinting Teahouse** (see p. 371) serves pots of tea. It is connected to the shore by a zigzag bridge (Jiuqu Qiao), a picturesque structure that also serves as a *fengshui* device to deflect bad spirits, which can only travel in straight lines. ■

Old Chinese City

Map: 181

Tourist Information & Service Centre

Address: 149 Jiujiaochang Lu, located a short walk southwest of Yuyuan Gardens

Phone: 021 6355-5032

Yuyuan Gardens

Price: $$

The centerpiece of Shanghai's most famous place of worship, Jade Buddha Temple, is its eponymous statue.

Jade Buddha Temple & other temples

FOR A CITY THE SIZE OF SHANGHAI, THERE ARE NOT MANY temples. In the northwest of town, however, you'll find the city's holiest spot, the saffron-colored Jade Buddha Temple (Yufosi).

Jade Buddha Temple
- 181
- 170 Anyuan Lu
- $

Jing'an Temple
- 181
- 1686 Nanjing Xilu
- $
- Nearest metro: Jing'an Si

Longhua Pagoda
- 181
- $
- Nearest station: Longcao Lu Light Rail Station

About 70 monks live in this temple, whose centerpiece is its jewel-encrusted white jade Buddha. Standing over 6 feet (1.8 m), the statue was brought back from Burma (Myanmar) in 1882 by a devout monk who hailed from the Buddhist island of Putuoshan.

Adorning the walls are 7,000 Buddhist sutras. At the rear stands a resplendent figure of Guanyin, surrounded by a host of little figures. Behind the main hall is a small courtyard attractively arrayed with plants; here you will see the tower where the Buddhist scriptures from India were stored.

The **Jade Buddha (Yufo)** can be found upstairs inside a small wooden hall. The gorgeous statue is clearly Southeast Asian in origin, with its luminous sheen and delightfully calm features. Unfortunately, a barrier prevents you from approaching the sacred effigy. It miraculously eluded the sledgehammers of the Cultural Revolution (1966–1976).

Downstairs in the **Reclining Buddha Hall** is a supine Buddha on a couch. It represents Buddha giving his last homily to his disciples before entering nirvana.

The **Jing'an Temple,** sitting above its namesake underground stop, is being slowly restored and boasts well-designed exterior walls and partially renovated interior walls. The Buddhist **Longhua Temple (Longhuasi)** in the south of town is Shanghai's largest temple complex; across the way rises its seven-story **Longhua Pagoda (Longhuata).** ■

French Concession

SHANGHAI'S MOST CHARMING STREETSCAPES, TRENDIEST shopping zones, most ultra-chic restaurants and bars belong to the former French Concession, an elegant swath of Paris-meets-Puxi that extends through the districts of Luwan to Changning, hinging north–south roughly on the shopping street of Huaihai Zhonglu.

One of the best ways to appreciate the charms of this area is to walk around its leafy backstreets. **Xintiandi,** an ambitious and ultra-trendy upscale retail, restaurant, and bar enclave south of Huaihai Zhonglu, is an excellent place to start exploring the eastern edge of the French Concession. Consisting of recently restored *shikumen* (literally "stone gate house") architecture, a kind of hybrid Chinese and European-style brick residential building divided up by *longtang* (alleyways), Xintiandi is ideal for sauntering. If you want to know more about shikumen buildings, pop into the **Shikumen Open House Museum,** a restored shikumen building situated here in Xintiandi.

Also located in Xintiandi is a crop of celebrated restaurants, including T8 (see p. 371 in Travelwise), and the **Site of the 1st National Congress of the Chinese Communist Party** (76 Xingye Lu), also housed in an attractive former shikumen house.

Wandering round the **Taikang Road Art Centre** on Taikang Lu to the south is an opportunity to check out some Shanghai art galleries, small boutiques, arts and crafts shops, and cafés, concentrated within a manageable area.

A fascinating diversion to the west of the French Concession, the **Propaganda Poster Art Center** can be found in the basement of a residential block. Hanging from the walls are excellent original examples of Mao-era propaganda art, lambasting the U.S. and celebrating the irrepressible onward march of Chinese communism. Many of the posters can be purchased.

At the time of writing, Shanghai's leading knock-off clothing bazaar Xiangyang Market had shut, but Huaihai Zhonglu remains an excellent street for window shopping. The French Concession is also one of the hubs of the expat drinking scene, with well-known drinking holes along Taojiang Lu and Dongping Lu (both off Hengshan Lu) and the south end of Maoming Nanlu. Hordes of popular restaurants similarly congregate along the streets of the French Concession cashing in on the district's indelible panache and easy sense of style. Explore the Western architecture and several notable buildings in this area (see the Shanghai feature pp. 192–93). ■

Xintiandi
Map 181
South Huangpi Rd. underground station

Taikang Road Art Centre
Map 181
Lane 210, Taiking Lu

Shikumen Open House Museum
Map 181
$ $

Propaganda Poster Art Centre
Map 181
Room B-OC, President Mansion, 868 Huashan Lu
021 6211-1845
$ $

Wandering the streets and alleys of the French Concession.

Western architecture in Shanghai

Before 1949, Shanghai's foreign enclaves existed for the very rich and the shockingly rich. The Western businessmen and financiers who effectively colonized Shanghai built a metropolis in their own image. Wall Street and the City of London came to Shanghai to sit on the Bund, the fine lines of Paris helped fashion the French Concession (see p. 191), and elsewhere Spanish, German, Japanese, Russian, Byzantine, and even Swedish flavors drifted in from abroad. An eclectic medley of Western building styles resulted that could only have converged in one city—Shanghai.

A stroll around Shanghai brings with it a fascinating taste of yesteryear. The concoction—a melee of venerable clubs, apartment blocks, churches, showy banks, hospitals, cinemas, and hotels—is an engaging brew. With styles ranging from the modest (villas) through the decorative and trendy (art deco) to the monumental (bank architecture), Shanghai is a yellowing photograph of late 19th-century and early 20th-century architecture.

The Japanese unfortunately destroyed many buildings, but today surviving heritage buildings are well preserved, due to their enormous real estate value and historical significance. Wherever you are in the former concession areas of Shanghai, keep your eyes open. Even a casual glance above the street level (often the best place to look) reveals a riot of Corinthian columns, European lintels, deco plasterwork, brick houses, red-tiled roofs, and carved facades. Throughout Shanghai, small ripples of Western styling gradually amass to result in the crashing wave of the Bund.

The Taipans (foreign owners of the *hongs,* or trading companies) constructed the most ostentatious buildings. The wealthy Jews (such as the Sassoons, Ezras, and Kadoories) also lived in regal style.

Much of the hotel architecture was fastidiously trendy. The 1934 **Park Hotel** (designed by Ladislaus Hudec) at 170 Nanjing Xilu has been robbed of a lot of its art deco finesse, but the **Peace Hotel** (see p. 184) still exudes sophistication. The **Pacific Hotel** *(104 Nanjing Xilu),* opposite what was the old Racetrack (now Renmin Square), displays considerable historic charm.

The eminent 1928 **Cathay Mansions** (Shanghai's first high-rise) on Maoming Nanlu, and the neighboring **Grosvenor House** are now owned by the nearby, glittering Jinjiang Hotel. The **Crystal Palace,** the **Astor,** the **Ritz,** and the **Metropole** were all cinemas. The deco outline of the **Cathay Theater** still stands, south of the Jinjiang Hotel at 870 Huaihai Lu (formerly known as Avenue Joffre).

Other extant deco edifices include the plaster-worked exterior of the **Savoy** apartments *(131 Changshu Lu),* near the junction with Huaihai Lu, and the brick **Astrid** apartments *(301–309 Maoming Nanlu).*

Suzhou Creek was lined with massive apartment blocks, such as the Sassoon-built **Embankment House** (equipped with its own artesian well). The huge **Post Office,** built in 1924 and adorned with Corinthian columns, is still on the corner of Sichuan Zhonglu (opposite stood the British American Tobacco Company).

Robust consular architecture, such as the **Russian Consulate,** also fringed the International Settlement north of Suzhou Creek. The **Chinese People's Association for Friendship with Foreign Countries,** a huge white affair at 1418 Nanjing Xilu, stands next to the Shanghai Exhibition Center. From the streets you can get a good view of the balconies and balustrades.

Wandering the French Concession's back streets—such as Julu Lu—is an excellent way to get a feel for the Shanghai of the early decades of the last century. The 1930s villas of the well-to-do are still preserved on leafy Xinhua Lu on the western borders of the French Concession. Other buildings to look out for are the former addresses of eminent people, such as Song Qingling's former residence at 1843 Huaihai Zhonglu and the former residence of Sun Zhongshan (Yat-sen)at 7

Xiangshan Lu, both serving as museums.

The fairy-tale towers of the **Moller Mansion** (now a hotel) rise surreally over the rooftops at 30 Shaanxi Nanlu. Both Lin Biao and Jiang Qing stayed at the European-style, red-tiled residence at 145 Yueyang Lu (south of the western end of Fuxing Zhonglu).

Much old architecture survives as department stores. The Sun Company long ago renamed the **No. 1 Department Store,** at the junction of Nanjing Donglu and Xizanglu.

The Catholics were also busy. The Jesuit-built **St. Ignatius Cathedral** *(158 Puxi Lu)* near the Xujiahui subway station is just along the road from the **Bibliotecha Zi-Ka-Wei** *(tel 021 6487-4095, ext. 208)*, the former Jesuit library, which can be toured between 2 p.m. and 4 p.m. on Saturday afternoons. The huge

Catholic church on Sheshan south of Shanghai was built between 1925 and 1935.

East of the Shanghai Museum on the corner of Hankou Lu *(No. 766)* is the charmingly simple **Mu-en Church (Mu En Tang),** formerly the Moore Memorial Church. Completed in red brick, this Protestant church was attacked in 1966 by Red Guards and its bibles damaged (a plaque outside in Chinese testifies to the event).

A Russian Orthodox church can be found on Xinle Lu in the French Concession. Sadly, most ecclesiastical stained glass was destroyed during the Cultural Revolution, but some remains in private houses (the Peace Hotel has wonderful examples).

Western architecture has entered a new age with the buildings on Pudong opposite the Bund. Many may have Chinese architects, but the inspiration is largely occidental. ■

Shanghai's Western buildings offer an intriguing glimpse back to the city's former heyday: St. Ignatius Cathedral (top); the dining room at the Jinjiang Hotel (above).

More places to visit in the Yangtze region

TONGLI

A day trip from either Shanghai or Suzhou, the town of Tongli on the Grand Canal is typical of the picturesque canal towns that dot Jiangsu Province. Rather less touristy than other canal towns that have been deluged, Tongli remains a charming portrait of old bridges, whitewashed houses, and traditional residences; weekends are busy so try to come during the week. One of Tongli's most famous assets is the **Chinese Sex Museum** *($)* famed for its honest look at the fascinating world of Chinese erotica. Not far from the museum, the **Tuisi Garden** *($)* is an attractive and retiring arrangement of rockeries and pavilions. There's a small entry fee for both.

141 E2 $$$

MUDU

Also accessible as a day trip from either Suzhou or Shanghai, Mudu is another canal town that

Ningbo's Ming dynasty Tianyige is China's oldest surviving private library.

has become popular for its canal scenes and gardens. Much less commercialized than Zhouzhuang, the best approach is to wander round the old town or ride one of the tour boats along the canal. Prime sights within the old town include the **Hongyin Mountain Villa** and the **Bangyan Mansion**.

141 E2 $$

NINGBO

The town of Ningbo lies huddled on the jagged Zhejiang coastline. It was an important port whose rising star was only eclipsed by Shanghai. Ningbo has a few notable buildings, including the **Tianyige,** an ancient private library.

Ningbo was partially dislodged into the hands of the powers by the treaty of Nanking in 1842. The domain north of Xinjiang Bridge provides walks among the old foreign concession. On Zhongma Lu, the **Portuguese Catholic Church** is a mummified slice of old Europe in China. The town is chiefly a port for the island of Putuoshan (see pp. 178–79).

141 E2

HUANGPU RIVER CRUISE

Pumping through Shanghai, the Huangpu River is the city's vital lifeline to the sea and the Yangtze. Boats leave from the wharf on the Bund for cruises to the mouth of the Yangtze River and shorter one-hour cruises.

141 E2 Dock: 239 Zhongshan Dongerlu 021 6374-4461 $$-$$$ 3.5-hour trip with dinner, $ one-hour trip

WUDANGSHAN

The temple-strewn Wudangshan Mountains stretch across the northwestern portion of Hubei Province and are wrapped in Taoist lore. They are also associated with the martial arts and are a pilgrimage destination for students of *gongfu* (see p. 122–23).

140 B2 & 141 C2

ZHOUZHUANG & CHANGZHOU

West of Shanghai awaits the ancient canalled town of Zhouzhuang. It is crisscrossed by very picturesque bridges and waterways and studded with traditional houses. Trains pass through Kunshan City, close to Zhouzhuang on the Shanghai-Suzhou railway.

Beyond Suzhou lies Changzhou, a town similarly threaded by canals and home to the refined **Tianning Temple.** The temple had a contingent of over 800 monks but suffered during the Cultural Revolution; its numbers are much reduced now. It has a collection of 500 gilded Luohan (see p. 72).

141 E2 ■

With its invigorating medley of moods, China's steamy south runs from the sandy beaches of Hainan Island to the sheer energy of Guangzhou or the enchanting concession-era legacy of Gulangyu Island.

The South

7th century porcelain Fo dog

South China's frontier town, Shenzhen is far removed from Beijing's conservatism.

The South

THE LANGUID TERRAIN OF SOUTH CHINA IS, FOR THE GREATER PART, strung out along a prosperous coastline. Down south, Beijing's political hegemony meets resistance, especially in the more experimental economies of Guangdong Province and Hainan Island. Beijing is further checked by a tangle of tongues that confounds Mandarin *(putonghua)* speakers. Shrewd business sense, savoir faire, diligence, and greater exposure to the West further shape a resourceful regional character.

Droopy and lush, China's rice-growing south sees abundant summer rains, typhoons that blast the ragged coastline ports, and green vegetation choking the land. This is a fecund and wealthy region.

The late Deng Xiaoping's maxim, "To get rich is glorious," allowed the free market to enter through Guangdong Province's backdoor. Guangdong is South China's heartland, a region forced open to trade by the foreign powers in the 19th century, and an exit point for legions of overseas Chinese. The return of Hong Kong in 1997 may have boosted China's gross domestic product by 25 percent, but the province had long prospered from its wealthy neighbor.

Guangdong's capital, Guangzhou, evinces a maelstrom of free enterprise, noise, and traffic. Shenzhen and Zhuhai continue to probe the waters of the free market and international finance. Together they typify the end of the altruistic economy built up by the older generation.

China's southernmost province, the island of Hainan, seems even more estranged from Beijing. A free-market haven, it is a place of greenery, beaches, and relentless summer sun.

East along the coastline lies the ancestral homeland of many Taiwanese—Fujian Province. Fujian's port of Xiamen squarely faces the Taiwan-controlled island of Jinmen, within artillery range off the coast. Xiamen is a peaceful place, however, further tranquilized by its picturesque island of Gulangyu, awash with colonial remains and fading history.

Hunan, to the north, is home to some of China's hottest food and a liberal sprinkling of Chairman Mao iconography (he was born and educated in the province). ■

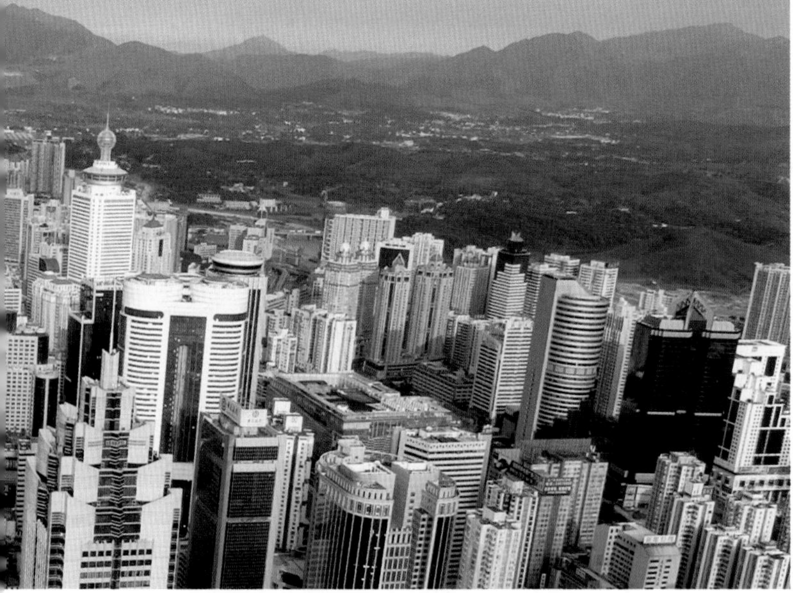

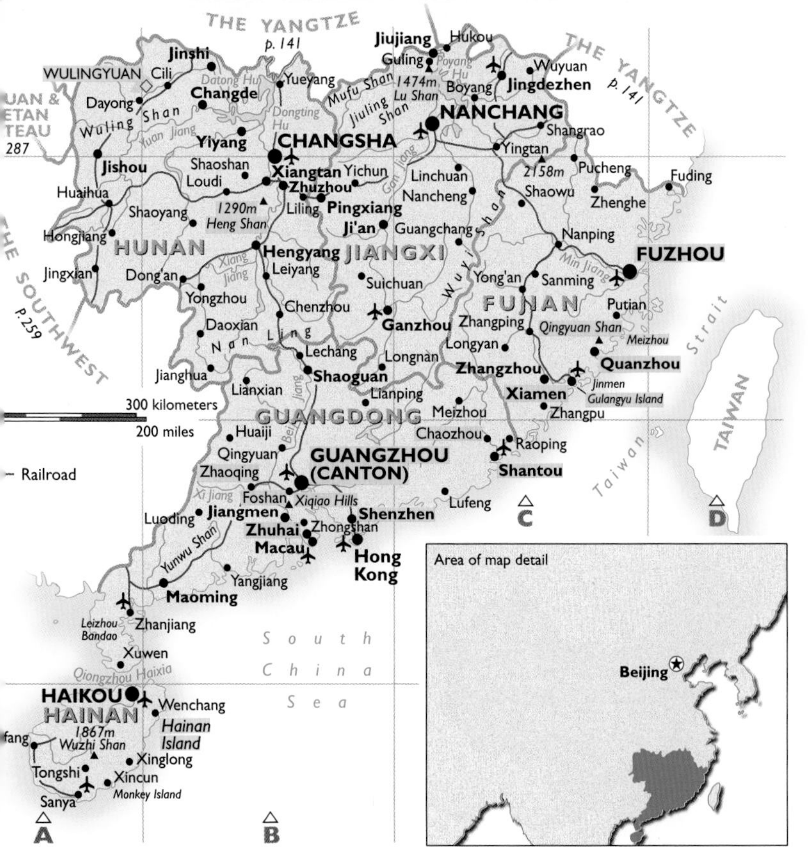

THE YANGTZE p. 141
Jiujiang
Hukou
Guling
Poyang Hu
Wuyuan
Jingdezhen
Boyang
Lu Shan
1474m
Mufu Shan
Jiuling Shan
NANCHANG
Shangrao
Yingtan
2158m
Pucheng
Fuding
Linchuan
Nancheng
Shaowu
Zhenghe
Guangchang
Nanping
Min Jiang
FUZHOU
Yong'an
Sanming
Wuyi Shan
FUJIAN
Putian
Zhangping
Qingyuan Shan
Meizhou
Quanzhou
Longyan
Zhangzhou
Jinmen
Xiamen
Gulangyu Island
Zhangpu
Taiwan Strait
TAIWAN
WULINGYUAN
Cili
Jinshi
Datong Hu
Yueyang
Dayong
Changde
Dongting Hu
Wuling Shan
Yuan Jiang
Yiyang
CHANGSHA
Jishou
Shaoshan
Xiangtan
Yichun
Loudi
Zhuzhou
Gan Jiang
Huaihua
1290m
Heng Shan
Liling
Pingxiang
Shaoyang
Ji'an
Hongjiang
HUNAN
Hengyang
JIANGXI
Xiang Jiang
Leiyang
Jingxian
Dong'an
Suichuan
Yongzhou
Chenzhou
Ganzhou
THE SOUTHWEST p.259
Daoxian
Nan Ling
Lechang
Longnan
Jianghua
Shaoguan
Lianxian
Lianping
300 kilometers
200 miles
GUANGDONG
Meizhou
Huaiji
Bei Jiang
Chaozhou
Raoping
Qingyuan
GUANGZHOU (CANTON)
Shantou
Railroad
Zhaoqing
Xi Jiang
Foshan
Xiqiao Hills
Lufeng
Luoding
Jiangmen
Shenzhen
Zhuhai
Zhongshan
Macau
Hong Kong
Yunwu Shan
Maoming
Yangjiang
Zhanjiang
Leizhou Bandao
Xuwen
South China Sea
Qiongzhou Haixia
HAIKOU
HAINAN
Wenchang
Hainan Island
1867m
Wuzhi Shan
Xinglong
Tongshi
Xincun
Monkey Island
Sanya
A
B
C
D
Area of map detail
Beijing

Mao Zedong legacies

More than 30 years after Chairman Mao's death, memories of the lumbering Great Helmsman remain fresh. His legacy is found all over China, a long shadow cast by his disingenuous experiments.

The ex-dictator is still held in high esteem by many elderly Chinese, who still commemorate him with a framed photo in their living room. Mao's face is no longer seen at every turn, but he often rears his head unexpectedly.

It must not be forgotten that the Chinese remember Mao more for his achievements than for his faults. A party consensus emerged in the 1980s that Mao's contributions to the revolution far outweighed his mistakes. Until recently, Mao Zedong Thought took precedence over Deng Theory in the hierarchy of Chinese socialist thinking.

Former president Jiang Zemin occasionally toasted his legacy by donning a stiff Mao suit (more accurately, a Sun Yat-sen suit), and Mao's massive portrait still smiles enigmatically over Tiananmen Square. Hawkers thrust gimmick Mao lighters into the protesting hands of capitalist visitors. Taxi drivers periodically adorn their car interiors with images of Mao, and there are few tourist street markets without piles of his collected quotations *(mao zedong quanji)*, the little red book.

Those on the lookout for Mao reminders will be in seventh heaven, for shrines are scattered all around China. His birthplace is Shaoshan village in Hunan Province, preserved in a time warp. You can traipse through his spartan childhood home and get an idea of the poverty of pre-Motorola China, which started Mao on the road to socialism. Shaoshan, 80 miles (129 km) southwest of Changsha, has its Museum of Comrade Mao (Maozedong Tongzhi Jinianguan), where his life is told through photographs and other exhibits.

Changsha, the provincial capital of Hunan, blows the dust off an assortment of Mao sites. Young Mao attended the Hunan No. 1 Teachers' Training School in the south of town. The Former Office of the Hunan Communist Party Committee on Bayi Lu contains mementoes of the Chairman's life and examples of his calligraphy. Not directly connected with Mao, but a component of his myth nonetheless, the heroic communist soldier Lei Feng, celebrated for his dedication to the revolutionary cause, is applauded at the Lei Feng Memorial Museum outside Changsha *(CITS visitor information, 160 Wuyi Dadao, tel 0731 446-8901)*.

Yan'an in Shaanxi Province was the headquarters of the Communist Party after the Long March (see p. 37) and is replete with revolutionary monuments and museums. Zunyi in Guizhou Province, the venue of the controversial Communist conference that crystallized Mao's authority, lay along the route of the Long March.

Mao's villa in Wuhan feels like a haunted hotel with a very damp cellar. The historic site of the 1st National Congress of the Communist Party is in Shanghai. Lushan makes it onto the Mao map for its communist heritage. Last, but not least, Mao made Beijing capital of the People's Republic of China and the seat of political power.

Mao statues abound throughout China, remnants of what was a very burdensome personality cult. Shaoshan and Changsha naturally have them, while

Above: Chairman Mao Zedong statute in Lijiang Yunnan. Right: The Mao memorabilia industry shows no signs of flagging.

Three girls dressed as Red Guards at the the Mao Family Bay restaurant in Wuchang, Wuhan

Dandong and Harbin in the northeast both sport them, but the most elaborate of all is in Shenyang. Other cities unexpectedly chip in: Lijiang in Yunnan Province has its own monument. Fuzhou and Guiyang have snow-white versions and Chengdu has one, but Hainan Island seems to have escaped. Even far-off Kashgar, on the wrong side of the Taklimakan Desert, boasts a huge likeness.

Mao was an expert calligrapher and his writing is truly excellent. Beijing Normal University's logo is his work, and it graces the Monument to the People's Heroes in Tiananmen Square.

Traces of the Cultural Revolution (1966–1976) have not been completely scrubbed away, and eagle-eyed travelers will spot the occasional relic. Ghostly propaganda still survives on walls in Xizhou and other towns around China, including Shanghai. ■

Lushan

THE MOUNTAINS OF LUSHAN TO THE SOUTH OF JIUJIANG rise to 4,827 feet (1,474 m). Poets and artists have immortalized their wooded slopes and distant views, and the pleasant summer climate has drawn vacationing visitors in growing numbers.

At the end of the 19th century, when it was known as Kuling, Europeans and Americans came in droves to clement Lushan in Jiangxi Province to escape the oppressive summer heat of nearby Jiujiang and the Yangtze River. Their houses remain, symbolic of a vanished era. As with other foreign centers in China, Lushan was almost a complete society, with post offices, hospitals, schools, and its own police force. Residents bought their provisions from stores along the road called the Gap.

The resort was divided into valleys—Russian Valley, Long Valley, Lotus Valley—and crisscrossed with streets bearing Western names such as Princeton Road, Cambridge Road, and Verdun Road. It was a veritable home away from home. A modest community of red-roofed bungalows, villas, and cottages was built in a mishmash of styles from Europe and America. Much of the charming and picturesque architecture survives.

The focal point of Lushan is the village of **Guling,** a cluster of wooden-fronted buildings, old cottages (many built by missionaries), and villas at the northeast end. Common motifs are the six-sided towers that spring up all around on the hillsides. Guling was originally a retreat for missionaries, and this is reflected in the church architecture that survives on the pretty streets (maps showing how to get around are plentiful in the village). The Red Guards swarmed through Guling adding their bit of desecration to the story of Lushan, but most of the churches were let off lightly.

A lot of gaily painted woodwork

Lushan

197 C4

$$ (entrance fee to Lushan)

CITS visitor information

48 Hexi Lu, Guling

0792 828-2497

Wuyuan

The villages round **Wuyuan** in northeastern Jiangxi Province—around 62 miles (100 km) east of Lushan and best reached from Jingdezhen or Tunxi—are beautiful snapshots of traditional Huizhou culture, similar to that seen in Yixian and Shexian (see p. 149). Set in lovely countryside, hunt out the old villages of **Likeng, Xiaoqi, Qinghua,** and **Jiangwan,** where scenic river views are vaulted by old stone bridges and simple accommodation is temptingly available for those who want to spend several days traveling from village to village. The settlements only became accesible a few years ago and remain, despite their newfound fame as some of the most attractive villages in China, in a relative state of authenticity, where communities still carry on regardless of the appearance of tourists. The town of Wuyuan can also serve as a useful base for exploring this region, although the town lacks the character of the surrounding villages. Beyond the villages, excellent opportunities also exist for trekking around the nearby countryside. ■

(most of it a soft blue) has survived decorating the porches, windows, and shutters. The stonework is worthy of close attention; the heavy blocks used in the construction have been fitted together with superb craftsmanship.

A creek runs through Guling and feeds a number of serene lakes. Here, too, past visitors built the occasional colonial house or now deserted boathouse.

Lushan is also much admired by the Chinese for its association with the politically powerful. Chairman Mao, Chiang Kai-shek, and Chiang's wife—Song Meiling—all had villas in Guling. One of the most famous buildings here is the **Meilu Villa (Meilu Bieshu),** Chiang Kai-shek's summer retreat. You can poke around his living quarters, but it's a bit forbidding inside. There are relics of Chiang Kai-shek found here; photographs of him and his wife still hang on the villa's walls.

The times are, however, catching up with Guling. Many of the villas have been sold and this could lead to its transformation. Some have been converted to guest houses to keep pace with demand for accommodations. The nobility of Guling is further under attack from relentless tour buses.

Thanks to its mountain position, Lushan has a pleasant climate in summer—the best time to visit weatherwise—but it also coincides with the tourist crush. It tends to be wet, cold, and misty during the rest of the year, and in winter a mantle of snow settles upon it. ■

Chinese poets have extolled Lushan's cool, mountainous landscape for centuries.

Meilu Villa

Hexi Lu

$

Chinese ceramics

Famed for centuries the world over, China's porcelain enjoys a long and splendid heritage. Designed as works of art, ceramics from the Middle Kingdom were also objects for daily use and of utilitarian value.

Pottery fragments in China date back to Neolithic times and to a primitive society known as Yangshao in North China. Surviving specimens from the Shang dynasty show a slow evolution to the important development of glaze, possibly during the Zhou dynasty. A relatively large number of pieces survive from the Han dynasty, which reveal a growing mastery of glazing techniques and stylistic energy, especially in statues and effigies.

Porcelain made its important appearance during the Tang dynasty as did colored glazes, most notably in the world-renowned *sancai* (three color) pieces that are typically green, yellow, brown, orange, and blue against an earthenware body. Song dynasty ceramics, which survive in fair number, are noted for their undecorated, monochrome simplicity.

The Yuan dynasty saw the arrival from the Middle East of underglaze cobalt blue (*qinghua*, or blue-and-white), a technique that flourished under the Ming and Qing dynasties. Blue-and-white is often seen to characterize the Ming period, but the style reached its peak during the Qing dynasty, which left us numerous pieces of perfection. The Qing dynasty is notable for colored porcelain and complex decoration. The luxuriously painted, often spectacular pieces are balanced by restrained monochromic ones.

Much Qing porcelain was destined for export to the European market, and consequently Western decorations were incorporated into Qing ceramics. Porcelain is still produced at numerous kilns today, but the golden days of porcelain production are over.

Porcelain Covered Jar with fish and seaweed design circa 1368-1644

Kilns

Ceramics were often named for the kiln where they were fired. In this way, ceramics are often named after Jingdezhen, Dehua, Ding, and Longquan.

Home to high-quality porcelain is the Jiangxi town of Jingdezhen. Records trace kiln activity here back to the Eastern Han (A.D. 25–225). The community of potters expanded during the Tang dynasty and flourished under the subsequent Song. Jingdezhen acquired a reputation for fine porcelain, with many pieces being specifically designed for imperial use. Production here continues today.

The Shiwan kilns in Foshan (see p. 220), near Guangzhou, first fired up in the Song dynasty. Demand increased in the Ming and Qing dynasties, and the kilns also continue to manufacture today. Yixing (see p. 168) teapots were made in vast quantities during the Ming and Qing dynasties. The range of colors (from purple to green) results from the high concentration of metallic oxides in the clay.

Symbols

At first glance, many ceramics are hidden behind a jungle of decorative motifs. An understanding of the prominent decorative symbols used on Chinese ceramics will help appreciation. The dragon often denotes the emperor and could indicate that the piece is imperial porcelain. The phoenix represents the empress. Peaches symbolize longevity, as do pine trees, tortoises, bamboo, and the bald-headed god of longevity. The Chinese character for long life *(shou)* is also a popular pattern.

Homophones are liberally used. Bats are common motifs. They are pronounced *fu*, the same sound as good fortune. Fish *(yu)* also appear, denoting abundance *(yu)*. Other designs include landscapes, flowers, and historical scenes. Literature often embellishes later pieces with a poem or a piece of prose in appropriate calligraphy. Religious imagery includes the eight immortals (see p. 72), the eight I Ching trigrams, and the eight Buddhist symbols.

Color, glaze, & mark

Chinese ceramics can be categorized by their color and glaze. Pale green celadon is a typically thick and creamy green glaze that the Chinese adore for its similarity with jade, symbol of both long life and purity. Qingbai, a transparent pale blue glazed ware was pro-

Above: Ceramic bowl decorated with cherry blossoms on a marbled background Qing Dynasty (1662–1722)
Right: One of two painted red pottery standing figures from the Tang Dynasty (ca. 618-907 A.D.)

duced mostly in Jiangxi Province and was very popular in the Song dynasty (960-1279). Crisp blanc de Chine *(dehua)* ware originated at the Quanzhou kilns in Dehua, Fujian Province. This pure white glazed ware is typically used for small Buddhist figures, such as Guanyin, the goddess of mercy (see p. 72), and mythological characters. Dehua's first appearance in the west is associated with Marco Polo's visit to China.

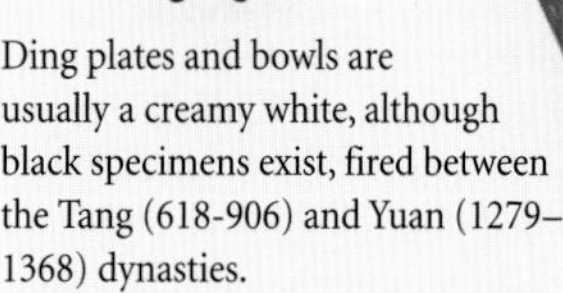

Above: A Chinese moon flask with designs from nature shows the delicacy of famille rose colors. Right: A glazed terra-cotta horse is from the Tang Dynasty. Below: Enameling comprises many different techniques and varieties, all requiring the process of firing at a constant and intense heat. The technique was almost certainly introduced from Europe.

Ding plates and bowls are usually a creamy white, although black specimens exist, fired between the Tang (618-906) and Yuan (1279–1368) dynasties.

The most famous colored porcelain is cobalt underglaze (a technique of painting the ware before it is glazed and fired) blue-and-white. Qing polychrome

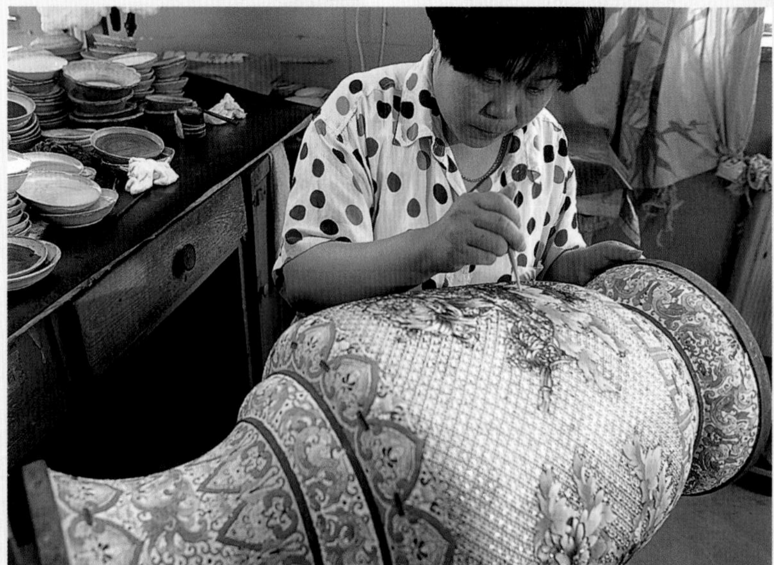

doucai (joined colors) pieces are characterized by green, blue, and red overglazed colored enamels on white porcelain backgrounds. Although often playful and simple, they can appear in a fantastic tangle of detail. *Wucai* (five colors) is a polychrome enameled decoration like doucai.

Famille rose, called *falangcai* (enamel colors) or *yangcai* (foreign colors), is a lush type of *ruancai* (soft colors). These are low-fired overglaze pieces finished in various shades of rose. Imperial monochromes are gorgeous pieces of uniform coloring; imperial Yellow *(minghuangse)* is a typical example, the bright yellow signifying the emperor.

Two calligraphic styles: The right hand mark attributes the piece to the reign of Ming emperor Hongzhi; the left hand to the reign of Qing emperor Qianlong.

The rough texture of Zisha (purple sand), produced in Yixing (see p. 168), is usually found in the form of teapots.

The mark, used to help identify the date of manufacture, is found on the foot of the ceramic. It is typically square or circular, with the name of the dynasty preceding the emperor, read vertically from right to left. It is, however, very risky to date a piece by the mark alone. Marks were often copied by later ages, and forgeries are manifold. Fake ceramics from China are improving technically all the time, often fooling inexperienced buyers and occasionally confounding the experts. The 1980s and 1990s saw an upsurge in the quantity of forgeries, and the majority of what you see in China's markets is fake. Most decent pieces are historical items that belong to private collections around the world.

The **Jingdezhen Pottery Culture Exhibition Area (Jingdezhen Taoci Wenhua Bolanqu)** is in the west of Jingdezhen. Tours of potteries can be arranged through the local branch of CITS *(tel 0798 851-5888)*. For those who appreciate fine ceramics, Shanghai Museum (see pp. 187–88) visit is essential. ■

Wulingyuan

THE MOUNTAINOUS RESERVE OF WULINGYUAN IS OFTEN touted as one of China's most magnificent karst landscapes. Officially named the Wulingyuan Scenic and Historic Interest Area, this park in northwestern Hunan is a magnet for hikers, rafters, and escapees from city life. The Chinese tout Wulingyuan as a geological museum, and it is also a UNESCO World Heritage site.

Wulingyuan's sky-reaching crags

Wulingyuan
197 B4
Zhangjiajie, Northwestern Hunan
$$

CITS visitor information
CITS Building, 631 Ziwu Lu, Zhangjiajie
0744 823-0110

Wulingyuan is known for its small communities of Miao, Bai, Tujia, and Hui (Muslim) minorities, as well as its spectacular forest of splintered, rocky columns. The huge grove of stone columns numbers in excess of 3,000. The park is cut by the Suoxi River, while waterfalls, limestone caves, and surface and subterranean pools add to the adventure. During the summer months, white-water rafting trips can be taken on the river.

Most visitors plunge into Wulingyuan from neighboring **Zhangjiajie Village,** which funnels hundreds of thousands of visitors into the region every year. You won't want to linger here, but it's useful for picking up maps and spending the night. The other two popular places to visit are Tianzi Peak and Suoxiyu Village.

Trails snake away from the entrance beyond Zhangjiajie Village, and you can take your choice of nearby peaks. Guides will pester you and porters will also press you to take a sedan chair.

Just beyond the entrance a path trails to the top of **Dragon Woman Peak.** To the north lies **Huangshizhai** (3,400 ft/1,035 m), a real clamber. Cable cars run up the sides of both, and from the summits you are treated to excellent views.

Surrounding Tianzi Peak in the north of the park are some of the loftiest pinnacles, alongside natural stone arches and bridges. The spectacle, generally draped in cloud and mist, is very steamy in summer.

A tangle of caves and underground streams perforates Wulingyuan. **Yellow Dragon Cave,** 12 miles (19 km) to the east of Suoxiyu Village, is a labyrinthine 7 miles (11 km) long, containing a subterranean waterfall and rivers. **Jiutiandong,** 10 miles (16 km) north of the park, is a massive cave.

Wulingyuan has a rich and varied collection of plants and wildlife. It is home to serows, clouded leopards, giant salamanders, Asiatic black bears, red magnolias (*honghua yulan*), and other rare and protected species. ■

Xiamen

CALLED AMOY BY WESTERNERS, THE ISLAND-CITY OF Xiamen has picturesque pockets of historical interest. The port, fortified in the Ming dynasty, is entwined with the Taiwanese, whose forces still occupy the nearby island of Jinmen. The neighboring island of Gulangyu (see pp. 208–210) is a delightful museum piece of meandering lanes and colonial history.

Xiamen became an important stronghold of resistance against the invading Manchu occupiers in the 17th century. It was later wooed by the European powers and the British prized it open with gunboats as a treaty port in the mid-19th century. Xiamen later became one of China's first special economic zones (SEZs; see p. 40).

The most attractive part of Xiamen is found in the port area that faces the island of Gulangyu. The colorful bustle of Zhongshan Lu runs east from the harbor front. Peek down its small side streets for a taste of a bygone age.

The famous **Nanputuo Temple** in the south of town is a wonderful complex, set against **Drum Hill (Gushan)** opposite Xiamen University. The Laughing or Future Buddha offers a welcome from **Tian Wang Hall;** backing onto him is Weituo, the protector of the Buddhist faith. Flanking them are the Four Heavenly Kings, awesome defenders of the temple.

The courtyard behind contains incense braziers, the **Drum Tower (Gulou)** to the west, and the **Bell Tower (Zhonglou)** to the east. The **Great Treasure Hall (Daxiongbaodian)** (north) houses three statues (Guanyin, the present Buddha, and Wenshu), while in adjacent halls sit the 18 Luohan (see p. 72) in ranks of nine. Behind stands the **Hall of Great Mercy (Dabeidian)** with four effigies of Guanyin, where most of the worshipers are women.

At the rear stands the **Hall of Sacred Scriptures,** where the original sutras were stored.

Across from the temple, **Xiamen University** has a pleasant campus that you can wander around. To the southeast of the university, along Daxue Lu (University Road), is the **Huli Cannon (Hulishan Paotai)** on **Huli Mountain (Hulishan).** The battery was installed by the Germans at the close of the 19th century. On a clear day, look east at **Jinmen** and **Xiao Jinmen,** the two islands still occupied by the "rebellious province" of Taiwan. ■

Worshipers at the Nanputuo Temple contemplate a huge character pronounced *FO*, meaning "Buddha."

Xiamen
Map 197 C3

CITS visitor information
✉ 335 Hexiang Xilu
☎ 0592 223-1259

Gulangyu Island walk

The enchanting island of Gulangyu (Drum Wave Island) is the real reason to come to Xiamen. It became a foreign concession in 1903, quickly acquiring a medley of building styles and textures. The island was blueprinted for churches, hospitals, schools, villas, consulates, and post offices—a home away from home for the foreigners who lived here. Crisscrossed with narrow, intriguing lanes, Gulangyu obliges with languorous walks amid palms, and a relaxed temperament holds sway.

Quiet, car-free lanes add to Gulangyu's allure.

Jump on a ferry from Xiamen's terminal (Lundu Matou) across the way from the waterfront Chinese-style Lujiang Hotel for the five-minute excursion to the island. The old ferry cuts diagonally across to the pier toward the south of the island. You will quickly notice that no cars are allowed on Gulangyu, and the only traffic noise is the whine of electric buggies straining to climb up the inclines—the island undulates with small hills, threaded through by little cobbled roads.

There are wonderful European-style villas on Gulangyu Island, a grand collection of columns, verandas, and red roofing surrounded by palms, banyans, and creeper-choked trees.

This walk is a rough guide only; it's easy to lose your way on Gulangyu, but because the island is so small, wandering around without a map or itinerary is just as much fun. If you do get lost, head for a high point and set your bearings in relation to Xiamen across the water.

Disembarking the ferry, you will see Xiamen Underwater World (a fun place for the kids), turn left and head south along Zhangzhou Lu. The hills on your right sport a cluster of imposing buildings from the foreign concession era. Situated here were the Amoy Telephone Company, the German Consulate, the King George Hotel, and the British Consulate (the latter can be seen on the first hill south of the pier).

Continuing south on Zhangzhou Lu takes you along a stretch opposite the Xiamen waterfront. On your right is **Flag Raising Hill (Shengqishan)**. At the southeastern tip of Gulangyu is a **statue of Koxinga ❶,**

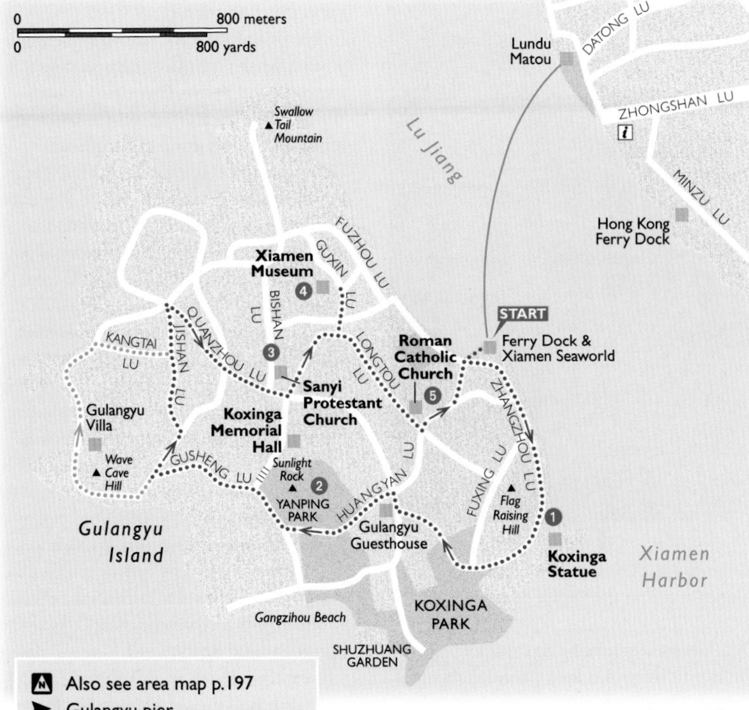

Also see area map p.197
➤ Gulangyu pier
3 miles (5 km)
1.5–2 hours
➤ Gulangyu pier

NOT TO BE MISSED
- Statue of Koxinga
- View from Sunlight Rock
- Gulangyu Guesthouse

otherwise called Zheng Chenggong. This hero pirate commanded a huge armada of junks, and with a massive army of fellow pirates at his beck and call he drove the Dutch from Formosa (Taiwan) in 1661. Koxinga championed the Ming cause and to his death defied the Qing government. His anti-Manchu motto was "resist the Qing and restore the Ming," often accompanied by the Shaolin salute (flat left palm pressed tightly over the right fist and held at chest level).

Zhangzhou Lu winds around to the right and climbs to a sports field. Turn left on Huangyan Lu (Bright Rock Road), passing by the large **Gulangyu Guesthouse** at No. 25, a magnificent old colonial building. The road then wraps around **Sunlight Rock (Riguangyan) 2,** the island's highest point. Buy a ticket and climb to its peak— where you look over the town's pretty tiles and redbrick buildings reminiscent of Qingdao (see p. 132) from this perspective. To the north of the island, the large, red-domed and colonnaded building is the Xiamen Museum. The locals call it the Bagua Lou or the Eight-Trigram Building, a Taoist description of its octagonal form. You will visit the museum later on this walk. Way off to the east lie the two Nationalist-held islands of Xiao Jinmen and Jinmen.

The small **Yanping Park** sits at the base of Sunlight Rock; also at the foot you will find the **Koxinga Memorial Hall (Zheng Chenggong Jinianguan),** where you can research the life of the mighty man. Keep an eye out for colonial architecture in the area.

South of Sunlight Rock and the Memorial Hall is **Gangzihou Beach,** just to the east of which is **Shuzhuang Garden (Shuzhuang Huayuan),** laid out in 1913

Gulangyu is a treasure trove of European architecture on the Fujian coast.

by a Taiwanese resident who came to Gulangyu having fled the Japanese invasion of Taiwan. The garden is the site of a fascinating **Piano Museum,** Asia's largest such museum collection. The island is well known throughout China as "Piano Island," as the music-loving island has the largest number of pianos per capita in the nation.

From Sunlight Rock, follow Gusheng Lu, which hugs the island's western shoreline. It wraps around **Wave Cave Hill (Langdongshan),** upon which sits the **Gulangyu Villa,** and continues on to Kangtai Lu. Otherwise, from Sunlight Rock, head along the enchanting Jishan Lu (Chicken Mountain Road) and turn right onto Quanzhou Lu. Both roads are bordered by a wonderful potpourri of architectural styles. Not far from the intersection of Quanzhou Lu and Bishan Lu (Pen Hill Road) is the **Sanyi Protestant Church** ❸**,** built in 1904, a year after the island was designated an International Foreign Settlement. A large plain building, it started out as the London Missionary Society hall.

Continue down Quanzhou Lu, bear left and join up with Guxin Lu, which leads to the **Xiamen Museum** ❹ mentioned earlier. At the time of writing a pipe-organ collection was due to move in. The path returning south along Guxin Lu reveals a fascinating collection of buildings that continues along Longtou Lu (Dragon's Head Road).

Near the intersection of Longtou Lu and Huangyan Lu is the old whitewashed **Roman Catholic Church** ❺**,** built in 1882. Follow Longtou Lu around the corner back to the pier and seat yourself at one of the many seafood restaurants for an appetizing treat. ■

Taiwan's golden gateway

The Taiwan-controlled island of Jinmen (Kinmen in Taiwan, Quemoy to westerners) lies 173 miles (278 km) from Taiwan, but it is just a few miles off the coast of Fujian Province. When the Nationalists withdrew to Taiwan (Formosa) in 1949 after fierce fighting, they managed to keep the island as an outpost. The name Jinmen means Gold Gate, which is perhaps appropriate considering that the Nationalist forces retreated to Taiwan with all of China's gold reserves.

Formed from granite, Jinmen belongs to an archipelago of 15 small islands that includes neighboring Xiao Jinmen (Little Kinmen); a number of these islands are in the hands of the People's Republic of China.

Jinmen has often found itself sheltering refugees, most notably those fleeing the Mongol invasion of China. It also harbored Ming partisans fighting the Manchus; the pirate Zheng Chenggong (see p. 209) was among them.

Along with the island of Matsu, Jinmen was heavily shelled for 44 days in 1958 by Communist forces, generating an international crisis. China's periodic sabre rattling is a fact of life on Jinmen, and the large military population of this fortress island is prepared for an overwhelming Communist onslaught should Taiwan (the Republic of China) officially declare independence from the mainland.

The island is open to tourism, but only if you approach it from the Taiwan side. ■

Zhaoqing

ZHAOQING IS AN ATTRACTIVE CITY 70 MILES (112 KM) WEST of Guangzhou. Noteworthy for its many tree-covered limestone peaks, set among lakes, it offers a pleasant contrast to the traffic of Guangzhou, as does the lovely wooded area of nearby Dinghushan.

Despite local comparisons with Guilin (see pp. 276–77), Zhaoqing has only a small number of peaks, but the city has its charms.

Seven Star Crags (Qixingyan) is the name given to the cluster of hillocks that are surrounded by lakes. Chinese myth ascribes the crags to a flock of stars that landed on Earth in the shape of the Big Dipper. The crags are picturesquely named: **Immortal's Palm Crag (Xianzhangyan), Jade Curtain Crag (Yupingyan), Toad Crag (Chanchuyan),** and so on. Catch a boat over to them from Paifang Square on the southern edge of Zhongxin Lake. Cross a bridge (paying a fee) to get into the main section; otherwise walk all the way around Li Lake (east of Zhongxin Lake) and view them from a distance.

Zhaoqing is not too large, and other areas can be taken in on foot or by taxi. In the southeast of the city is the **Chongxi Pagoda (Chongxita),** overlooking the Xi River. Not far from here stands the restored **Yuejiang Tower (Yuejianglou).**

Twelve miles (19 km) east of the city you will find the charmingly wooded **Dinghushan,** a retreat of peaceful and sheltered walks, streams, springs, temples, and pools. From the bus station, paths follow streams, skirting peaks and passing an assortment of temples. To the east is the **Leaping Dragon Nunnery (Yuelongan)** and the **White Cloud Temple (Baiyunsi);** in the north lies **Qingyun Temple (Qingyunsi).** A resort near this temple offers accommodations. ■

Local legend recounts that seven stars plunged from the heavens to form Zhaoqing's peaks.

Zhaoqing
197 B2

CTS visitor information
✉ CTS, Duanshou Wulu
☎ 0758 226-8090

GETTING TO DINGHUSHAN

To reach Dinghushan, take the No. 15 or No. 21 bus from Paifang Square. ■

Strolling the Guangzhou's flower festival (Xihu lu) during the Chinese New Year

Guangzhou

ASTRIDE THE PEARL RIVER, GUANGDONG PROVINCE'S CAPital has a long history of exposure to the West. This helps explain its sky-high economic figures, its special economic zones (SEZs), the breakneck piracy of everything from DVDs to designer clothes, and its sweatshops. China's gravy train set out from Guangzhou in this corner of the south, but in its wake, thankfully, it left charming pockets of history and a distinctive cuisine.

Guangzhou
197 B2 & 213

CTS visitor information
179 Huanshi Xilu
020 8666-6889

There has been a settlement here since the time of the Qin (221–207 B.C.); by the Tang dynasty (618–907) it had evolved into a flourishing market town. Foreign trade, first with the Middle East and Central Asia, focused the attention of the West. By the late 17th century, Guangzhou (also called Canton by Westerners) was partially opening its doors to the West. In time, the Cantonese through trade and emigration established Chinatowns the world over. Their culture harbored revolutionary forces in the Taiping leader, Hong Xiuquan (see p. 158–59) and republican Sun Zhongshan (see p. 36). Both were influenced by contact with the West. Guangdong Province was later earmarked by Deng Xiaoping as vanguard to China's modernization.

The dry run of capitalist experimentation nosed Guangdong Province into a commanding lead over the rest of China. Guangzhou epitomizes the success and failure of the country today. Vast new hotels sparkle, and building projects shape the skyline. Simultaneously, China's jobless migrants race to the city to swell unemployment figures and the crime rate, stretching the creaking infrastructure in the process.

Getting about can be difficult. The city is a grid-locked sprawl of honking cars, although the subway is changing this. Sights are scattered around haphazardly, and negotiating a route to encompass them all can fray tempers. The best advice is to make a choice, and stick to it. For Western visitors, Shamian Island (see pp. 216–17) in the south part of Guangzhou is a blessed sanctuary of quiet streets.

TEMPLES, MOSQUES, & CHURCHES

Although history takes a backseat to Guangzhou's modernization drive, nuggets glint from the fog of construction dust. The **Temple of the Six Banyan Trees (Liurongsi Huata)** is Guangzhou's most celebrated temple. Devoid of its fabled eponymous trees, the temple receives shade from the 17-story Flower Pagoda. Dating from the mid-sixth century, the temple was built to provide a reliquary for some of Buddha's ashes.

Entering, you are greeted by a statue of chubby Milefo, the Laughing Buddha. To his right are the Chinese words"The big belly can endure all that is unendurable"; on his left the words read: "He opens his mouth and laughs at all the laughable people in the world." Behind him stands Weituo (see p. 72), with his staff to the ground.

The three golden Buddhas in the back of the temple represent the Buddhas of the past, present, and future. Within the main temple are two others: The small **Sixth Ancestor's Temple** has the words "One Flower, Five Leaves" embroidered above it. Inside it stands an effigy of the sixth patriarch of the Chan Buddhist sect, Huineng (637–731). The **Guanyin Temple** houses a huge statue of the Buddhist goddess of mercy.

The octagonal **Flower Pagoda (Huata)** is the tallest pagoda in Guangzhou; previously it held the aforementioned sacred ashes of Buddha. It has 17 floors, despite the external illusion that it only contains nine. You can climb the pagoda for excellent views over the city. The road leading to the temple bustles with stalls selling

Temple of the Six Banyan Trees

- Map 213
- Liurong Lu
- $
- Ximenkou subway station

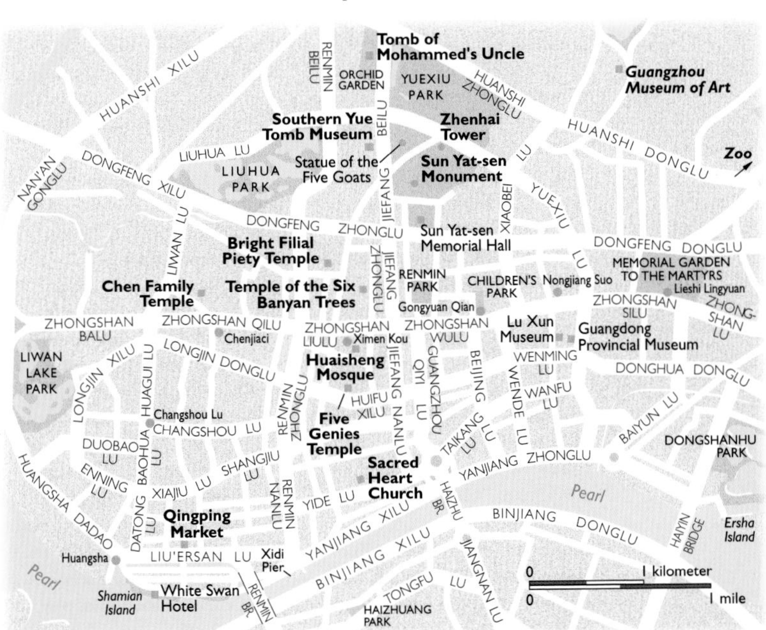

Bright Filial Piety Temple
213
Guangxiao Lu
$
Ximenkou subway

Huaisheng Mosque
213
Guangta Lu
$
Ximenkou subway

Five Genies Temple
213
Off Huifu Xilu
$
Ximenkou subway

souvenirs, religious accessories, and jade objects.

Not far away is **Bright Filial Piety Temple (Guangxiaosi),** parts of which date from the fourth century. The Laughing Buddha again greets you with the jovial message "Spirited eyes, full chest." To your left as you enter is the **Drum Tower** and to your right is the **Bell Tower.** A reclining Buddha lies in the **Fahua Altar (Fahuatan).** The characters on the entrance read: "As if asleep, but not asleep; sex is empty, empty is sex" and on the left the words read: "Truly awake, pretending to be awake, the heavens connect with water, water connects with heaven."

The main temple contains three golden Buddhas under a vast, beamed roof. To the rear, the ancestor temple is pleasantly shaded by trees. Women file into the Guanyin Temple to burn incense and pray to Guanyin, the goddess of mercy, while monks wander around in saffron robes.

Nearby, **Huaisheng Mosque (Huaishengsi Guangta)** testifies to the penetration of Islam into Guangdong. The mosque traces its lineage back to the Tang dynasty (618–907) and is notable for a smooth minaret, which lends its name to the neighboring street, Guangta (Smooth Minaret) Lu.

To the south, the **Five Genies Temple (Wuxianguan)** is a Taoist complex and site of the mythical creation of the city. The Five Genies correspond to the five elements (fire, water, earth, wood, and metal), the five planets (Venus, Mercury, Jupiter, Saturn, and Mars), and the five seasons (spring, summer, autumn, winter, and middle). If the clapperless, five-ton, Ming dynasty bell rings, it means affliction will hit the city. The bell was apparently struck by a shot from an English gun during the Opium War.

Down by the Pearl River, the Gothic-style **Sacred Heart Church (Shishi Jiaotang)** was designed in the 19th century by the French architect Guillemin and built in granite. Unfortunately, as with most churches in China, much of its stained glass is missing. The Cantonese call it the Church of the House of Stone.

The **Chen Family Temple (Chenjiaci)** was built at the end of the 19th century with funds donated by the families of that name (it is a common name in Guangdong Province). This traditional complex *(west off Zhongshan Lu, Chenjiaci subway)* contains a main hall, lesser halls, courtyards, and sculptures. The temple survived the Cultural Revolution, when many others dedicated to ancestor worship were destroyed. Today, handicraft exhibitions are held here.

OTHER SIGHTS

Qingping Market (Qingping Shichang), opposite Shamian Island, is an institution. This legendary market, a menagerie of Cantonese cooking and medicinal ingredients, is a Noah's Ark of the exotic and bizarre, both alive and dead: Vegetarians should avoid it. The market sprawls through a labyrinthine checkerboard of streets; you could spend an afternoon with your eyes popping out.

Starting innocently enough with the pungent aroma of dried herbs—an A–Z of Chinese medicine—and fungi, things soon move into squeamish territory. Owls are crammed into cages, skinny cats sit stuffed into tight boxes, and turtles rasp in the heat. Animal products galore are scattered hither and thither, including deer horns, bear paws, unidentifiable tendons, piles of dried animal parts; sea horses, geckos, and bluebottles all play their part. The moving, heaving, and slithering end of the market may turn some stomachs; but then again, as they say in China, the Cantonese will eat anything on four legs, unless it's a table.

Yuexiu Park (Yuexiu Gongyuan) is a vast diversion where you will find the rather ghastly Statue of the Five Rams, symbolic founders of the city, and the **Zhenhai Tower,** a pagoda built in 1380 and once part of the old city wall. Today it houses the city museum, devoted to the history of Guangzhou. In the south section of the park lies the **Sun Yat-sen Monument,** dedicated to China's famous revolutionary.

To the west of the park, the **Southern Yue Tomb Museum (Nanyuewangmu)** stands on the site of the tomb of the second king of Yue, a breakaway kingdom that lasted until 111 B.C. with Guangzhou as its capital. Yue is the name given to the whole province of Guangdong to this day. On display is an array of jade funeral objects found in the tomb.

If you want to voyage south of the river, visit restored **Haizhuang Park (Haizhuang Gongyuan),** which is home to the Ocean Banner Monastery.

You will find the **Guangzhou Museum of Art (Guangzhou Yishu Bowuguan)** south of Luhu Park in the north of town *(13 Luhu Lu, $)*. Displayed here is a collection of modern and traditional works by Chinese artists and sculptors.

The **Pearl River cruise (Zhujiang Youlanchuan)** takes you along Guangzhou's main artery, the Pearl River. The neon hoardings of the southern shore illuminate the evening trip (April–October). The boats depart from Xidi Pier, or you can book through your hotel (the White Swan Hotel has its own tour). ■

Sacred Heart Church
- Map 213
- Yide Lu
- Closed Mon.–Sat.
- $

Southern Yue Tomb Museum
- Map 213
- 867 Jiefang Beilu
- $

Pearl River cruise
- Xidi Pier, Yanjiang Xilu
- $$

With its cages of live animals, Qingping market is not for the squeamish.

Shamian Island walk

Shamian Island, a captivating museum of colonial architecture, sits on a half-mile-long (0.8 km) lozenge of sand in the Pearl River just south of Qingping Market. This is Guangzhou's equivalent to London's Kensington and Chelsea, a preserved snapshot of 19th-century Europe in the Far East.

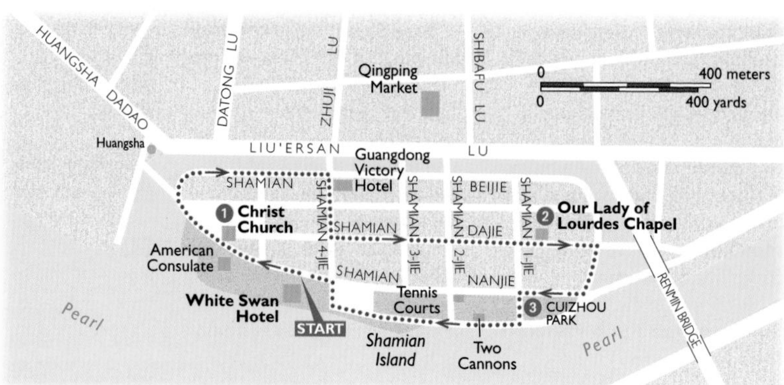

Spearheaded by the British, the West carved this little slice of Europe for itself after forcing open the doors of China to trade in 1843. The island quickly assumed a foreign guise, with banks, churches, administrative offices, and all the trappings of Western culture.

The British policed their domain with Sikhs, and the island was joined to Canton by the "English Bridge," which was closed nightly at 10 o'clock to keep the locals out. Symbolic of the power and organization of the "foreign barbarians," Shamian remained in Western hands until being salvaged by the founding of the People's Republic in 1949.

Shamian Island (Sameen Do in Cantonese; the name means "sand surface") is another world when compared to the traffic-locked snarl elsewhere in Guangzhou. Set against the background roar of ceaseless construction in the city proper, Shamian languishes in a delightful reverie that dwells upon a faded era. As towering five-star hotels erupt from the ground across the river, Shamian crumbles slowly away in the melancholic Canton damp.

Many buildings have been restored and several now bear plaques detailing their history. The real estate value of the island can only be guessed at and cafés and restaurants add to the European feel, while several hotels can be found on the island if you want to overnight.

Also see area map p. 197
- White Swan Hotel
- 1 mile (1.6 km)
- 30–40 minutes
- White Swan Hotel

NOT TO BE MISSED
- Christ Church
- Shamian Dajie
- Our Lady of Lourdes Chapel

Only a mile (1.6 km) in circumference, the island makes for a leisurely stroll. Start at the **White Swan Hotel** (one of the few distinctly modern structures on the island) and head west along Shamian Nanjie.

Ahead on your right is **Christ Church** **1**, managed by the Guangdong Christian Council. It is disappointing that you can't just walk in, but visitors are welcome to the service each Sunday from 9:30–10:45 a.m. Continuing west, you will also pass the American Consulate, with the usual lines of people applying to emigrate. This stretch of road was the former waterfront promenade.

Time's bell jar has been dropped over Shamian's delightful European architecture.

You will pass the occasional tree flagged for its age and rarity. Small residential streets lead into very tranquil backwaters; follow them if you wish. They offer a glimpse into courtyards and the occasional open doorway leading to old, sturdy, wooden stairs that climb into cavernous interiors.

At the western tip of the island is the modern and heavyset former German consulate building, its bombastic styling hardly a nod to the local character. Continue around the western tip of the island, and walk along Shamian Beijie, with the city to your left over a black sludge of river water. At the **Guangdong Victory Hotel,** opposite the bridge, turn right onto Shamian 4-Jie, a lively street with restaurants, antique galleries, souvenir stores, and bars (the island sports a flourishing crop of Western watering holes).

Turn left onto **Shamian Dajie,** the main boulevard running through the middle of the island. Along its length are a motley collection of prestigious buildings with a pleasant green strip of grass, trees, and park benches down the middle.

Once full of dilapidated and roofless houses rotting away through neglect, the main road, Shamian Dajie, is a very pleasant and genteel stretch of restored buildings and tranquil street scenes. The overgrown trees and palms recall a time when Shamian was shrouded in greenery. Farther down Shamian Dajie, the central parks become tidier and better groomed. There is even a small running track.

Walk on east along Shamian Dajie, and after crossing Shamian 1-Jie you will find **Our Lady of Lourdes Chapel** ❷ *(14 Shamian Dajie)*, a late 19th-century French church, which remains open for services. Check the blackboard outside for details of the next sermon, if you would like to attend.

Turn right onto Shamian Nanjie and follow the road south, where you will pass **Cuizhou Park** ❸**.** Take the road alongside the park to the riverside, and stroll past the tennis courts. Here you will encounter **two cannons.** Inscriptions on them reveal that they were forged on nearby Foshan, or Buddha Mountain, and used against the "imperial invaders." You are also told that they are 6,000 *jin* (6,600 pounds) each in weight and were moved to Shamian Island in 1963. Continue walking west back to the White Swan Hotel, your starting point. ■

Bleached by the sun, a fisherman's boat lies on the sands of Sanya's magnificent Yalong Bay.

Hainan Island

HAINAN (SOUTH OF THE SEAS) IS A LARGE TROPICAL island and erstwhile place of exile. Disgraced officials were (permanently) dispatched here, and it was only in the late 1980s that the island was reinvented as a special economic zone. A new free-market prescription galvanized Hainan's economy, and the blend of a sultry climate, the proximity to increasingly lawless Guangdong Province, and the political and geographical removal from Beijing encourages a lax atmosphere.

Hainan Island
197 A1–B1

CTS
Haifu Dadao
0898 6530-6003

Sweltering in greenhouse temperatures from March onward and typhoon-lashed in summer, Hainan attracts a massive influx of winter visitors from the mainland. At a time when Hong Kong Chinese venture to glacial Harbin (see pp. 344–47) in northernmost Heilongjiang Province to see snow, half of Manchuria comes to Hainan to catch some rays.

The mountainous and forested central belt that forms the spine of the island supports minority Li and Miao tribes, whose communities can be visited by the more adventurous (see p. 219).

HAIKOU

The capital, Haikou (Sea Mouth), is the island's access point. Elements of colonial architecture have survived the damp climate, and there are a few historical sites of note, but a day here at most will suffice. Strolling around Haikou quenching your thirst with coconut milk, readily available from streetside sellers, is fun.

The attractive **Five Officials Memorial Temple** lies in the southeast of town and is dedicated to five unfortunate officials who were exiled to Hainan. The temple was built in the Ming dynasty, though it was later restored.The memorial temple is surrounded by pleasant walkways, ponds, and greenery. The **Tomb of Hairui** *(off Haixiu Dadao)* is dedicated to an honest and well-respected 16th-century official. Recent restoration has given it a thoroughly modern and bright new look.

AROUND THE ISLAND

Wenchang, on the island's east coast, is famed for its coconut plantations, beaches, and seafood.

Hotels have sprung up around the famous hot spring baths at **Xinglong,** farther down the east coast toward Sanya. The nearby Indonesian Village celebrates Indonesian culture with music and dance. Xinglong is also renowned for its coffee, a major crop here.

Monkey Island, a narrow peninsula on the coast, is home to over a thousand Guangxi monkeys *(Macaca mulatta)*, but they are elusive and numbers are beginning to shrink. A wildlife research center has been established to study them.

SANYA

The beaches of Sanya, on the south coast, are the principal reason for coming to Hainan. By far the best is the long curve of **Yalong Bay (Yalongwan)**—a white ribbon of sand over 4 miles (6.5 km) long, on the hook of land east of Sanya. This is the southernmost reach of China, and it feels like it. If you come here any time other than winter, bring plenty of sunscreen, as the sun can be ferocious.

The bay is reached via Yalong Bay Square in Sanya, where an 88-foot (29 m) **totem pole** has been erected. The primitive totemic engravings on the pole are of auspicious animals and gods, including the dragon, Pangu (see p. 22), and the Great Yu (see p. 22), who harnessed the floodwaters.

Ferry service on Hainan Island evokes bygone days.

Closer to Sanya lies the smaller and more crowded beach at **Dadonghai,** just south of town. Running along the edge of the Luhuitou Peninsula are other beaches, while a half-hour bus ride away is the beach of **Tianya Haijiao,** west of Sanya. A stone etched with the characters *tianya* (edge of sky) and *haijiao* (rim of sea) stands on the beach. The stone is famed, as it is pictured on the back of the old Y2 note.

LI & MIAO MINORITY VILLAGES

Perched up in the Limuling Mountains is the town of **Tongshi,** (also called Wuzhishan), putting you within reach of Li and Miao minority villages. Some communities have been requisitioned by the tourist industry, which parades them for the benefit of visitors. Other communities farther in the interior are more genuine. Not far from Tongshi is **Five Fingers Mountain (Wuzhishan),** at 6,122 feet (1,867 m) the island's highest peak. ■

TOURS

The best way to see the outlying parts of the island is to join one of the tours that depart from Haikou. They race to Wenchang, Xinglong, Monkey Island (sporadically), and Sanya, and then do a whistlestop return via Tongshi. Tours can be arranged with English guides through the tourist office, and they are expensive; a Chinese tour is much cheaper—but only viable if you speak the language. ■

More places to visit in the South

CHAOZHOU

Chaozhou, a trading city in Guangdong Province, is probably most famous for its cuisine, a tasty regional rival to Cantonese food. The Tang dynasty **Kaiyuan Temple** is not far from the remains of the old city walls.
197 C2

FOSHAN

Buddha Mountain or Foshan (Fatsan in Cantonese), 17 miles (27 km) southwest of Guangzhou, is home to the intriguing **Ancestor's Temple (Zumiao).** The temple oversees a huge bronze statue of Beidi, the Emperor of the North, and a wonderful panoply of colorful ceramic figures. Shiwan, famed for its porcelain, lies southwest.
197 B2 **CTS visitor information** 14 Zumiao Lu 0757 222-3828

HENGSHAN

The southernmost of the five sacred Taoist Mountains, Hengshan rises above the interior of Hunan Province. The mountain is a constellation of peaks rather than a single mount, famed for its greenery and temple architecture, an important example being the **Nanyue Temple (Nanyue Damiao).**
197 B3

MEIZHOU

The small island of Meizhou, one of the myriad islands along the shore of Fujian Province, shelters delightful temples. It is celebrated as the birthplace of Tianhou, the goddess of seafarers, an important deity on China's coast.
197 C3 **CTS visitor information** 0753 225-9650

QINGYUANSHAN (QINGYUAN MOUNTAINS)

This mountain cluster just north of Quanzhou has been associated with the Confucian, Taoist, and Buddhist orders from the Tang dynasty onward. Sites include a Song dynasty **statue of Laozi, Buddhist caves (Qingyuandong),** and a **Muslim tomb (Lingshan Shengmu)** dedicated to two Islamic missionaries. It is known by the Chinese Muslims as the "third Mecca."
197 C3

QUANZHOU

Pretty Quanzhou in Fujian Province was formerly a port city on the maritime silk route. *Dehua,* or "Blanc de Chine," porcelain originated here. Tang dynasty **Kaiyuan Temple** leads to a museum with the remains of a Song dynasty junk. Quanzhou has a number of temples, and **Qingjing Mosque** testifies to its once flourishing Muslim community.
197 C3 **Kaiyuan Temple** Xi Jie $

SHANTOU

Shantou in Guangdong Province is another stitch in the fabric of foreign maritime outposts on China's coast. Although it is a special economic zone, like Zhuhai, the Midas touch has somehow eluded it. Pockets of disintegrating colonial architecture near the quayside make for engaging walks; a boat trip to Mayu Island brings pilgrims to its Tianhou Temple.
197 C2

XIQIAO HILLS

The Xiqiao Hills (Xiqiao Shan), 42 miles (67 km) southwest of Guangzhou, are a scenic area of caves, waterfalls, and peaks. Trails start from Xiqiao town, reached by bus from Foshan.
197 B2

ZHUHAI

Zhuhai (Pearl Sea) is an SEZ on the border with Macau. A labor force from Zhuhai washes in and out of Macau in droves (including prostitutes and hit men). Most people are either en route to somewhere else or on business. Haibin Park has pleasant walks, and the **New Yuan Ming Palace (Xin Yuanmingyuan),** a reproduction of Beijing's Old Summer Palace (see p. 79), offers a Chinese theme-park experience. The old house of **Dr. Sun Yat-sen (Sun Zhongshan Guju)** can be visited in Cuiheng, north of Zhuhai.
197 B2 **CTS visitor information** 33 Shuiwan Lu, Gongbei 0756 888-6748 **CITS visitor information** 1034 Fenghuang Nanlu 0756 212-0028 ■

Both Hong Kong and Macau blend pockets of colonial and historic charm with full-on modernity. Hong Kong is a dynamic outpost fringed with sleepy islands; Macau a romantic port city with Portuguese charms and a mushrooming casino circuit.

Hong Kong & Macau

Hong Kong taxi

Hong Kong & Macau

HONG KONG AND MACAU SHARE UNIQUE HISTORIES BUT ARE VERY DIFFERent. Hong Kong, the robust ex-colony perched on an uncertain political faultline, is a success story of magnificent proportions. Macau, the former Portuguese enclave, is blessed with a Latin mood and a charm that eludes Britain's former territory.

"ONE COUNTRY, TWO SYSTEMS"

The return of Hong Kong and Macau to the "motherland," in 1997 and 1999 respectively, ended a humiliating chapter for China, and it couldn't have come at a more opportune moment. Coinciding with a period of unprecedented Chinese economic development, the restoration of colonial spoils at the end of the 20th century was an apt finale. Of course, there were other reasons to celebrate; Hong Kong's return to China automatically increased China's gross domestic product by 25 percent.

Hong Kong and Macau are Special Administrative Regions (SARs) within China, retaining their own laws, tax systems, budget, and freedom in all areas except defense and foreign policy. The promise of the "one coun-

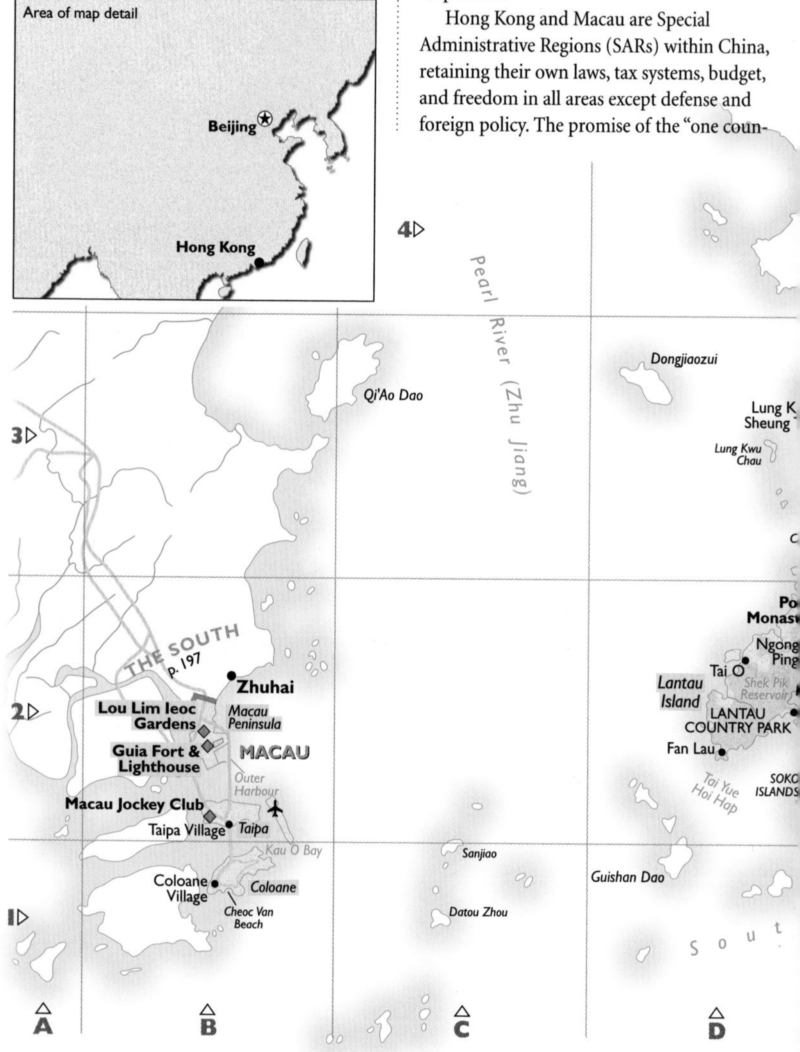

try, two systems" policy—which China wants to get right in a bid to lure Taiwan back into the fold—will protect the Hong Kong way of life for 50 years from 1997, and Macau has a similar proviso.

What is remarkable is that part of the West has been successfully grafted onto Communist China. This is because it occurred at a time when China was more open to the West than ever before.

HONG KONG TODAY

Is Hong Kong the ultimate Trojan Horse of Western values? Or is the Hong Kong and Macau way of life hostage to an unpredictable power? To date, Hong Kong's free press, freedom of speech, and its evolved and fair legal system have had negligible impact on China. Apart from capitalist know-how, China has shunned Hong Kong's more progressive formula; but as ever, how the fickle winds of Chinese politics will blow in the future is anyone's guess.

For the moment, China is happy to maintain the colonial institutions that garner both money and international respect. It needs to impress Taiwan that it can act responsibly, in the hope that the "rebel province" will return.

If the ploy fails and Taiwan continues to shun Beijing's courtship, a more desperate policy could emerge. An invasion of Taiwan would signal a shift to "one country, one system" and consequent panic in Hong Kong and Macau. ■

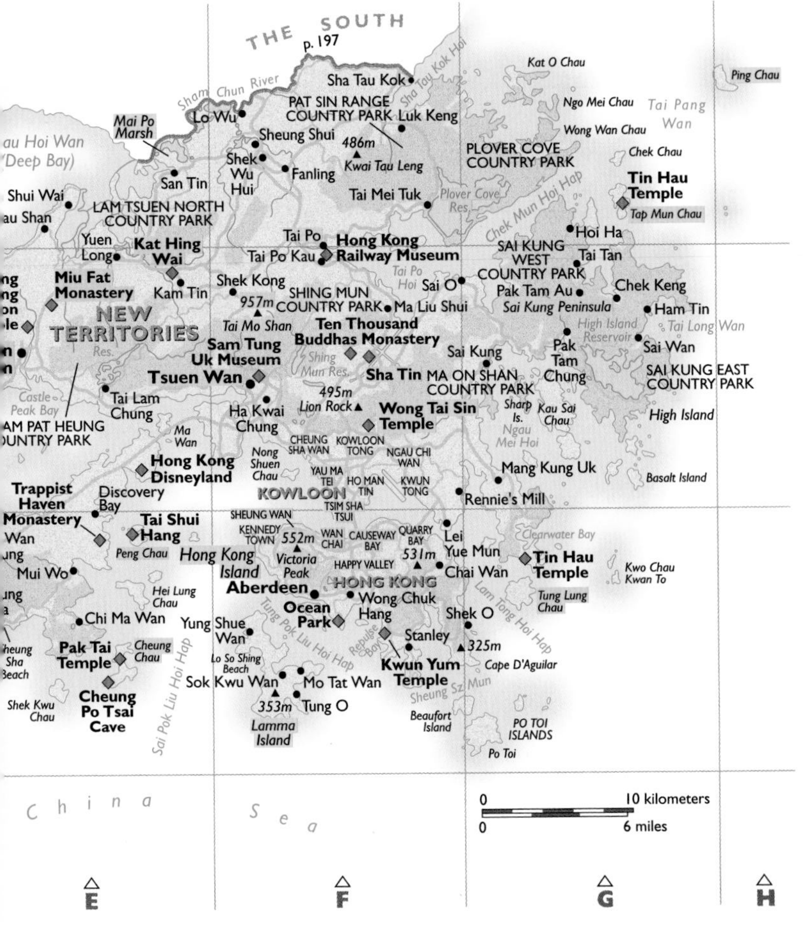

Hong Kong

Hong Kong panders to its cosmopolitan image with international restaurants at every turn, five-star hotels, shopping malls, plush bars, horse racing, and more. But it is the unexpected side to Hong Kong—a territory of overgrown islands, temples, hills, beaches, and wild walks—that makes this destination so rewarding.

Hong Kong Island was originally ceded to the British "in perpetuity" with the Treaty of Nanking in 1842, which concluded the first Opium War (see p. 35). This was expanded to include Kowloon in 1860, mushrooming later to embrace the New Territories in 1898, on a 99-year lease. China understandably nursed feelings of grievance for many years. During the Cultural Revolution (1966–1976), Hong Kong braced for the Chinese invasion that never quite came: Mao Zedong was keenly aware that Hong Kong was a useful portal to the outside world and a fundamental source of foreign exchange.

The year 1997 signaled the expiration of the 99-year lease for the New Territories, and the idea was that the whole colony should be handed back. The only demand was that Hong Kong's way of life be guaranteed for the next 50 years. The Sino-British Joint Declaration was signed between the then British Prime Minister Margaret Thatcher and Deng Xiaoping in 1984, and a basic law was drawn up for Hong Kong.

The decade preceding the handover was fraught with tension. The Tiananmen Massacre (see p. 41) sent a chill through the territory, and the last British governor, Chris Patten, regularly locked horns with Beijing as both sides maneuvered to shape Hong Kong's postcolonial future.

The handover on July 1, 1997, was a rainy,

Hong Kong's symbols of wealth remain untarnished since the handover.

melancholic affair. The immediate aftermath of return to Chinese sovereignty and the ensuing years saw Hong Kong going pear-shaped, albeit in unpredicted fashion. A long-term economic downturn, bird flu, and SARS all conspired to knock the stuffing out of the territory, but in recent years Hong Kong has recovered its confidence and economic drive, while Chief Executive Donald Tsang has proved popular.

Hong Kong, more fully called the Hong Kong Special Administrative Region (SAR), is an ambivalent city. While the outward guise of British culture—the wigged judges, historic buildings, and afternoon tea in postcolonial hotels—remains intact, the city has always been Chinese; the people, language, food, and culture are predominantly Cantonese.

If you are planning to visit Hong Kong as part of your trip to China, it is best to come having seen the rest of the mainland. If this is your first port of call, it may be too redolent of the West to surprise you; but after idiosyncratic mainland China, the city's forthright blend of Occident and Orient will make perfect sense. ■

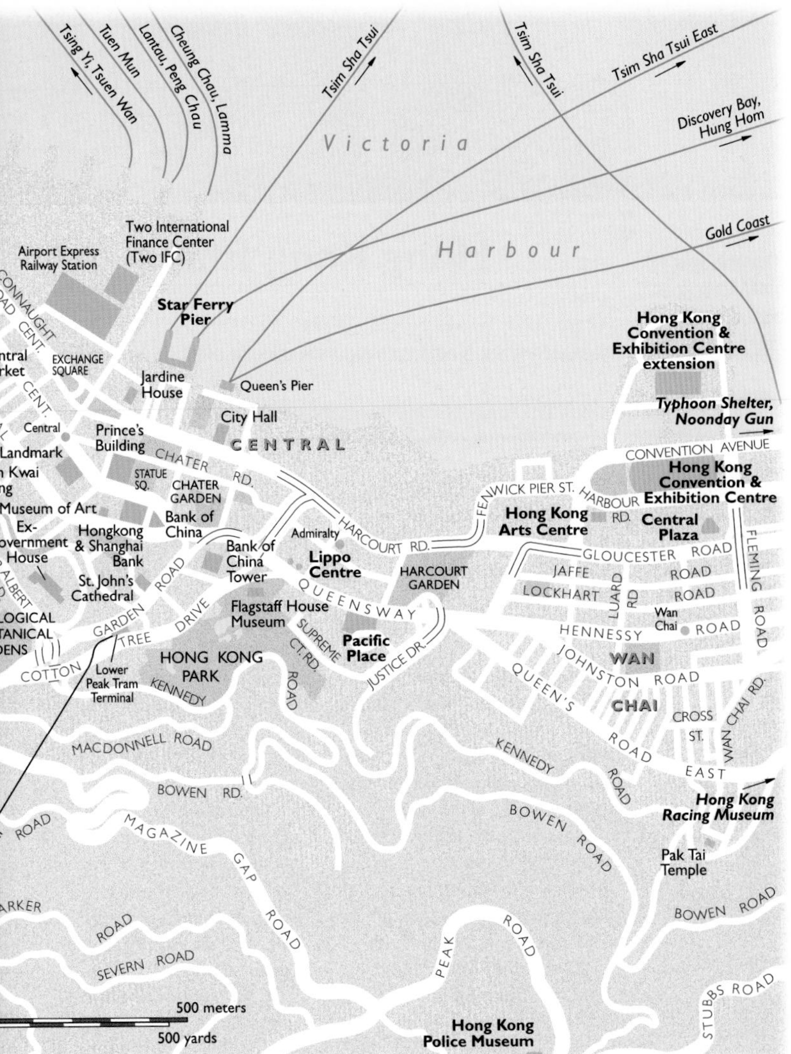

The only way to build is up in high-density Hong Kong.

Hong Kong Island

TAKE THE STAR FERRY FROM TSIM SHA TSUI ON THE southern reaches of the Kowloon Peninsula to Hong Kong's Central District for a classic approach to one of the world's most photographed vistas. The Bank of China Tower and other landmarks of modern architecture that thrust skyward define the sophistication of Hong Kong.

Hong Kong Island
223 F2

Hong Kong Tourism Board (HKTB)
www.discoverhongkong.com
Ground floor, The Centre, 99 Queen's Road, Central
0852 2508-1234

To the east and jutting out from Wan Chai is the splendid **Hong Kong Convention and Exhibition Centre extension,** poised as if to take wing. Nearby **Central Plaza** is another piece of audacious, uncompromising architecture, as is the colossal **Centre** building to the west—Hong Kong's tallest. The trip by night is something else: Central, Wan Chai, and Causeway Bay are transformed into a technicolor splash of neon.

Hong Kong Island defines the territory. This is where you can find the stock exchange, the financial district, the legislature, government offices, the most exclusive hotels (apart from the Peninsula) and restaurants, the most expensive real estate, plus the best stores and nightlife in town.

Nevertheless, it's not all business and commerce. Above the futuristic landscape of Central rises the most expensive piece of real estate in the world: the Peak. **Victoria Peak,** at 1,810 feet (552 m), is home to Hong Kong's elite, and the closer to the summit you get, the more stunning the cost. Property prices here, like the mist-wreathed paths that circle the Peak, are well and truly in the clouds.

To the south of the island lies a scattered retreat of small communities, seaside restaurants, and beaches. Tempting walks snake across the island, and several bus rides pass very dramatic and inspiring scenery.

Hong Kong Island is also the springboard to the picturesque outlying islands (see pp. 245–48). ■

Central walk

This walk through Hong Kong's Central District explores the territory's extrovert face. It's a splendid crush of refined shopping malls, cosmopolitan restaurants, and triumphant skyscrapers with relaxing diversions of parks and historic buildings.

Disembarking the ferry at the Star Ferry Pier, take the underground walkway that exits by the **Cenotaph ①,** where British servicemen formerly held daily ceremonies for raising and lowering the flag. The Cenotaph is dedicated to Hong Kong residents who gave their lives during the two world wars.

The impressive, 52-story, 1973 **Jardine House** (formerly the Connaught Centre) rises across Connaught Road Central, to the northwest. Built on reclaimed land, this is the sophisticated and towering aluminum-clad building with the circular windows. Square windows were avoided to maximize the strength of the lightweight structure.

An overhead walkway links Jardine House with **Exchange Square,** three towers encircling a public area of statues and fountains. To the north is Two International Finance Center (Two IFC), currently Hong Kong's tallest building at 1,378 feet (420 m), next to which is the luxury IFC Mall, an exclusive zone of brand-name outlets, attracting Hong Kong's indefatigable shoppers.

Also see area map p. 223
- Star Ferry Pier
- 2 miles (3 km)
- Half a day
- Lan Kwai Fong

NOT TO BE MISSED

- Hong Kong and Shanghai Bank building
- Bank of China Tower
- Zoological and Botanical Gardens
- Lan Kwai Fong

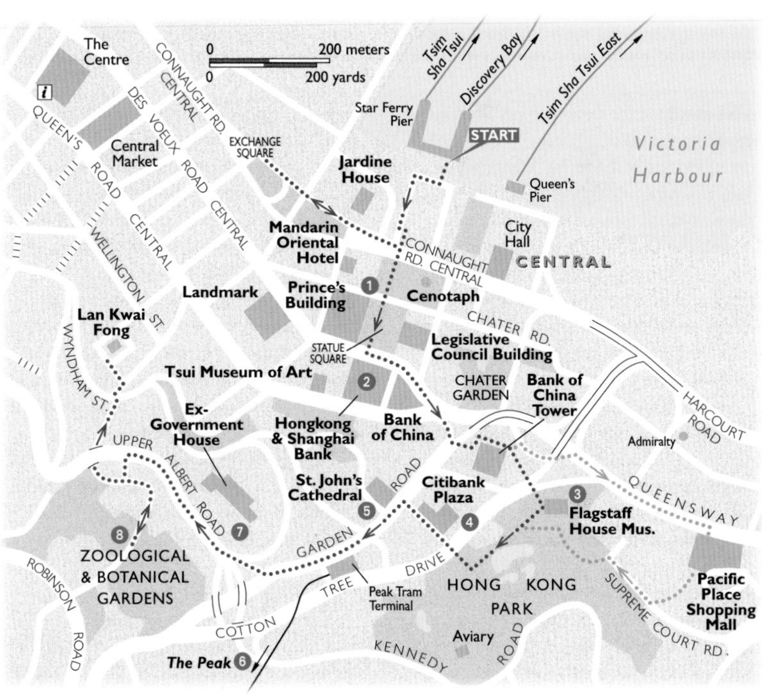

The Hong Kong and Shanghai Bank building (far right) rates high among Central's acclaimed architecture.

Southwest of the Cenotaph lies **Statue Square,** with the premier shopping experience of **Prince's Building** *(Chater Rd., Underground: Central)* to the west. The full-on shopping experience is a further hallmark of Central. The **Landmark,** southwest of Prince's Building, plays host to a further spread of elegant outlets, supported by the Galleria and Alexandra House. Many of these buildings are linked by overhead walkways, rising above the traffic.

Northwest of Statue Square lies the **Mandarin Oriental Hotel** *(5 Connaught Rd., tel 2522-0111, Underground: Central),* one of Hong Kong's exclusive hotels. Facing Victoria Harbour to the northeast stand the **Furama Kempinski** and the **Ritz-Carlton** hotels.

The colonial building to the east is the **Legislative Council Building (LegCo).** The statues that used to populate the square are gone (Queen Victoria's statue now stands in Victoria Park), and the only survivor from the Japanese occupation during World War II is a figure of Sir Thomas Jackson, a previous manager of the Hong Kong and Shanghai Bank.

Cross Des Voeux Road Central to visit the elaborate genius of Sir Norman Foster's **Hong Kong and Shanghai Bank building** 2 *(1 Queen's Rd., Underground: Central).* The space under the edifice is a public area, and two escalators feed into the belly of the structure. When it was completed in 1985, it was the world's most expensive building at almost a billion dollars. Note the two huge bronze lions that guard the entrance.

Foster's masterpiece looks down upon the structure to its east, the old **Bank of China building.** The top three floors play host to the ostentatious China Club (note the two sets of lions outside—one traditional, the other 1940s).

Not to be outdone, the building resurrected itself farther to the east in 1990 (beyond the mighty, gleaming Cheung Kong

Center), with the help of architect I.M. Pei, in the dramatic guise of the 70-story **Bank of China Tower** *(1 Garden Rd., Underground: Central).* The Tower thrusts up like a gleaming crystal, challenging with its sharp lines and ingenuity. It's designed to withstand typhoon stresses four times the equivalent for earthquake requirements in Los Angeles. The landscaping on either side of the shaft and the lobby are muted Chinese gestures that remain smothered in the building's overall modernity. Take the express elevator to the 47th floor for sweeping views over Victoria Harbour. Admiralty, to the east, feeds into famous Wan Chai, but not before making its pronouncement with the huge **Pacific Place Shopping Mall.**

South of the Bank of China Tower is **Hong Kong Park,** an escape from the overwhelming presence of tall buildings and busy streets. The park contains an aviary with a fascinating collection of brilliantly plummaged tropical birds, a visual arts center, and a *taiji* garden. The **Flagstaff House Museum** ❸ *(Hong Kong Park, 10 Cotton Tree Dr., tel 2869-0690, closed Tues. & some public holidays, Underground: Admiralty),* with its display of Chinese tea ware, dates from 1846. It's a great place to spend an hour or so. You can access the park via Cotton Tree Drive, or alternatively enter via its main entrance on Supreme Court Road, accessible by the huge Pacific Place Shopping Mall in Queensway (follow the tram lines or take a tram).

Overlooking the park south of the Bank of China Tower is another wonderful example of architecture—**Citibank Plaza** ❹ *(3 Garden Rd., Underground: Central).* The interplay of curved and straight lines lends a powerful grace to this 1992 building.

Take the park exit to Cotton Tree Drive and cross over to Garden Road and **St. John's Cathedral** ❺**.** Built in 1847, this is one of the last colonial pieces of architecture left in Hong Kong. It was badly damaged during the Japanese occupation in World War II. Services are still held here regularly, and an information booklet is available inside the church. Farther up Garden Road, you can hop aboard the Peak Tram, which drags itself up an impossible angle to the summit of **The Peak** ❻ (see p. 232).

Visitors to the aviary enjoy the view.

Alternatively, walk south up Garden Road, turn right on Upper Albert Road, and pass **Ex-Government House** ❼**.** Dating from the mid-19th century, this was the residence of colonial governors during British rule. Hong Kong's present chief executive refused to live here, complaining that the *fengshui* was not up to scratch. The house is not open to the public, except for one Sunday in March; contact the Hong Kong Tourism Board for details (*Ground floor, The Centre, 99 Queen's Rd., tel 0852 2508-1234*).

Albany Road runs south from Upper Albert Road to the splendid **Zoological and Botanical Gardens** ❽**,** home to a surprising number of exotic creatures, including a family of orangutans and a black jaguar.

Backtrack along Albany Road and feed into Glenealy. At D'Aguilar Street turn left to reach **Lan Kwai Fong.** This is a tight jam of pubs, clubs, discos, restaurants, sandwich places, and cafés. Hong Kong's bright young things converge here to parade themselves and escape the stresses of office life. Farther west are the bars, cafés, and restaurants of SoHo, abbreviated from "South of Hollywood Road," and NoHo, or "North of Hollywood Road," *(Gough St.)*—two of Hong Kong's most popular drinking and eating spots. ■

Wind & water

The sacred science of *fengshui* (literally "wind water" in Mandarin) is a conservative tradition that reaches back to the earliest origins of Chinese civilization. You may consider it rather surprising, therefore, that fengshui should cast such a spell in modish, technocratic Hong Kong.

Despite the territory's innovative modernism, Hong Kong is rife with superstition. The Hong Kong Chinese are more credulous than their mainland counterparts. The number four *(sei),* for example, is obsessively avoided for its similarity with the word for death *(sei),* despite having a different tone. The number eight *(baat),* on the other hand, is fortuitous —associated with good luck and health. Few Hong Kong Chinese will live in a place overlooking a graveyard.

The Cantonese culture's penchant for the occult spawns a massive film industry revolving around ghosts and vampires. Fengshui, or *fungsui* in Cantonese, accommodates itself easily to this spontaneous persuasion for things mystical.

But what is fengshui? Put simply, it is an understanding that one's life and destiny are shaped by one's physical surroundings. Man and his environment react with each other via *qi,* or energy (Cantonese *hei),* a relationship that fengshui seeks to harmonize. This relationship is also called *dao* (Cantonese *do*) or the Way, and any action that helps cultivate the Way is beneficial.

Fengshui is most importantly used for the siting of buildings, for interior design, and for the positioning of graves (you will see graves in Hong Kong pointing out to sea). With buildings, the *fengshuishi* (fengshui expert or geomancer) looks for places with *ling,* or spirit. Ling is also a kind of elemental form of qi. Temples are generally well sited and charged with ling. Qi is channeled by certain landscape features, which become veins of energy, and these can be tapped. Some places are intrinsically luckier and more positive than other places, for they positively channel qi, improving our physical and spiritual existence. Such places tend to be open, airy, elevated, and hilly; green with vegetation; and near a water source (waterfalls, rivers, lakes, or ponds). Despite the specific vocabulary, fengshui is often just common sense.

Hills accommodate two mythical animals—the Green Dragon (in the east) and the White Tiger (in the west)—from which large amounts of qi can be harvested. Houses should ideally be positioned in the lap between the two and never at the crest of the hill.

Places that are dark, dank, dull, and stagnant, where qi is largely absent, should be avoided. Rocky soil is shunned and loamy, airy soil is preferred.

Harmony is of paramount importance. *Yin* (the female, dark, cold, quiet, shadowy, and lunar realm) should be balanced with *yang* (male, light, warm, noisy, solar, and bright) for the optimum amount of qi. A glut of either is best avoided.

A further system of relationships that must be observed is the *wu xing* (five elements). Wood, fire, earth, metal, and water exist in a cycle of mutual creation and destruction, and their importance in fengshui can best be seen by the colors associated with them. Wood is green, fire is red, earth is yellow, metal is gold, and water is black. If an element needs to be emphasized, its color can be accentuated. A skilled fengshui master can quickly ascertain the elemental condition of a place and identify imbalances.

In temple architecture, the five elements are represented by the fabric of the buildings. The Wong Tai Sin Temple in New Kowloon (see p. 240) pays them due respect.

Fengshui is taken very seriously in Hong Kong. As it endows a business location with good luck, it is a further weapon in Hong Kong's highly competitive armory. If your business is ailing, a fengshui master can maximize the arrangement of your office to attract good fortune. ■

Even the modern geometry of contemporary Hong Kong architecture pays homage to the old laws of fengshui.

NEC

Victoria Peak

Victoria Peak
223 F2 & 224

THE PEAK IS THE MOST EXCLUSIVE RESIDENTIAL AREA IN Hong Kong, a confluence of huge bank accounts, massive real-estate value, and panache. It was rapidly colonized by a British establishment eager to escape the suffocating summer heat below.

Victoria Peak houses the most expensive residential property in Hong Kong.

The best way to get up here is by the Peak Tram, a unique ride. The angle of the railway slope approaches 45 degrees; just try not to think what might happen if the cable snaps! In fact, the tram has never had an accident since opening in 1888. It operates from 7 a.m. to midnight, running every ten minutes. A one-way trip takes about eight minutes.

The Peak Tram terminus is located in Garden Road, Central, and is connected to the Star Ferry Pier by a free shuttle bus that runs every 20 minutes between 9 a.m. and 7 p.m. (till 8 p.m. on Sundays and public holidays).

The impressive, dissonant, and renovated **Peak Tower** (designed by British architect Terry Farrell) doubles as the upper tram terminus, and this is where to leave the kids. Tucked away in this shimmering structure are theme rides and shows. The rest of the tower has galleries to take in the views, shops, and restaurants. The upper tram terminus is not the Peak per se; that's farther uphill and you'll have to walk. Apart from the views, however, there is little to see at the actual summit.

The nearby **Peak Galleria** has another collection of shops and the excellent **Peak Lookout** (see p. 375). If you can get a table for dinner here, do so; the nocturnal view down to the neon foothills of the Peak is unforgettable.

Harlech Road and Lugard Road run around the Peak, and make for an attractive, if undemanding, walk. More strenuous walks lead away from the Peak downhill, one of which takes you along Pok Fu Lam Reservoir Road and past the reservoir. The brisk **Hong Kong Trail** commences here as well (see p. 236) for the more adventurous.

On a misty day, the trails around the Peak make for a very refreshing and atmospheric day out. On a clear night, the twinkling view down to Central is simply bewitching. You can understand why residents are willing to pay so much to live here. ■

Sheung Wan

THOUGH SHEUNG WAN IS MORE DOWN-AT-THE-HEELS than Central, it is also more authentically Cantonese in flavor. Located to the west of Central, this ramshackle area comprises temples, shops, and pungent pockets of dried-seafood stores.

Sheung Wan
223 F2 & 224

Hollywood Road, a fascinating jumble of antique stores, burrows into Sheung Wan from Central. Sift through a sea of ceramics, Ming furniture, Tibetan artifacts, and relics from the Cultural Revolution. Half a day can be spent here, trawling for those elusive treasures.

Note the **escalator** (the world's longest) that ferries shoppers and commuters up to the Mid-Levels from Central—it's over 2,600 feet (790 m) long. It descends from 6 a.m. to 10 a.m. and ascends from 10:20 a.m. to midnight. Jump on if you want (the total journey time is 20 minutes).

The **Man Mo Temple,** one of the oldest temples in Hong Kong, also lies on Hollywood Road. It predates the British arrival and is dedicated to the civil and the martial (in Cantonese *man* means "literature" and *mo* means "military"). Hanging from the roof are huge, picturesque incense coils. Farther into Sheung Wan, on Tai Ping Shan Street, are two smaller temples, the **Pak Sing Temple** and the **Kuan Yin Temple.** Nearby Possession Street marks the spot where the Union Jack was first raised over Hong Kong on land that was then shoreline.

The Edwardian **Western Market,** on New Market Street at the corner of Des Voeux Road, is built on what was one of Hong Kong's busiest food markets. The brick building is a nostalgic nod to the past, equipped with an old London phone booth, cafés, and trinket stalls (with fabrics upstairs).

Jetcats travel the route to Macau (see pp. 249–53) from the Ferry Terminal behind the twin-towered **Shun Tak Centre** at 200 Connaught Road.

Toward Kennedy Town along Des Voeux Road West, stores spill over with dried seafood—squid, scallops, and the like. Jump on an eastbound tram back to Central, and go on to Admiralty, Wan Chai, Causeway Bay, or Happy Valley if you want (check the front of the tram). Grab a seat at the top and sail back through a forest of store signs. ■

The Man Mo Temple on Hollywood Road is one of Hong Kong's most ancient sacred sites.

Wan Chai, Happy Valley, & Causeway Bay

HEAD EAST ON THE DOUBLE-DECK TRAM FROM CENTRAL to Wan Chai, a knot of Western bars, sandwich parlors, and brisk side streets. Causeway Bay beyond caters to eager shoppers and diners, while Hong Kong's gamblers converge on Happy Valley's racecourse.

The buildings get progressively more frayed and tarnished to the east, with the hulking twin towers of the **Lippo Centre** a reminder of the shameless 1980s.

Wan Chai itself is a tacky strip of bars, clubs, and pubs, its reputation still feeding remorselessly off its red-light association with the 1950s novel *The World of Suzie Wong*, by Richard Mason. Wan Chai is a *gwailo* (foreign devil) stomping ground, jammed with snack bars and cafés.

One of the best sights here is the **promenade** around the **Hong Kong Convention & Exhibition Centre extension.** The promenade allows fabulous views over Victoria Harbour to both Kowloon and Central. The new wing itself is a gorgeous extension of the waterfront; pop inside and stroll around its spacious interior.

Not far away is the **Hong Kong Arts Centre** *(2 Harbour Rd., tel 2582-0200)*, where contemporary art exhibitions are held. The **Police Museum** *(27 Coombe Rd., tel 2849-7019, closed Mon., Tues. before 2 p.m.)* is devoted to the history of Hong Kong's police force.

For a diversion, jump on a tram with the destination Happy Valley and visit the horse-racing track. If you fancy a flutter on the horses, the racing season is from September to May. Otherwise, you can glean some of the history of racing in Hong Kong at the **Hong Kong Racing Museum** *(2nd floor, Happy Valley Stand, Happy Valley Racecourse, tel 2966-8065, closed Mon.)*. West of the track lies a collection of well-tended Catholic, Muslim, Parsee, and Hindu cemeteries.

Continue by tram to Causeway Bay. Much of this former warehouse district was under water until a land reclamation program transformed it into a vast restaurant and retail zone. A lasting symbol of the departed colonial presence is the **Noonday Gun.** Fired daily at noon, it can be found in a garden by the **Typhoon Shelter** on Gloucester Road.

Farther to the east are **Quarry Bay** and **Chai Wan.** Not far from the Chai Wan Underground station is the **Law Uk Folk Museum,** a restored Hakka dwelling *(14 Kut Shing St., tel 2896-7006, closed 1–2 p.m. Tues.–Sat.; Sun., public holidays closed before 1 p.m.)*. One of the traditional Chinese groups living mainly in the New Territories, the Hakka are recognizable by their distinctive broad-rimmed, black hats. ■

Wan Chai, Happy Valley, & Causeway Bay

223 F2 & 225

Left: Horse racing is the only legitimate form of gambling in Hong Kong, and the Happy Valley racecourse is the territory's most famous venue.

Around Hong Kong Island

Beaches and quiet settlements fringe Hong Kong's south coast.

HONG KONG ISLAND'S SOUTHERN COASTLINE HARBORS AN enticing world of seaside retreats and beach life far removed from the strip of urban congestion on its northern shore. The thrills and spills of Ocean Park and Water World make for a fun family destination.

Most of the small communities sheltered along the coast are lined with beaches, but a casual glance at Hong Kong's pollution figures should deter you from flinging a towel into your luggage. The beaches make for attractive strolls, with swimming only for the thick-skinned.

On the southeast coast is tiny **Shek O.** A tip: Go during the week; it's not easy to get to, but it's worth it, and you will have a lot of space to yourself (including the excellent beach). The No. 9 bus from Shau Kei Wan Underground takes an attractive route there.

Another popular hamlet on the south coast of the island is **Stanley,** a *gwailo* (foreign) refuge famous for its market. Again, the weekends see the place crammed with visitors, so try a weekday. The nearby **St. Stephen's Beach** is an attractive stretch of sand, and the village is packed with a choice of popular restaurants and bars. To the west of Stanley is a small

Hong Kong Island
Map: 223 F2

Ocean Park and Water World
Map: 223 F2
Address: Ocean Park Rd.
Tel: 2552-0291
Hours: Water World closed Nov.–May
Price: $$$

A statue of Guanyin stands in Repulse Bay.

Tinhau temple, and a temple to **Kuan Yin (Guanyin)** perches on a hill overlooking the sea.

West along the coast is **Repulse Bay,** Hong Kong's most popular beach, though it suffers from sludgy water. Its popularity guarantees it an ever present audience of sunseekers. An enticing feature of the bay is the **Kwun Yum Temple** at the eastern end, where you will find a fascinating collection of Buddhist effigies wreathed in pearls and jewelry. **Deep Water Bay** is a quieter beach farther around the coast to the west.

The big, fun **Ocean Park** and **Water World** sit west of Deep Water Bay. Ocean Park, a huge marine/amusement park, makes an ideal outing for children. The shark aquarium is particularly instructive and exciting. Water World is a fun complex of swimming pools and water slides.

Aberdeen, opposite the island of **Ap Lei Chau (Duck's Tongue Island),** was where boat-people lived on junks and sampans, but many have now moved ashore. It is worth noting that you can get to **Mo Tat Wan** and **Sok Kwu Wan** on the south of lovely **Lamma Island** (see pp. 245–46) from Aberdeen. You can take tours of the harbor from one of the private sampans, which will take you on a meandering chug past the houseboats. Walk along the water-front and you will be quickly encircled by sea dogs offering rides. Otherwise, find the pier for the harbor's outsize floating restaurants and get a free ride (boats leave every five minutes).

HONG KONG TRAIL

If you want to get the blood pumping and see a rawer side to the island, this 31-mile (50 km) trail will guide you through the nature spots. It winds from Lugard Road on Victoria Peak, down to **Pok Fu Lam Reservoir** (you can join this section from Aberdeen), before snaking through country parks in the east of the island and coming to a halt in Shek O.

WILSON TRAIL

Walking the Wilson Trail offers a further chance to decompress from the strain of the city. It cuts across Hong Kong Island, submerges under Victoria Harbour, and re-emerges in the New Territories. The trail commences just above **Stanley** on the south of Hong Kong Island, cuts roughly north, straddles Violet Hill, traverses **Mount Butler,** and drills through the Eastern-Harbor Tunnel (take the Underground from Quarry Bay to Lam Tin) to the other side. Once in the New Territories (see pp. 241–44), the trail charts a breathtaking course through **Lion Rock Country Park** (bisecting the MacLehose Trail, see p. 242), over hills, and on to the **Pat Sin Range Country Park.** ■

MAPS

A very useful Hong Kong Trail map, published by the Country Parks Authority, is available from the Government Publications Centre, Rm. 402, Murray Building, 22 Garden Rd., Central (*tel 2537-1910*). A map of Hong Kong Island is published by Universal Publications and is available at most bookstores. Universal Publications also has a map of the Wilson Trail. ■

Tsim Sha Tsui walk

Tsim Sha Tsui in Kowloon (Kowloon or Gaulong means "Nine Dragons" in Cantonese) is altogether a land of rougher textures than Central. This walk takes you past hallmark locations of sophistication (the Peninsula) and culture (the Hong Kong Cultural Centre), with a dazzling view over to Hong Kong Island. Kowloon Park patiently waits for those exhausted by the shopping frenzy of Nathan Road.

Start at the **Star Ferry Pier** in Tsim Sha Tsui, and go into the Hong Kong Tourism Board *(Star Ferry Concourse, tel 2508-1234)* if you need extra information. Follow the promenade along to the east. The splendid waterfront walk along the edge of Victoria Harbour offers an ideal view over to the sparkling districts of Central and Wan Chai on Hong Kong Island. The nighttime vista is one of the most breathtaking urban sights imaginable (the final leg of this walk brings you back along the promenade, so you will have a chance to stroll most of its length).

Also see area map p. 223
- Star Ferry Pier
- 2.5 miles (4 km)
- Half day, with museum visits
- Star Ferry Pier

NOT TO BE MISSED
- Waterfront Walk
- Hong Kong Cultural Centre
- The Peninsula Hong Kong
- Nathan Road
- Hong Kong Museum of History

You will pass the **Hong Kong Cultural Centre** *(10 Salisbury Rd., tel 2734-2009)*, one of Hong Kong's landmarks, and the **Clock Tower** ❶. The clock is a remnant of the old Kowloon-Canton (Guangzhou) Railway station, built in 1915 and demolished in 1978. The Cultural Centre houses an impressive range of cultural amenities, including a concert hall, a theater, and an arts library. The bookstore has a varied selection of books on art and is worth a browse.

Part of the Cultural Centre is the **Hong Kong Museum of Art** *(10 Salisbury Rd., tel 2721-0116, closed Thurs. & some holidays)*,

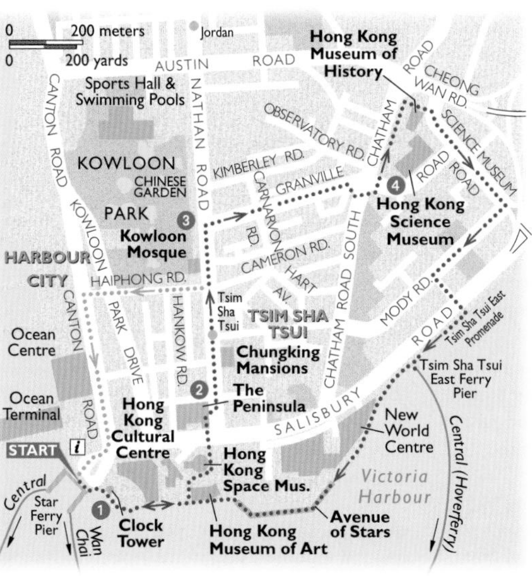

Hong Kong's popular Star ferry shuttles between Central and Tsim Sha Tsui.

which holds regular exhibitions of homegrown and international art. The adjacent **Hong Kong Space Museum & Theatre** *(10 Salisbury Rd., tel 2721-0226, closed Thurs.)* has a constellation of facilities, including a planetarium (where films are regularly screened).

Cross over Salisbury Road to the fabled **Peninsula Hong Kong** ❷ *(Salisbury Rd., tel 2920-2888)*. This is the grandest building in Tsim Sha Tsui, boasting an equally luxurious view over Victoria Harbour. If you ever have the good fortune to be a guest here, it will put an ornate frame around your memories of Hong Kong. If not, catch a glimpse of this sterling establishment through its ritual of afternoon tea in the foyer. Peruse the lobby and the excellent shopping arcades, both buffed to a high shine. The hotel is an oasis of luxury in a rather run-down neighborhood.

Turn left onto **Nathan Road** (called the Golden Mile for its sky-high real-estate value), cutting a mercantile swath through Tsim Sha Tsui to Mong Kok. This is the place to come if buying a copy Rolex is on your list; you're bound to be approached by street sellers.

The notorious **Chungking Mansions,** firetrap capital of backpackerland, is at 36–44 Nathan Road, with its hideous stairwells and minute rooms. Be careful if shopping for cameras or electrical goods at one of the many outlets here: They prey off the tourist market (note the absence of price tags on items in the windows). But Nathan Road has to be experienced because it is pure, unadulterated Hong Kong.

Kowloon Park ❸ provides a nearby retreat from exhaust fumes and the general chaos of Tsim Sha Tsui. The swimming pools are open between April and October, but go during the week when they are not a heaving mass of limbs and waterwings. The park sits at the edge of some of the priciest real estate in the world, so you can imagine its development value. Like other parks in Hong Kong, it is a sculptured, rather contrived garden, but it is still attractive and an essential refuge for local residents. On the southeast corner of the park rises **Kowloon Mosque,** which you can only enter if you are Muslim.

If you want to return to the Star Ferry Pier to go to Central (see pp. 227–29), turn left onto Haiphong Road, which skirts south of the high wall of Kowloon Park. The network of streets south of Haiphong Road is another sanctuary of *gwailo* (foreigner's) watering holes and international restaurants that come alive at dusk. Beyond lies Canton Road, hemmed in on either side by cinemas, top-end hotels, and shopping arcades, taking you south back to the Star Ferry Pier. Otherwise, from the southeast corner of Kowloon Park you can take the MTR (Mass Transit Railway) north to Yau Ma Tei and Mong Kok (see p. 256).

Back on the main walk, the roads running off to the east of Nathan Road (Carnarvon Road, Mody Road, Hanoi Road, etc.) journey through an energetic domain of Western pubs, clubs, discos, and restaurants. These roads are the commercial arteries that help feed the masses trudging up Nathan Road.

Follow Granville Road, opposite the Parklane Shopper's Boulevard (a wall of designer names), and take the walkway from the Ramada Hotel Kowloon over Chatham Road South, which accesses Energy Plaza before traversing north to the **Hong Kong Science Museum** ❹ *(2 Science Museum Rd., tel 2732-3232, closed Thurs. & some holidays)*. Imaginative and up-to-date displays and exhibits make for a lively experience that will keep the kids amused. Farther on, north of the Science Museum, is the **Hong Kong Museum of History** *(100 Chatham Rd. South, tel 2724-9042, closed Tues.)*, a thorough and resourceful chronicle of the ex-British colony.

This area is Tsim Sha Tsui East, a domain of nightclubs, hotels, restaurants, and shopping emporiums built on reclaimed land salvaged from Victoria Harbour. Walk south from the Museum of History down Science Museum Road, and turn right onto Mody Road. At the Urban Council Centenary Garden about 150 yards (140 m) down Mody Road, take the walkway to the Tsim Sha Tsui East Promenade and walk past the **Avenue of the Stars** (a tribute to the Hong Kong film industry and its famous faces) back to the Star Ferry Pier. Alternatively, catch a ferry to Central from the Tsim Sha Tsui East Ferry Pier. ■

Shops line Nathan Road—the Golden Mile—in Tsim Sha Tsui.

位元堂
位元堂
新新
SUN SUN

GLORY

夜總會

Wong Tai Sin Temple

Wong Tai Sin Temple
223 F3
Exit B, Wong Tai Sin MTR

BRINGING A SPLASH OF VIBRANT COLOR TO NEW KOWLOON is Wong Tai Sin Temple, which swarms with worshipers casting *chim*—bamboo sticks used to interpret the future—amid pungent clouds of incense.

Wong Tai Sin (Huang Daxian in Mandarin) is a Taoist deity much lauded in Hong Kong and the surrounding region, and he reigns from this fabulous temple. The deity, a shepherd who lived in Zhejiang Province, was taught the art of healing by an immortal. Consequently, those who are ill seek his guidance and restorative powers. The temple is a splendid mishmash of faiths. The main temple contains an image of Wong Tai Sin and the Monkey God, a mythical being who appears in the classic tale *Journey to the West*. The **Three Saints Hall** behind has a statue of the Buddhist Guanyin (pronounced Kwan Yam in Cantonese), Guandi (Kwan Ti), and one of the Eight Taoist Immortals (see p. 72). There is also a Confucian Hall, called the **Qilin Pavilion (Linge).** The Qilin is a mythical animal often associated with Confucius and royalty.

Come at the weekend, when the temple is most active, to catch the faithful praying (but be unobtrusive). A carnival atmosphere also reigns during Chinese New Year and on Wong Tai Sin's birthday, the 23rd day of the 8th lunar month.

THE FIVE ELEMENTS

The fabric of the temple taps directly into the *fengshui* lore. The **Bronze Pavilion** to the east represents metal (which produces water and is itself produced by earth in the phase of creation and destruction of the five elements). The other elements (wood, fire, earth, and water) manifest themselves in other halls.

The **Yue Heung Shrine (Yue Heung Ting)** contains a portrait of the Buddha of the lighting lamp; the portrait embraces fire and the brick wall in front of the hall represents earth. The **Scriptures Hall (Ging Tong)** preserves the teachings of Wong Tai Sin; its wooden structure represents wood in the elemental cycle, and the fountain in front represents water.

FORTUNE-TELLERS

If you want your fortune told, there are booths of commercial fortune-tellers (some speak English) who will read your palm or consult the *I-Ching* (see p. 50). ■

CHINESE DIVINATION

Chim are an assortment of numbered bamboo sticks placed in a bamboo container. After lighting incense and kneeling in front of an altar, the worshiper shakes the container in both hands until one of the sticks escapes and falls to the ground. The number is then interpreted for its message. ■

A group prays at Wong Tai Sin Temple in Kowloon displaying their bamboo sticks.

New Territories

THERE'S MUCH MORE TO HONG KONG THAN THE BRIGHT lights of the big city. The rural New Territories introduces a more pastoral side, a pressure valve for the grinding stresses of high-density living. Along with the outlying islands, this is Hong Kong's garden.

New Territories
223 E3

Technically speaking, all that lies between Boundary Street in Kowloon and the border with China proper is the New Territories (leased to Great Britain in 1898 for 99 years). The area embraces a wide range of sights and activities, and a potentially vast region in which to explore. To see it all would take several days of rigorous trekking, so it pays to make a judicious selection.

SAI KUNG PENINSULA

The ragged expanse of the Sai Kung Peninsula out to the east offers a number of opportunities for exploration. The old fishing town of **Sai Kung** acts as a launchpad to the surrounding region, and boats venture out to a scattered assortment of small islands.

Pak Tam Chung, on the borders of the **Sai Kung East Country Park,** ushers you onto the start of the **MacLehose Trail** (see p. 244). The 62-mile (100 km) route winds its length through the New Territories. South of Sai Kung town, the road penetrates to the rough tip of land around **Clearwater Bay (Tsing Sui Wan),** where you can find pleasant beaches and an aged **Tin Hau Temple** overlooking Joss House Bay. The island to the south is **Tung Lung Chau** (see p. 256).

SHA TIN

The **Ten Thousand Buddhas Monastery** lies west of Sha Tin, a town easily accessed by taking the KCR (Kowloon Canton Railway). A steep 15-minute climb brings you to the temple, so named because hoarded there are roughly 13,000 statues of Buddha. The **Heritage Museum** (*1 Man Lam Road, tel 2180 8188, closed Tues.*) is one of Hong Kong's best museums, with displays on traditional Hong Kong culture.

The Ten Thousand Buddhas Monastery west of Sha Tin actually houses close to 13,000 effigies of Sakyamuni.

Sha Tin will also be of note to gamblers, because Hong Kong's second racecourse can be found here. There's an entrance charge on days when there are races.

TAI PO

Farther north on the KCR is Tai Po, a new town that has little value for the traveler apart from the **Hong Kong Railway Museum** *(13*

The Sam Tung Ulk Museum in Tsuen Wan shows Hong Kong's more rustic heritage.

Shung Tak St., tel 2653-3455, closed Tues.), which should be of interest to railway enthusiasts and children.

TSUEN WAN

Tsuen Wan is easy to reach from either Kowloon or Hong Kong Island, being at the end of the MTR (Mass Transit Railway) line. The main draws here are the **Yuen Yuen Institute** *(tel 0852 2492-2220)* and the Buddhist **Western Monastery** *(tel 0852 2411-5111);* both are worth a look. The Yuen Yuen Institute is a Taoist temple with a vegetarian restaurant and panoramic views.

A taste of simple, traditional Hakka (the "guest people," and one of Hong Kong's minority groups) life can be gleaned by visiting the **Sam Tung Uk Museum** *(2 Kwu Uk Lane, tel 2411-2001, closed Tues.),* also in Tsuen Wan. The name means "three beam house" and was originally peopled by a migrant Hakka community from Fujian Province (adjoining Guangdong to the east). It is actually a small, walled village, of which there are other examples in the New Territories. The setting wins acclaim due to its authenticity.

The **Airport Core Programme Exhibition Centre** *(410 Castle Peak Rd., closed Mon.),* west of Tsuen Wan, guides

you through the civil engineering feat of Chek Lap Kok airport and the stupendously long Tsing Ma, a joint railroad suspension bridge.

TAI MO SHAN

Big Misty Mountain, or Tai Mo Shan, is Hong Kong's tallest peak at 3,139 feet (957 m). It lies on the MacLehose Trail (see p. 244), but you can also reach the peak from Tsuen Wan to the south (take bus 51 from Tsuen Wan MTR station).

TUEN MUN

Tuen Mun is a new town to the west of the **Tai Lam Pat Heung Country Park.** In the north of town is the **Ching Chung Koon Temple,** a Taoist house of worship dedicated to a Taoist Immortal, replete with ancestral hall and

drum towers. The most active time to visit is during the Ching Ming Festival, a period of remembrance for the dead, which occurs at about the same time as Easter (Easter is known as the Foreigner's Ching Ming in Hong Kong). Tuen Mun is best reached by hover ferry from Central, but you can get there by bus from Tsuen Wan. It can also be accessed along the MacLehose Trail as Tuen Mun marks its culmination.

MIU FAT MONASTERY

Take the Light Rail Transit (LRT), whose terminus is Yuen Long, to Lam Tei from Tuen Mun, where you can find the Miu Fat Monastery. Three huge, golden Buddhas preside over its top floor. The vegetarian restaurant here makes for a healthy diversion.

MAI PO MARSH

Bird-watchers and nature enthusiasts will hardly expect Hong Kong to host a thriving wetland in the northwest of the New Territories. However, Mai Po is a hidden natural gem full of bird life—at least for now. It's under threat from Shenzhen's chronic pollution. Trips to the marsh, north of Yuen Long, can be arranged through the World Wildlife Fund *(1 Tramway Path, Central, tel 2526-4473).*

KAT HING WAI

The walled village of Kat Hing Wai, with its traditional architecture, will bring you face to face with old Hakka women in traditional garb, bunching together for photo ops. A donation box is set up at the gate where you are

The walled Hakka village of Sam Tung Uk dates from 1786.

The Hakka (Guest People) are one of Hong Kong's Chinese minorities. Hakka women wear distinctive black, wide-rimmed hats.

MAPS

Universal Publications print the excellent **Hong Kong Guidebook** (HK$60), with a highly detailed map of the entire territory of Hong Kong; look for it in Hong Kong bookshops. Arm yourself with this guide if prospecting for far-flung sights in the New Territories and islands. Taking plenty of food and drink, sunscreen lotion, sun hat, and a basic medical kit is advisable. ■

encouraged to submit a small fee. Outside Kam Tim is **Shui Tau,** another walled village.

WILD WALKS

With some 40 percent of Hong Kong being country parkland, sweeping views are a world away from the fractured urban cityscape of Tsim Sha Tsui, Central, and Wan Chai. The true fresh air, great outdoors experience can be had along invigorating walks that penetrate these parks and wild places. Get off the beaten shopping track and into wild and hilly countryside with rugged scenery, campsites, far-flung temples, and villages.

MacLehose Trail

The complete 62-mile (100 km) MacLehose Trail is a daunting prospect if you only have a few days in Hong Kong. Don't be put off though; it can be chopped up into manageable sections or stages and is a bracing antidote to the grind of the shopping malls. The MacLehose Trail (named after one of Hong Kong's former British governors) starts in Pak Tam Chung in the Sai Kung Peninsula and finishes in the western New Territories town of Tuen Mun. The trail can also be done in reverse.

The first section takes you from **Pak Tam Chung** and initially skirts south around High Island Reservoir, before winding through the tiny villages of **Ham Tin (Salty Field)** and **Tai Long (Big Wave)** along the shoreline. Both villages have small beaches. The trail curls on up through the village of **Chek Keng (Red Path)** and on to **Pak Tam Au,** where you can get a bus to **Sai Kung town** (see p. 241) if you don't wish to continue. The path then enters the **Ma On Shan Country Park** and leads up the mountain of **Ma On Shan.** The mountain climb can be exerting so if you want, you can jump on bus No. 99 to Sai Kung town.

Persevering on the trail through Ma On Shan Country Park, you will come to the next peak of **Tai Lo Shan** (1,892 feet/576 m). The trek (stage 5 of the MacLehose Trail) then passes **Lion Rock** (a path north leads to Amah Rock), the ancient lookout post of **Beacon Hill,** and **Eagle's Nest. Kowloon Reservoir** lies ahead (where you can catch a bus back to civilization on Tai Po Road) and beyond that, to the north, **Shing Mun Reservoir.**

You are now wandering around **Tai Mo Shan Country Park.** Pause for breath before clambering up **Tai Mo Shan** (see p. 242). This is stage 8 of the trail, and you still have almost 14 miles (22 km) to get to **Tuen Mun.** Alternatively, catch bus No. 51 to Tsuen Wan MTR station from Tai Mo Shan Road.

Stretching ahead to the west, the trail wraps itself around the north of **Tai Lam Chung Reservoir,** before breathlessly halting in Tuen Mun. ■

Outlying islands

A VOYAGE TO THE OUTLYING ISLANDS THAT SPECKLE THE waters around Hong Kong is essential for a complete perspective on the territory. Take a breezy boat ride to one of the islands to dispel any lingering impressions that Hong Kong is just a city.

Although Hong Kong takes its name from one island, the territory comprises more than 260 outlying islands dotted throughout the South China Sea.

Along with the New Territories (see pp. 241–44), the outlying islands show the rural side of Hong Kong, a rich and diverse aspect to the ex-colony often overlooked by travelers. They are a treasure chest of charm, and essential for anyone who wants fresh air, lush vegetation, and superb views out to sea.

Before embarking for the islands, it pays to get hold of a copy of the Hong Kong and Yaumati Ferry Co.'s timetable from the outlying islands' ferry piers, in Central. If you plan to do some hiking while on the islands, drop in on the Government Publications Centre in Central, which publishes a useful series of detailed regional maps (see p. 236).

LAMMA ISLAND

Lamma Island, a hilly patch of land crisscrossed with atmospheric pathways, bordered with beaches, and supporting two vibrant villages, makes for a superb half-day trip.

Yung Shue Wan, in the north of the island, is the hub of the *gwailo* (foreign) community—a lively strip of bars, seafood restaurants, cafés, and stray dogs. Surrounding it is a host of smaller villages (such as Tai Peng to the north), slotted in among the patchwork of hillocks and fields.

The walk from Yung Shue Wan to the southern community of **Sok Kwu Wan** will take you across the backbone of the island, passing the small but unspoiled beach of **Hung Shing Ye** on the west of the island. The walk should take you about an hour to complete. The beach is protected by a shark net, which is (supposedly) checked daily during the swimming season.

Lamma Island
223 F2

A bustling community that makes a living from the sea, Cheung Chau's bay teems with sampans and houseboats.

Note the conspicuous industrial addition to the skyline, the Lamma Island Power Station (the cables of which burrow through the island and provide electricity to the whole of Hong Kong Island). Farther on is the small, but attractive, **Lo So Shing beach.**

If you plan your walk right, you will come into **Sok Kwu Wan** in time for either lunch or dinner. The community has a row of seafood restaurants that are popular with locals. The **Lamma Hilton Shum Kee Seafood Restaurant** *(tel 2982-8241)* enjoys a loyal following. Once you have finished washing that lobster down with chilled white wine, you can take the ferry from Sok Kwu Wan to either Aberdeen or Central.

The more adventurous can clamber over the hills to the lovely driftwood-littered bay of **Tung O** on the southeast coast (no shark net), and from there cut your way west through to unspoiled **Sham Wan (Deep Bay).** From Tung O Bay, there is a superb walk through bamboo groves and banana trees to **Mo Tat Wan,** where you can catch the ferry out to Aberdeen.

Ferries for Yung Shue Wan and Sok Kwu Wan generally leave hourly from the Outlying Islands ferry piers in Central on Hong Kong Island. The last boats to Central leave from Sok Kwu Wan and Yung Shue Wan at 11:40 p.m. and 12:30 a.m. respectively.

CHEUNG CHAU

Cheung Chau (Long Island) has lovely walks, temples, and a bay filled with sampans and junks. Pirates once used the island as a base, and some historical remnants can be found. The main event of the year is the Cheung Chau Bun Festival, which takes place in May, climaxing in a procession of costumed children, some of whom ingeniously appear to float down the streets (suspended by invisible wires). The famous bun towers were banned after one of them collapsed, injuring participants.

Praya Street, running north and south from the ferry pier, overlooks the bay—a colorful stretch of junks and sampans. An assortment of cafés and restaurants has grown up around the view. Walk north along Praya Street and pay homage to the brightly painted **Pak Tai Temple.** Built in 1788, it is dedicated to a thoughtful god who rescued the inhabitants of Cheung Chau from a plague. Inside the temple are relics associated with Pak Tai: a Song dynasty sword, and a sedan chair that was used to ferry aloft an effigy of the god on festival days. A marvelously dilapidated altar, depicting a coiling dragon, sits in a roofless chamber under the sun.

Cheung Chau Village is worth exploring for its mix of herbal stores, shrines, mahjongg parlors, traditional Chinese houses, sacred trees, and shops selling brightly colored decorative paper for funerals. Tung Wan Beach, on the village's east coast, is a popular venue for windsurfing. The smaller beach farther south is **Kwun Yam Wan Beach** (Afternoon Beach), named after Guanyin, the Buddhist goddess of mercy; a temple dedicated to her is nearby.

Peak Road winds in a long loop around the south of the island, and it is worth exploring for magnificent scenery and vistas out to sea. Lined with trees and shaded from the sun, the road passes sea-facing cemeteries and makes its way to **Sai Wan (West Bay).** Here you can see a **Tin Hau Temple** and the **cave of Cheung Po**

Cheung Chau
223 E2

Lantau Island
222 D2 & 223 E2 & E3

Tsai, a notorious pirate who frequented Cheung Chau and stashed his booty here. From Sai Wan, hop aboard a sampan back to the pier at Cheung Chau Village in time for lunch or dinner.

Ferries for Cheung Chau leave hourly from the Outlying Island ferry piers in Central on Hong Kong Island. The last boat returns to Central at 12:30 a.m.

LANTAU

Not as easy to negotiate your way around as Lamma and Cheung Chau, Lantau is the huge island that greets you as you fly into Hong Kong. **Chek Lap Kok airport** was built on a huge mass of reclaimed land north of the island, and the airport express shuttles over the vast Tsing Ma bridge that straddles the waters across to Kowloon. Lantau's size makes for challenging walks. Harboring a number of important temples and monasteries, the island boasts the world's largest outdoor, seated bronze Buddha and a sprinkling of seaside communities.

The ferry from Central drops you at **Mui Wo (Plum Nest)** on Silvermine Bay (named for the abandoned silver mines there), which has an attractive stretch of beach and a waterfall north of the village. Buses to the rest of the island radiate from Mui Wo.

Tricky to reach but perhaps worth the hike for devout Catholics is the **Trappist Haven Monastery,** a 90-minute clamber north of Mui Wo. Alternatively, you can grab a ferry to the island of **Ping Chau** (see p. 256) from Mui Wo and then take a *kaido* (small ferry) to the monastery (destination **Tai Shui Hang**).

Most people who visit Lantau make a beeline for the **Po Lin Monastery** *(www.plm.com.hk),* a large Buddhist complex on the Ngong Ping Plateau. Weekends see the monastery throbbing with visitors from the rest of Hong Kong and beyond, so a weekday trip is essential if you want a more unhindered view of monastic life. The colossal **statue of Buddha,** on the hill overlooking the monastery, is a staggering 111 feet (34 m) and the focus for tour groups.

Lantau Peak, the highest mount on the island, rises southeast of the monastery. Dawn-watchers race energetically to the 3,063-foot (934 m) summit for panoramic views that stretch as far as Macau.

The seaside village of Tai O, on the western shore is a mildly charming diversion, while most of the local and mainland Chinese crowds surge to **Hong Kong Disneyland** *(tel 1-830-830, www.hongkongdisneyland.com).*

Cheung Sha Beach on the southern fringe of Lantau is a popular magnet for the weekend crowd, so be warned. More secluded are the beaches at **Fan Lau,** on the **Lantau Trail.** Fan Lau is also host to an ancient fort, near which rest the timeless remains of a primitive stone circle.

Ferries to Mui Wo leave roughly every hour from the Outlying Islands ferry piers in Central. The last return boat departs at 12:20 a.m. During the week, faster hover ferries also make the trip.

Lantau Trail

The Lantau Trail provides dramatic scenery. You can do short sections or the whole knee-wobbling 43 miles (69 km). Starting from Mui Wo, it does a long loop over Lantau Peak, passing south of Tai O, hooking around Fan Lau, threading through Shek Pik and its reservoir, and running alongside Cheung Sha beach before returning to Mui Wo. Remember to take enough liquids and sunscreen along. ■

Gambling is Macau's major drawing card, especially for big spenders from Hong Kong.

Macau

The romantic enclave of Macau may be back in the hands of the People's Republic of China, but its atmosphere is still heady with the flavors of Portugal. Moreover, despite its customary pairing with Hong Kong across the water, Macau comfortably stands alone as a unique travel destination in China. A leisurely mood here helps you unwind after the breathlessness of the former British colony.

Macau, the successful result of Portugal's foraging for trade routes in the 16th century, was leased from China in 1557. The territory was called Macau after the local name: Amagao, or island of A-Ma. The local name for Tianhou (Tinhau or Mazu), the goddess of seafarers, is A-Ma (see p. 73).

Macau thrived on its trade of sandalwood, tea, and other commodities, but by the 19th century Canton (Guangzhou) had become an important rival. Macau further lost its shine to Hong Kong, whose star was on the rise, and the gradual fading of the Portuguese Empire. By the early 20th century, its significance had dwindled to the mere picturesque.

Macau—never a colony like Hong Kong—was only under the temporary administration of Portugal, which twice tried to hand it back, with no success. With an agreement on Hong Kong's return on the table, the question of its future arose again, and a settlement was made with China in 1987.

On December 20, 1999, Macau returned to China and was ushered in as a Special Administrative Region (SAR) enjoying a high degree of autonomy (in official parlance). As with Hong Kong, Macau has a level of self-determination denied other areas of China.

Macau consists of a peninsula and two islands, capped by the city of Zhuhai to the north. Beyond its many casinos, the peninsula is a charming checkerboard of Portuguese ruins, decaying churches, and colonial buildings. The islands of Taipa and Coloane each shelter small communities where life continues in an unhurried and traditional way. In recent years the enclave has emerged as a major casino center (see p. 253), luring ever growing crowds of gamblers for a throw of the dice and the chance to strike gold. ■

Macau's enduring symbol is St. Paul's, a typhoon-ravaged cathedral façade designed by an Italian, built by Japanese, and attended by Portuguese.

Macau Peninsula

THE MACAU PENINSULA IS A WONDERFUL CANVAS OF grand colonial monuments, interesting church architecture, and charming side streets.

CENTRAL MACAU

Cutting an impressive slice across the peninsula, the **Avenida de Almeida Ribeiro** runs east to west and south of the grand **Largo do Senado,** the main tiled square of fountains, colonnades, and Portuguese architecture. Here you will find the Macau tourist office. Opposite is the **Leal Senado,** the august seat of the municipal government. North of the main square on Rua de São Domingo sits **St. Dominic's Church,** a 17th-century Dominican building that is open to the public.

Probably the most awe-inspiring sight is the glorious ruin of **São Paulo (St. Paul's),** just to the west of Monte Fort. The crumbling façade is all that remains of the church, an apt metaphor for the decline of European ecclesiastical power in Asia. The wooden church was destroyed by fire during a typhoon, and this is all that remains. The structure becomes even more inspirational at night, when it is illuminated.

The annals of Macau's past unfold at the **Macau Museum.** Hollowed from the slopes of the hill capped by Monte Fort, the museum is a comprehensive and well-equipped chronicle of the enclave.

Monte Fort (Fortaleza do Monte), above the museum, was built by the Jesuits. Its cannons only roared once, in 1622, repelling the Dutch who had designs on Macau. Today, the muted weapons remain, standing silent guard over the fort.

Macau Peninsula

Map: 251 & 222 B2

Macau Government Tourist Office

www.macautourism.gov.mo

Map: 251

Address: Edificio Ritz, 9, Largo do Senado

Tel: 315566 or 333000 (hotline)

Macau Museum

Map: 251

Address: Monte Fort

Tel: 357911

Hours: Closed Mon.

Price: $$

The odd bell still hangs, muffled. As a strategic location, the fort offers sweeping views out to sea, and the best time to come here when the city darkens into twilight.

The **Camoes Gardens,** located toward the Inner Harbour, are dedicated to Luis de Camoes, the 16th-century Portuguese poet. There is no substantial proof that the writer ever came to Macau, but the gardens offer a pleasant departure from the streets. Come in the morning to see old men walking their caged birds; stroll to the top where old practitioners perform *taiji* and *qigong* in the cool air to traditional Chinese music. Middle-aged folk walk over the pathways of rounded pebbles, massaging acupressure points in the feet. Botanists will love the wealth of flowers and vegetation; there's a splendid collection of trees, many festooned with long, hanging creepers.

Nearby is the **Old Protestant Cemetery,** the final resting place of artist George Chinnery (1774–1852), renowned for his depictions of the China coast. Also buried here is British missionary Robert Morrison (1782–1834), who had the unenviable task of translating the Bible into Chinese.

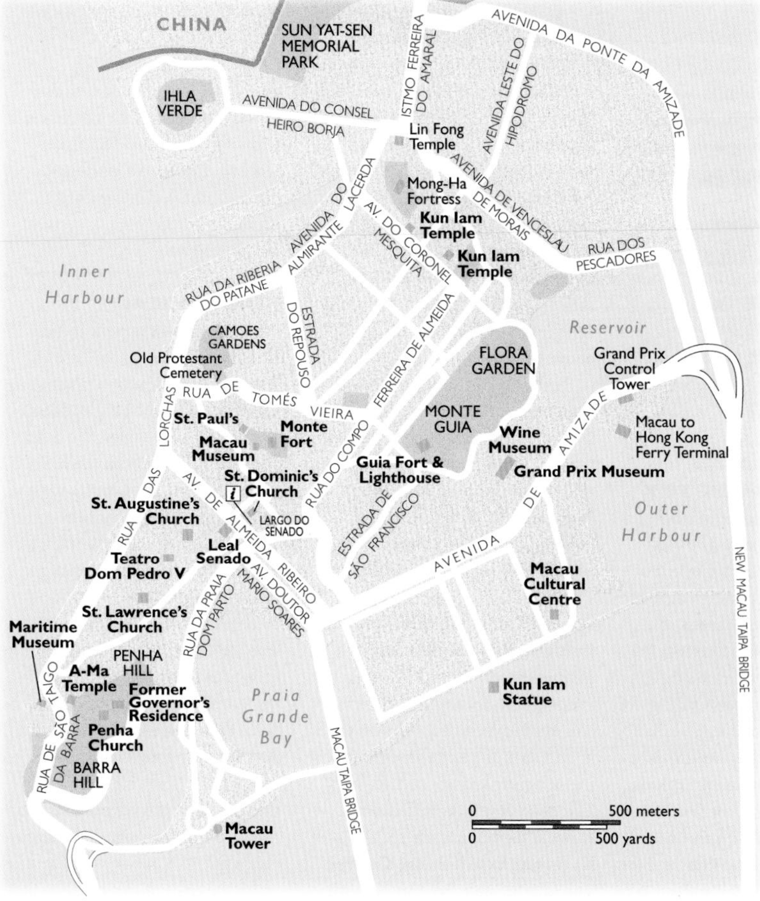

Chinese and Portuguese traits mingle in Macau's bustling streets.

Wine Museum & Grand Prix Museum

- 251
- Macau Forum
- 7984108
- Closed Tues.
- $

MACAU GRAND PRIX

This November race, watched by some 70,000 people, first screamed around the sleepy streets of Macau in 1954. The main race is the FIA International Cup for Formula Three, but other events include customized touring cars (the Guia Race), saloon cars (the Macau Cup), and the Super Car Race. ■

Wine enthusiasts will have their prayers answered at the **Wine Museum,** a celebration of the wine industry; the ticket price includes a tasting. It's located near the outer harbor. The **Grand Prix Museum,** housed in the same building, lets you try out some simulation rides (without the acrid smell of burnt rubber and petrol fumes).

Part of the **Macau Cultural Center,** a noteworthy architectural experiment that contains three museums and two auditoriums, is the rewarding **Macau Museum of Art,** well worth exploring for its temporary exhibits as well as its permanent collection.

Nearby, a walkway stretches across the water to a gargantuan **golden effigy of Kun Iam (Guanyin),** built in 1999. It is immediately obvious that the statue has Western elements; this was the intention of the Portuguese sculptress Christina Maria de F. R. Leiria. The effigy is wonderfully illuminated at night. Beneath it is the **Kun Iam Ecumenical Center.** The interior walls are painted with excerpts from the great Chinese classical philosophers: Confucius, Mencius, and Laozi. The center seeks to embrace all faiths under one roof, with a common expression of spirituality permeating its design.

NORTH MACAU

You can join worshipers at the **Kun Iam Temple** on Avenida do Coronel Mesquita, a fascinating temple dedicated to the goddess of mercy. The complex opens onto a small courtyard with the main temple behind. In front stands a large copper incense burner. Trees pleasantly shade the courtyard and stone lions lie among creeping vegetation.

Signs on the pillars exhort those who are dirty (of conscience) not to enter. The effigy of Guanyin is in the temple at the rear, and above her is the customary inscription *daci dabei,* or great charity, great compassion. The 18 Luohan worship her from glass cages on either side. Incense hangs in spirals from the ceiling.

To the right of this building lies

a gorgeous little garden temple, and around it is a fascinating assortment of smaller temples. Fortunetellers offer their magical wares in the temple. Farther west on Avenida do Coronel Mesquita is another, smaller **Kun Iam Temple** that is equally appealing.

SOUTH MACAU

Just south of Leal Senado is **São Agostinho (St. Augustine's Church),** near the cool green of the **Teatro Dom Pedro V,** built in 1873. The ravaged paintwork of the square-towered **São Lourenço (St. Lawrence's Church)** farther south shows the effects of Macau's humid climate.

Running along the eastern seaboard is the picturesque **Rua de Praia Grande,** the location of the **Governor's Residence.** Painted bright rose, the building can only be admired from outside. Nearby is the stately colonial building that was once Macau's finest hotel—the **Bela Vista.** This eight-room former pensione is characteristically colonial and sophisticated.

A steep climb up the hill behind takes you to the granite **Penha Church,** which affords extensive views of the southern reaches of the peninsula.

Around the hook of land at the tip of the peninsula is the **A-Ma Temple (A-Ma Miu),** elements of which have a 600-year-old history. A-Ma is the goddess of the sea and the queen of heaven (also called Tinhau), it is she who lends her name to Macau. Come here during the spring festival for an explosive display of bangers, crackers, and cymbals. In addition, A-Ma has her own festival in April or May.

Nautical enthusiasts will find what they are looking for at the **Maritime Museum,** opposite the A-Ma Temple. Macau's rich and glorious maritime history is on display in the form of vessels, equipment, clothing, techniques of boatbuilding, and more. ■

Chinese women traditionally worship Guanyin (Kun Iam), the compassionate bodhisattva who has temples dedicated to her throughout Macau.

Maritime Museum

- 251
- Opposite A-Ma Temple
- 595481
- Closed Tues.
- $

Kun Iam Temple

- 251
- Avenida do Coronel Mesquita

Las Vegas of the East

Macau's gambling revenues are reportedly outstripping even Las Vegas, and with pundits expecting Macau's gambling market to expand from its current US$9 billion to US$12 billion over the next five years, the former Portuguese enclave is going places that nowhere else in China is destined. Casinos are multiplying to feed China's insatiable appetite for gambling: With Chinese salaries on the rise and the number of mainland arrivals mushrooming as travel restrictions are relaxed—Macau saw 18 million visitors arrive in 2005—many say the only way is up for Macau's casinos. ■

Macau's islands

THE TWO ISLANDS OF TAIPA AND COLOANE, JUST LIKE THE outlying islands of Hong Kong, are refuges of tranquil charm (albeit easier to reach). Their Mediterranean-like pace invites you to saunter through pastoral villages and enter a long-lunch frame of mind.

TAIPA

Originally two islands but now fused by silt, Taipa still musters considerable rural appeal despite the threat posed by the new airport and the metropolitan aspirations of Taipa City. Make a beeline for **Taipa Village** in the south and skirt around the construction.

In permanent siesta, Taipa Village seems oblivious to the construction roar besieging it. The leisurely mood inspires a desire to take root and buy a chicken farm on the edges of the village.

Near the waterfront, the **Avenida da Praia** used to border the sea, but a tide of silt has pushed it back. Regardless, this promenade of trees, benches, and colonial buildings is a restful and picturesque synopsis of Macau. Take your time languishing here and enjoy the postcard view.

The **Taipa House Museum** on the promenade has preserved the life enjoyed by a middle-class family in the last years of the 1900s. Period furniture and authentic decorations take you on a historic tour.

West of the museum and elevated on a rise of land, the ubiquitous presence of Portuguese Catholicism appears in **Our Lady of Carmel Church (Igreja Nossa Senhora do Carmo),** which overlooks gardens leading down to the silted seafront. In the west of the village you will find the small **Tinhau** and **Pak Tai temples.**

The village has a famous assortment of Portuguese restaurants that can serve as an indulgent conclusion to your visit. **Rua de Fernao Mendes Pinto** is a picturesque walk of restaurants, and **Rua do Cunha,** at right angles to it, is a pleasing stretch of eateries.

You can rent a bike cheaply from a few places in Taipa Village. This is an excellent way to see the rest of the island, and you can even cycle over to Coloane.

If the thought of being separated from Macau's casinos (see p. 256) leaves you cold, a gambling rush can be had at the **Macau Jockey Club** *(tel 820868),* west of Taipa Village. Races are held twice a week, so call beforehand to check dates.

Taipa
222 B2

Macau Government Tourist Office
www.macautourism.gov.mo
Edificio Ritz, 9, Largo do Senado
315566 or 333000 (hotline)

Taipa House Museum
Avenida da Praia
Closed Mon.
$

Hakka Chinese in front of the Chapel of St. Francis Xavier, Coloane

The explosive clatter of Mahjongg pieces echos throughout Hong Kong and Macau.

COLOANE

Coloane is joined to Taipa by a causeway swollen through land reclamation that is fusing the two islands together. **Coloane Village** has some colonial treasures worth exploring.

The **Chapel of St. Francis Xavier (Capela S. Francisco Xavier)** is subtropical Christianity's bastion in the village. The white church rises magisterially from the dusty streets and can be carefully contemplated over a coffee from one of the cafés opposite. The chapel dates from 1928 and is dedicated to St. Xavier, a missionary who trawled the Far East for converts to Christ. Among relics previously sheltered here was the saint's elbow bone, which had been held at St. Paul's until the big fire (see p. 250); it was returned to the museum there in the mid-1990s.

Other temples in the village are the **Kun Iam Temple,** the **Sam Seng Temple,** and the interesting **Taoist Tam Kong Temple,** housing a detailed whalebone carving of a boat with oarsmen.

At **Cheoc Van Beach (Bamboo Bay),** about a mile (1.6 km) around the coast to the south, you can take a dip in the silted waters. There's a swimming pool and a few restaurant/cafés, but it's altogether a bit dormant.

There's more of a sense of activity and beach life, at the **Hac Sa Beach,** on Coloane's eastern fringe. Not only can you find one of Macau's best restaurants, **Restaurante Fernando** *(tel 882531),* but the whole area is attractive, the views are excellent, and a recreation park is bursting with activities. Here you will find tennis courts, ping-pong tables, football, and badminton courts; you can also rent sailboards and jet skis. ■

Coloane

222 B1

More places to visit in Hong Kong & Macau

HONG KONG

PENG CHAU

The small island of Peng Chau, home to a large, active community, is assailed on weekends by day-trippers to neighboring Lantau Island. The island has a handful of small seafood restaurants and a **Tin Hau temple**; its highest point is the diminutive **Finger Hill** (310 feet/95 m). You can look out over to the *gwailo* glitter of **Discovery Bay** (otherwise known as Disco Bay) to the west.
223 E2

PING CHAU

Just within the orbit of Hong Kong, Ping Chau has a dash of Chinese temple architecture, small sandy beaches, and shells of deserted buildings. There's also a radiation shelter in case an accident occurs at China's Daya Bay nuclear power station, 7 miles (11 km) away.
223 H4

PLOVER COVE RESERVOIR

This is excellent hiking territory, up in the wilder reaches of the northeast New Territories. You can follow the **Pat Sin Leng Nature Trail,** which starts at Tai Mei Tuk and ends at Bride's Pool, or hike around and join the **Wilson Trail** (see p. 236) and head south. Weekends see the area crawling with evacuees from the city, so time your trip well.
223 F4 & G4

TAP MUN CHAU

Tap Mun Chau is one of the more far-flung islands, a grassy knoll in the northwest of the New Territories. It has a Qing dynasty **Tinhau temple** and a sense of seclusion.
223 G4

TUNG LUNG CHAU

South of Joss House Bay on the Clearwater Bay peninsula is the uninhabited island of Tung Lung Chau. A **fort** was built in the 18th century on the island's northeast fringe to protect it from pirate attack. The fort's remains can still be explored. Rock carvings show traces of early inhabitation.
223 G2

YAU MA TEI & MONG KOK

The overhyped **Jade Market** sells its wares from Kansu Street, Yau Ma Tei, a dilapidated area north of Tsim Sha Tsui (see pp. 237–38). Unless you know your subject, it is very easy to buy inferior jade, so do some research before you haggle. North of the market is a **Tinhau temple.** A wander around the **Temple Street Night Market** reveals a profusion of stalls, their wares spilling over under the feet of eager shoppers. Some real bargains surface from the bustle, but be prepared for a tide of pirated goods.

The Chinese fascination with birds can be explored in the **Yuen Po Street Bird Garden,** Mong Kok. It has hundreds of birds, many of which sing from the confines of exquisitely carved, wooden cages. The garden is a short walk from Prince Edward Subway.
223 F3 **Hong Kong Tourism Board (HKTB)** Star Ferry Concourse, Tsim Sha Tsui; or Ground Floor, The Centre, 99 Queen's Rd., Central or Hong Kong International Airport 0852 2508-1234

MACAU

GAMBLING

With 26 casinos, Macau makes more revenue from gambling than Las Vegas. Casinos are the principal reason there's such a weekend exodus to Macau from Hong Kong.

GUIA FORT & LIGHTHOUSE

The fort, sitting on Guia Hill in the east of the peninsula, was built between 1637 and 1638 on Macau's highest point. It also has a 17th-century chapel and excellent views spanning out over the territory. Hiking trails encircle the hill, while a small cable car ascends to the top.
222 B2 & 251

LOU LIM IEOC GARDENS

This quiet enclave can be found to the west of Guia Hill. The gardens, dating from the 19th century, are a profusion of plants, interspersed with ponds, paths, and pavilions. It is named after a famous merchant of Macau.
222 B2 **Lou Lim Ieoc Gardens** Avenida do Conselheiro Ferreira de Almeida $

Teeming with minorities and rewarding travelers with some breathtaking landscapes, the Southwest is one of China's must-see regions. Guilin, Yangshuo, Dali, and Lijiang are unique attractions, while Xishuangbanna abounds with trekking opportunities.

The Southwest

Dai girl, Xishuangbanna

The Southwest

IF YOU THOUGHT CHINA WAS IN DANGER OF BECOMING A WASHED-OUT blur of socialist housing, the Southwest throws color back into the mix. Historically under vacillating Chinese control, it's a magnificent patchwork of minority cultures stitched into a dreamy landscape. This is an enthralling region if you want to explore rather than tour. Guilin, Yangshuo, Dali, Lijiang, and Xishuangbanna are a roll call of China's must-sees.

The Southwest's secret lies with its unique combination of geography and ethnic culture. Yunnan, situated high up on the Yunnan–Guizhou plateau, is overlooked to the north by the roof of the world—Tibet. The jungles of Myanmar (Burma) encroach from the west, while the flavors of Laos and Vietnam spill over from the south. The province's sheltered relief endows it with clement weather in both winter and summer; the provincial capital, Kunming, is called Spring City.

Half of China's 55 ethnic minorities call this area home, from the industrious, blue-clothed Naxi of Lijiang (see pp. 268–71) to the often elusive tribes of the southern border regions. Together they cling to a colorful way of life that 50 years of Communist supervision has failed to bleach.

Not long ago, backward transport and terrible roads put many important destinations in the Southwest tantalizingly beyond reach of those with little time. Dali and Lijiang should be savored slowly, but airports long ago opened them up to whistle-stop approaches.

Xishuangbanna, in the lush south, lures visitors with the chance to explore tropical jungles. The regional pivot, Jinghong, is surrounded by a domain of ethnic villages, deep in the green tangle of foliage.

Guilin, in adjacent Guangxi Province, has suffered from overpopularity and the resultant plague of trinket sellers and insistent guides, but popular nearby Yangshuo has much more to offer in its enticing dreamland karst scenery, which is simply spellbinding.

Opportunities exist in all these regions to jump on a bicycle and work out a route as you go along. And you will find an energetic service sector dedicated to entertaining and feeding Westerners. In most of China visitors tend to be left to fend for themselves; in the Southwest, a lively tourist industry has equipped itself with the trappings of banana pancakes, cappuccino, and not half-bad English. ■

Classic pastoral scenes characterize China's southwest corner.

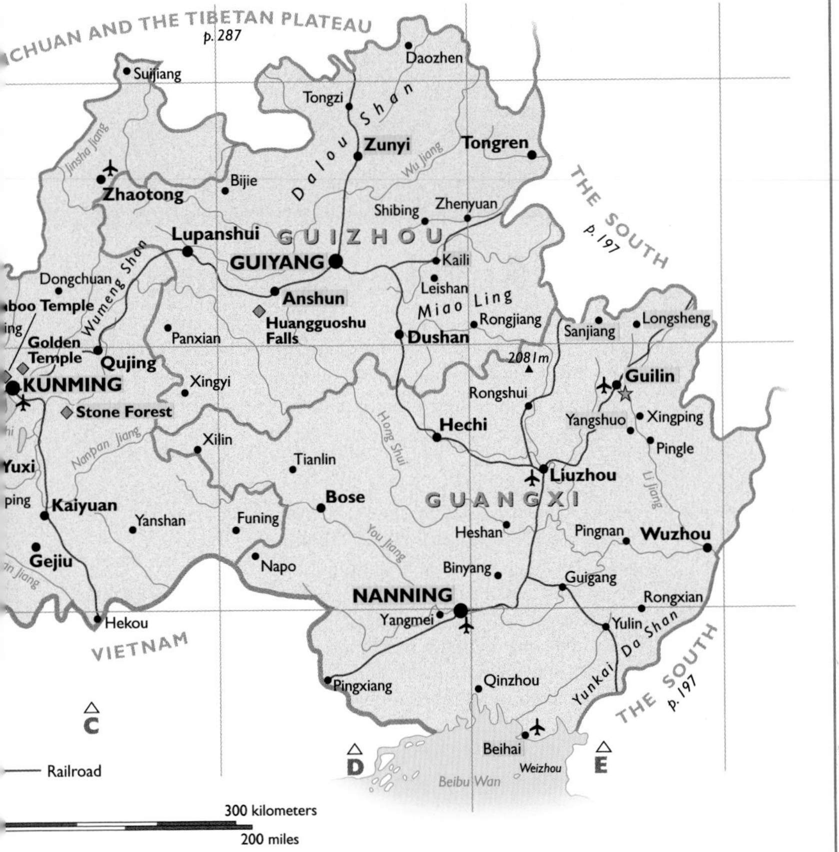

Clement Kunming is a well-placed center for visiting Yunnan Province.

Kunming & around

THE NAME KUNMING COMES FROM A VANISHED MINORITY group called the Kunmi. Capital of Yunnan "South of the Clouds" Province, it has historic temples and pagodas and is an ideal springboard to the rest of this area.

Kunming
259 C2

CITS visitor information
285 Huancheng Nanlu
0871 356-6730

Today, the city has long prospered from being drawn into the whirlwind of economic change sweeping China. This may be the kiss of death for Kunming's more historic architecture, which is being moved aside for modern building projects.

Foreign involvement came with British and French influence in Burma and Indochina respectively. In the 1930s, the daring Burma Road cut 625 miles (1,000 km) through the mountains here, enabling the British and Americans to funnel supplies through Kunming to aid the resistance against the Japanese.

TEMPLES & MOSQUES

The **Yuantong Temple,** in the north of the city on Yuangtong Jie near the zoo, is a huge and fascinating Buddhist complex worthy of an hour or two. Through the secondary gate and past a refreshing stretch of gardens you come to the main "courtyard." From the center of the large, square pool rises an

octagonal temple to Guanyin. Inside are two statues of the goddess of mercy standing back to back; one is a thousand-armed Guanyin (Qianshou Guanyin), the other an offering-child Guanyin (Songzi Guanyin). In the main temple lies a white marble statue of Buddha, presented by the king of Thailand in 1985.

Hui (Muslim) Chinese worship at the rebuilt **Nancheng Ancient Mosque (Nancheng Gusi),** on Zhengyi Lu. If you hanker for lamb kebab sprinkled with cumin, then search the surrounding streets, which abound with Islamic restaurants.

The **West Pagoda (Xisita),** tucked away in the south on Dongsi Jie, was built during the Tang dynasty and can be found in an original part of town. Not far away, on Shulin Jie, are the remains of its brother, the **East Pagoda (Dongsita),** which was toppled by an earthquake in 1833 (tremors are common in Yunnan Province). Both pagodas were once accompanied by now vanished temples.

AROUND KUNMING

The region surrounding Kunming is more tempting than the city itself. The **Golden Temple (Jindian),** also known as the Copper Temple, is a Taoist place of worship 7 miles (11 km) northeast of Kunming on a pine-forested hill. This double-roofed, Ming dynasty structure (completed in 1604) replaces the original that was transported to Dali prefecture. It is amazingly made of copper, built upon a base of marble. The panels are intricately created and decorated: A stylized motif of the character *shou,* or "long-life," is plentifully employed. There isn't an abundance of metal temples in China, but another exists in Wutaishan (see p. 105). You can climb the steps and examine the Golden Temple close up, if you can wedge yourself between the visitors; it's a good idea to get here early to avoid the crowds. The surrounding forest offers inviting walks, threading along paths among the trees.

The Tang dynasty **Bamboo Temple (Qiongzhusi),** 8 miles (13 km) northwest of Kunming, contains 500 eccentric clay Luohan modeled at the end of the 19th century by the Chinese sculptor Li Guangxiu and his students. The Luohan usually appear in a dignified assembly of 18; when portrayed in a group of 500, they tend to be a wilder bunch. Other Chinese temples host such plentiful Luohan, but none have the mannerisms and energy of these. The full range of human emotion is

Yuantong Temple

✉ Yuantong Jie

$ $

SHOPPING

Shopping comes to you in Kunming, rather than the other way around. A vast population of hawkers sell pipes, trinkets, costumes, hats, ceramics, tea, and "angel hair" (Yunnan tobacco) from the city's streets. ■

Some of Li Guangxiu's 500 Luohan statues that inhabit the Bamboo Temple

fashioned in clay by Li's creative fingers. Some are grotesque, others mad, sad, or joyful.

Lake Dian (Dian Chi) is heavily promoted in tourist literature as a worthwhile destination, but it's best avoiding its industrial southern edges. A trip to **Daguan Tower (Daguanlou)** in Daguan Park (Daguan Gongyuan), 2 miles (3 km) to the southwest of the city on Daguan Jie, offers excellent views over the water. An inscription by the Qing dynasty poet Sun Rangwen lauds the view, but that was before industry began polluting the lake. The tower was torched by Muslim rebels in the mid-19th century and later rebuilt.

Also on the shores of the lake is the **Yunnan Nationalities Village (Yunnan Minzu Cun),** a concentration of ethnic minority exhibits from around the province. There are a number of places like this in China, but if you are interested in China's minorities and want to learn about their customs, the best strategy is to visit the areas where the people live (such as Xishuangbanna and northern Yunnan). You can drift over to the summit of the Western Hills, on the western flank of Lake Dian, by cable car from near the Village.

It's more fun to explore the **Western Hills (Xishan)** on foot. From the bus station at Gaoyao, you can make your way up the paths and steps to the summit and the waiting **Dragon Gate (Longmen).** Expect the ascent to take three or more hours. The cliffs on the way up bristle with temples, including **Huating Temple** at the base, **Taihua Temple** farther up, and, as you approach the summit, the Taoist **Sanqing Temple (Sanqingge).** Farther on still, a cluster of grottoes, statues, and pavilions clings to the sheer cliff face, carved by Taoist faithful. Plunging views sweep over Lake Dian below. ■

South of the Clouds cuisine

Kunming is a virtual delicatessen. *Guoqiao mixian* (across-the-bridge noodles) has a nationwide reputation: it's a hot chicken, chili, and vegetable noodle broth that seethes beneath a layer of insulating oil. Served throughout the province is black, gritty, and strong Yunnan coffee *(yunnan kafei)*. Toasted goat's cheese (which you dip into herbs and spices), Yunnan mushrooms, and Yunnan ham could well rob you of the motivation to do anything else but eat during your stay. Interestingly, *nailao* (cheese) is eaten here; it is generally shunned by Chinese, who opt instead for Chinese cheese *(furu)*, a kind of fetid tofu preserved in oil. If you buy a chicken drumstick from a street vendor, check first that it's well cooked. ■

Stone Forest

Weathered, rocky pillars crowd the Stone Forest.

THE LIMESTONE OUTCROPS KNOWN AS THE STONE FOREST (Shilin) bristle 75 miles (120 km) southeast of Kunming. The ashen stone pillars, abandoned by the sea as it receded hundreds of millions of years ago, bunch together into a geological thicket. Their twisted and shattered form is the result of excessive weathering, a natural oddity similar to that found at Wulingyuan (see p. 206).

The journey to the forest is as beautiful as the landscape that surrounds it. Scattered around the stone forest are villages populated by the local ethnic minority, the Sani. They also congregate at the entrance to the Stone Forest and will gladly accompany you as tour guides; you may prefer to go at your own pace. Paths bore between the limestone pillars, past pools, pavilions, and peaks.

Visiting Chinese are enchanted by the game of identifying shapes among the columns, an activity that has given names to many of the formations (e.g., **Buddha Stone** and **Rhinoceros Gazing at the Moon).** The shapes act as points of reference around which you can explore the domain.

The forest, for many Chinese, is Yunnan's main attraction. Visitors give it mixed reports; some say it's a waste of time, while others sing the praises of penetrating into the inner regions. Late in the day is the best time to visit, when the tourists drift away and twilight creates a shifting mood.

You can spend the night at one of the onsite hotels or in the nearby **Five-Tree Village.** The **Stone Forest International Youth Hostel** *(tel 0871 771-0768)* has clean single and double rooms. In the evenings, Sani singing and dancing troupes often perform.

A highway enables visitors to get rapidly to and from Kunming. Many hotels in the city can arrange trips to the Stone Forest. ■

Stone Forest

Map 259 C2

$ $$$$

CITS visitor information

✉ 285 Huancheng Nanlu, Kunming

☎ 0871 356-6730

STAYING HERE

If you want to go independently to the Stone Forest or stay the night there, catch a bus leaving from the bus station or the long-distance bus station on Beijing Lu in Kunming. ■

Dali

Dali
258 B3

Dali Museum
111 Fuxing Lu
$

Visitor Information
Huguo Lu (Foreigner's St.) has travel agents and cafés for tours, tickets, and local information.

DALI IS ONE OF THOSE FEW PLACES IN CHINA WITH AN infectious ambience that waylays those who pass through. Travelers sit back with foaming cappuccinos and banana pancakes, tell tales of their travels, strum guitars, and swap their hiking gear for ethnic togs. Some come to stay for a few days but remain for months.

Dali was once the capital of the Nanzhao Kingdom, a powerful entity separate from China. The region was invaded and subjugated by the Mongols in the 13th century. The largest ethnic minority is the Bai, who speak a Tibetan-Burmese language and whose traditional architecture can be seen at Xizhou, north of town. Dali is famous for its marble, lending its name to the Chinese word for the stone (*dalishi*). Marble pictures can be bought along the main shopping street or viewed at the Dali Museum.

Spring Festival greetings adorn a traditional Dali doorway during Chinese New Year.

DALI MUSEUM

Most of the bronzes and ceramics featured in the Dali Museum (Dali Bowuguan) are from the Nanzhao and Dali state period (8th to 10th century A.D.), and some of the Ming period blue-and-white porcelain is interesting. But the layout is yesteryear Soviet style, and the museum is hampered by a lack of English captions. Luckily, you can escape to the courtyard outside where decapitated statues (probably victims of Red Guard sledgehammers) preside over rows of steles (inscribed stone slates).

At the rear is an enticing (although, again, Englishless) gallery of polished marble slabs whose grain resembles mountains in the clouds and rivers. Try to find the one called "Mountain Devil," an image of a demon caught in stone.

FOREIGNER'S STREET

Foreigner's Street (Yangren Jie) is where visiting Chinese come to watch foreigners eating Western food and buying souvenirs. The real name of the street is Huguo Lu. If you want a change from rice and noodles, you will love the homemade apple pie, cheeseburgers, pizzas, and more offered in all the little restaurants. Some of the food is only vaguely recognizable at best, but some is spot on. The shops

along either side of the street are important to Dali's economy.

ERHAI LAKE

Dali sits near the shore of Erhai Lake (Erhai Hu), a ten-minute cycle ride away. The best views of it are from the Zhonghe Temple (see below). Cormorant fishing is popular here, and your hotel in Dali can arrange this for you.

The lake also acts as a waterway to **Wase,** a traditionally built village on the eastern shore that throws together a lively market on the 5th, 10th, 15th, 20th, 25th, and 30th of each month. **Putuo Island** supports a small community with a temple dedicated to Guanyin. Check in one of the cafés on Foreigner's Street before voyaging over, because a group could well be going. Otherwise, you can jump aboard a boat at the Caicun dock 3 miles (5 km) directly to the east of Dali.

ZHONGHE TEMPLE & BEYOND

The countryside around Dali has dazzling scenery, fascinating temples, and the occasional village showcasing exquisite traditional Bai architecture. A good start is to visit the **Zhonghe Temple,** right outside Dali, up the hillside. You can climb the paths that snake their way up, but it's far better to take a

East of Dali awaits Erhai Lake, popular among cormorant fishermen.

Much of Dali's traditional architecture has been preserved.

Three Pagodas
$$$$

CORMORANT FISHING

The cormorant *(Phalacrocorax carbo)* has long been trained for fishing in China. The sleek swimming birds have rings or tight cords fitted around their throats before fishing. The ring constricts the throat so the bird does not swallow the fish and the fisherman can retrieve his catch. Cormorant fishing continues today, albeit largely for the tourist market. ■

20-minute cable car ride and see the marvelous view of Erhai Lake. The cable car trims the pine trees on the way up, passing numerous Chinese tombs, the occasional tumbledown house, and streams.

At the top, you'll be at the gate to the temple, which embraces both Taoist and Buddhist features. The people guarding the temple are welcoming, and guides (armed with bad English and ponies) will offer to lead you into the woods and on to distant springs, creeks, and waterfalls. These are in the marvelous **Cangshan Mountains,** which form the backdrop to Dali. You can hike out by yourself, but be prepared for changeable weather. A good walk begins from the cable car: Head left on the path through the pine forest and, after about 6 miles (10 km), you will reach seven pools and waterfalls. From here, you can either walk back the way you came or down to the road and get a bus back to Dali.

THREE PAGODAS

The famous Three Pagodas (Santasi) stand a short distance northwest of Dali. They are attractive from a distance, especially early in the morning or at dusk, although hardly worth visiting. The tallest of the three has 16 tiers, reaching 234 feet (72 m) high, and was originally constructed in the ninth century. The cable-car trip to the Zhonghe Temple affords an excellent view of the Pagodas.

GUANYIN TEMPLE

Three miles (5 km) south of Dali is a fascinating little Guanyin Temple (Guanyintang), dedicated to the Buddhist goddess of mercy. In the small shrine in front of the main temple (Daxiong Baodian) is an effigy of the goddess worshiped by the 18 Luohan (arhat). The Luohan stand on little niches carved into a cliff face, all exhibiting vivid and lively facial expressions. One has a huge, extended arm that grabs at what appears to be the moon in the clouds. Another holds his trousers up and has telescopic legs. On his left swoons a drunken arhat; another rides a tiger, while yet another pulls open his stomach to reveal a Buddha inside. Spot the one with the extra-long eyebrows.

The complex is an active nunnery. The large hall at the rear houses a collection of *pusa* (bodhisattvas), while the inner courtyard has a small, square temple built over a boulder and encircled by a pond crossed by a bridge. The boulder was apparently rolled into position by the goddess to stall an advancing army.

The two golden characters on the right-hand door as you enter the compound mean "Wheel of the Law," or *falun* in Chinese.

GANTONG TEMPLE & JIZHAO NUNNERY

Tucked away in the pine-clad mountains above the Guanyin temple is the tiny Buddhist **Gantong**

Temple. It's quite a hike up the hill (about an hour; come out of the Guanyin Temple, turn into the first right and keep going). Horse carts often plod by, however, and will take you up for a small fee.

Just above the temple in the trees is a small **dagoba,** where you may find monks practicing *gongfu*. Another five minutes into the woods is the **Jizhao (Quiet Illumination) Nunnery,** with a peaceful courtyard laid out with beautiful gardens.

XIZHOU

Fifteen miles (24 km) north of Dali is this gem of a village, a must-see for architecture enthusiasts. Much of the original Bai architecture is well preserved, and that which is not crumbles into picturesque decay. A few interesting Bai courtyards have been sectioned off and here there is an entry fee. A slow amble through the streets is by far the best approach.

Doors with colorfully painted eaves yield to active courtyards where children play, chickens squawk, dogs fight, and all the rhythms of family life play out. Here and there, amazingly, you will see a 19th-century Western door, complete with marble pillars and classical pomposity, relic of an early European presence.

The village is exceptionally photogenic and the maze of little streets a charming place to get lost in. Cultural Revolution buffs will revel in hunting down the former local party headquarters and graffiti of the Cultural Revolution era. One such, on a gaunt and lifeless building, proudly declares "Serve the People," in Mao's calligraphy with his signature next to it. Flanking it are the scrubbed-out characters "Study Mao Zedong Thought." They remain ghostly, indelible shadows.

SHAPING MARKET & BUTTERFLY SPRING

The town of Shaping, about 20 miles (32 km) north of Dali, buzzes with a popular market on Mondays. You can visit the **Butterfly Spring (Hudie Quan)** en route *(3 miles/5 km south, west of road)*; it swarms with butterflies in spring. ■

The tallest of Dali's Three Pagodas, Qianxun Pagoda dates back to the ninth century.

Jade Dragon Snow Mountain rises over Lijiang, suggestive of Tibet to the north.

Lijiang

IN THE FOOTHILLS OF TIBET LIES LIJIANG, IN NORTHWEST Yunnan Province, a splendid little town that is home to the ancient Naxi people. Almost bursting at the seams with visitors, the town has undergone considerable transformation—including a pounding from an earthquake in 1996—since drifting onto the tourist radar in the 1980s. The town is worth a visit, and valiant efforts have been made to preserve disappearing arts such as its timeless Naxi music. The stunning Jade Dragon Snow Mountain hints at the Land of Snows to the north, and Tiger Leaping Gorge awaits the adventurous.

Lijiang

258 B3

Visitor information

Any of the hotels or cafés in the old town

OLD TOWN

The old town of Lijiang is a wonderful maze of traditional Naxi architecture, pitted against the new section, an encroachment of breeze blocks and ceramic tiling. It's a marvel at night, when the Chinese roofs are festooned with lights and sparkle against the evening sky; the old quarter is a dreamscape of dark cobbled streets, gushing canals, and paths trailing away from the main street. Wooden doors are thrown open to reveal the cozy interiors of Naxi and Western restaurants.

Study the architecture. Many of the traditional structures survived the 1996 earthquake, which measured 7 on the Richter scale and leveled other areas in the town. The buildings charm you with their engaging and satisfying harmonies. Substantial half-timbered and earthen houses have solid wooden gates, central courtyards, and eaves carved with fish and symbols for good luck. Wander around to your heart's content and get lost if you wish; there aren't many parts of China such as Lijiang.

The morning sees a bustling local market animating the streets of the old town, providing a lively montage of blue-clothed Naxi women. As well as local produce, you can buy tourist staples such as embroidery, hand-beaten copper pots, or carved wooden birds.

Black Dragon Pool (Heilongtan) in the north of town is a large park containing a pond, pavilions, and a museum dedicated to the shamanistic Dongba religion that the Naxi people brought with them from Tibet.

If you are out for a twilight stroll, walk along the narrow street south along the canal that borders the main street to the west, and try one of the restaurants here. Several of these serve traditional Naxi food such as *baba,* a local flatbread; others celebrate food from around the world. Western cafés are common in the old town, providing Internet access and knowledgeable advice on jaunts into the surrounding region. Round off the evening by taking in one of the shows featuring Naxi music (see sidebar p. 270).

For a panoramic view of Lijiang take one of the roads west away from the canal, climb up the hill past the radio station, and go on to **Wangulou,** a pavilion that overlooks the town. The rooftops of Lijiang stretch out below.

JADE DRAGON SNOW MOUNTAIN

If the weather is clear, a visit to the breathtaking Jade Dragon Snow Mountain (Yulongxueshan), 21 miles (34 km) north of Lijiang, is mandatory. The mighty mountain rises raggedly above Lijiang, encrusted with snow and (if you're lucky) set against a sharp, blue sky. It's an alluring sight that can make for dramatic photography. Be warned that the elevation can make some people feel queasy: Lijiang sits at 7,924 feet (2,415 m), high enough to affect some, and the mountain's summit soars to 18,354 feet (5,596 m).

Blue-clothed Naxi throng Lijiang's picturesque streets.

If it's cloudy or misty, don't bother. During the rainy season at the end of summer, it's often exactly that; late autumn and winter are the ideal seasons. Cable cars (one from the Snow Flower Mountain Village, itself reachable by local bus from Lijiang) take you to idyllic spots for the best views.

Jade Dragon Snow Mountain
$ $$$

BAISHA

Baisha village, about 5 miles (8 km) north of Lijiang, is noted for its collection of faded religious frescoes (*bihua*) that took a hammering during the Cultural Revolution. As with many Buddhist treasures around China, the collected scars tell a more vivid story than the relics themselves. In Baisha, some of the figures have had their faces bluntly scratched away, while here and there vandals have etched their names into the paintwork (a Mr. Yang is proudly recorded).

You can't photograph the frescoes; expect a big fine if you do. If this is an attempt to protect the works of art, it is laughable considering their condition. The lighting is very gloomy and it is

NAXI MUSIC

For good evening entertainment, a highly recommended cultural event is presented by Naxi orchestras in Lijiang. Currently there are two venues; both begin at 8 p.m. One is the Naxi Ancient Music Palace *(75 Xingwu, tel 0872 518-3710, $)*; the other is the Dayan Naxi Music Association *(74 Mishi Alley, tel 0872 512-7971, $)*. Many

of the played tunes were rescued from oblivion by elder members of the band (some in their 70s and 80s). Colorful ethnic dancing and solo singing spice up the show, and a venerable Naxi sage does a sword dance. You can take photographs. ■

difficult to make any coherent sense of the pictures without a guide. Naxi dancers perform for a fee as you exit.

The other gem of Baisha is the legendary Dr. Ho, an enthusiastic Taoist physician who operates from his Clinic of Chinese Herbs in Jade Dragon Mountains of Lijiang. Patients come away wide eyed with sachets of a powdery tea. Some people swear by his potions.

Generally, visitors rent bikes and pedal out on unpaved roads to visit the sites around Lijiang. To reach the nearby unspoiled village of **Longquan,** turn left off the road about 2 miles (3 km) north of Lijiang. In the village, the Ming dynasty **Dajue Temple** still retains its frescoed walls. Across a narrow bridge over roaring water lies the **Nine Vessel Dragon Pool (Jiuding Longtan),** a clear blue pool otherwise simply called Dragon Spring; behind it is an attractive hall.

TIBETAN MONASTERIES

Also in the foothills of Jade Dragon Snow Mountain is the **Yufeng Monastery,** a Tibetan lamasery about 3 miles (5 km) north of Baisha. The monastery is famous for a 500-year-old camellia tree that flowers profusely in spring.

A number of other Tibetan temples survive in the region. You will find frescoes at the **Fuguo Monastery** not far from Baisha, and the **Puji Monastery** just northwest of Lijiang contains some original Tibetan features.

TIGER LEAPING GORGE

The adventure of visiting Tiger Leaping Gorge is the main reason many visitors come to Lijiang. If the weather is fine, it is one of the most striking treks in China.

With Jade Dragon Snow Mountain as a breathtaking backdrop, the Jinsha River flows through the gorge, later swelling into the mighty Yangtze River. The gorge is a dramatic and thrilling journey, but traversing it is not a picnic. Changeable weather (especially during the rainy season at the end of summer) can catch hikers without warning, and periodic landslides and falling rocks can be lethal. Several travelers have been killed while navigating the gorge.

That said, the majority of ramblers experience no mishap. Time is a factor, and you will need two days for the trip, but if you have a generous schedule this can be extended to three or four days, or as long as you like. You can stay the night at

one of the hostels at the midpoint, **Walnut Grove,** and prepare for the next leg.

To tackle the gorge, embark from either **Qiaotou** or **Daju,** both of which are connected to Lijiang by bus. The most popular route sets out from Daju across the field and then goes over the river by ferry. This crossing can be hard to find, so it might be a good idea to find a guide either in Lijiang or in Daju to accompany you. It's a 10-mile (16 km) hike to Walnut Grove, and from there you have a choice of two paths. The lower one is a proper road and is quicker, but it is prone to periodic landslides, which can make trekking hazardous. Figure on about six hours to reach Qiaotou following this route. The upper road—slower but safer (although it can also be treacherous after heavy rain)—should take you about nine hours. Take water.

It's advisable to check at one of the foreign cafés in Lijiang for news on conditions in the gorge before you set out. A number of cafés have hand-drawn maps of the gorge, as well as addresses and phone numbers of guesthouses in Walnut Grove, Daju, and Qiaotou. They can also offer sound advice to travelers. Some of what they tell you can be essential—for example, news of a temporary stoppage of the ferry service across the river. ■

Tiger Leaping Gorge
$ $$

The Yangtze River, here called the Jinsha River, crashes through Tiger Leaping Gorge from the heights of Tibet.

Xishuangbanna

The name Xishuangbanna is derived from Sip Sawng Panna—Twelve Rice Growing Districts.

YUNNAN MERGES WITH SOUTHEAST ASIA IN THE REGION of Xishuangbanna. Bordering Laos and Myanmar (Burma), it is an abundant, though dwindling Eden of plant and animal life. Hiding off trails that snake into the forest are scattered temples, stupas, and a host of minority communities, some of which have marginal contact with the outside world. The farther you delve, the more you will discover. Arm yourself with decent mosquito repellent, food, and water, and leave the provincial capital, Jinghong, to track down some of these occasionally elusive villages. Between June and August Xishuangbanna is a sauna, raining violently almost every day.

Xishuangbanna
 258 B1

JINGHONG

At the hub of the Xishuangbanna (or just "Banna") region, Jinghong is best used as a base from which to explore the surrounding territory. The Lancang River, otherwise known as the Mekong River, flows through the city before coursing into Myanmar.

Jinghong has a varied ethnic mix (the Dai are the largest minority), which finds expression in the food, skin color, and bone structure of its residents. But much of the

more traditional, regional architecture is missing. It's best to treat the city as a communications center.

At the **Tropical Flowers & Plants Garden (Redai Huahuiyuan),** you can leaf through an encyclopedia of tropical plant life. There are over 1,000 species of plants here, many under threat in their natural habitat. The institute, lying off Jinghong Xilu in the west of Jinghong, vividly captures the range of Xishuangbanna's diverse plant life.

Manting Park (Manting Gongyuan), on the city's southern edge, can make for a reasonable distraction. The local tourist authorities dress up visiting Chinese in ethnic costumes to pose in front of a statue of ex-premier Zhou Enlai (also garbed in local costume). There's an aviary here with hundreds of peacocks strolling around: Spring is the best time to catch them in boisterous plumage. A couple of Buddhist temples on the grounds are worth a visit, including the Buddhist **Manting Temple** just next to the path. As with most temples in the region, you have to remove your shoes before entering.

The **National Minorities Park (Minzu Fengguangyuan),** off Minhang Lu in the south of the city, is a rather tired tribal gala that should be avoided.

AROUND JINGHONG & SURROUNDING VILLAGES

The secret to getting the most out of Xishuangbanna is to put on your explorer's hat and get off the beaten path. Around Jinghong is a plethora of small villages and towns on forest fringes, many of which are reachable by bus or bike. You have to reign in your wanderlust, as some destinations (such as Demenglong) are virtually on China's borders and trespassing without a visa may not go down too well with the Myanmar (Burma) or Lao authorities.

Before you bolt into the undergrowth, do yourself a favor and work out a plan of attack on the region. A good idea is to call in at the **Mei Mei Café** *(tel 0691 212-7324)* at the top of Manting Lu (running south to Manting Temple) in Jinghong, the nearby CITS office, or any Western café nearby. The Mei Mei Café has books of collected wisdom from travelers and excellent advice from those who have explored the region. This is also a great place to meet others and negotiate a strategy for tackling Xishuangbanna.

Traveling by bike is feasible and puts you within reach of a number of adventures. It's important to check the tires and brakes carefully

CITS visitor information

✉ Luandan Lu, or try the cafés along Manting Lu

☎ 0691 663-8459

Tropical Flowers & Plants Garden

✉ 28 Jinghong Xilu

$ $

Treasures such as the golden stupa at the Ganlanba Temple entice adventurers out of Jinghong.

Saffron-robed Dai monks represent the pronounced influence of Southeast Asian Buddhist culture in Xishuangbanna.

before you set out. You can head for Ganlanba by bike (which should take you about three hours) and cross the Mekong River at Ganlanba by barge, where you will find a cluster of little villages on the other side.

If you do head into the wilds for a few nights, it's imperative to take sunblock, a flashlight, insect repellent, toilet paper, food, water, and water sterilization tablets. Despite the low incidence of malaria, antimalarial tablets should also be taken if heading into village areas, and be on your guard against snakes.

Ganlanba

Ganlanba (Menghan), south along the Mekong River, is an exciting minibus drive away, following the great river. The **Ganlanba Temple (Menghan Chunman Dafosi),** originally built in A.D. 583, was badly damaged during the Cultural Revolution and last restored in 1997. The building features traditional Dai architecture, with cross beams, ocher-and-gold paint, and expertly laid roof slating. The huge statue of Buddha inside is surrounded by a group of smaller effigies.

Part of the main temple is put aside as a classroom for the children of the Buddhist school in the compound. Outside the temple, hedged in by plants and shrubs, stands a bright golden stupa. The monks seem very relaxed about visitors passing through; they have a souvenir desk in the main temple.

The temple is set on the grounds of a **Dai minority garden (Daizuyuan).** If you head away from the temple, you can explore the countryside and visit traditional Dai communities (the road follows the riverside and you might find a boat that will ferry you to small, inhabited islands in the river).

Heading farther out of town will take you into agricultural countryside. Travelers report joining tours such as a three-day expedition from Ganlanba back to Jinghong, via Jinuo and Mengyang. Mengyang has a banyan tree *(rongshu)* shaped like an elephant that attracts tour groups. You may well get the opportunity to stay with Dai families in the area.

Mengla

The countryside around Mengla, 125 miles (200 km) southeast of Jinghong (six hours by bus), has exciting treks and traditional Yao villages. People are sometimes welcomed into minority homes to spend the night, although invitations should be accepted cautiously; there are a few negative tales.

Damenglong

In and around Damenglong, 43 miles (69 km) south of Jinghong, are the rather gaudy **Black Pagoda** and **Manfeilong Pagoda.** The Black Pagoda sits on the hill above town, and the Manfeilong Pagoda is a short motorbike taxi ride out of

town. The sight of saffron-robed monks wearing sunglasses and riding motorbikes around town is a treat.

Striking out in almost any direction from the main road of Damenglong, however, will take you into a countryside of forests and farmland, with occasional temples twinkling from the foliage (but remember the border is only a few miles to the south). Other temples crumble and return to nature.

Alternative expeditions from Damenglong can be made by the more intrepid to **Manguanghan village** and **Guangmin,** where the Hani minority lives, or to **Manpo,** and its Bulang people.

Menghai, Menghun, & Xiding

Other villages reachable by public transport west from Jinghong include Menghai, Menghun, and Xiding. All have Sunday markets that are full of ethnic flavor. The Thursday market in Xiding starts in the morning, with Dai and Hani villagers coming in from the surrounding area. Take the bus from Jinghong to Menghai and Xiding.

SANCHA RIVER NATURE PRESERVE

Sancha River Nature Preserve (Sanchahe Ziran Baohuqu), 15 miles (24 km) north of Jinghong, is a vast protected forest region that can be explored. ■

Dai street vendors

Water-splashing Festival

The traditional Dai minority Water-splashing Festival is held every year in mid-April. The Buddhist Dai celebrate the occasion by drenching everything that moves in a bid to cleanse away the dirt and ills of the old year. This is the most popular time of the year, and Jinghong is generally packed with visitors. The event is a three-day gala that culminates with the great soaking. The ritual has been hijacked by the local tourism industry, which performs daily Water-splashing events at select sites, including Manting Park. ■

Guilin

Guilin
259 E2 & 276

CITS visitor information
41 Binjiang Lu, and tourist information booths can be found around town
0773 286-1623 or 282-8314

Wave-subduing Hill
276
Binjiang Beilu
$

Folded Brocade Hill
Diecai Lu
$

FOR CENTURIES, CHINESE POETS, PAINTERS, AND AESTHETES have used Guilin and its environs in Guangxi Province as a yardstick for natural beauty. Celebrated for its karst limestone pinnacles, the city was unsuccessfully besieged by Taiping rebels in 1852; some complain that tour groups have put the city under similar duress. Nonetheless, Guilin has considerable appeal and Yangshuo, a boat trip away along the scenic Li River, is a delight.

Rising from the center of Guilin, **Solitary Beauty Peak (Duxiufeng)** commands stunning views over the town and down to the Li River sparkling to the south. Not far to the east is **Wave-subduing Hill (Fuboshan),** whose slopes are punctuated with a number of caves.

Folded Brocade Hill (Diecaishan) is an attractive hike north of Solitary Beauty Peak. Hot, summer climbs are cooled by the refreshing **Wind Cave** to your right soon into your ascent. Actually, there are two caves here that funnel the wind between them in a fresh breeze. Putting your arms around the small, supine laughing Buddha (Milefo) will reputedly bring you good luck. A larger Milefo sits joyously in the other cave.

At the summit of **Four Views Hill,** climbers enjoy excellent views of other Guilin peaks. A museum at the base of the mount houses a fine collection of colorful butterflies.

Seven Star Park (Qixing Gongyuan), east across the Li River by way of Liberation Bridge, is a well-tended park studded with seven peaks thought to resemble the Great Bear constellation. The many caves that honeycomb the hills are geologically garish, but picturesque scenery, bridges, woods, and lily-choked ponds can also be found. The grass is lush and well managed, especially in front of **Camel Hill,** where a plinth commemorates a speech made at this spot in 1998 by former President Bill Clinton (he spoke on environmental issues).

The geological oddity of **Elephant Trunk Hill (Xiangbishan),** with its "trunk" in the Li River, is worth a peek. You can be photographed standing under a seething mass of pigeons or with local Zhuang minority props, but it's more fun to paddle in the clear waters of the Li River (unless

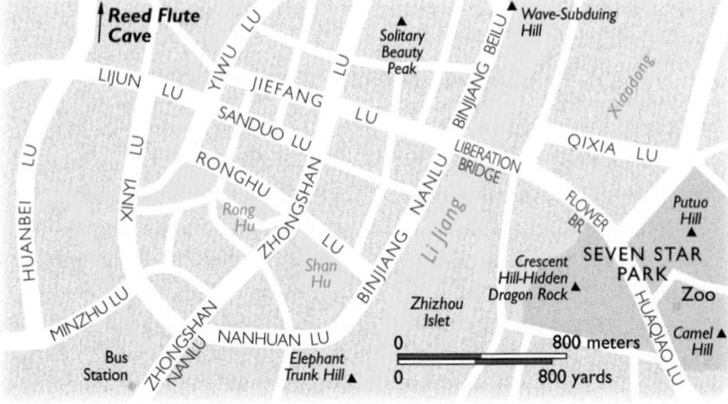

Calligraphy and Buddhist statuary decorate the walls of breezy Wind Cave on Folded Brocade Hill.

it's winter). You can then dry your feet on the banks and eat a toasted Li River fish bought with small change. Clamber up to a cave, take a trip on a bamboo raft into the river for more comprehensive views, or take to the waters watching cormorants fishing.

A pleasant bike ride takes you to **Reed Flute Cave (Ludiyan),** northwest of town. The cave has some of the most arresting scenery in Guilin. The whistle-stop tour gushes through a cavernous labyrinth of stalactites and stalagmites gaudily illuminated by disco lights. Water drips, covering the rocks in a cold sheen. The way can be slippery, so hold on to the rails. The tour leader casts a torch beam here and there, illuminating a snowman, a lion, or a giant sunflower leaping out from the gnarled formations. It's a magnificent product of nature, especially the vast crystal palace of the Dragon King, a huge aircraft hanger of a cave, partially suspended over a very cold lake. Unfortunately, the production-line tour commercializes the mystery out of the place: Ignore the sales pitch and enter without a guide, if you can.

The **Li River** flows right through Guilin, and two lakes (Banyan Lake and Fir Lake) rest next to each other in the center of town. The Li River makes for a fascinating stroll in the early morning, its banks dotted with a crowd of *taiji* enthusiasts, ballroom dancers, and sun worshipers.

About half a mile (0.8 km) north of Seven Star Park is the **Minorities Cultural Park,** an artificial tour through the minority realms of the Guangxi Zhuang Autonomous Region (the full name of this province).

Crime is a flourishing reality in Guilin, primarily because of the large number of foreign tourists, and the illegal economy runs from pickpocketing to prostitution and beyond. Never forget the fact that showcase tourist destinations such as Guilin are frontier towns that attract itinerant thieves and pimps. Try to establish prices (such as taxi fares) before committing yourself. ■

Reed Flute Cave
Map 276
Ludi Lu
$$

Li River cruise

One of the most popular trips in China, the Li River (Lijiang) cruise takes you past a panorama of bamboo groves, sleepy villages, and karst peaks. This is also the most picturesque way to reach fabled Yangshuo to the south of Guilin. The scenery en route is a splash of coffee-table book colors and, as you approach Yangshuo, some of the most idyllic in China.

A cruise to Yangshuo takes between five and six hours. The river is not navigable along its complete length through the year, and the best seasons are spring and autumn. Winter waters are too low to allow boat tours, and the summer heat is oppressively sticky. If you are lucky enough to have a clear day, the flat water offers a two-fold reflection of the idyllic scenery.

Your ticket should include a buffet meal and a return bus ride to Guilin. Getting aboard one of these boats, however, may put you at the cutting edge of the Guilin market economy. The boat trip down the Li River to Yangshuo is considered by many travelers to be extortionately priced *($$$$)*, which may leave you cold. As a result, some travelers take the bus to Yangshuo for a more piecemeal, but cheaper, look at the surrounding region. Once you get there, Yangshuo has the advantage of being far more easygoing than Guilin.

The boats will carry you slowly down the 52-mile (83 km) stretch, taking you past rock formations fancifully christened by painters and poets. The names of the mountains comprise a dictionary of the fantastic, religious, and decorative: Look for Dragonhead Hill, Boy Worshiping Guanyin, Bat Peak, and Nine Horses Painting Hill. Nestling between the peaks are sleepy villages, while fishermen move along the riverbanks.

Elephant Trunk Hill (Xiangbishan) is clearly identifiable as the ungainly formation appears to drink from the river. **Pagoda Hill (Tashan)** drifts by to the east, a peak topped by the tapering form of a Ming dynasty pagoda. **Cock-Fighting Hill**

A centuries-old way of life accompanies the timeless karst landscape along the Li River.

(Douji) 1 gives the impression of battling roosters, while Moon Cave drills through the side of **Tunnel Hill (Chuanshan).**

Rising south of Millstone Hill (beyond the riverside town of Daxu) is **Bat Peak (Bianfushan)** 2**,** its sheer cliffs resembling the airborne mammals. Bats are fortuitous symbols in China; the words for bat and good fortune are homonyms.

Farther down the river are **Dragons Play in the Water (Qunlong Xishui),** rocky outlines of the magical dragons dispatched by the Jade Emperor (see p. 73) to gather sweet-scented osmanthus flowers.

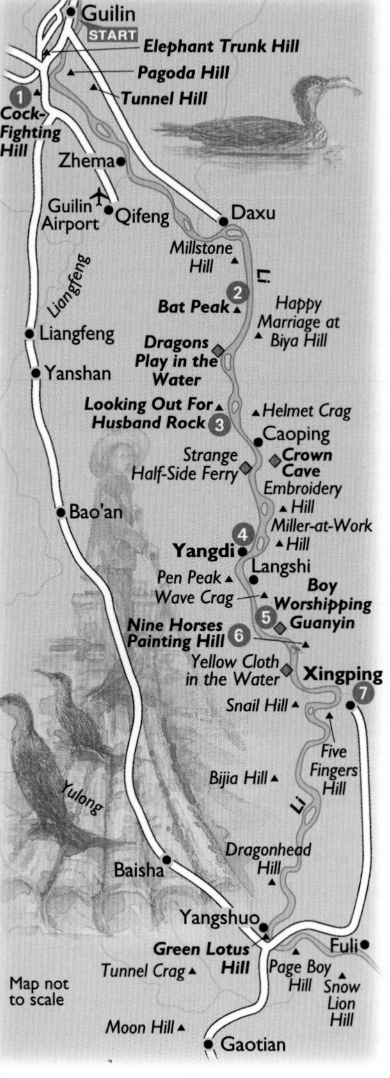

Looking Out For Husband Rock (Wangfushi) 3 resembles a maiden with a young child on her back. She gazes into the distance, awaiting the return of her spouse.

The boat nudges past **Caoping** village and the dark depths of **Crown Cave (Guanyan)** on the eastern bank. Beyond lies the thatched village of **Yangdi** 4**,** among the dense bamboo fronds that stretch out over the river. **Wave Stone Misty Rain (Langshi Yanyu)** is a hazy phenomenon conjured up by the mists that cloak the river in autumn, absent in clear weather.

The **Boy Worshiping Guanyin** 5 is supposed to resemble a respectful toddler communing with the goddess of mercy. Before you reach Xingping you will see **Nine Horses Painting Hill (Jiuma Huashan)** 6**,** a jagged monument to the forces that molded this landscape. Among the sharp lines and dramatic fissures dance the images of nine horses. The full herd of steeds is elusive, but those with a good imagination can usually count seven.

Surrounding picturesque **Xingping** 7 is some of the most breathtaking scenery on the voyage. You can easily return to it from Yangshuo for a closer inspection.

Wave good-bye to **Five Fingers Hill (Wuzhishan),** creep by **Snail Hill (Luoshishan),** and float on to **Dragonhead Hill (Longtoushan).** This marks the arrival of the boat in Yangshuo, where it moors under **Green Lotus Hill (Bilianfeng).** ■

Also see area map p. 259
Guilin
52 miles (83 km)
5–6 hours
Yangshuo

NOT TO BE MISSED

- Looking Out For Husband Rock
- Boy Worshiping Guanyin
- Nine Horses Painting Hill

Yangshuo & around

Yangshuo
259 E2

CITS visitor information
Travel agents & Western traveler-oriented cafés line Xi Jie & Pantao Lu

YANGSHUO IS A LEGENDARY CORNER OF CHINA, A pastoral patchwork of fields, rivers, and limestone peaks. Its uniqueness has attracted a mixture of Western cafés, dazed travelers, musicians, poets, and itinerant idealists. It is the China that some travelers make the journey specifically to find. Green Lotus Peak (Bilianfeng), Yangshuo's most famous peak, overlooks the Li River, with long views up- and downstream.

There are a few peaks in Yangshuo itself, but you will soon learn that the true gems lie outside town. By renting a bike, you will throw open the entire surrounding countryside to exploration.

The otherworldliness of **Moon Hill** is about a 30-minute bike ride to the south *(take Pantao Lu out of town)*. This journey alongside the Li River from Yangshuo is a dream. Towering karst peaks surround, rivers glitter, and herds of water buffalo munch lazily at the wayside. After you arrive at the base of Moon Hill and jostle past the gaggle of water sellers at the gate (stock up), it's a solid half-hour ascent up the steps, through tunnels of bamboo and a crescendo of cicadas, to the top. Here rises **Moon Arch,** which gives the hill its name. The

The limestone outcrops around Yangshuo are China's largest and most beautiful cluster of peaks.

Fishermen on the Li River tame cormorants—glossy underwater swimmers—to help them catch fish.

true summit, a further five-minute climb, offers breathtaking views: Below is a canvas splashed with rivers, emerald-green karst peaks, and little hamlets. The best time of day is early in the morning or approaching twilight. Hawkers will draw your attention to an ancient **Big Banyan Tree,** visible on the land below, selling postcards of it in every conceivable season.

Near Moon Hill, guides pounce to show you **Black Buddha Caves, New Water Caves,** and **Dragon Cave.** The cave networks include underground streams, waterfalls, and huge subterranean pools.

Yangshuo also puts you within range of villages along the Li River. Pretty **Fuli** can be reached by boat, bus, or bike; an alternative is to rent an inner tube (in summer) from one of the cafés or perhaps a raft or kayak. Market day is a tempting occasion to catch the local minorities: It's held twice a week.

The other road much traveled is to **Xingping** (see p. 279), which you will have passed if you took the Li River cruise from Guilin (see pp. 278–79). The scenery around Xingping is a condensation of this attractive region, enveloped by peaks. The picturesque village is hewn from stone and has a few places where you can overnight. Farther up the Li River you will come to the village of **Yangdi** (see p. 279), which you can also reach from Yangshuo.

Back in Yangshuo, **Pantao Lu** and especially **Xi Jie** are the crossroads of the Yangshuo Western food industry. Taking a stroll in this neighborhood is essential to get laidback Yangshou in perspective. Here you will find a constellation of funky little cafés with intriguing names: Under the Moon Café, Minnie Mao's, and the Meiyou Café. These are, along with Dali (see pp. 264–67) and Lijiang (see pp. 268–71), a frontline against an endless diet of rice and noodles. There are plentiful Chinese restaurants for local food.

Xi Jie is also a mildly anarchic way forward for China's holiday industry. The café owners speak English, mimic Western cooking, and arrange tours to the surrounding areas. They respond to the needs of Western travelers, a significant improvement over other parts of China. Guided tours of the area are available, which could be worthwhile if you don't have the time to tackle the area single-handed.

Xi Jie also swarms with souvenir stores, silk bargains, calligraphy, and leechlike trinket sellers who will doggedly pursue you. Eating al fresco at any of the cafés will invite them to stand next to you during your meal, bleating occasionally.

An evening attraction in Yangshuo is cormorant fishing (see p. 267); tours to accompany the fishermen can be taken from the pier. The sleek birds are deft at catching prey, lured to the surface by bright lamps. ■

Beihai

A fishing family dries its take under a scorching sun on Dijiao.

POKING INTO THE SEA ON A STUB OF LAND EAST OF Vietnam, Beihai and its beaches are still a backwater, but the city was once a treaty port, swarming with British, Dutch, and German traders. It preserves its crumbling concession architecture so typical of port towns along China's coast to the west.

If you're planning a trip to Hainan Island (see pp. 218–19) from Yangshuo, Guilin, or Nanning, spend a day here before you hop on a ferry to the southern climes. The city is awash with pearls that have been cultivated here for thousands of years, and sea breezes funnel through the boulevard's banyans.

The historic Western quarter of embassy buildings, schools, and churches was shoehorned into an area along Zhongshan Lu in the north of town, rather like Shamian Island in Guangzhou. The old shells remain, now requisitioned by a new breed of merchants. The sunny streets are redolent of Macau in the shaded sidewalks that run under arcades created by the overhanging upper stories supported on pillars. The grand old **British Embassy** building, somewhat derelict these days, is not far from **Zhongshan Park. Dijiao,** a nub of land in the northwest of town, is the heart of Beihai's fishing community.

Silver Beach (Yintan), just 6 miles (10 km) to the south of Beihai, is touted as one of China's best, but remember that beach culture is still in its infancy in China. That said, this is a clean stretch of white sand.

A 22-mile (35 km) boat trip to the south will bring you to the small volcanic island of **Weizhou (Weizhoudao).** The island supports a French cathedral attended by a respectful congregation. Chinese Catholics sought sanctuary here after persecution, and many of the local population are still nominally Roman Catholic. ■

Beihai
259 E1

CITS visitor information
3rd floor, Shangri-La Hotel
0779 8060

GETTING TO WEIZHOU

Ferries from Weizhou at 8:15 a.m. from the Beihai International Ferry Terminal (Beihai Guoji Keyun Matou) on Yintan Lu. ■

More places to visit in the Southwest

ANSHUN

The pleasant city of Anshun, in Guizhou Province, is close to **Huangguoshu Falls (Huangguoshu Pubu).** Formerly involved in the opium trade, Anshun has a **Confucius Temple (Wenmiao)** south of Hongshan Reservoir. Huangguoshu Falls, 28 miles (45 km) to the southwest, is the highlight of a vast scenic area riddled with caves and decorated with karst peaks. The falls cascade (most vigorously in the rainy summer season) through a region populated by the Bouyei minority, distinguished by their batik-making skills.

259 D3 **CTS visitor information**
Tashan Donglu 0853 323-4662

GUIYANG

This little-visited city, capital of Guizhou Province, is a useful stopover en route to the provincial drawing card, the Huangguoshu Falls. The city also puts you within reach of other parts of Guizhou rich in ethnic culture, most notably Kaili (see below) and the southeast. Guizhou's many minorities include the Miao, Bouyei, Zhuang, Dong, and Hui.

Near the summit of the mount in **Qianling Park (Qianling Gongyuan),** in the northeast section of town, is the **Hongfu Temple,** a very impressive early Qing dynasty monument with excellent views over the city. The **Qianming Temple** is just north of the Nanming River, near a flourishing market selling birds and flowers, and the **provincial museum,** in the north of town, focuses on the life and culture of Guizhou's ethnic minorities.

259 D3 **CITS visitor information**
20 Yan'an Zhonglu 0851 690-1660
Guizhou Provincial Museum Beijing Lu
$ Closed Mon.

KAILI & AROUND

Kaili opens the southeast of the province to exploration if you are interested in Guizhou's colorful ethnic world. This region remains less popular than Yunnan Province and is less commercialized (although this means more primitive facilities). Probe the small towns and villages such as Chong'an, Shibing, Zhenyuan, Leishan, and Yongle.

259 D3 **CITS visitor information**
Yingpan Hotel, 53 Yingpan Donglu
0855 822-2506

NANNING

Capital of the Guangxi Zhuang Autonomous Region, Nanning hardly sparkles with interest, but it is a useful juncture for those bound for Vietnam. **Guangxi Provincial Museum (Guangxi Bowuguan)** on Minzu Dadao ($) in the southeast of the city introduces elements of regional minority culture and history. Fifteen miles (24 km) to the northwest are the stalactite-encrusted **Yiling Caves.** The attractive and historical Qing dynasty town of **Yangmei,** 16 miles (26 km) west of Nanning, makes for an interesting and popular day trip.

259 D2 **CTS visitor information**
40 Xinmin Lu 0771 280-4960

SANJIANG & LONGSHENG

While these two towns in north Guangxi Province are featureless conurbations in themselves, they are portals to enticing minority villages and the stunning landscape that seasons the region. Sanjiang is an enclave of the Dong minority, while Longsheng is an authentic jumble of Zhuang, Dong, Yao, and Miao minorities.

The undulating region surrounding Longsheng (a 3- to 4-hour bus ride from Guilin to the northwest) is delightfully sculptured with rice terraces, but the highlights for their sheer scale are **Dragon's Spine Rice Terraces** at Longji, 12 miles (19 km) from Longsheng. Yao farmers are behind the genius of these layered slopes, and climbing to the top is essential to get a wide-angle view.

Another 30 miles (48 km) to the west of Longsheng lies the covered **Chengyang Wind and Rain Bridge (Fengyuqiao),** not far from Sanjiang. Set in a fertile valley amid Dong villages, the bridge was built by the villagers in 1916 and is a perfect example of local craftsmanship, constructed with a beautiful thoroughness and without the use of nails.

259 E3 ■

The strong religious persuasion of Sichuan finds expression in the temples of Chengdu, Dazu's Buddhist statuary, the mountains of Emeishan, and Leshan's colossal Buddha. The mountain fastness of Tibet overlooks Sichuan to the west.

Sichuan & the Tibetan Plateau

A giant panda

Sichuan & the Tibetan Plateau

DESPITE BEING DISTINCT ENTITIES, SICHUAN AND TIBET (COLLECTIVELY called *chuanzang diqu* in Chinese) culturally and geographically fuse at their mountainous seam. Many travelers clamber onto the roof of the world from Sichuan (Four Rivers), sampling some of the land's spiciest food en route.

Settled at an early date by the Han Chinese, the populous province of Sichuan was known as the Kingdom of Shu during the Three Kingdom era (A.D. 220–265). The name Shu still refers to Sichuan today.

Sichuan's encompassing mountainous fringe and remoteness were strategically attractive to the Nationalists, who made it their stronghold during the war with Japan between 1937 and 1945. Its geographic isolation has not stopped it from becoming one of China's wealthier provinces (the fact that Deng Xiaoping hailed from the province probably helped).

The province's capital is Chengdu, a pleasant city that sidesteps the worst that industrialization can throw at it. It's an attractive portal to the Buddhist shrine of Leshan, where you can size up the world's largest stone Buddha statue and take rigorous hikes up the holy mountain of Emeishan. Outside Chengdu, Qingchengshan tempts with its Taoist mysteries. The reserve of Jiuzhaigou is a bracing slice of scenery in the far north, and the Tibetan influence grows steadily the farther west you proceed.

Sichuan's most abiding impression could well be its food. The local cuisine *(chuancai)* is a smoldering concoction of herbs and spices that frequently puts curry in the shade. Many travelers passing through the province develop a lifelong appreciation.

Tibet, Sichuan's great western neighbor, towers across its eponymous plateau alongside. A remote, high-elevation society for so long preserved by the rarefied atmosphere of Tibetan Buddhism, its idiosyncratic way of life wrestles with the long arm of Beijing, especially now that the railway to Lhasa has been completed, bringing in huge influxes of outsiders. Even so, Tibet remains an enthralling land of mountains, monasteries, and monks with one of the most extraordinary cultures in the world and a remoteness that has long seduced Western travelers.

The Tibetan capital, Lhasa, is physically dominated by the looming grandeur of the Potala Palace and animated by the spiritual presence of the Jokhang Temple. Explorations beyond the capital will bring you to more monastic societies and the great Buddhist temples at Gyantse and Shigatse.

The huge province of Qinghai, famed for its Ta'er Monastery and Qinghai Lake, sits to the north of both Tibet and Sichuan.

Mighty Chongqing (see p. 146) was cleaved from Sichuan Province in the 1990s, and is now a municipality with the world's largest metropolitan area and population of over 30 million.

Dressed in magnificent robes, Tibetan monks assemble to dispel the shadows of the old year and usher in the New Year.

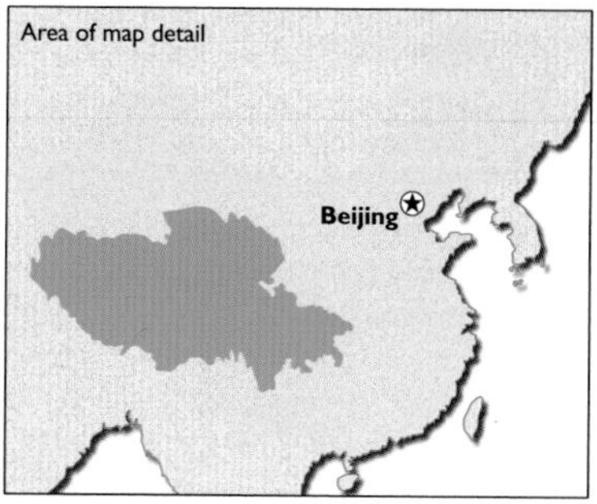

Chengdu

CHENGDU, CAPITAL OF SICHUAN PROVINCE, MANAGES TO preserve a sense of history despite wholesale modernization. Apart from its fine temple architecture, teahouse atmosphere, and giant pandas, it provides an intriguing gateway to Tibet. The city is also the heartland of searing Sichuan cuisine and a springboard for Buddhist pilgrims to Leshan and Emeishan.

Founded by the Qin before they completely unified China in 221 B.C., Chengdu prospered as a major commercial center during the Tang dynasty. It later introduced paper money in the tenth century. The city also earned a reputation for its brocades and satins, winning it the name Jincheng, or "Brocade City."

Industrialization is usually the Chinese kiss of death. The city is blessed, however, with some fine temples and diversions. Its layout is redolent of Beijing with its wide streets, but the town center is a perpetual logjam of vehicles, presided over by a gargantuan statue of Chairman Mao. Charming backstreets of traditional timber houses have somehow eluded the construction ball.

Qingyang Temple (Qingyanggong), "Green Goat Temple," is an important Taoist temple in the western part of the city. A typical Taoist motif here is the octagonal Eight-Diagram Pavilion, a design reflecting the eternal principle of the Bagua, or the eight trigrams of Taoist philosophy. The eight trigrams represent all natural phenomena, combining to form the 64 hexagrams of the *Book of Changes (Yijing* or *I-Ching)* (see p. 50).

In front of the pavilion, a stone tablet depicts the Yin/Yang symbol (for the female/male, dark/light principle in nature), surrounded by the Bagua. Inside, a statue of Laozi, the founding father of Taoism, rides through the Hangu Pass on his green ox. Laozi compiled his mystical musings into a succinct volume

Chengdu
287 E2 & 288

CITS visitor information
65 Renmin Nanlu
0288 666-4422

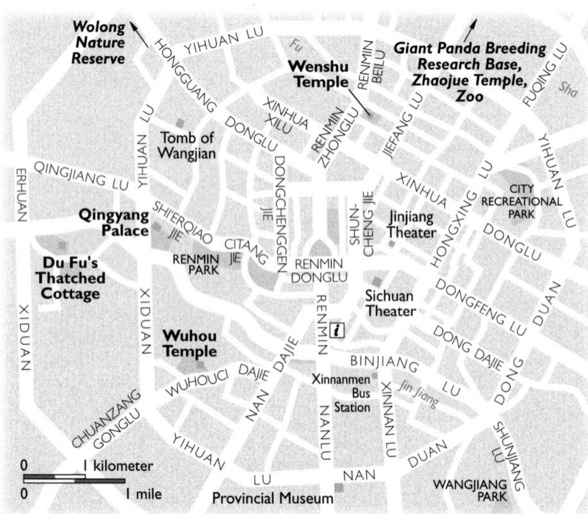

Qingyang Temple
288
Erduan Yihuan Lu
Closed after 6:30 p.m.
$

Wenshu Temple
288
Wenshu Yuan Jie
0288 674-2375

Above: Worshipers cast red incense sticks *(xiang)* into a conflagration at the Wenshu Temple.

and deposited them with the gatekeeper at the pass, before continuing on his journey west (to become the Buddha, some say).

In front of the San Qing Hall is another plaque representing the Yin/Yang symbol, circled by the 12 animals of the Chinese zodiac. The golden characters on the right-hand lintel of the hall, which houses two vast statues of Taoist deities, note "The sun and moon, the two wheels, are the eyes of heaven and earth."

Wenshu Temple (Wenshuyuan) is a large Buddhist complex in the northern section of the city. The four massive guardians, two on either side as you enter, are vividly painted. Inside the compound lies a cluster of temples and a large teahouse where Chengdu citizens gather to relax and read the paper. The rear of the temple complex has a small network of paths through greenery that makes for a pleasant sojourn. The most fascinating spectacle at the temple is the number of worshipers who congregate here to *baifo* (pray to Buddha); the best time to witness this is on a weekend. The market street outside throngs with stalls selling religious accoutrements.

An essential place of homage for Chinese is **Du Fu's Thatched Cottage,** to the west of the Qingyang Palace. Du Fu was a Confucianist poet of the Tang dynasty and is widely considered to be China's greatest poet. He is revered for his lyrical rendering of a lifetime of great suffering. Li Bai (see p. 49), his hard-drinking and

Du Fu's Thatched Cottage
288
Waixi Caotang Lu
\$\$

errant confrère, is often mentioned in the same breath, although the two were very different in character and style (see p. 49).

For the curious, you will find Du Fu's thatched cottage and places described by him in the 200 or more poems he composed here. An

Chinese socialize and escape the stresses of life at a Chengdu teahouse.

interesting sideshow chronicles visits to the cottage by a number of statesmen and politicians, including Mao Zedong, Zhu De, Liu Shaoqi (the disgraced ex-Communist Party chairman), Deng Xiaoping, Li Ruihuan, the great playwright Cao Yu, and others.

There are also models of how the estate changed over the centuries, with English captions.

Giant Panda Breeding Research Base
288
Xiongmao Dadao
0288 351-6748
\$

Wuhou Temple
288
231 Wuhou Ci Jie
\$\$

The Giant Panda Breeding Research Base, located about 7 miles (11 km) north of Chengdu, tries to preserve the lineage of the giant panda. The animals are free to wander through a sizable domain of bamboo groves and forest. Probing their kingdom along pathways affords an occasional glimpse of the protected animals. The best time to catch sight of them is during feeding hours in the morning (between 8 and 10 a.m.); at other times, they are likely to be sleeping. The base has largely supplanted the attraction of trying to sight elusive pandas at the **Wolong Nature Reserve,** 87 miles (140 km) northwest of Chengdu.

TEAHOUSES

Chengdu has long been famous for its steamy teahouses (*chadian*), where customers recline on bamboo armchairs and meet with friends. The lid came down on the teapot during the Cultural Revolution, when many of the teahouses, former stomping grounds of the intelligentsia, were closed. Apart from quaffing *cha,* legitimate activities include playing cards, reading the newspaper, and debating; it's an excellent panorama of Chinese social life.

The **Wenshu Temple** has an active teahouse, and a large convention of tea drinkers descends on **Renmin Park,** west of the center of town. A number of teahouses also line the Jin River, which runs through the city.

OTHER ATTRACTIONS

Zhaojue Temple, a much restored Tang dynasty structure in the northeast section of town, has a main hall with three gilt Buddhas and is more interesting than the adjacent **zoo (Dongwuyuan).** Somnolent pandas reside at the zoo, but if you want to see one of these lovable creatures, it is better to visit the Giant Panda Breeding Research Base.

Wuhou Temple, situated southwest of the Jin River, is a monument to the Three Kingdoms period of Chinese history. Wuhou translates as "minister of war" and refers to Zhuge Liang, a famous military tactician of the period. ■

Around Chengdu

IF YOU HAVEN'T THE TIME OR ENERGY TO CLIMB THE HOLY Buddhist peak of Emeishan (see pp. 292–93), the Taoist mount of Qingchengshan, 40 miles (64 km) west of Chengdu, is a much smaller-scale, more manageable alternative.

Qingchengshan is a sacred Taoist destination, and the climb is bordered by pines, pools, cool streams, and wayside temples. It isn't as rigorous as Emeishan, but the climb can still be grueling.

A number of Taoist temples dot the mountainside. Just by the main gate at the foot of the mountain you'll find the **Jianfu Temple (Jianfugong),** a sanctuary of peace and seclusion. It evokes all the feeling of a hillside Taoist retreat with huge pines soaring above and moss and grass carpeting the roof and paving stones. The black statue draped in robes backing onto you as you enter is Caishen (god of wealth).

From here, the less energetic can ride a cable car up to **Yuecheng Lake,** take a boat over to the other side, and continue by cable car to the summit.

At the top is **Shanqing Hall (Shanqinggong),** a Taoist temple sheltering travelers recovering from their climb, and a community of blue-clothed monks. (The temple guardians are sensitive to photography.) There's a Taoist restaurant here, but a cursory look at the menu reveals the standard Chinese fare. As you descend again toward the cable car, you will see four large characters on the wall facing you. They are pronounced *dadao wuwei,* which literally means that the "the great way achieves all through inaction."

Unfortunately, the usual blitz of hawkers lines the route as well; some of them serve a useful purpose, keeping you going with cucumbers, corn cakes (*yumi gao*), and mineral water. The sedan chair carriers are particularly vocal, pouncing on you as you exit the cable car, wanting to carry you to the summit.

Behind Qingchengshan is **Qingcheng Houshan,** a wilder mountain area threaded with hiking trails and traversed by gorges.

The **Monastery of Divine Light (Baoguangsi)** in Xindu, 11 miles (17 km) north of Chengdu, is a vast and alluring Buddhist complex. The Tang dynasty temple suffered a string of calamities before reemerging in its present, reconstructed incarnation. It hosts an assembly of 500 Luohan (see p. 72), a statue of Buddha made from white jade, and a leaning pagoda. ■

A spider explores a stone carving on the shores of Yuecheng Lake, Qingchengshan.

CITS visitor information

288

65 Renmin Nanlu

0288 666-4422

Pilgrims greet the sunrise at Emeishan; historically, some threw themselves into the radiant clouds.

Emeishan
287 E1

Tourist Service Center
Emeishan
0833 559-2404

Emeishan

EMEISHAN, ONE OF THE FOUR SACRED BUDDHIST MOUNTAINS of China, originally teemed with Taoist hermits and recluses, but it was appropriated by partisans of Buddha in the sixth century. The philosophical founder of Taoism, Laozi, is said to have lived here in a mythical incarnation.

The four Buddhist mountains are protected by the Four Heavenly Kings (seen guarding the entrance to temples) of the four directions. Emeishan, the westernmost mountain, is the highest at 10,170 feet (3,099 m). Jiuhuashan is 4,400 feet (1,342 m), and Wutaishan is 10,036 feet (3058 m), while the island of Putuoshan is more of a hill.

Myth swarms around the name Emei itself. Some say it means Moth-Browed Mountain (though this doesn't match the characters for its name); others insist it echoes the first two syllables of the Buddhist invocation E-Mi-Tuo-Fo; while others assert that the original characters for the mountain have been lost. There is agreement that the deity ruling this mountain is Puxian, who is generally depicted riding an elephant or holding a lotus flower.

CLIMBING EMEISHAN

The best seasons for climbing are spring to autumn—the winter climb can be treacherous. The mountain is often misty, and a sudden change in the weather is possible in any season. Waterproof clothing is important, as are an umbrella, decent shoes (with a good grip), water, and toilet paper. From the town of Emei, 90 miles south of Chengdu, buses take you to Baoguo at the foot of the mountain (elevation 1,800 feet/547 m).

Most climbers ascend by way of the Wannian Temple, via Xixiang Pond, and up to the summit at almost 10,168 feet (3,100 m); they descend past the pond, Xianfeng Temple, and the Qingyin Pavilion. You will need a day for your ascent and a day to clamber back down.

Minibuses speed you to Wannian Temple from Baoguo Monastery, and from there it's about a ten-hour climb to the summit. Buses from Qingyin Pavilion return to Baoguo Monastery. Those with aching feet, lethargy, or a plane to catch can take a minibus to Jieyin Pavilion and then transfer to a cable car going to the summit. Many temples provide food and spartan shelter, so you can put a roof over your head and plan your next day's scramble up or down the mountain.

TEMPLES

Many of Emei's temples have vanished in the swirl of time, but some gems remain. **Baoguo Monastery** was originally built by a Taoist, and some Taoist elements remain. A feature of the **Fuhu Monastery (Crouching Tiger Monastery),** farther on, is its Ming dynasty copper pagoda with a plethora of Buddhist images and a complete text of the Garland Sutra (almost 200,000 characters) of the Hua Yan Buddhist school.

Qingyin Pavilion (Pure Sound Pavilion) echoes the sound of the nearby confluence of the **Black Dragon** and **White Dragon** waters. Higher up the path at 3,345 feet (1,020 m) is the **Wannian Temple (Temple of Ten Thousand Years).** Founded in A.D. 268, it was embellished during the reign of Wanli (see p. 34) with a huge beamless hall to house an enormous copper and bronze figure of Puxian on his elephant. The original wooden structure burned down, so the present one was made of brick. The hall was apparently modeled on a tower at Kublai Khan's summer lodge in Chengde (see pp. 114–16), and it is Middle Eastern in appearance.

Xianfeng Temple (Immortal Peak Temple) is located near a network of formations known as the **Jiulao Caves (Nine Immortals Caves).** Near the intersection of the two major trails, **Xixiang Pond (Washing Elephant Pond)** is where Puxian bathed his elephant; bathing the elephant is a Buddhist metaphor for the cleansing of the world from one's mind.

It's an exhausting hike to the **Golden Summit (Jinding),** with its vertigo-inducing rock faces and eponymous temple. En route, you pass a number of temples that have fallen victim to the ravages of time and weather, including the **White Cloud Temple** and **Hall of the Thunder God.**

If you're lucky, you will see **Buddha's Glory (*foguang*),** a light effect in the clouds below. Sunlight shining on water droplets cause rainbows. In ages past, devotees overcome by the ethereal lights would cast themselves into the glow, only to be dashed on the rocks below. A chance of this glimpse of the divine is still the reason many climb Emeishan.

The mountain sees an eclectic mix of pilgrims winding their way to the top. It is a victim of its own popularity and it's difficult to stake your claim to areas of tranquility without a hawker trying to sell you something. Don't be deterred, for the landscape is spectacular. ■

The spirit of the deity Puxian infuses the temples, rocks, and trees of Emeishan, enticing devotees up its grueling heights.

Leshan

Leshan
287 E1
$$

Leshan Tourism Bureau
Binhe Lu, Leshan
0833 213-6926

PRESIDING OVER THE CONFLUENCE OF THE TWO RIVERS that sweep past the foot of Lingyun Hill at Leshan, not far from Emeishan, is a huge statue of Buddha. Carved from the rock face, it is a staggering 233 feet (71 m) high and is even more impressive for having been created over 1,200 years ago during the Tang dynasty.

The Chinese have a saying: "Buddha is a mountain, mountain is Buddha." This Buddha's head alone is an awesome 50 feet (15 m) high; his ears come in at a lengthy 20 feet (7.5 m), and his sizable feet can hold an audience of 100 sightseers, while he looks down with his 10-foot-wide (3 m) eyes. The Buddha represented is the Maitreya

Buddha, the Buddha of the future. The outsize deity (*dafo*) is more of a marvel to behold for its scale rather than for any exquisite carving. Haitong, a devout monk from nearby **Lingyun Temple (Lingyunsi),** made this his labor of love, starting in 713, but he died before its completion 90 years later. He embarked on the project so that Buddha's presence would calm the turbulent waters of the Dadu and Min Rivers below, which had claimed lives.

Amazingly, the big Buddha—the world's largest stone Buddha statue— has survived a combined assault of civil war, weathering, and bouts of anti-Buddhist hooliganism. The statue was at one time covered by a protective wooden building, but this was destroyed during the Ming dynasty. An elaborate drainage system was built into it to prevent the worst effects of weathering.

Steps cut into the rock next to the statue funnel visitors up and down. Above Buddha's crown and at the top of the stairs is the **Great Buddha Temple (Dafosi).**

From Leshan ferry pier, boats go south to the Buddha, so that you can make your climb up to it on the north side. First you pass the impressive halls of the Tang dynasty **Wuyou Temple.** Across a bridge you come to the **Oriental Buddha Park (Dongfang Fodu),** with its assembly of Buddhist images, including a vast reclining Buddha. A nearby museum displays Han dynasty tomb relics, while continuing north brings you to Big Buddha. ■

Left: A huge statement of faith, the big Buddha at Leshan is the world's largest carved stone Buddha.

Above: A walkway allows you to examine the colossus from many angles.

Dazu

THE BUDDHIST CARVINGS AT LONGMEN, DUNHUANG, AND Yungang are loudly trumpeted as the most important monuments to Buddhist art in China, but Dazu County in Sichuan has an equally important, if more scattered, collection.

Above: The vivid carving at Dazu relates stories culled from Taoist, Buddhist, and Confucian beliefs.

Opposite: The Wheel of Life is suspended from the mouth of the Lord of Death at Baodingshan.

Dazu
287 E2

CITS visitor information
151 Zourong Guangchang
023 6903-7560

The carvings differ stylistically from the others because they meditate more on the human subject. The most successful carvings in Dazu, 70 miles (112 km) northwest of Chongqing (see p. 146), are recognizably human and less preoccupied with the concept of divinity. The tribe of figures includes Taoist and Confucian parables among the Buddhist allegories.

Carved between the late Tang and Qing dynasties, principal pieces emerged from the hands of Song dynasty craftspeople. The main figures are clustered in two groups, one on Beishan (North Hill) and the other on Baodingshan (Precious Summit).

BEISHAN

Beishan, located just over a mile (1.6 km) north of Dazu, is home to a large community of weather-beaten effigies in niches carved from the hillside. Far from disappointing, some niches shelter exquisite faces—delicately featured Guanyins amid other tender-looking bodhisattvas.

The pantheon is a varied cast: Samantabhadra, Manjushri, Ksitigarbha (god of the underworld), and others, plus crowds of small effigies of Buddha. In the **Thousand Buddha Cave** (niche No. 155), the Peacock King presides over a dominion of miniature carved Buddhas.

BAODINGSHAN

Baodingshan, situated 10 miles (16 km) northeast of Dazu, boasts a universe of 10,000 figures, a massive project initiated in the Southern Song dynasty by Zhao Zhifeng, a monk of the Tantric or esoteric school of Buddhism. The statues are located on a horseshoe-shaped cliff beneath a hill, capped by temples.

The most commanding piece is the reclining Buddha, a 100-foot (30 m) depiction of Sakyamuni (see. p. 72) issuing his final teachings. Surrounded by his disciples, the effigy radiates a compelling feeling of power.

Other stories are charmingly told. The baby Buddha, for instance, bathes in a stream of water issuing from a dragon's mouth (niche No. 12). Some, such as the assembly of figures stressing filial piety (niche No. 15), are instructive parables, while others caution with fear. The illustration of hell (niche No. 21) is a ghastly presentiment of what awaits evildoers. ■

Invocations are carried aloft on the wind from prayer flags during the Tibetan New Year.

Tibet

A vast land of high plateaus and towering mountain peaks, Tibet has long captivated the Western imagination. Its epithets—Roof of the World, Shangri-La, and the Land of Snows—divulge a tempting otherworldliness. After the monarch Trison Detsen enshrined Buddhism as the state religion in the eighth century, Tibet long devoted itself to spiritual ways, but its troubled modern history and ongoing development has sadly diluted much of its mystery. Travel to the land remains difficut, but with the completion of the railway to Lhasa in 2006, transportation has become easier.

After centuries of isolation and little communication with the outside world, Tibet's conservatism and backwardness left it unable to resist the Chinese invasion of 1951. A Tibetan revolt in 1959 was mercilessly crushed, and more than 100,000 Tibetans fled the country, including the Dalai Lama. Tibetan culture faced annihilation during the Cultural Revolution, when thousands of monasteries were destroyed.

Today Tibet exists as an autonomous region within China. Periodic splutters of revolt are ruthlessly suppressed, and China wages a constant propaganda war against the "Dalai clique" government in exile.

Travel for foreigners within Tibet can be difficult. Permit requirements are imposed on all foreign travelers (which must be arranged through a travel agency) to Tibet, and other areas outside Lhasa Prefecture and Shigatse require further permits (see p. 353 for details). This could change with the opening of the railway to Lhasa, but at the time of writing it was still too early to say, so it is best to check with a travel agent in China or with the Public Security Bureau. Transport beyond the main sights around Tibet is basic and many travelers opt instead to rent a four-wheel drive.

Nonetheless, with its magnificent scenery and unique culture, the mountain kingdom offers an unforgettable experience. It's worth the extra effort. ■

Its roof ornamented with gold, the Jokhang Temple is Tibet's holiest temple; in the distance lies the Potala Palace.

Lhasa

LHASA, HOLY CAPITAL OF TIBET, GUARDS THE FLICKERING flame of Tibetan heritage that Chinese rule has failed to extinguish. Potala Palace gazes down on a city stormed, but not completely ransacked, by Han Chinese culture while the beguiling portals of Lhasa's myriad temples, especially the fabulous Jokhang Temple, access the mysterious realms of Tibetan Buddhism.

Sitting in a valley on the Kyi-chu River, the historic districts of Lhasa do battle with a final, drab encroachment of Chinese government housing. The old Tibetan town in the west has a footing back in the distant seventh century, and it is here that traditional culture flourishes. This is also where Lhasa keeps her cultural jewels.

JOKHANG TEMPLE

One of the oldest buildings in Lhasa, the labyrinthine Jokhang Temple (Dazhaosi) is also the holiest of Tibet's temples. A palpable sense of reverence accompanies a visit here. The temple was consecrated in A.D. 647 on a strict geomantic scheme, and it has undergone considerable embellishment and renovation through the centuries. A major period of restoration followed great damage during the Cultural Revolution. Now literally deluged with Tibetan art, the building is illuminated by a constellation of guttering candles.

The temple is divided into inner and outer sanctums. A prayer wheel-lined pilgrim route called the **Nangkhor (Inner Pathway)** surrounds the quadrangular **inner Jokhang,** itself a sacred repository of chapels, halls, and highly precious statuary on a number of floors. You can visit the ornamented roofs that cap the Jokhang.

Lhasa
Map 287 C1

Lhasa Tourism Bureau
Address: 33 Jiangsu Lu
Phone: 0891 634-2884

Jokhang Temple
Map 287 C1
Address: East of Barkhor Square
Hours: Closed p.m.
Price: $$

Norbu Lingka
Mirik Lam
Closed 1:00–2:30 p.m.
$$

Ramoche Temple
Xiaozhaosi Lu
$$

A Khauipa woman trades at Barkhor's market.

An extension of chapels and halls, the **outer Jokhang** wraps around the holy inner core. On the periphery of the outer Jokhang is the **Barkhor,** the middle pilgrim circuit, a holy place of perambulation, around which pilgrims circle in a clockwise direction (don't go against the flow). It has also become a focus for market stalls and a crush of hawkers and traders from other parts of Tibet. The whole melts into a fusion of color and activity, where you can pick up that prayer wheel you were after, or a double-*dorje* (scepterlike object).

OTHER LHASA MONASTERIES

Near the Barkhor and the Jokhang are other temples worth seeking out. These include the **Meru Nyingba Monastery** and the **Ani Tshamkhung Nunnery. Tengyeling Monastery,** northwest of Barkhor Square, was built in the 17th century after Lhasa was reinstated as capital of Tibet. Lhasa also shelters a Muslim community. The largest mosque is the **Gyel Lhakhang,** towering southeast of Barkhor Square.

Ramoche Temple, half a mile (0.8 km) north of Barkhor Square, is about the same age as the Jokhang. It was burned down early on, rebuilt, damaged by the Mongols, and then served time under the local Communist division in the 1960s.

Norbu Lingka (Luobu Linka), in the western part of Lhasa, has been used as the Summer Palace since the mid-18th century. It's a 98-acre (40 ha) park split into palaces, opera grounds, and government buildings; it also contains a zoo. As with the Potala Palace, the complex has mushroomed over the centuries.

AROUND LHASA

Five miles (8 km) north of Lhasa, **Drepung Monastery (Zhebangsi)** was founded in the 15th century. At one time over 10,000 monks lived here in what was the largest monastery in the world. It has managed to survive amid flames fanned by civil war, Mongol incursions, and the Cultural Revolution.

The temple's *($$)* contingent of monks is sadly much reduced today, with only 600 remaining. Numerous halls and chapels constitute the complex, including the large golden-roofed **Assembly Hall (Tsokchen Lhakhang).** The holiest site is the **Jampa**

Yellow and Red Hat Sects

The Gelukpa (Model of Virtue), or Yellow Hat Sect, was founded by Tsongkhapa in the late 14th century. Tsongkhapa wanted to establish a Tibetan Buddhist order that was strictly disciplined and scholarly. The Red Hat Sect opposed the hegemony of the Yellow Hat Sect, but the Yellow emerged as the leading order in Tibet, with the Dalai Lama at its head, and remained the supreme power until 1959. ■

Tongdrol Lhakhang, adorned with a 50-foot (15 m) image of the Maitreya Buddha.

Less than a mile southeast of Drepung Monastery is **Nechung Monastery,** traditional home of the State Oracle and Pehar, defender of the faith (Dharmapala), who resided for 700 years at the Samye Monastery and then relocated to Nechung Monastery. Pehar is most actively worshiped by followers of the Yellow Hat Sect.

A disciple of Tsongkhapa (creator of the Yellow Hat Sect) founded **Sera Monastery** *($$)* in 1419. On the northern outskirts of Lhasa, it was formerly a major community. The largest building is the Great Assembly Hall, in which hang vast *tangkas* (Buddhist banners). Sera also contains three colleges devoted to esoteric Tantric study.

Pawangka Monastery, 5 miles (8 km) northeast of Lhasa, is possibly older than the Jokhang Temple. The current three-tiered structure was originally a tower built by the pioneering king of ancient Tibet, Songtsen Gampo.

Ganden Monastery *($)*, 28 miles (45 km) east of Lhasa off the Lhasa– Sichuan road, was built by Tsong-khapa in 1409. This flourishing monastery suffered enormous destruction during the Chinese invasion. Many structures are associated with Tsongkhapa, including a stupa that contains his relics.

Lying among magnificent mountain scenery 120 miles (193 km) north of Lhasa is **Namtso Lake (Namucuo),** the world's highest lake, with accommodation available near the lakeside **Tashidor Monastery.** At an elevation of more than 15,000 feet (4,570 m), only attempt this trip after long acclimatization in Lhasa.

Samye Monastery *($)* was Tibet's first monastery. Probably founded between 775 and 779, its founding symbolized the vanquishing of primitive belief in Tibet by Buddhism. The very earliest of the monastery's structures have succumbed to an unfortunate concoction of fire, civil war, earthquake, and Chinese politics. Difficult to reach (and a permit is officially required), it lies 19 miles (30 km) northwest of Tsetang, north of the Yarlung Zangbo (Brahmaputra) River. The journey there involves a multiple bus-ferry-truck trip.

Yumbu Lagang, 7 miles (11 km) southwest of Tsetang, is a reconstruction of Tibet's oldest building. The palace was built on a hilltop for the first king of Tibet, Nyatri Tsenpo, in the 2nd century B.C. and has been frequently reconstructed. ■

The much restored Yumbu Lagang rises from its hilly perch above a picturesque valley.

TANTRIC BUDDHISM

Tantric Buddhism is a creed that seeks enlightenment through inner experience and growth; it is symbolized by exotic images of male and female coupling. ■

One of the defining images of Tibet, the Potala Palace is a colossal sanctuary for the goddess of compassion, Avalokiteshvara.

Potala Palace

A HUGE WALLED CASTLE OF A BUILDING TOWERING ON the slopes of Red Mountain (Mount Marpori), the Potala Palace (Budalagong) is Lhasa's dominating feature. With the Dalai Lama in exile, the Potala has been put on show, but the palace remains a potent symbol of Tibetan nationhood.

Potala Palace
287 C1
$$$$

This awesome fortresslike palace springs from the hillside above Lhasa, occupying your first impressions of the city. It takes its name from Mount Potalaka, sacred home of the bodhisattva of mercy, Avalokiteshvara, known in China as Guanyin. Two distinct sections comprise Potala, the **White Palace** (built between 1645 and 1653) and the **Red Palace** (between 1690 and 1693).

The outer and larger section, the White Palace constituted the winter residential quarters of the Dalai Lama (who is the physical incarnation of Avalokiteshvara) and the governmental headquarters. The Red Palace within is a magnificent realm of temples and spiritual buildings.

The huge walls surrounding the labyrinthine palace of 1,000 rooms are fortified, with watchtowers on the two southern corners.

The Potala Palace's first stones

Right: The exiled Dalai Lama's private apartments at the Potala Palace patiently await his possible return.

were laid in the seventh century A.D., but time has taken its toll and only a few structures remain from that period. The building underwent a great period of reconstruction with the fifth Dalai Lama in the 17th century, when Lhasa was restored as the capital of Tibet. The palace's dimensions grew during the 18th century, and it was considerably renovated in the 20th century. Though shelled during the 1959 uprising, the building survived the tumult of the Cultural Revolution. Many rooms remain off-limits.

WHITE PALACE

Overlooking the **Eastern Courtyard,** the White Palace was the administrative hub. Visit the Dalai Lama's private quarters on the top floor for a fascinating look at the lineage of some of the men who achieved Buddhahood, and access the well-preserved apartments of the 13th and 14th Dalai Lamas for a taste of their rarefied world. Portraits of the former occupants hang in the chambers, intriguing murals cover the walls, and small chapels bristle with statuary. Many of the chambers formerly served as government boardrooms. The largest chamber here is the **East Main Hall,** which served as a reception hall and the venue for the observance of religious festivals.

RED PALACE

The religious sphere is enclosed within the four-story Red Palace, itself enclosed by the White Palace. This sacred plot is made up of numerous temples and the reliquaries for the remains of former Dalai Lamas. The core structure is the West Main Hall.

For a glimpse into Tibetan Buddhism, investigate the chapels. All four levels of the Red Palace lead to a stunning display of

mandalas (mystic diagrams), sacred images, and an encyclopedic display of deities. Stupas containing the relics of past Dalai Lamas contribute to the reverential character of the Red Palace.

On the fourth floor, the **Phakpa Lhakhang—**holy nucleus—enshrines a sandalwood effigy of the bodhisattva Avalokiteshvara, discovered miraculously in Nepal in the seventh century. A cohort of other sacred images join the effigy.

The **Chogyel Drupuk,** on the third floor, is a venerable old columned chamber replete with images of Avalokiteshvara, Maitreya, Sakyamuni, and portraits of Tibetan royal personages. The second floor consists of closed chapels but displays murals relating to the Potala Palace.

The largest chamber in the palace is the pillared **West Main Hall** on the first floor, which contains the throne of the sixth Dalai Lama, murals on Buddhist and royal themes, *tangkas* (paintings on cloth), and tapestries. ■

Tibetan Buddhism

Chinese and Tibetan Buddhism widely diverge in both doctrine and ritual. Chinese Buddhism can seem mundane compared with the more exotic, wondrous images that characterize the Tibetan way. Within Tibetan Buddhism lie elements of the older Bon, a primitive Shaman religion indigenous to Tibet that was steered onto the Buddhist path.

Buddhism originally penetrated Tibet in the fifth century A.D. Tibet inherited the cream of Indian Buddhism, partly due to the proximity of the two countries. Buddhism's resulting fusion of Tantric and more esoteric elements with Bon forged Tibetan Buddhism, though Bon still survives as an independent faith. The religion ultimately pervaded the whole of Tibetan society. It is startlingly different in culture and belief from the Buddhism followed outside Tibet, and is composed of a number of schools.

Peculiar to Tibetan Buddhism is the doctrine of the reincarnating Lama (see p. 306) and its idiosyncratic pantheon of deities. A number of the latter have terrifying characteristics not associated with Chinese Buddhism, but it should be remembered that Buddhism is a compassionate religion.

Bon

The primitive Bon religion is governed by a priestly class of mediums, exorcists, and miracle workers. Tibetan Buddhism has preserved much Bon technique, including faith healing and miracle working. The ecstatic dances, belief in human flight, spirit languages, and mythical lore of Bon Shamanism were successfully transplanted into Tibetan Buddhism. The Tibetan *Book of the Dead* (a book to be read by a lama to the recently deceased, without touching the body) is shaman in organization.

This helps explain why Tibetan Buddhism is replete with netherworld images. Human skulls and bones have a symbolic and magical function that reaches out from the Bon psyche. Undoubtedly, what survives of the Bon religion in its Buddhist constitution has come under the corrective of Buddhist theology, removing much of its potency. Buddhist elements were also absorbed by Bon.

Accoutrements & motifs

Tibetan Buddhism has a number of talismans and ornaments that serve sacred purposes.

The Wheel of Life Often found decorating temples in Tibet, the Wheel depicts the cycle of suffering and rebirth. It hangs from the mouth of the lord of death, who oversees the drama unfolding within its circuit.

Prayer Wheel This decorated, hollow metal tube on a rod accommodates a roll of paper upon which is written a mantra or invocation. The turning of the wheel is a substitute

for the recitation of the mantra. Photographer James Ricalton noted, while visiting China in the early 20th century, that prayer wheels can be attached to windmills, a strong breeze allowing the lama to "consign himself to the arms of Morpheus, and in the morning find himself the very *ne plus ultra* of holiness."

Prayer Flag Similar to the Prayer Wheel, the mantra on the Prayer Flag is carried aloft by the wind.

Phur-bu This ritual dagger was formerly used for human sacrifice. It is symbolically employed to exorcise evil spirits. The blade is three-sided, and the handle generally sports the head of a deity or some other fierce design.

Kapala A cup made from a human skull (*kapala* is Sanskrit for "skull"), the Kapala is often used in ceremonies to offer food and drink resembling flesh and blood to deities.

Dorje This small scepterlike object (*vajra* in Sanskrit), made from either brass or bronze, represents a thunderbolt. A male symbol, it is balanced by the bell, or *dril bu*, a female symbol. The dorje sometimes appears in double form, in the shape of a cross.

Festivals

Monlam, or Great Prayer Festival, is the most momentous festival of the year, held during Tibetan New Year. The celebration reasserts faith in Buddhism and was initiated by the founder of the Yellow Hat Sect, Tsongkhapa. The Tibetan New Year is a great event, starting on the first day of the first month (usually February or March in the Gregorian calendar). ■

Tibetan Buddhism differs in both form and function from other Buddhist schools.

Gyantse & Shigatse

THE OLD TOWN OF GYANTSE DWELLS UNDER AN authentic Tibetan spell much sought after by travelers to this land. It can easily be visited going to, or returning from, Tibet's second largest city, Shigatse.

The vast image of Maitreya gazes out from its sanctuary at the Tashilhunpo Monastery in Shigatse.

Founded in the 15th century, the **Pelkhor Chode Monastery** *($)* is the most famous sight in Gyantse (Jiangzi), 162 miles (260 km) southwest of Lhasa. The marvelous octagonal **Kumbum (Place of 100,000 Images)** stupa rises up within the walls, with nine tiers, 75 chapels, and 108 gates. Containing a lengthy pilgrim circuit past magnificent murals, the stupa was completed in 1427. Gyantse's hilltop fort, the **Dzong,** dates back to 1268, and has superb views. A museum records the damage done to the fortress by the British Younghusband expedition in 1904 (this expedition forced the flight of the Dalai Lama to Mongolia).

Shigatse, at a slightly higher elevation than Lhasa, was historically an important monastic center and a former capital of Tibet. It is noted for its **Tashilhunpo Monastery (Zhashilubusi),** seat of the Panchen Lama. The first Dalai Lama founded the monastery *($$)* in 1447. Although it once housed nearly 5,000 monks, it now has many fewer. Displayed here is a massive 85-foot (26 m) beatific effigy of Maitreya, the Future Buddha (see p. 72).

Currently undergoing renovation, Shigatse's hilltop fortress ruin combines a wrecking inflicted in the 18th century with later damage. ■

Gyantse & Shigatse
286 B1 & 287 C1

ALIEN TRAVEL PERMIT

To obtain an Alien Travel Permit to Gyantse, see p. 353.

Lamas

The Dalai Lama is the head of the Yellow Hat Sect of Tibetan Buddhism (see p. 300). The name means "Ocean of Wisdom," and he is the physical manifestation of Avalokiteshvara, the salvationary bodhisattva of mercy (called Guanyin in China). Until he fled Tibet in 1959, the current Dalai Lama was the spiritual and temporal ruler of the land.

The Panchen Lama is a physical incarnation of the Amitabha Buddha. The Panchen Lamas enjoy successive reincarnations like the Dalai Lamas. When the 10th Panchen Lama died in 1989, after spending most of his life in Beijing, the Dalai Lama chose the reincarnated Panchen Lama, as was the custom. Beijing ignored this decision and chose a different contender. ■

Xining & around

Ta'er Monastery, set amid the fields and hills of Qinghai Province, is one of the most significant Tibetan monasteries outside Tibet.

QINGHAI IS THE HUGE PROVINCE NORTHEAST OF TIBET, situated on a part of the Tibetan Plateau. One of China's poorest provinces, it is also where the mighty Yellow, Yangtze, and Mekong Rivers begin as snow water. The capital Xining has little to offer in itself, but it's a gateway to the Ta'er Monastery and Qinghai Lake and is a staging post for travelers taking the train to Tibet.

The **Great Mosque (Qingzhen Dasi)** on Dongguan Dajie is the place of worship for Xining's Hui Muslim community. In the mountains northwest of town lies the **Beishan Temple.**

Ta'er Monastery is one of the six great Yellow Hat Sect lamaseries. This monastery, 16 miles (26 km) south of Xining in the town of Huangzhong, is revered for its association with the founder of the Yellow Hat Sect, Tsongkhapa, who was born here in the 14th century. Its cluster of buildings include a fine temple roofed with gold-plated tiles, several stupas, and a hall containing yak-butter statues, a historic Tibetan art form.

Important festivals that attract pilgrims are celebrated in the first, fourth, sixth, and ninth lunar months. Ta'er Monastery is easy to reach by bus from Xining.

Twelve miles (19 km) south of Ledu, a small town 40 miles (64 km) east on the Xining–Lanzhou railway line, is the **Qutan Temple,** a Lamaist temple with some attractive and well-preserved frescoes.

Qinghai's other main attraction is the huge **Qinghai Lake (Qinghaihu),** China's largest salt-water lake. Most travelers explore **Bird Island (Niaodao)** in the western part of the lake, where thousands of seabirds descend during the breeding season (March to June). Some tours from Xining to the lake pass the Ta'er Monastery, useful if time is limited. Check the latest bird flu reports before visiting. ■

Xining, Qinghai Province
Map 287 D3

CITS visitor information
✉ 156 Huanghe Lu
☎ 0971 613-3844

Ta'er Monastery
Map 287 D3
✉ Huangzhong
$ $$$

Bird Island
$ $$

Pearl Shoal Falls roars into a remote cleft in Jiuzhaigou, in north Sichuan.

More places to visit in Sichuan & the Tibetan Plateau

SICHUAN

Hailuogou Glacier Park

Part of Mount Gonggashan, this (sadly commercialized) glacier in western Sichuan has breathtaking views over a mountainous backdrop. Autumn offers the best weather, but take warm clothes. A guide is included in the entrance fee, but if trekking take food and water.
287 D1 $ $$$$$

Jiuzhaigou

This huge nature preserve in northern Sichuan is both remote and blessed with some stunning scenery. With its airport connected to Chengdu (with flights to other major Chinese cities planned), Jiuzhaigou attracts huge numbers of domestic travelers, but the reserve remains a gorgeous panoply of lakes, forest, and alpine scenery. In summer and autumn tours from Chengdu usually include the **Yellow Dragon Temple (Huanglongsi),** between the town of Songpan and Jiuzhaigou. The reserve lies high up, so take warm clothes.
287 D2–E2 $ $$$$$

Kangding

One popular, but risky, route into Tibet runs along the Sichuan-Tibet highway, which trundles through Kangding in western Sichuan. If you simply want to reach Tibet, fly or take the train; the land route is officially closed to foreigners and accidents are commonplace on the bad roads. Kangding is dominated by 24,798-foot (7,556 m) **Mount Gonggashan,** and several Tibetan lamaseries and mountain lakes can be found in the surrounding region.
287 D2 **Sally's Knapsack Inn**
Kangding 0836 283-8377

TIBETAN PLATEAU

Everest Base Camp & Rongbuk Monastery

If you are Nepal bound, you can stop at Rongbuk Monastery and the Everest Base Camp for some simply unforgettable mountain scenery. A guest house next to the monastery offers accommodations and a restaurant, and tents are available at Everest Base Camp.
286 B1

Sakya

The route from Shigatse to the Nepalese border passes through Sakya. Its huge monastery is sublime, with gargantuan walls thrusting out of the earth. The immense structure is a remarkable sight. Political power crystallized here 700 years ago during the period of Yuan Mongol patronage, a relationship aimed at protecting the country from destruction. Sakya lies at the outer limits of the public transport system for foreigners within Tibet, and if you wish to go farther, you will have to rent your own vehicle. You will also need to obtain an Alien Travel Permit (see p. 353) for visits to Sakya.
286 B1 $ $$ ■

From Ürümqi to far-off Kashgar lies an epic territory of desert, mountain lakes, and the debris of ancient civilizations. The Silk Road led here via Dunhuang and Lanzhou. Hardy Inner Mongolia stretches east beyond Gansu Province.

Inner Mongolia & the Silk Road

Festival riders, Inner Mongolia

Inner Mongolia & the Silk Road

CHINA'S FIRST OPEN-DOOR POLICY NOURISHED THE COUNTRY with the trade, religion, and outside contact that flowed along the historic Silk Road (Sichou Zhi Lu). The merchandise traveled in both directions. Bouncing west along the routes out of China were bundles of silk, while ivory, gems, fruit, glass, precious metals, and a variety of religions and creeds crept east.

Departing from Xi'an, the silk-laden caravans passed through Lanzhou, nudging through the Jade Gate (Yumen) near Jiayuguan before forking at Dunhuang to skirt the dry menace of the Taklimakan Desert (Takelamagan Shamo). Watered by the oases of Turpan, Kuqa, and Hotan, the trails followed northern and southern arms before reuniting at Kashgar. Caravans that blindly strayed into the desert were quickly swallowed up by sand and heard from no more. One route of this ancient highway slipped out of China over the Pamir Mountains to destinations as far away as the Mediterranean. From the southern arm, another road fed into northern India through the lofty Karakoram Highway.

The Silk Road brought riches to several pre-Islamic, Buddhist civilizations that flourished in these regions. Surrendering later to the remorseless desert sands or simply forgotten, many were plundered by intrepid European, Russian, and American archaeologists in the early 20th century. The sacred caves at Dunhuang in Gansu Province were singled out for particular attention.

China's arid northwest is a tamer world today, but it remains a place of hostile desert dappled with green oases. A desert for all seasons, the Taklimakan is a searing griddle in summer and frozen wasteland in winter, forcing life to the oasis towns on its boundaries. East of the desert is the lake of Lop Nur, a body of water that has drifted over the ages. Oasis towns, tranquil lakes, snowcapped mountains, Buddhist caves, and remnants of ancient cities add allure to this wilderness. Bumpy bus rides, long train journeys, and less exciting, but quicker, airplane trips cover the huge distances.

Ürümqi is the capital of the Xinjiang Autonomous Region (formerly far more grandly called Chinese Turkestan), a region that only came under absolute Chinese control in the Qing dynasty. The city is a communications hub to the rest of Xinjiang, including nearby Heaven's Lake, or Tianchi, the oasis town of Turpan, and Kashi (Kashgar).

The long east–west strip of Inner Mongolia is a very separate cultural and historical entity, an autonomous region bridged to Xinjiang by Gansu Province. Its eastern extremities abut Jilin, Heilongjiang, and Liaoning Provinces.

As in parts of Xinjiang, the huge influx of Han settlers into Inner Mongolia has put a much resented Chinese stamp on the local culture. Mongol pride finds concrete expression in the Mausoleum of Genghis Khan, a memento of those glory days when the Mongol Empire enslaved China. Lamaseries in Hohhot point to the historic allegiance between the Mongols and Tibetan Buddhism.

Pinched between barren Gansu Province and Inner Mongolia, the tiny Ningxia Hui Autonomous Region has a large minority of Hui Chinese, Muslim descendants of Middle Eastern merchants who plied the Silk Road. ■

Mountains, plateaus, lakes, and deserts punctuate the "New Borderland."

Ürümqi is a very Chinese gateway to Xinjiang, the mighty northwestern province formerly known as Chinese Turkestan.

Ürümqi

ÜRÜMQI, CAPITAL OF THE VAST, DRY EXPANSE OF THE Xinjiang Autonomous Region in China's remote northwest, can be disappointing. The expected thrill of arrival in Xinjiang is dissipated by this very typical Chinese city. No matter, it is an essential staging post to sparkling Tianchi, thirsty Turpan, and exotic Kashgar (Kashi), and there's some excellent Uighur food to be found.

Ürümqi
310 B2

CITS visitor information
38 Xinhua Nanlu
0991 282-1428

Xinjiang Autonomous Region Museum
Xibei Lu
Closed 1:30–3:30 p.m.
$

Xinjiang is best explored with an understanding of the local culture. One excellent step toward this can be found at the newly-restored **Xinjiang Autonomous Region Museum,** which has recently benefited from a huge renovation that has banished the stale exhibits and seen the creation of a multi-hall replacement. This is an essential learning curve for anyone interested in the region: Xinjiang's vanished Buddhist civilizations and cities are all examined, along with Buddhist frescoes, while fascinating pieces of trivia round out the picture.

Some interesting facts can be gleaned. Did you know that more than 8,000 Chinese Russians live in Xinjiang, mainly in the north and that 18,000 Manchurians also call the region their home?

But the highlight of the museum is its star collection of mummified bodies, preserved by the desiccating effects of the arid desert. The body of one woman is about 4,000 years old, unearthed from the region of the Tieban River in 1980. She and several others are of European extraction, revealing a nomadic intrusion into these parts millennia ago by a tribe who spoke a language called Tocharian. The bodies—some of which are children, including a baby—are well preserved and sealed in airtight perspex containers. The main excavation sites are illustrated on a map on the wall.

For those who would like to dis-

Silk Road minorities

Xinjiang's largest Turkic group is the Uighur minority, a Turkic-speaking people of Turkish descent. They are also scattered throughout Kazakstan and Kirgizstan.

The **Uighurs** are a Sunni Muslim people who resent the influx of the Han into their province. The more conservative Uighur males parade themselves in long coats, knee-high boots, and fur-trimmed hats, while the women swathe themselves in shawls. Far-flung Kashgar, on the western rim of the parched Taklimakan Desert, is predominantly Uighur.

A hardy Turkic group, the nomadic **Kazaks** number over a million in Xinjiang; many fled to China after the 1917 Russian Revolution. The shores and mountains around Tianchi outside Ürümqi teem with Kazak families.

Another Turkic-speaking Chinese minority, the **Kirgiz** are also Muslim by faith and nomadic like the Kazaks. Huge numbers of Kirgiz fled to China from Kirgizstan (Kyrgyzstan) after a 1916 revolt against Russian hegemony; they are concentrated north of Kashgar. Other Turkic-speaking tribes exist in Xinjiang, and these include the agricultural **Uzbeks** and **Tartars.**

The **Mongol** tribes were united by Genghis Khan, and their descendants are scattered through the provinces of Inner Mongolia, Xinjiang, Qinghai, Tibet, and the northeast. They are typically stocky, short-limbed, and round-faced with flat features. Tibetan Buddhism was historically their chosen religion.

The face of this Tajik girl discloses the non-Chinese bloodline common to this part of northwest China.

The **Hui** (also known as Dungan) are Muslims descended from Chinese converts to Islam. They can be found throughout China but are most concentrated in Gansu, Xinjiang, Qinghai, and Ningxia. Hui men are recognizable for the white caps they wear.

The **Sibo,** a **Manchu** tribe, live in the northwest with descendants of Manchu troops stationed in Xinjiang during the Qing dynasty.

Originally from Iran, the **Tajiks** live in far west Xinjiang around the border with Tajikistan, particularly in the town of Taxhorgan (Tashkurgan). They number about 35,000 and speak a form of Persian.

The small community of **Russians** who were living in China was bolstered by refugees from the 1917 Russian Revolution. ■

cover more about the mummies, Elizabeth Wayland Barber, who is an expert on ancient textiles, is the author of *The Mummies of Urumchi* (Macmillan, 1999). The book is a fascinating and exhaustive piece of forensic detective work, in which the author posits a possible Celtic ancestry for the mummies, after a highly-detailed examination of their garments and analysis of the mummified corpses. ■

Many Kazak families live on the shores of Tianchi.

Tianchi

FROM THE DESERT-DRY AND SAND-BLOWN TERRAIN around Ürümqi, capital of Xinjiang Province, rises an unexpected alpine treat—mountains surrounding Tianchi, Heaven's Lake, perched at an elevation of 6,560 feet (2,000 m).

Tianchi

310 B2

$$$

CITS visitor information

38 Xinhua Nanlu

0991 282-1428

Not to be confused with Tianchi in China's northeastern Jilin Province (see pp. 340–41), the lake, located 70 miles (112 km) east of Ürümqi, is spectacularly at odds with the low-lying, arid terrain below. It is filled with melted snow from the surrounding mountains and ringed by forest. In summer, Tianchi is a breath of fresh air in one of China's oven territories.

You should aim to spend a day here at least, that is unless the weather, which usually obliges with postcard blue skies, is foul (the lake is only really accessible between spring and autumn). The punishing Xinjiang winter clamps the lake in ice and puts it out of reach to travelers.

Some people are so enamored with the lake that they spend months here, shacking up in the Kazak yurts that hug the shores. It's easy to understand why: The lake area is a pastoral pleasure with trails winding through deep pine forest, crossing flowery meadows over-looked by mountain goats on

precarious perches, skirting streams, and passing Kazak herders and cattle. If you have time (and not necessarily money) on your hands, this could well be the best way to experience China—one long, unique impression rather than as a kaleidoscopic series of tourist sights.

You disembark the bus from Ürümqi at a point you will want to leave quickly. This is where the Chinese tour buses grind in, disgorge travelers who clump together for photos and troop off to nearby restaurants for lunch before speeding back to base. (As always, try to avoid weekends and public holidays.) Aim to head off quickly around the paths that ring the lake, climbing and descending the undulating contours of the surrounding pine forest.

SUGGESTED ROUTE

Take the road to the right, and when you encounter the Kazak horsemen who are generally on hand (they will offer you tours up to the snowline for a price), turn left onto a concrete path. This soon gives way to a rough path, covered in hoof prints, which guides you into the pine forest carpeting the slopes around the lake. You will probably run into wide-eyed cattle munching vegetation on the slopes. Threading through the forest, you should find yourself alone, apart from the occasional fellow traveler. After about 20 minutes, the path leads downhill to a small glade beside the water, where cattle graze and yurts form a little community.

Just beyond is an exceptionally tranquil stretch with only the occasional cow for company. If you continue on the trail, you may meet a Kazak herder or two. A hillside invites you to clamber up, or you can continue on the lower path, as mountain goats scramble over the loose rocks, watching your ascent.

The boat cruises are tempting but not essential, for they only take you on a tour of what is far better to tramp through yourself. For a reasonable fee, Kazak riders will take you up to the snowline, which takes about ten hours.

You'll probably see a number of travelers dragging hiking gear into the region to fully explore what it has to offer, and this is a good option if you have the time.

If you find the two and a half-hour bus ride back to Ürümqi too daunting a prospect, you should quite easily be able to organize a stay in a yurt for the night; just ask around. These are very cheap, and three daily meals are included in the price. Otherwise, there's a guest house on the shores of the lake where you can stay in reasonable comfort. ■

YURTS

The shores of Tianchi are dotted with pie-shaped yurts (also called *gher*), nomadic tents favored by the Kazaks who dwell here. They are made from a thick outer skin of hide or thick felt thrown over wooden poles, and they are easily erected and taken down as herders moves to other pastures. Felt is the preferred material for nomads because

it is quick and easy to produce, not being a woven fabric. Yurts are cozy in the winter and cool in the summer. ■

Turpan

Turpan
311 B2

CITS visitor information
Oasis Hotel, 41 Qingnian Beilu
0995 852-1351/52

John's Information Café
Opposite Turpan Guesthouse, Qingnian Nanlu
0995 852-4237

Around Bezeklik Thousand Buddha Caves

A SENSATIONAL JOURNEY ACROSS A STARK LANDSCAPE from Ürümqi lies the green oasis town of Turpan, thirstily surviving on irrigated snowmelt water from Tianshan (Tian Mountains). The 30,000-square-mile (77,670 sq km) Turpan depression is China's lowest spot below sea level, a baking kiln in summer (temperatures can soar to 130°F/55°C) and a blistering freeze in winter.

THE DRIVE TO TURPAN

This is an unforgettable and invigorating experience. The town of Turpan was a luxuriant staging post on the northern arm of the Silk Road, imprisoned in the sterile void of the surrounding terrain. The expressway initially passes a long stretch of the **Tianshan range**—a dramatic backdrop that eventually flattens out into a featureless, sweeping plain.

On either side of the road extend huge desiccated swaths of desert. You pass a massive windmill field swept by forceful gusts. Some of the scenery here is remarkable—vast plains, snowcapped mountain

ranges, and an overwhelming sense of aridity. Step from the air-conditioned chill of your taxi into the summer oven of the Turpan basin, and feel the heat hit you like a frying pan. Farther south at Loulan was the testing range for China's nuclear weapons.

VINEYARDS

As well as being a well-irrigated oasis, Turpan is also a premier wine-growing region of China. Driving up toward the vineyards, you could almost think that you had accidentally stumbled upon a French wine-growing colony. Vine trellises shade the city, and the prime grape-picking season is from August to September. The viticulture is worth perusing for a taste of the sweet grapes and the comfortable shade that the vines offer.

Wander around the grape markets that cluster about the tourist-designated vineyards and sit down for a typical Uighur meal: crispy roast lamb skewers (fat clumps of grapes are thrown in for free). If you have developed a taste for kebabs *(yangrouchuan)*, these are some of the best around. The market is a hive of activity, especially at lunchtime: Chefs fan thick clouds of smoke from glowing coals spitting with lamb fat, while hawkers bellow and shout.

The market is presided over by ethnic traders overseeing huge bags that spill over with raisins and grapes. They will also draw your attention to rows of locally fermented wines.

The characteristic buildings with the missing bricks that you see all over Turpan are for drying grapes to make raisins.

SUGONGTA

Sugongta *($)* is a minaret and mosque, also known as Emin Minaret, on the southeast edge of town. Built in 1778, the tower is very simple and rather unspectacular.

KAR WELLS

The vines in Turpan are watered by an elaborate irrigation project that feeds water in from the melting snows of the Tianshan. The impressive channels were first engineered 2,000 years ago, based on a Persian design. Without them, Turpan would rapidly join the desert. The longest channel is over 6 miles (10 km) in length, and the system in total runs to 3,100 miles (4,990 km). You will probably get an idea of the wells and channels just by visiting the city, but a few kar wells *(kaner jing)* can be accessed as tourist sights. These unfortunately give little insight into the huge engineering entailed in the project, despite accompanying exhibits, but at least you can climb down the steps and run your fingers through the icy waters.

JIAOHE RUINS

The strategically located ruins at Jiaohe *($)*, about 4 miles (6.5 km) west of Turpan, were built on a plateau, originally occupied in the second century B.C. From 108 B.C. to A.D. 450, the city was the capital of the kingdom of Jushi, which was

GETTING AROUND

The best strategy is to rent a car or take a taxi from Ürümqi to Turpan and drive to most of the sights. The total distance is about 370 miles (595 km). Otherwise, buses run regularly between Ürümqi and Turpan, departing every 20 minutes or so for the two and a half-hour journey. ■

Dried fruits for sale at a local market hint at the bounty of produce culled from Turpan's well-irrigated land.

Bezeklik Thousand Buddha Caves

✉ 6 miles (10 km) north of Gaochang ruins

$ $

The surrounding land's rich textures echo in the ruins of Gaochang, the ancient Uighur capital.

destroyed by fire in a rebellion in the 14th century. There is not much to see here, and the remains of the buildings have taken on the appearance of the eroded landscape. But it is an atmospheric place and pleasant to walk around.

BEZEKLIK THOUSAND BUDDHA CAVES

Most of the sights are found outside the pleasant Uighur town itself. The Bezeklik Thousand Buddha Caves (Baizikelike Shiku), 35 miles (56 km) northeast of Turpan, are a network of grottoes featuring badly damaged Buddhist figures and wall paintings. They are eclipsed by some breathtaking scenery. Take your time to wander around the landscape, sculptured by the wind and redolent of an out-take from an Indiana Jones epic.

The poor condition of the caves can be traced to the energetic and wholesale removal of frescoes by Albert von le Coq (1860–1930), a German Oriental specialist, and Theodore Bartus, his assistant. The grottoes were also defaced by Islamic Uighurs, who had little time for the idolatrous Buddhist art.

Cave No. 27 shelters faintly discernible frescoes. The best preserved examples cling to the ceiling. Many of the faces are scratched away, while others appear caked in mud. One of the grottoes pitifully displays the huge figure of a toppled Buddha. Bad lighting in many of the caves doesn't help demystify the divine images. The experience unfortunately speaks more of the destruction of Buddhist art than its preservation.

The surrounding hills and dunes make for hot and energetic climbs. These are recommended for their stunning views over the arid rock formations (camels will carry you over short distances for a fee). If you are there in summer, don't forget sunscreen, and plenty of water.

As you drive to the Thousand Buddha Caves, you will pass the **Flaming Mountains (Huoyanshan),** which radiate a fiery hue under the relentless sun.

GAOCHANG & THE ASTANA TOMBS

To the south of the Bezeklik caves are the ruins of Gaochang, an ancient Uighur capital and later regional capital during the Tang dynasty. The city was destroyed in the 13th century, but outlines of the buildings and other shadows of habitation remain. The Astana Tombs lie to the northwest of the ruins of Gaochang. This is where the dead of Gaochang were buried over a period of 500 years from A.D. 273 to 782. The remains (some corpses, fabrics, and paintings) are remarkably well preserved by the aridity, as are all archaeological sites in the region. They were robbed centuries ago, however, and later turned over by Aurel Stein, a Hungarian-British Orientalist in the early 20th century. ■

Kar wells

⊠ Yaer Village, Turpan

Gaochang ruins

Map 311 C2

⊠ 28 miles (45 km) east of Turpan

$ $

Astana Tombs

Map 311 C2

⊠ North of the Gaochang ruins

$ $

A local Kuqa family watches television in a simple dwelling in this ancient Silk Road town.

Kuqa

FED BY SNOW WATER, THE OASIS OF KUQA (KUCHE) WAS formerly the seat of a prosperous Silk Road kingdom. The ancient shells of the nearby Kizil Buddhist caves are still decorated with frescoes despite the voracious attentions of European archaeologists.

The area was an important juncture on the northern arm of the Silk Road and a center of Buddhist activity. Kumarajiva (A.D. 344–413), one of the most diligent translators of Buddhist sutras, worked here (in charge of a huge band of translator monks). The great Chinese traveler Xuanzang, who passed through in the seventh century bringing Buddhist scriptures back to China, described a wealthy kingdom. To the south extends the fierce dryness of the Tarim Basin and to the north, the immense Tianshan Mountains.

As with any Xinjiang town worth its salt, Kuqa hosts a market that draws traders from surrounding desert outposts. Its bazaar is held on Fridays in the old town to the west of the new district. This is a seasoned part of town, decorated with old mosques. Kuqa is a harbor for a throng of minorities, including Uighurs, Sibo, Hui, Kirgiz, Manchus, and Mongolians.

The **Tomb of Molana Eshding Hoja,** in the west part of town, honors this 14th-century Muslim missionary. But Kuqa's showpiece is the **Kizil Thousand Buddha Caves (Kezier Qianfodong),** 43 miles (69 km) to the west. There are 236 caves scraped from the rock, many representing the earliest of their type (third century), although only a few are open. Many frescoes were removed and taken to Europe along with other antiquities by Von le Coq. Despite these attentions, many paintings remain.

At **Kizilgaha,** north of Kuqa, is an early **beacon tower (*fenghuotai*)** that was a link in a chain of signal posts across the region. ■

Kuqa
310 B2

Kizil Thousand Buddha Caves
$

GETTING THERE

It's quite a journey to the caves, which generally involves renting a vehicle (CITS can arrange) or taking a taxi. Take plenty of food and water in case of a breakdown. You could get a bus to Baicheng and sort out transport there for the remaining 7 miles (11 km). ■

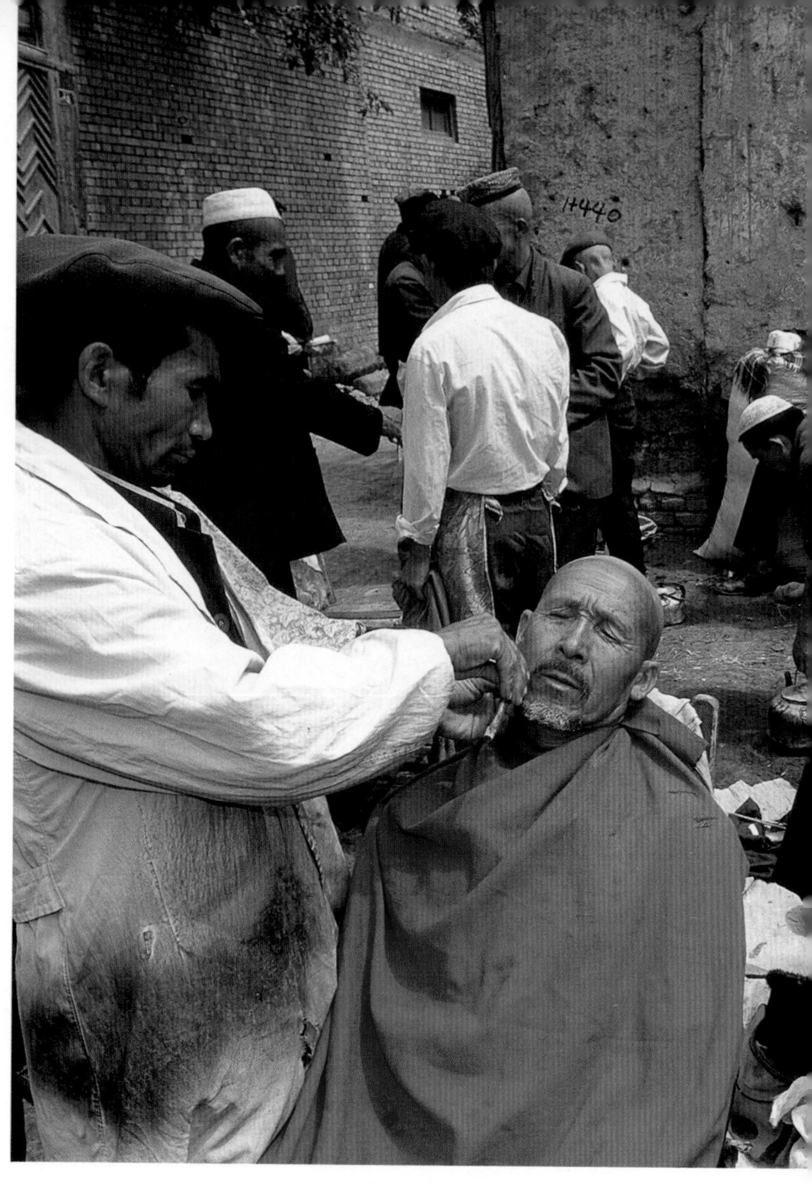

Kashi (Kashgar)

Kashgar
310 A2

John's Information Café *(see p. 383)*
Seman Hotel, 170 Seman Lu
0998 258-1186

OASIS OUTPOST, PLAYING FIELD OF THE GREAT GAME, AND Silk Road junction, Kashgar—despite the growing Han Chinese stamp—is a Central Asian town that has somehow drifted with the sand over the Chinese border from Central Asia. It is the focal point of this western region of what was called Chinese Turkestan, a city of silk markets, exotic bazaars, camel traders, and Islamic aromas. The farthest west of China's towns, Kashgar is pressed up toward bordering Kirgizstan and Tajikistan by the arid sands of the Taklimakan Desert.

Unlike Ürümqi to the east, Kashgar's persona is overtly Islamic, as 90 percent of the population are Uighur Muslims. Beijing's power diminishes in sandstorms somewhere east of here, although Kashgar somehow musters together a Mao statue and a People's Square. The socialist-housing style that defines the rest of China is delightfully absent.

A few miles east of Kashgar is the sacred resting place of the descendants of Abakh Hoja, a 17th-century Muslim holy man and ruler of this region. The 17th-century hall is capped with a green-tiled dome. It is also believed that Xiangfei, the Fragrant Concubine, is buried here. This Muslim princess was captured by Qing forces and taken to Beijing to serve

Open-air shave at the Sunday market. Unlike Ürümqi, Kashgar is deeply Uighur in character and custom.

as the emperor's concubine. The Qianlong emperor (*R.*1736–1795) built her a tower facing her homeland because she pined for her country, but palace intrigues compelled her to commit suicide under coercion from the empress dowager.

Kashgar's famous **Sunday market,** a busy confluence of trade traversing the old Silk Route, has been held here for the past 1,500 years. It rolls dustily into town every Sunday from the desert and throws up an enormous bazaar. This is the trading event of the week, a bustle of farmers and merchants bargaining over camels, sheep, goats, and fabrics; it fans out along Aizilaiti Lu in the east part of town.

Cattle are herded into crowded pens as farmers swarm amid an enthusiastic and boisterous swell. The market offers a wide variety of goods: kitchenware, multicolor fabrics, knives, embroidered rugs and carpets, handicrafts, and food; streetside vendors, serving up flat breads and yogurts, feed the throng.

During the week, a permanent bazaar peddles its wares on lanes that sprout east and west from **Id Kah Square.** The side streets glitter with jeweled knives and ornate boxes, while piles of rugs and carpets, hats, and embroidered caps attract souvenir hunters. Metal is hammered out and shaped on the spot, alongside jewelry shops that twinkle with precious metal, necklaces, and rings.

Id Kah Mosque (Aitigaer Qingzhensi) magnanimously overlooks its eponymous square, and is probably the most illustrious example of Islamic architecture in China. A glance at its dome and minarets, tiled in blue and red, reveals an aesthetic that would look at home in Islamabad.

The entry of Buddhism into China along the Silk Road left traces in the **Three Immortals Cave (Sanxiandong),** 8 miles (13 km) to the north. The frescoes have virtually vanished, and all that remain of the figures are a few minute statues of Buddha.

Twenty-five miles (40 km) west of Kashgar is the simple **Tomb of Mahmud Kashgari,** an 11th-century Uighur academic. ■

Above: A Xinjiang horseman tests his new mount at the Kashgar Sunday market.

Left: Uighur bookstall owner, Kuqa. The Uighurs use their own script (*weiyu*), although many can also read Chinese.

Right: A mechanized convoy snakes through the Taklimakan Desert.

Taklimakan Desert

The Taklimakan Desert, or Takelamagan Shamo, was historically a hostile wilderness and graveyard for foolhardy explorers and disoriented caravans. The desert dryly consumes the rivers that penetrate it from the Kunlunshan to the south and the Tianshan range to the north. The ancient Chinese called it the *liu sha*, or "moving sands," for the dunes that crawl across its face. Caravans wisely skirted it along the oasis-stringed perimeter, lest they be led to a dusty death or lashed by one of the epic sandstorms. Winters are freezing and summers searing, with negligible precipitation. ■

Karakoram Highway

Karakoram Highway
310 A2
Border at Khunjerab Pass officially opens Apr. 15–Oct. 31

THE KARAKORAM HIGHWAY FEEDS DRAMATICALLY through the mountains over the Khunjerab Pass and across the border into Pakistan. If you plan to visit Pakistan, this can make for an unforgettable entrance, but if you're just plain adventurous, the region offers a spellbinding display of awesome mountain scenery filled with lakes, canyons, and cliffs.

A breathtaking mountainous backdrop accompanies the road from Kashgar to Tashkurgan.

THE GREAT GAME

This is the name given to the colliding spheres of influence in Central Asia, played out by the great powers (most notably Great Britain and Russia) in the latter half of the 19th century and the early part of the 20th century. ■

Surging through Afghanistan, Pakistan, Kashmir, and China, the Karakoram mountain range boasts **K2 (Qoghir),** the world's second highest peak (28,250 feet/ 8,611 m). The Khunjerab Pass (named after the river) is the historic channel that funneled caravans and treasures into and out of China from present-day Pakistan. Today, if you are Pakistan bound, a more modern road will take you there.

From Kashgar (see pp. 320–23), the road as far as the town of Tashkurgan is wild, feeding between the staggering mountain heights of Kongurshan (25,280 feet/ 7,719 m) and Mustagh Ata (24,600 feet/ 7,500 m).

Between the two lies the icy beauty of **Karakul Lake (Kalakuli Hu)** *($$),* about 100 miles (160 km) southwest of Kashgar. The lake, at 12,464 feet (3,800 m), is dwarfed by towering peaks on either side. The waters are breathtakingly serene, and a sight to be witnessed. You can overnight here in one of the lakeside yurts for a proper assessment.

Opportunities exist to spend weeks here, and five-day hikes can be arranged from Kashgar. Otherwise, locals will gather with horses for ventures around the lake. Beyond the lake, the road to Tashkurgan passes gorgeous pastures.

Tashkurgan is an eight-hour bus ride from Kashgar. The town is the capital of an autonomous Tajik county, a fascinating borderland of cultures and moods. Though diminutive, Tashkurgan's importance was once greater than its size suggests; it often acted as a cornerstone of Great Game politics. Its most famous attraction is the **ruined fort.** Beyond lies the Khunjerab Pass and Pakistan. On the Pakistan side, things get rougher, and there's greater danger from falling rocks (and stones thrown by children). The best season to visit is summer; Tashkurgan lies at an elevation of more than 11,000 feet (3,350 m).

Vehicles can be hired in Kashgar to take you to both the lake and Tashkurgan. Remember to schedule a return for the next day (ask at John's Information & Café in Kashgar, see p. 383). ■

Hotan

ALSO KNOWN AS KHOTAN, THE OASIS CITY OF HOTAN (Hetian) lies at the southern extremity of the Taklimakan Desert, washed by a number of jade-bearing rivers. To the south are the ragged Kunlunshan, and the surrounding land is scarred with the withered remains of ancient cities. Hotan is celebrated in China for its indigenous jade, silk, and carpet production.

Hotan
310 BI

Like many Silk Road cities in Xinjiang, Hotan lay along the sweep of Buddhism as the religion journeyed east and was a thriving center for it before the arrival of Islam in the eighth century.

The **Hotan Museum (Hetian Wenbowuguan),** just south of the remains of the old city walls, contains relics from Hotan's kingdom past that eluded the antique collectors. Among the clutter lie two fascinating mummified bodies like the ones that can be seen in Ürümqi (see pp. 312–13).

Drop in on **Hotan's Sunday market** in the east part of town for its textures of local life. Hotan, one of the principal suppliers of nephrite jade in China, is renowned for the quality of its green silicate. You may see jade being carved and polished around town. The main street has a large number of shops and stalls selling it.

At the beginning of the 20th century, European adventurers explored the ruined cities around Hotan, unearthing Roman coins. Hotan's rich pre-Islamic kingdom was formerly embellished with fabulously ornamented Buddhist temples and monasteries. The nearest remains of this prosperous epoch are the ruins at **Yurturgan (Yuetegan),** 6 miles (10 km) to the west, and **Malikurwatur (Malikewate),** 16 miles (25 km) to the south. Despite their former importance, both ruined cities have collapsed under the weight of time, leaving little to posterity. ■

A Hotan silk worker uses a traditional method to starch his material.

Chinese jade

Despite being synonymous with China, jade is surprisingly not found in China proper. Nephritic jade was first discovered in river deposits in Xinjiang, or Chinese Turkestan.

Its color (generally green) depends on the concentration of metallic oxides present. It can be differentiated from jadeite by its oily feel. Jadeite has a glassy smoothness and impurities that make it white, emerald green, and blue, and it is found most abundantly in Myanmar (Burma). The jade often seen in Hong Kong is generally the much cheaper and more abundant fluorite (calcium fluoride). ■

CITS visitor information
- 23 Tamubake Xilu
- 0903 202-6090

Dunhuang

DUNHUANG IS AN ANCIENT OASIS TOWN IN THE PARCHED deserts of western Gansu Province, sheltering one of the most significant capitals of early Buddhist art in China. The caves are only equaled in renown by the grottoes at Longmen and Yungang.

Dunhuang
311 C2

CITS visitor information
32 Mingshan Lu
0937 882-3312

John's Information Café
Next to Fei Tian Hotel, 22 Mingshan Lu
0937 882-7000

Mogao Caves
311 C2
15 miles (24 km) southeast of Dunhuang
$$$$

International Dunhuang Project
www.idp.bl.uk
For information on cave treasures at Dunhuang

VISITING THE CAVES

Getting there and back is easy by minibus from Mingshan Lu in Dunhuang. Bear in mind that you will probably need at least a whole day here as there is a vast amount of detail to explore. Winter trips are not advisable because of the extreme cold. ■

When Buddhism first entered China, Dunhuang lay on a principal trade route along which flowed emissaries from myriad cultures: Turkish, Mongolian, Christian, Manichean, and Buddhist from Central Asia. The town marked a confluence of artistic styles and philosophies, becoming an important center of Buddhism and a place of devout pilgrimage. Even Hellenistic elements made their way into the art of Dunhuang, via Gandhara in North India.

The most famous grottoes are the **Mogao Caves (Mogao Shiku)** that pierce the desert cliff faces 15 miles (24 km) southeast of Dunhuang. Begun in the fourth century A.D., the caves were gradually adorned over a period of six centuries with paintings and effigies of Buddha, filled with religious manuscripts, and then mysteriously sealed in the 11th century.

It was not until 1900 that the caves were rediscovered, revealing a collection of 50,000 drawings and scrolls. Among these were not only Buddhist sutras but Taoist, Nestorian, and Zoroastrian documents. Collectors acting for large museums in the West were among the first to get wind of their discovery. The archaeologist explorers Aurel Stein and Paul Pelliot are vilified by the Chinese for their acquisition of bundles of priceless texts from Abbot Wang, who stumbled upon the find. Further damage was done by refugee White Russians who were forced by the Chinese to hole up in the caves. Subsequent efforts have been made to preserve the color and condition of the frescoes in the 492 caves. Some 45,000 frescoes remain, together with more than 2,000 statues.

THE GROTTOES

The Mogao Caves are kept behind locked doors, which makes access troublesome. A guide unlocks the caves in sequence, a service included with the ticket price. Each cave contains statues of Buddha or bodhisattvas. Representations of Buddha changed over the centuries, with Sakyamuni being popular in earlier ages, evolving into a later preference for the salvationary Buddhas, such as Guanyin.

The caves of the Northern Wei are replete with the otherworldly and delicately featured Buddhas characteristic of this era. The earlier figures reveal foreign influence, giving way to the more noticeable Chinese effects of the Sui caves.

The caves of the Tang dynasty tell different stories from their earlier Northern Wei counterparts, with a strong emphasis on the art of bodhisattva statues. Tang craftsmen were responsible for almost half of the caves. Other caves, such as **Cave 465,** show figures engaged in Tantric sexual union and are off-limits, unless you pay a hefty fee.

Highlights

Cave 96 contains a statue of Buddha, 113 feet high (34 m), seated behind the frame of a huge wooden pagoda. This is the Buddha of the future, the Maitreya Buddha. Inside the huge **Cave 16,** figures stand on a platform. It is reached by

a passageway adorned with Song bodhisattvas. The adjoining **Cave 17** contained many of the manuscripts that were plundered when the grottoes were rediscovered. **Cave 257** displays typical work from the Northern Wei, telling stories of Buddha's life (in this case the Deer King fable). In **Cave 259,** effigies of Buddha have that distant look sought by Wei craftsmen, and a definite Indian influence in the contours and styling. **Cave 148** has a 55-foot (16.5 m) Buddha, dispensing a final piece of wisdom before entering Nirvana.

The entry fee includes an English-speaking guide, who can cast light on these parables in stone. Photography is not allowed. Take a torch. It might be worth visiting the Dunhuang Research Centre at the **Mogao Caves** before you go around them. Exhibits explain how the caves were discovered and what remains in them.

CRESCENT MOON SPRING & SINGING SAND DUNES

About 4 miles (6.5 km) south of Dunhuang is the **Crescent Moon Spring (Yueyaquan),** a lake fed by a spring, set among colossal sand dunes that swirl around the oasis town. You can climb the **Singing Sand Dunes (Mingshashan)** for breathtaking views, wander through the setting on camelback, paraglide, or sand surf, all for a fee. Bikes can be rented from John's Information Café in Dunhuang (see p. 384); it's advisable to make the trip late in the afternoon when the dunes are cooler. ■

European archaeologists stripped Dunhuang's caves of their sacred scrolls in the early 20th century but spared the marvelous frescoes and statues.

Singing Sand Dunes

Map 311 C2

$ $$$

The snowcapped Qilian Mountains frame the magnificent spectacle of Jiayuguan Fort.

Jiayuguan Fort & around

WHILE THE INDUSTRIAL TOWN OF JIAYUGUAN HOLDS FEW surprises itself, its fort 4 miles (6.5 km) to the east is a monumental culmination to the story of the Great Wall. This spectacular structure traditionally marks the barrier's westernmost extremity.

Jiayuguan Fort
311 C2
Closed 12:30–2:30 p.m.
$$

Overhanging Great Wall
311 C2
$

July 1st Glacier
311 C2
$$

Despite the fort's fame as the terminus of the Great Wall (see pp. 86–89), older Han dynasty sections stretched farther west into the Gobi Desert, only to dissolve later into fragments. The vast structure was not built until 1372, soon after the establishment of the Ming dynasty.

The strategic importance of the fort's position is obvious. It controls the route through the Jade Pass that threaded the Silk Road between the Qilianshan and Black Mountains into this part of Gansu. The Taoist sage, Laozi (see p. 42), apocryphally journeyed on his ox through this pass en route to the west. Some say he reached India and became Buddha.

Jiayuguan Fort is a marvelous outpost to behold, its illustrious gate towers rising 35 feet (10.5 m) from the desert. Inside is an assortment of buildings, including a temple, and a theater where Qing troops were entertained. You can climb the walls and stroll along the battlements. Also included in the price is admission to the informative **Great Wall Museum**. A reconstructed section of wall, the **Overhanging Great Wall (Xuanbi Changcheng),** lies a few miles north of the fort.

Twelve miles (19 km) east of Jiayuguan is a group of **tombs.** The area is studded with burial mounds, but only some are open, 20 miles (32 km) northwest of Jiayuguan. Most were built during the Wei and Western Jin dynasties.

To escape the summer heat, take a taxi or minibus 80 miles (129 km) south to the **July 1st Glacier** in the chilly heights of the snowcapped Qilianshan. ■

Lanzhou & around

LANZHOU, CAPITAL OF IMPOVERISHED AND RUGGED Gansu Province, was an important staging post on the Silk Road. The corridor of commerce fed through the province, leaving a strong regional culture of Buddhist cave art in its wake.

There's not much to see in Lanzhou itself, but the **Gansu Provincial Museum (Gansusheng Bowuguan)** on Xijin Xilu displays an intriguing collection. The world-famous Han horse of Wuwei, a statue of a flying steed, is the show-piece item. It has an exhibition charting the history of the Silk Road, marked by compelling pieces that made their way into China from Byzantium.

White Pagoda Hill (Baita-shan) is an attractive climb capped by a temple of the same name. It lies on the northern bank of the Yellow River on which Lanzhou sits. **Five Spring Hills Park** to the south is linked to the heights of **Lanshan Park** above by a cable car.

Forty-six miles (74 km) to the southwest of Lanzhou, at Yongjing, are the carved Buddhist caves of **Binglingsi** *($$)*. The works are chiseled from the walls of a gorge above the Yellow River. The feat was begun in the Northern Wei dynasty, with additions by succeeding dynasties—especially the industrious Tang, Song, and Ming. On display are large effigies of Buddha with attendant wall paintings. The caves can be visited as a day trip from Lanzhou by taking a three-hour bus ride from Lanzhou followed by a one-hour speedboat ride to the grottoes; ferries also ply the route, but are much slower (seven hours return). Winter puts an icy clamp on all ferry tours to the caves because the water is too low.

Xiahe and the **Labrang Monastery** (see p. 330) can also be reached from Lanzhou. ■

Lanzhou

311 D1

CITS visitor information

10 Nongmin Xiang

0931 883-5566

Gansu Provincial Museum

Xijin Xilu

Closed Mon.

$

Work on the well-preserved Buddhist carvings at Binglingsi was carried out over a period of a thousand years.

Something in the air

The air in Lanzhou (which has a large petrochemical industry) is some of the worst on this planet. It's worth bearing this in mind if you are asthmatic or have another breathing difficulty. A report by the Washington-based World Resources Institute lists Lanzhou as having the world's most polluted atmosphere. The institute discovered that nine out of ten cities with the worst air pollution were in China. Jilin and Taiyuan both suffer from appalling levels. ■

Xiahe
311 D1

Labrang Monastery
311 D1
Xiahe
$

Xiahe & Labrang Monastery

THE PRAYER FLAG-GARLANDED TOWN OF XIAHE NESTLES deep in southwestern Gansu Province, a spiritual beacon turned toward Lhasa. For many, arrival at the Lamaist Labrang Monastery is akin to setting foot in Tibet. Most wayfarers depart Xiahe with fertile memories of a divine enclave and an enchanting sanctuary.

Labrang Monastery, the most famous Lamaist monastery outside of Tibet, is beautifully situated in a mountain valley.

Almost 10,000 feet (3,045 m) above sea level, Xiahe is a long strip of a town abutting the Daxia River. The community wraps itself around the **Labrang Monastery (Labulengsi),** huddled in the center of the town, ringed by a pilgrim's way. Worshipers shuffle around this sacred route, compelled by an ancient devotion that makes all outposts of Tibet so remarkable.

The Labrang Monastery, a flourishing retreat of Tibetan sacred culture far removed from the Chinese knot surrounding it, managed to escape the worst excesses of the Cultural Revolution. It dates back to 1709 and the time of the first Jamyang (the reincarnating Buddha of the monastery). Approximately one thousand monks live here, and six institutes delve into the arts of Buddhism, religious philosophy, astrology, and other esoteric disciplines. There are devotional temple buildings, the monks' living quarters, and a museum, in addition to the institute buildings.

The interiors of the Tibetan monastery buildings are lit with the soft glow of candles, which pick out Buddhist effigies and sacred volumes, monks at prayer, and frescoes. A disastrous electrical fire in 1985 gutted the **Assembly Hall,** but it has since been rebuilt.

Many Western travelers report being warmly received by monks at Labrang and welcomed into their living quarters; you can only enter the monastery, however, as part of a tour with a guide.

At festival time nomads and pilgrims swarm to the monastery and pitch tents in the surrounding grasslands. The most significant event is the Monlam Festival (4th to 16th day of the first lunar month, just after the Tibetan New Year). It includes the custom of displaying a huge cloth painting or *tangka* of the Buddha, dancing, and an exhibition of Tibetan butter sculpture.

Other noteworthy festivals are held in the second, sixth, seventh, and ninth lunar months (like the Chinese, Tibetans use the lunar calendar).

Opportunities also exist for bicycle and bus trips to the valley, lakes, and yak-grazing grasslands around Xiahe. Most hotels offer bicycle rental. ■

Yinchuan

YINCHUAN (SILVER RIVER) IS AN ATTRACTIVE, CLEAN, and easygoing city, capital of the poor and parched Ningxia Hui Autonomous Region. Summers are ferociously hot and winters savage; the unrelenting aridity of the region drives communities to cluster along the life-giving artery of the Yellow River.

Situated on the Lanzhou-Beijing railroad line, Yinchuan is divided into a new town (Xin Cheng) and an old town (Lao Cheng) with most of the city's features and areas of interest in the old town. The two towns are situated approximately 5 miles (8 km) apart.

A number of monuments in the old town recall Yinchuan's moment of glory as capital of the nomadic Tangut Xi Xia dynasty, which was wiped out by Ghenghis Khan. The predominant ethnic group here are the Hui, Muslim descendants of the merchants who traveled the Silk Road.

Many sights can be seen on foot. The **Ningxia Museum (Ningxia Bowuguan)** is part of the old **Chengtian Monastery** on Jinning Nanjie, running north– south. It assembles fragments from the Xi Xia dynasty and items from Hui culture. You can climb up the monastery's brick pagoda.

The old **Drum Tower (Gulou),** on Jiefang Dongjie (the main road running east–west), is just to the west of the **Yuhuang Pavilion (Yuhuangge),** a tower dedicated to the Jade Emperor (see p. 73) and formerly a museum.

Haibao Pagoda (Haibaota), also called the **North Pagoda (Beita),** lies in the north of the city. It is housed among temple buildings, inside one of which reclines a 23-foot (7 m) supine Buddha.

Historical remains scatter throughout the countryside around Yinchuan. The Xi Xia emperors are entombed about 30 miles (48 km) to the west. These **tombs (Xixiawangling)** can be visited by trips arranged by CITS *($)* or by hiring a taxi. Dusty and solemn crypts lack the majesty of other imperial tombs, but they evoke the passing of the dynasty.

Buses run the 12 miles (19 km) to **Yongning** to the south of Yinchuan. Outside town you can find the impressively constructed **Najiahu Mosque (Najiahu Qingzhensi).** This imposing Ming dynasty mosque is very busy on Fridays but quiet at other times of the week.

The **Yuhuang Pavilion** in **Pingluo,** 37 miles (60 km) to the north, is another temple structure dedicated to the Jade Emperor. ■

A member of the local white-capped Hui minority enters a mosque.

Yinchuan
311 D1

CITS visitor information
116 Jiefang Xijie
0951 504-8006 or 0951 504-5555

Ningxia Museum
32 Jinning Nanjie
$

Originally populated by more than one thousand monks, Wudangzhao Monastery is Inner Mongolia's largest lamasery.

Baotou & around

THE CITY OF BAOTOU, ON THE NORTHERN LOOP OF THE Yellow River, may seem little more than an industrial smudge across the map of Inner Mongolia, where few travelers linger, but there is a satisfying assortment of temples. More significant, the symbol of Mongolian national identity, Genghis Khan's Mausoleum near the city of Dongsheng to the south, urges exploration.

Baotou
311 D2

CITS visitor information
14 Shaoxian Lu
0472 511-6824

Dongsheng
0477 834-1075

Mausoleum of Genghis Khan
311 D1
$$$
One and a half hours to Dongsheng by bus, then two hours by minibus to mausoleum.

Temple hunters should head out of town for the Qing dynasty **Wudangzhao Monastery (Wudangzhao)** in the mountain foothills 40 miles (64 km) northeast of town. The Tibetan-style Yellow Hat Sect lamasery *($)* is wonderfully laid out along passages dividing buildings, with gloomy halls and dark interiors. Staring into the darkness slowly brings the occasional ogrelike statue and diabolical painting to life, along with a host of Buddhist effigies.

For those with an interest in the bloodthirsty chieftain, homage can be paid at the **Mausoleum of Genghis Khan (Chengjisihanling)** outside the city of **Dongsheng,** 68 miles (110 km) to the south. This is the place to get the core of the Mongolian identity in focus. Mongolians travel from all over the far-flung and disparate lands of Inner and Outer Mongolia to pay their respects to the man who set the world ablaze and placed China under the yoke of the Yuan dynasty. The mausoleum has naturally taken its place as an icon of Mongolian nationalism and cultural identity.

The domed buildings, dating from the 1950s, were restored after Cultural Revolution damage. Inside, offerings from visitors are laid in front of a statue of Genghis Khan. Adjacent halls accommodate the remains of his wife and one of his sons. Periodic ceremonies at the mausoleum further indulge the legacy of the man. ■

Hohhot

HOHHOT IS THE CAPITAL OF STEPPE-COVERED INNER Mongolia, lashed by merciless and forbidding winters. A thriving corner of temple architecture survives here, demonstrating the Mongolians' energetic liaison with Tibetan Buddhism.

The name Hohhot originates from its Mongolian name, meaning "blue city." The prospering modern city is today largely Han in character, but evidence of its Mongolian identity can be discerned in the occasional Mongolian script on street signs.

Temples lie in the old part of town to the southwest. **Dazhao Temple** *($)*, off Danan Jie, is the region's premier lamasery, albeit tainted by commercialization. The hall at the rear is a compelling, authentic feature.

The active **Xiletuzhao Temple** nearby, a rather dusty relic with mild Tibetan features, includes a large white **dagoba (stupa).**

On Wutasi Houjie lies the **Five Pagoda Temple (Wutasi)** *($)*, a group of orphaned brick pagodas abandoned by their temple. They rise together from a stone base, carved with Tibetan, Mongolian, and Chinese script. There is a small fee.

The Chinese-style **Great Mosque (Qingzhen Dasi),** on Tongdao Jie to the north, marks the confluence of Hohhot's Muslim community. Opposite, on Binhelu, the brisk **Bird Market (Binhe Lu Niaoshichang)** chirps throatily and sets up its stall on the weekends. Binhe Lu is to the west of Tongdao Jie.

For an understanding of the local culture, visit the intriguing **Inner Mongolia Museum (Neimenggu Bowuguan),** where you'll find yurts (see p. 315), clothing, and even a mammoth skeleton dug up in the northern part of the province. The museum *($)* is on Hulunbei'er Lu, at its intersection with Zhongshan Donglu. The **Zhaojun Tomb (Zhaojunmu),** 6 miles (10 km) south of the city, is the crypt of a Han dynasty imperial concubine. There are fine views of the surrounding countryside here.

The **grasslands** beyond town lure tour groups. Most of these tours offer contrived evenings in yurts. The nearest grasslands are at **Xilamuren,** 50 miles (80 km) away; taxis can take you there. Shop around for the best price.

The lively summer festival of Naadam, usually held in mid-August, is marked by traditional Mongolian sports such as wrestling and horse racing. ■

Hohhot

Map 311 E2

CITS visitor information

Inner Mongolia Hotel, Wulanchabu Lu

0471 230-8056

The rearing horse is a symbol of Mongolian freedom.

More places to visit in Inner Mongolia & the Silk Road

GRASSLANDS

For those who want a glimpse of yurts and a more authentic way of life, CITS , CTS, and hotels in Hohhot, can arrange tours to the grasslands. The consensus is that the trips are not the real thing—you'll need to visit Outer Mongolia to see that. Nonetheless, this is the closest you'll get in China itself.

CTS visitor information ✉ Inner Mongolia Hotel, Wulanchabu Lu ☎ 0471 230-8056

HAMI (KUMUL)

The predominantly Han city of Hami in the east of Xinjiang is famed for its melons. It has an attractive Uighur quarter that resists creeping industrialization. If traveling on the Lanzhou/Ürümqi railway, you could jump off here and seek out the **Muslim King Tombs (Huiwangmu)** in the southwest part of town.

Map 311 C2 **CITS visitor information** ✉ Building No. 1, Hami Binguan

LANGMUSI

The Gansu village of Langmusi attracts visitors to its two Tibetan monasteries. Situated near Sichuan, the community has strong Tibetan traditions. Langmusi can be reached from the nearby town of Hezuo.

Map 311 D1

LINXIA

Formerly an important Silk Road staging post, Linxia is a busy Muslim town southwest of Lanzhou (see p. 329). The minaret-studded town is today noted mainly for its markets and Muslim Hui character. The busy streets throng with people of the Dongxiang and Bao'an minorities. A climb away up **Beishan Park (Beishan Gongyuan)** is the **Taoist Wanshou Temple** that offers views over town.

Map 311 D1

MAIJISHAN

The Maijishan **Buddhist cave carvings** are not far from the town of Tianshui in the southeast corner of Gansu Province. Two cliffs are pockmarked with 194 caves ornamented with figures of Buddha and religious frescoes, ranging from Northern Wei work to the Qing dynasty. The rock face is webbed with staircases and platforms. The effigies in cave No. 133 of the Western Cliff are the most renowned. Some caves are inaccessible, but you can cut the gloom with a flashlight.

Map 311 D1 $ $$

ZHANGYE

Midway between Wuwei and Jiayuguan in Gansu is the old garrison town of Zhangye. Marco Polo passed through and called the town Campichu, followed centuries later by the Anglo-Hungarian adventurer Aurel Stein and the American archaeologist and art historian Langdon Warner (1881–1955). The story of the **Giant Buddha Temple (Dafosi)** begins during the tribal Xixia dynasty, further unfolding under the Ming and Qing. The spectacular 111-foot (34 m) reclining Buddha is the largest of its type in China.

Forty miles (64 km) south of Zhangye is the village of **Mati (Horse's Hoof).** Activity centers on the cliffside **Mati Temple** *($$)*, a regional focus of the Yellow Hat Sect of Tibetan Buddhism. The temple encircles a hoofprint left by a sacred horse.

Map 311 D1 **CITS visitor information** ✉ 60 Xianfu Nanjie ☎ 0936 824-3445

ZHONGWEI

The impressive Gao Temple is the main reason to come to Zhongwei in Ningxia Province. The temple, a chance for the three major Chinese faiths to rub shoulders with each other, shows stupendous design and detail. A hall dedicated to the chambers of hell is a particular freak show, indulging in the unpleasant horrors awaiting evildoers.

Comprehensive tours around Zhongwei include the **Shapotou Desert Research Institute,** a chance to see a traditional water wheel at Beichangtai, trips along the Yellow River on leather rafts, and fragments of the **Great Wall** in the Tenger Desert. **Shikong,** not far east of Zhongwei, contains some rather neglected ancient **Buddhist cave art.**

Map 311 D1 **Ningxia Zhongwei Travel Service** ✉ 7 Xi Dajie ☎ 0953 701-2620 ■

Dalian brings sophistication to the conservative Northeast—the three provinces formerly known as Manchuria. Manchu artifacts survive in Shenyang, while Harbin displays its Russian heritage alongside a glittering winter ice festival.

The Northeast

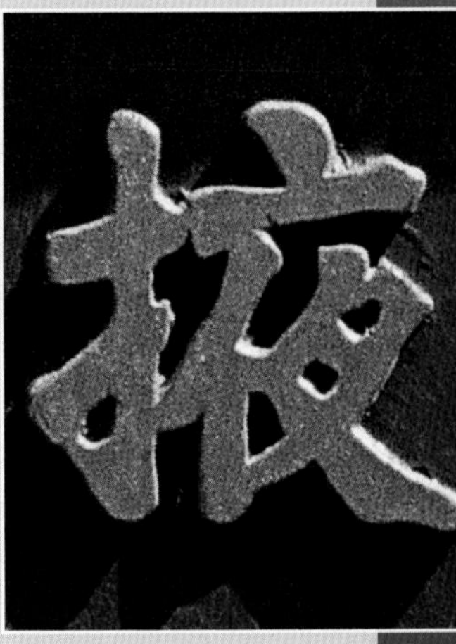

Detail from the Imperial Palace in Shenyang

The Northeast

COMPARED WITH ENTREPRENEURIAL, STEAMY SOUTH CHINA, THE HARDY Northeast is the other side of China's coin. Blasted by staggeringly cold winters and cast as an industrial hinterland—it has a reputation for being rather pedestrian. The toughness of the people, however, finds dramatic reflection in an often savage landscape of frozen rivers, volcanic lakes, jagged mountains, and rugged borderlands. The Northeast is also the cradle of the magnificent Manchurian civilization with a piecemeal history of Russian control that has left a grand inheritance of dashing architecture.

Autumn along the Yalu River Jilin Province

While perhaps this should not be your first port of call in China, the Northeast is often unjustly sidelined by travelers. The temple-watcher and sunseeker may leave the Northeast feeling cheated, but if you're in search of wilder climes and textures, you will be fully rewarded.

The dynamic port city of Dalian drags the whole of the southernmost Manchurian province of Liaoning behind it. The city has preserved museum-piece Russian architecture while being a blueprint for a new and adept China. This southern upstart eclipses its land-locked provincial capital, but Shenyang discloses a precious vein of imperial splendor in its Manchurian palace and tombs.

Border fanatics can traipse over to Dandong to gaze North Korea in the face and

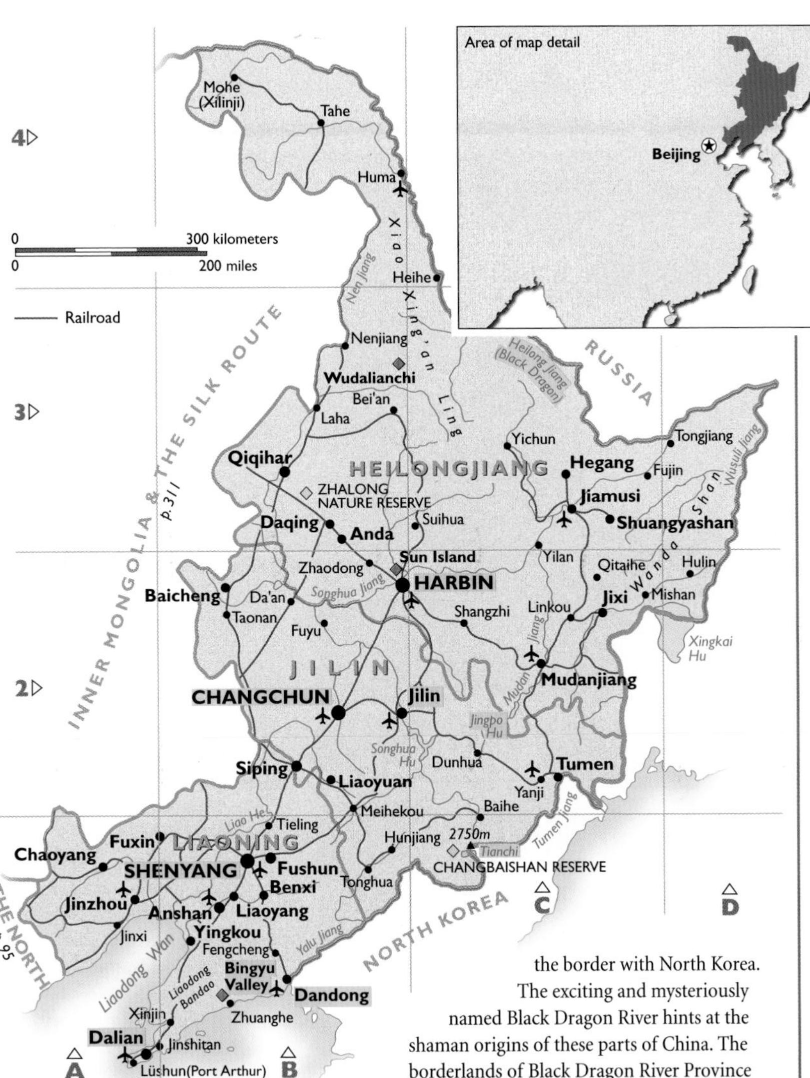

possibly even penetrate the idiosyncratic state.

The large cities of Jilin Province, sandwiched between Russia, Inner Mongolia, and North Korea, are of the heavyset industrial cast, but the volcanic lake of Tianchi fires the province with mystery. High up in a beautiful alpine landscape of firs and flowers, the lake is within a sublime range of ragged rocks, with crystal waters and melting snow, straddling the border with North Korea.

The exciting and mysteriously named Black Dragon River hints at the shaman origins of these parts of China. The borderlands of Black Dragon River Province (Heilongjiang) indeed still support shaman-believing minorities.

Winter's big chill puts many transportation options literally on ice. The icy season, however, yanks the curtain off the glittering Ice Festival in the province's attractive capital, Harbin. This unlikely but very popular tourist season drags Chinese from all over the land to watch the locals swimming in thick holes cut into the ice-bound river. You will need a strong constitution, but some people say it's very good for the heart. ■

Dalian & around

Dalian
337 A1

CITS visitor information
145 Zhongshan Lu
0411 8367-8019

THE PORT CITY OF DALIAN FOSTERS AN UPBEAT SPIRIT forged from the zeitgeist of reform. This oasis of enviable prosperity, clean buses, lawns, and streets is loved by its citizens. With some grand examples of Russian and Japanese architecture, Dalian is also famed for having China's sole unit of policewomen patrolling on horseback.

Dalian's Bank of China Building in Zhongshan Square is an example of the city's architectural heritage.

The ice-free port of Dalian was granted to Russia as a concession in 1898, only to slide into the jaws of the Russo-Japanese War (1904–1905). **Port Arthur** (now known as Lüshan), just to the south, was the scene of Russia's humiliating naval defeat in 1904. Dalian remained under Japanese control until the end of World War II, when it again passed into Russian hands, returning to China in the 1950s.

Much of Dalian's charm is a result of its architecture, and building enthusiasts will enjoy the spectacle of **Zhongshan Square** (actually a circle). The city converges on this point, with major streets radiating from here. The wonderful **Dalian Hotel** is a picture. Across the way is the domed Bank of China Building, and the classical pile next to it is the **People's Cultural Hall.**

Decorated with beautiful lawns, **People's Square (Renmin Guangchang)** to the southeast of Zhongshan Square is a popular congregation point for Dalian's citizens. Much of the architecture in what was formerly called Stalin Square is of the monumental, Soviet-style variety. Tianjin Jie, east of Shengli Square, is a popular shopping drag.

AROUND DALIAN

Dalian is surrounded by a wealth of beaches, and there's some dramatic scenery down by the coast. About three miles (5 km) southeast is the pebbled beach of **Bangchuidao.** In the vicinity are some splendid vistas, including a stirring stretch west along the coastal road to Laohutan Park, overlooking the sea from the clifftops. Farther along the coastline to the west is a small string of sandy beaches—**Fujiazhuang, Silver,** and **Gold.** Farther westward again lies the attractive beach of Xinghai Park.

Thirty-seven miles (60 km) north of Dalian is **Jinshitan (Golden Stone Beach),** a popular weekend getaway. The area is noted for its rocky landscape formations, caves, and beach area. ■

Shenyang

SHENYANG IS THE CAPITAL OF LIAONING PROVINCE AND IS the most southerly of the three provinces that made up Manchuria. Historically, the city was fought over by the Russians and Japanese and was left a ragged mess after World War II. Today it is principally driven by heavy industry.

Shenyang
337 B1

Liaoning Tourism Bureau
113 Huanghe Dajie
0428 8680-7316

Strong echoes of the Forbidden City (see pp. 56-62) exist in the design of the walled **Imperial Palace,** dating from 1625, although it is mainly Manchu in concept. The palace is smaller than its counterpart in Beijing, but it was here that the Qing dynasty was inaugurated in 1636 (before going on to consume the rest of China).

The buildings are laid out on a north–south axis, with halls on either side displaying weapons and exhibitions of ceramics and jade. Notable halls are the the **Dazheng Hall,** the **Chongzheng Hall,** and the **Wensu Hall.** Some were used for the shamanistic rites that formed the belief system of the Manchu (see pp. 34–35).

Historically bedeviled by a lumbering state enterprise sector, Northeast China has, in recent years, been confronting the harsh truths of economic reform by heavily shedding industrial jobs. Shenyang has its own potent symbol of political backwardness, a **Mao statue** in Zhongshan Square in the center of town—evocative of all that was wrong with China, the proletariat gaily reached for a future that never quite dawned. Inspect it closely, for there are numerous stories etched into the stone, but the overall message is the unmistakable folly of megalomania.

In the northern suburbs is the magnificent **North Tomb (Beiling).** Entombed here is Abahai (1592–1643), founder of the Qing dynasty, and his wife. Built in the mid-17th century, with later additions, the tomb rests at the end of a statue-lined avenue inside a vast park. Southeast of North Tomb, off Chongshan Lu, is the restored North Pagoda, with halls that are decorated with a series of celestial images and statues.

Five miles (8 km) east of Shenyang is East Tomb, the final resting place of Abahai's father, Nurhachi (1559–1626). The Manchurian chieftain (also known as Kundulun Khan) brought together the scattered northeastern Jurchen tribes into the capable fighting force that invaded China. ■

Manchu splendor marks the Imperial Palace in Shenyang, with the dragons symbolizing the emperor.

Imperial Palace
Shenyang Lu
$$

North Tomb
Taishan Lu
$

Tianchi

Tianchi
337 C1

Changbai Mountains
$$$$

TIANCHI (HEAVEN'S LAKE) IN JILIN PROVINCE IS A volcanic lake on the North Korean border in the Changbaishan (Ever White Mountains) Reserve. It is one of the prime sights of China's northeast. The perfect antidote to congested cities, it is a blessed retreat for volcanologists, geologists, and adventure seekers. Its panorama of photogenic opportunities includes snarling rock formations, a mirror-smooth lake, emerald green pines, and all the drama of a volcanic presence.

China's largest nature reserve is a treasure chest for the natural scientist. The region is thickly covered in deciduous and coniferous forests, with alpine meadows on the higher reaches. There is also a wealth of medicinal plants and animal species, along with rare sightings of the Manchurian tiger (see p. 340).

Waterfalls drain the chilly lake of Tianchi in summer, plunging dramatically past as you ascend to the volcanic rim.

The peaks of the **Changbai Mountains (Changbaishan)** cluster around a number of dormant volcanoes and crater lakes in a belt that has heavy precipitation. The highest peaks (8,000 feet/2,438 m) of the range are covered by snow for half the year. Rivers plunge from Tianchi cascading into spectacular waterfalls.

The lake is the goal for most travelers, but many do not take the time to fully appreciate the spectacle. At 7,200 feet (2,195 m), the air is getting thin, but not dangerously so. Three miles (5 km) from north to south and just over 2 miles (3 km) from east to west, the lake is 8 miles (13 km) in circumference. Clear weather adds sharp definition to the jagged rocks and peaks and makes for dramatic images.

A word of warning: The Changbai Mountains cleave Liaoning and Jilin Province from North Korea. Tianchi straddles the North Korean border, and the lake cannot be circumnavigated, so stick to the northern perimeter. The whole region on the Chinese side in Jilin is called the Korean Autonomous District, populated by Chinese of Korean ancestry.

Another word of warning: Chinese tour buses descend on Tianchi for swift assaults on the area. Chinese visitors habitually discard styrofoam lunch boxes, chopsticks, and plastic water bottles, festooning the crags with detritus. To escape the main concentration of tourists, chart your own route around the immediate reaches of the lake. It's relatively simple to get away from tourists; they tend to herd together at the main assembly point.

If you set off on your own, watch out for sharp rocks, as well as dense cloud cover that can suddenly appear. Weather at such high elevations can change quickly, and what was a fine day can become cold and miserable. You can hire PLA (People's Liberation Army) overcoats and waterproof jackets from the gaggle of women who wait at the Tianchi bus stop.

Guides are at hand for those who want to access the highest reaches of the lake for sublime views down to the water. Take a wide-angle lens to encompass the whole circle of the volcano's rim (but don't bother to hike up if the weather is not good).

Getting to Changbaishan, formerly called Puxianshan after the bodhisattva, is quite a journey. The lake is only realistically accessible from late June to September, when the ice and snow that grip the volcano for the rest of the year melts. The occasional snowmobile makes the trek out from Baihe (a very small town closest to the mountains) during the frozen months, but this can be extremely hazardous. For the intrepid, however, guest houses are plentiful in the Changbaishan region.

You can get to Baihe either by train from Shenyang (see p. 339) via Tonghua, or from Dunhua (see map). Alternatively you can fly to Yanji, head back to Antu, and then get a bus to Baihe. From Baihe, buses leave from the square in front of the train station (from 6 a.m. to noon); for more freedom, you can always rent a car with a driver. ■

Overlooking the border with North Korea and only accessible in summer, the volcanic lake of Tianchi is a dramatic destination.

Tigers in China

China offers a precarious abode to the tiger, one of the world's most fascinating and majestic species. As in other countries, the tiger in China is on the verge of extinction in the wild. The 20th century saw three subspecies wiped out completely in other countries, largely because of hunting, forest degradation, and encroachment on habitat.

Chinese tigers are being enticed to return to sanctuaries, reserves, and zoological parks created for their protection.

The tiger casts a spell over the Chinese imagination. It belongs to one of the 12 animals of the Chinese astrological calendar and is represented by wood in the cycle of the five elements (see p. 230). The white tiger denotes the guardian of the eastern direction in *fengshui* (see p. 230). The markings above and between a tiger's eyes resemble the Chinese character for "king" (*wang*), three horizontal lines joined by a vertical line. The tiger lends its movements to one of the more vigorous of Shaolin *gongfu* (see pp. 122–23) styles, where the tendons of the forearm and hands are conditioned like steel and the legs strengthened for leaping.

Tiger parts are prized in the Far East for their alleged medicinal properties, and consequently Chinese tigers have been trapped to feed the traditional medicine market in China, Taiwan, Japan, Korea, and Chinese communities the world over. China is a signatory to the Convention on International Trade in Endangered Species of Wild Fauna and Flora (CITES). The market within China has been banned, but illegal hunting continues.

It's hard to determine exactly how many tigers still exist in the wild in China. They are careful to live as secretively as possible and are therefore elusive. Siberia Tiger Park (see p. 346) is part of a large program to breed animals in captivity and release them back into the wild. There are problems of inbreeding with captive animals, especially where there is a very small natural population in the wild.

Siberian tiger

The world's largest tiger, the Siberian (Manchurian or Amur) tiger (*Panthera tigris altaica*), is a fascinating specimen. Sadly, it dwindles on the cusp of extinction in its homeland of Manchuria, Russia, and North Korea, but it has been seen in the Changbaishan region of China's northeast, which adjoins North Korea.

A far larger and heavier cat than the other Chinese tigers, with males weighing up to 800 pounds (360 kg) and reaching 9 feet (2.8 m) in length, it has a yellowish-orange fur ribbed with black stripes. Its eyes are yellow and its night vision is excellent (for hunting).

Siberian tigers are on the Endangered Species List, and considerable conservation efforts have rescued them from certain obliv-

ion. These animals are not very sociable, tending to lead solitary lives. They mate in winter and spring, and the litter typically consists of two to four cubs.

Only 200–300 tigers survive in the wild (mostly in Russia), with another 1,000 or so in zoological parks and reserves such as the Siberia Tiger Park in Harbin (see p. 346). In captivity, they can expect to live much longer than in the wild and yield offspring.

Indochina tiger

The Indochina tiger (*Panthera tigris corbetti*) is possibly vanishing more rapidly than any other subspecies. About 1,200 to 1,800 of these animals survive in China, Vietnam, Laos, Myanmar (Burma), and Thailand. The only specimens that now exist in China are a handful of animals that live in reserves in Xishuangbanna in southern Yunnan Province (see pp. 272–75).

South China tiger

About 30 South China, or Amoy, tigers (*Panthera tigris amoyensis*) survive in the wild, with about 50 in captivity. This is the only tiger indigenous to China. It numbered 4,000 in the early 1950s but was almost bludgeoned into extinction when it was hunted as a pest. Evidence of its existence has been found in the provinces of Hunan, Fujian, Guangdong, and central Jiangxi. ■

Hunted virtually to extinction, the huge Siberian tiger is a protected species struggling for survival in China's northeast.

Thickly swaddled Harbin residents battle against the winter cold.

Harbin & around

A STATELY MEMENTO OF RUSSIA'S FORMER INFLUENCE here, Harbin is capital of Heilongjiang (Black Dragon River) Province. The city's visual appeal is great: Russian Orthodox churches, onion domes, and fancy pockets of cobbled streets. Take a deep breath of the glacial Harbin winter and feel it punch you in the chest. This is the season when Harbin's picturesque streets swarm with out-of-towners, lured by the twinkling of the city's renowned ice festival.

Harbin
337 B2

CITS visitor information
68 Hongjun Jie
0451 5366-1191

The attractive historic quarter lies north of the train station. The China Eastern Railway put Harbin on the map, linking it to Vladivostok (250 miles/402 km southeast) and to Russian-controlled Dalian (see p. 338). Russian influence periodically waned (such as after the disastrous Russo-Japanese War), but there was a continual presence here (with Russians outnumbering the Chinese for a while). Today, the hotels that flank the train station overflow with Russian visitors who flock to Harbin to shop.

The **Church of St. Sophia (Dongzheng Jiaotang),** on Toulong Jie near Diduan Jie, is the premier example of Russian

Orthodox church architecture in China. Some churches, most notably the small, wooden **St. Nicholas,** failed to survive the battering of wars and the Cultural Revolution. Fortunately, this proud and charismatic church remains despite the foliage that indiscreetly pokes from rooftop niches.

Built in 1899, the church is a gorgeous pile of round arches and red brick capped by a turquoise dome and adjacent towers, where Byzantine curls and flourishes confidently assert themselves. Within the church is the **Harbin Architecture & Arts Centre,** with photographs on local history.

Zhongyang Dajie, in the heart of **Daoliqu,** Harbin's most graceful neighborhood, is the main boutique-lined street that conveys shoppers to the Songhua River. Take your time to wander past Russian spires and turrets and around the side streets that lazily meander off Zhongyang Dajie.

The misnomer of the **Modern Hotel** disguises its more historic origins in 1906. This civilized Russian hotel is a stylish place brimming with character. Pop inside for a feel of the place and a glance at the lobby, or reserve a room. The hotel sits on a street undergoing a defiant modernization of boutiques and fast-food restaurants, yet the local mood has not been completely trampled.

Standing at the northern end of the street by the Songhua River, the modern **Flood Control Monument** is a reminder that Harbin often suffered serious flooding. The embankment that runs along the river has a ponderous Russian ring to it: **Stalin Park** (much of the Northeast still has one foot in the era of Sino-Soviet camaraderie). This is the main area of Harbin's summer tourist industry, jammed with vendors of all description selling hot sweet potatoes and cooked river snails. Boats of all shapes and sizes chug to and fro across the river to Sun Island.

In winter, arctic temperatures transform the river into a glacier decorated with ice skaters (and other winter sports enthusiasts). The locals show their contempt for the cold by carving holes in the ice and swimming in the slush beneath.

The winter also ushers in Harbin's tourist season. To the east is **Zhaolin Park (Zhaolin Gongyuan),** the annual venue for the **Ice Lantern Festival (Bingdengjie).** This fairyland extravaganza sees carvers shaping ice to look like animals, fantastic creatures, and famous historic buildings. The sculptures are colorfully illuminated from within (it's

The Modern Hotel

✉ 89 Zhongyang Dajie

☎ 0451 461-5846

Ice Lantern Festival

✉ Zhaolin Park

$ $$

Siberia Tiger Park

✉ 88 Songbei Jie, Songbei District

☎ 0451 8808-0098

$ $$

even more enthralling if you've had some of the local firewater to stave off the cold). The festival is held from January to March, but it's worth phoning a hotel in Harbin to check before you sled over. If you do visit Harbin in winter, prepare yourself for the extreme temperatures; buy a good padded down jacket, thick gloves, lip salve, long johns, and warm boots.

Sun Island (Taiyangdao), on the opposite side of the Songhua River, sounds welcoming, unless you happen to arrive in midwinter. Spring and especially summer promise long walks and camping opportunities. The island is a huge expanse of parks, paths, and the excellent **Science and Technology Museum (Kejiguan) Siberia Tiger Park (Dongbeihu Linyuan).** Ten miles (15 km) north of town, the park is a noble attempt to stave off extinction for the massive Manchurian tiger (see pp. 342–43).The objective is to rear tigers for their eventual release into the wild, where numbers are precipitously low.

Visitors are driven through the reserve in vehicles for close-up views of the huge mammals. With over 100 cubs born here every year, the park—China's largest reserve for the breeding of the Manchurian tiger—currently has over 620 tigers and aims to rear 1,000 tigers by 2010. ■

Harbin's glittering Ice Lantern Festival draws visitors from all over China.

Unit 731

This horrible scar of the war with Japan is exposed to view around 10 miles (16 km) to the south of Harbin *(closed 11:30 a.m.–1 p.m.)*. The remains of the infamous Unit 731 Japanese Germ Warfare Division were left behind by fleeing Japanese troops at the end of World War II.

The base served as an experimental germ-warfare laboratory, with human subjects (Chinese, British, and Korean POW) used as guinea pigs.

Japan's goal was to leapfrog the West in the nonconventional warfare race. The operation aimed to develop a host of pathogenic weapons (including anthrax, plague, typhoid, and cholera) with prisoners as lab specimens. Prisoners were experimented on to further medical knowledge.

The display is not as engrossing as its equivalent in Nanjing (see pp. 154–57), as it consists only of a few rooms and remnants of the base, but for historians of the war with Japan, and for those keen to better understand why many Chinese still harbor suspicions about the Japanese, it is essential viewing. ■

More places to visit in the Northeast

BINGYU VALLEY

About 150 miles (240 km) north of Dalian, Bingyu Valley (Bingyu Gou) is a gully of precipitous rock formations pinched by forested mountains. It's an impressive natural wonder but only worth considering if you have a lot of time, because traveling there is a lengthy operation. The best way to reach Bingyu Valley is by bus from Dalian to Zhuanghe, and then by minibus.

337 B1 $$$$

BLACK DRAGON RIVER

Snaking along the border between China and Russia, this river lends its dark name to Heilongjiang Province. The Black Dragon River penetrates areas of Siberian forest, and summer boat trips can be made between **Tongjiang, Heihe,** and **Huma.** This is the shrinking homeland of minorities such as the Shaman Oroqen and the Daur. You can't go farther north than **Mohe,** also on the river, from where you can witness the aurora borealis (northern lights). Winter trips are out of the question as the temperature can fall as low as low as -60°F (-50°C).

337 C3

CHANGCHUN

Changchun is the rather dull capital of Jilin Province. Its **Puppet Emperor's Palace & Exhibition Hall** is where you can unearth vestiges of the life of Henry Puyi, the last emperor. His lamentable life was retold by Italian film director Bernardo Bertolucci in his epic film *The Last Emperor.* The puppet king was manipulated by the Japanese and stage-managed as emperor of Manchukuo (Japan's policy of taking over China began with Manchuria) in 1934, with Changchun as its capital. The palace was his residence and is a spiritless reminder of the tragicomedy of Puyi's life. You can walk through his domain of small rooms and trace his unfortunate story through the photos on the walls. An exhibition at the rear deals frankly with the Japanese occupation of Manchuria.

337 B2 **CITS visitor information**
Changbai Shan Hotel, 1448 Xinmin Dajie
0431 566-6541

DANDONG

Bordering North Korea on the Yalu River, Dandong's main attraction is the opportunity to get up close to that monolithic entity—the Democratic People's Republic of Korea (DPRK). This can be done by taking a speedboat along the river to peer at a sad panorama of idling soldiers and barking dogs. The half-destroyed bridge crossing the river was the work of the U.S. Air Force during the Korean War, during which 200,000 Chinese died.

Fenghuangshan is a mountain decorated with charming temples. It lies 32 miles (51 km) to the northwest of Dandong.

337 B1 **CITS visitor information** 20 Shiwei Lu 0415 213-5854

JILIN

The city of Jilin (known in the West as Kirin) is most famous for its winter phenomenon of ice-rimmed trees. Water from the nearby hydroelectric plant flows into the river and keeps it from freezing; the evaporating water condenses on the frozen branches of riverside trees, encrusting them with ice.

Locals are proud of the **Catholic church,** on the north shore of the Songhua River by Jilin Bridge, which suffered a dressing-down during the Cultural Revolution. Not far east of the church, the magnificent **Confucius Temple (Wenmiao)** displays an interesting exhibition featuring the archaic methods of the imperial examinations (see p. 83). The main temple presents a statue of Confucius surrounded by sacred objects.

337 B2 **CITS visitor information**
1 Chongqing Jie 0432 244-1304

JINGPO LAKE

As with many natural marvels in China, Jingpo Lake (Jingpo Hu) is a victim of its own popularity. Legions of Russians and Chinese descend here to navigate boats around this island-studded lake on the Heilongjiang–Jilin border, and a resortlike character results. To capture a more meditative mood, rent a fishing rod (in summer) and find yourself a quiet perch on the shore.

337 C2

Travelwise

Out for the day at Dounag Flower Market

TRAVELWISE INFORMATION

PLANNING YOUR TRIP

CLIMATE & WHEN TO GO

China is a vast land with large disparities in climate, so you have to decide where you are going before deciding when. Summer is hot the land over, humid along the southern coastline and the Yangtze region, and arid in the northwest. Rains are generally heavy in July and August, especially in the south. The southern reaches of Guangdong, Guangxi, and Yunnan Provinces, Hong Kong, Macau, and Hainan Island all lie in a tropical zone, with sweltering summer humidity. Late autumn, winter, and early spring are comfortable seasons to visit Hong Kong and Macau.

Typhoons can scuttle travel plans, blowing in along the southern coastline (and Hainan Island) during the summer.

Winters north of the Yangtze River are bitterly cold, especially in Tibet, the Northwest, Inner Mongolia, and the Northeast. High elevation destinations will be very cold in winter, and many places such as Jiuzhaigou and Tianchi are inaccessible during winter months. You would not want to visit Jiayuguan or Dunhuang in Gansu Province during winter, and the Turkic northwest is just as inhospitable. On the other hand, Harbin in the Northeast makes a tourist season out of its harsh winter. Beijing endures hot summers and bitterly cold winters, but it can realistically be visited in any season, although autumn—a very short season in the capital—is definitely the best. Shanghai is miserable in winter and extremely hot and muggy in summer, with spring and autumn the best seasons to visit. Central and southern Yunnan Province experience a relatively mild winter. Hainan Island is very comfortable in winter.

China's festivals are times to see the land celebrating. The Chinese New Year, or Spring Festival, is a nationwide holiday that can extend to a week off for China's citizens. The May 1 (May Day) and October 1 (National Day) holidays now both typically run to a week. All of these festivals see hotel prices rising; train, plane, and bus tickets can be in very short supply, especially at the Chinese New Year. Moreover, tourist sights around China are flooded with domestic tourists during these holiday periods, making it a very busy time to be traveling for leisure.

WHAT TO TAKE

Travel as light as possible. A collapsible umbrella is useful. Take jeans, or a light pair of quick-dry travel trousers, a waterproof jacket, waterproof or durable shoes. A sun hat, sun screen, sunglasses, first-aid kit, bug repellent, and lip salve are also needed. You will find a phrase book, money belt (essential), Swiss army knife (important), alarm clock, small flashlight, and camera helpful. Diarrhea tablets can be lifesavers on a long-haul bus trip. Also pack antiperspirant/deodorant (hard to find). A thick, padded jacket, long johns, warm socks, and gloves are essential if traveling to North China, Tibet, the Northeast, Inner Mongolia, or the Northwest in winter. A durable backpack is recommended for more independent travel. Most hotels provide disposable toothbrushes and toothpaste, but it's best to bring your own. Name or business cards are a good idea as the Chinese take giving and receiving cards very seriously.

Reading material is essential: Much of the fiction available in China is hard-going (see Media, p. 355). Hong Kong is a good place to stock up on literature. Take an MP3 player or your own CDs, as the selection in China is limited.

If you enjoy photography, stock up with film, color-slide film, and batteries in the cities (Kodak stores are widespread), as they can be either expensive or difficult to obtain elsewhere.

INSURANCE

Make sure that medical coverage in your travel insurance is adequate. If your stay in China is extended, take out international medical insurance before going (see p. 360).

FESTIVALS & HOLIDAYS IN THE PEOPLE'S REPUBLIC

Yuandan (Western New Year) January 1
Chun Jie (Chinese New Year, Spring Festival) Falls within January, February (most significant festival of the year; five-day holiday)
Yuanxiao Jie (Lantern Festival) 15th day of first lunar month (usually mid- to end of February)
Qingming Jie (Tomb Sweeping Festival) First week of April, often around Easter
Wuyi Laodong Jie (Labor Day, May Day) State holiday
Wusi Qingnian Jie (International Youth Day) May 4
Duanwu (Dragon Boat Festival) Fifth day of fifth lunar month (normally held in June)
Liuyi Ertong Jie (Children's Day) June 1, holiday for school children
Communist Party Founding Anniversary July 1
Zhongqiu Jie (Mid-Autumn Festival) 15th day of the eighth lunar month
Guoqing Jie (National Day) October 1, state holiday (normally for three days)

Both Hong Kong and Macau celebrate other festivals; for details phone either the Hong Kong Tourism Board (tel 0852 2508-1234) or the Macau Government Tourist

Office (tel 0853 340390 or 0853 315566).

FURTHER READING

It's worth reading a few titles to arm yourself with a vision of your destination. Suggestions include the following:
The Hermit of Peking, by Hugh Trevor-Roper. Classic investigative scholarship into the colorful life of Edmund Backhouse, the eponymous hermit and Sinologist.
The Way and its Power (Daode Jing), by Laozi. Taoist classic.
Tao: the Watercourse Way, by Alan Watts. An enlightening and insightful introduction to the Way and its mysteries.
Three Chinese Poets, translation by Vikram Seth. Three Tang dynasty poets (Wang Wei, Li Bai, and Du Fu) expertly translated.
Foreign Devils and the Silk Road, by Peter Hopkirk. Thrilling history of antique hunters in Chinese Turkestan in the early 20th century.
Red Dust, by Ma Jian. Off-beat China travelogue
Mao: the Unknown Story, by Jung Chang and Joh Halliday. Outspoken exhumation of the former tyrant.
The Search for Modern China, by Jonathan Spence. Huge post-Ming history lovingly executed by well-known Sinologist.
The Tyranny of History: The Roots of China's Crisis, by W.J.F. Jenner. Critical look at the tyrannical nature of China's traditions and her conservatism.
Wild Swans, by Jung Chang. Popular biography charting the trauma of recent Chinese history.
Concise English-Chinese, Chinese-English Dictionary, Oxford University Press. Excellent, exhaustive, concise dictionary.

HOW TO GET TO CHINA

PASSPORTS & VISAS

A valid passport and visa are required for entry to China. Your passport must be valid for at least six months after the visa expiration date. Thirty-day tourist visas (type L) are usually issued, visa prices are rising steadily. Contact your nearest Chinese embassy for more information. Make a photocopy of your passport (the page with your photo, passport number, and other details) in case of loss or theft while in China; contact the Public Security Bureau (see p. 360) and your nearest consulate or embassy immediately. If you are planning to stay for a long period, register your passport with your nearest embassy or consulate (see p. 357). Your passport will also serve as an invaluable proof of identity while in China, but don't hand it over as a deposit if you can avoid it. If you want to extend your visa, take it to the Public Security Bureau for consideration (they will charge a small fee). You will need a letter of invitation from a host company if you wish to work in China.

Hong Kong

A valid passport is needed to visit Hong Kong. British citizens can stay visa-free for six months. Australian, Canadian, United States, New Zealand, Western European and EU citizens can stay for three. Citizens of a number of Middle Eastern, Southeast Asian, and former Soviet-bloc countries require a visa. Chinese citizens need a visa. Hong Kong Immigration Department: Immigration Tower, 7 Gloucester Road, Wan Chai, tel 0852 2824-6111, fax 0852 2877-7711; e-mail: enquiry@ immd.gcn.gov.hk; www.info.gov.hk/immd/english

Macau

A valid passport is needed to visit Macau. Vistors from the EU can stay for 90 days; citizens from the U.S.A, Canada, Australia, New Zealand, Israel, and South Africa can stay for 30 days. Hong Kong residents and Portuguese passport holders can stay for one year without a visa. Nationals of other countries need a visa, which can be obtained on arrival in Macau. Chinese citizens need a visa.

AIRPORTS

Most international flights arrive in Beijing, (Capital Airport: tel 962-580, within Beijing only; flight info tel 0106 454-1100), Shanghai or Hong Kong (and to a much more limited extent, Macau). In Beijing you will have to take a bus or a taxi (45 minutes) from the airport to the city.

Shanghai's Pudong Airport (tel 021 3848-4500) is linked to the city by bus, taxi, and Maglev (the latter connecting with the No. 2 metro line). Shanghai's other airport—Hongqiao Airport—is on the other side of town, with flights to domestic destinations.

Hong Kong's airport is joined to Lantau Island and connected to the city by airport train, airbus, or taxi.

RAIL

China can be reached by rail from Europe aboard the Trans-Mongolian or the Trans-Manchurian express that terminates in Beijing. Both routes connect Beijing to Moscow, from where you can continue to Western Europe. This is a fascinating, though time-consuming, means of reaching China (five or more days). Returning to Europe this way is popular; contact CITS (China International Travel Service) in Beijing (Beijing International Hotel, 9 Jianguomennei Dajie, tel 010 6512-0507). Tourist or transit visas must be arranged. A number of travel agents outside of China can arrange tickets; White Nights (www.wnights.com) is an example.

GETTING AROUND

Be warned that getting around China can be exhausting (but fun) unless you are part of a tour. Shortage of tickets, communication difficulties, bureaucracy and inefficiency can conspire to make things hard going. Using an agency might make it easier: Travelchinaguide .com is China's largest online tour operator 800/892-6988 (US or Canada) or (0086-29) 8523 6688 in China.

TRAVELING AROUND CHINA

BY AIR

This is the most sensible option for those who have little time to take the train or the bus, but tickets are expensive. China's airline, CAAC, has been split into regional airlines (such as China Southern Airlines, China Southwest Airlines) with a much improved safety record over the past decade. Air tickets can generally be bought quickly through CITS, your hotel travel desk, or air ticketing offices (in all cities with airports). Discounting is common on domestic air tickets, although you may have to pay the full price to large cities on the weekend. Tickets are one-way and delays are common.

All provincial capitals have their own airports, as do numerous large cities and popular tourist destinations. Airports vary in distance from the city center, but most have airbuses that convey passengers to air ticketing offices in town; taxis are abundant. The better hotels have shuttle buses that wait for passengers at the airport. Departure tax (Y50) is generally included in the ticket price. Insurance is offered as an optional extra. Airline meals on domestic flights are generally of very poor quality.

BY BICYCLE

Bike (*zixingche*) travel is one of the best ways around town, unless you are in Chongqing (the only city without cycles due to its steep inclines). Ask if your hotel has bike rental—check the brakes and the tires before setting out.

Many large cities and tourist destinations, such as Beijing, Hangzhou, Suzhou, Nanjing, and Yangshuo, have cheap bike rental. If you plan to stay in China for a while, buy a bike and join the throng. Bicycle repairmen line the road throughout Chinese cities and are generally very cheap and efficient. Theft is very common, so lock your bike.

BY BOAT

Maritime and river boat routes are dwindling due to alternative forms of transport. Jetfoils ply the waters between Hong Kong and Macau, and boats still journey to Hainan Island, from Yantai to Dalian, and from Shanghai to Putuoshan, but many other routes have ground to a halt. The most popular river route is along the Yangtze River; boats can be taken along the Li River and the Grand Canal, but elsewhere routes are limited.

BY BUS

Large government-run buses (*gonggong qiche*), private buses, and minibuses travel inter-city routes all over China. Tickets are easier to procure than rail tickets, but as with rail tickets, you can only travel single and not round-trip. State-owned buses leave on schedule and are the cheapest, but are the most uncomfortable. Private buses offer more comfort and often have such luxuries as on-board toilets. Sleeper buses navigate the night roads through the land. Private minibuses (*xiaoba*) are faster but run mainly on local routes, often departing only when completely full. Private minibuses become very crowded, making it both uncomfortable and dangerous. Buses can be very dangerous in the more peripheral regions (Tibet, Yunnan, Hainan Island, parts of Sichuan, etc.) and should only be taken if there is no other alternative. Driving standards are appalling and accidents are common. Keep a close eye on your bag and belongings, especially on sleeper buses.

Urban bus fleets in the larger cities are being slowly modernized but aged beasts survive. Cities such as Beijing, Shanghai, and Dalian sport modern fleets. Pay the driver as you board or pay the ticket seller on the bus. Trips within cities are cheap and most trips should cost around Y1–Y2 (about 12 cents). Some cities also have electric trams (e.g. Hong Kong).

Outside Hong Kong and Macau, bus stops have signs only in Chinese, making successful navigation difficult. Keep a close eye on your belongings, as the crowded environment is perfect for pickpockets.

BY CAR

China's roads are anarchic and the cause of 600 deaths per day (according to the WHO), or the equivalent of two airplane disasters daily. Even if you wanted to drive, only foreign residents in China could hire cars to drive (as of 2006) in Beijing and Shanghai, with tourists effectively barred from the roads. If you are a resident in China, you will be required to obtain a Chinese driving license if you wish to drive. Cars in China drive on the right-hand side of the road. Cars can be rented however, in Hong Kong and Macau.

Car rental with driver

It is easy to rent a car with a driver—the best thing is to ask at your hotel; alternatively negotiate a fee with a taxi driver. See the By Taxi section p. 353. In Beijing, try Hertz at Jianguo Hotel, 5 Jianguomenwai Dajie, tel 0800 810-8833; or ask at your hotel.

Hong Kong

Cars can be rented at a number of places in Hong Kong, but the excellent public transportation system obviates the need. If you want to drive, try Avis, Ground Floor, Bright Star Mansions, 93 Leighton Rd., Causeway Bay, tel 2890-6988, or contact the HKTB for further information.

Macau

Vehicles can be rented from Avis Rent-A-Car at the Macau Ferry Terminal, tel 726-571, www.avis .com.mo

BY PEDICAB

Pedicabs, or three-wheeled bicycles (*sanlunche*), offer a relatively cheap but slow amble around town. Because they are often operated by old men, it's usually cheaper, and far quicker, to take a taxi. Remoter regions are serviced by motorbikes.

BY SUBWAY

China's metropolitan subway system (*ditie*) is growing. Beijing, Shanghai, Hong Kong, Shenzhen, Guangzhou, Tianjin, and Nanjing all have systems, of varying complexity. Of them all, Hong Kong has the best network. Light rail systems are also becoming increasingly widespread (e.g. Beijing, Wuhan, Shanghai). Trains are punctual, reliable, and cheap.

BY TAXI

This is by far the fastest and most hassle-free way around town. Taxi rates vary but typically cost Y5–Y10 for the first 4 km (2.5 miles), and from then on Y1.4 per kilometer (0.6 mile). Prices vary depending on the city and the size of the taxi, but you will quickly realize that it costs very little to travel around town by cab. Taxis are ubiquitous and display a light when unoccupied. Insist that the driver uses the meter (*dabiao*). Take a note of the taxi driver's number, which is displayed, if you have any reason to complain. Tipping is unnecessary, and sometimes refused. Do not expect any English to be understood, except the names of the larger hotels.

Taxis can often be used to take you to places out of town cheaper than joining a tour. Drivers will charge a flat fee and may well expect you to pay for lunch.

BY TRAIN

Traveling around China by train (*huoche*) is a fun and exciting way to chart the land; the larger part of the country (including Tibet) is enmeshed in a punctual rail system. The Beijing to Kowloon (Hong Kong) journey is an excellent way to bridge the two cities. Traveling by train is also the best way to practice your Chinese.

Try to buy your tickets early through your hotel travel desk—otherwise you can try your luck at the station, but expect a long line. Don't expect to obtain a ticket on the day of departure unless it's for a local train, and plan a few days ahead at all times (buying your outward ticket as soon as you arrive at a destination is very good forward planning). Tickets are typically single trip, rather than return.

Standards of comfort on trains are gradually improving, but the system is overstretched with too many customers.

Tickets come in various classes: hard seat (*yingzuo*), soft seat (*ruanzuo*) on certain routes, hard sleeper (*yingwo*), and soft sleeper (*ruanwo*). Hard/soft seat is fine for short journeys, but you will find yourself among watermelon seed shells, cigarette ends, and the staring masses.

For journeys of more than five hours, a sleeper ticket is important. A hard sleeper ticket puts you on a reasonably comfortable bunk bed in a crowded, doorless, six-bed compartment in a carriage. You have a choice of upper (*shang*), middle (*zhong*), or lower (*xia*) berth. The middle berth is generally the best option as the lower bunk is used as a bench by all and sundry while the top bunk is quite a climb and space is more limited.

Soft sleeper (much more expensive) puts you in your own four-berth compartment (with door). If traveling by sleeper, the ticket collector will come and exchange your ticket for a metal version, which will be swapped before you arrive at your final destination. You can often upgrade (*bupiao*) your ticket once aboard the train.

TRAVEL RESTRICTIONS

Most of China is open to travelers (including all destinations covered in this book), but some areas remain closed. Off-limits areas are usually ethnic border regions or militarily sensitive regions. If you wish to visit an area that you suspect may be closed, contact the PSB (Public Security Bureau) for clarification (see p. 360). In certain cases, travel permits will be issued.

Tibet

Reaching Tibet is not too difficult, but travel within the land is restricted, apart from those areas that are designated accessible to travelers. First, you will need a valid China visa. When applying for a visa in a Chinese embassy, the form will ask you to list which provinces and cities you plan to visit. If you plan to visit Tibet, putting this on your application may raise eyebrows. Suffice to say, you can modify your itinerary in China as you see fit once you are there.

Because of Tibet's desire for autonomy from the PRC (People's Republic of China), China is highly sensitive to individual Western travelers roaming around the land. To control movement within Tibet, individuals are forced into tour groups (charging high rates) on travel permits. Such permits can be purchased through travel agencies in China. This will get you to the Tibetan Autonomous Region (TAR).

Some parts of Tibet will require the acquisition of a further Alien Travel Permit (ATP), issued by the PSB. The best way to obtain the permit is through a travel agency in Lhasa (see pp. 299–301) so that you are officially part of a tour group. Destinations that do not require an Alien Travel Permit (at the time of writing) include Lhasa and Shigatse; travelers to the Everest Base Camp, Gyantse, and Samye Monastery will need a permit.

With the new railway, Lhasa is now linked by train to numerous stations in China, including Shanghai and Beijing. Flights to Lhasa depart from numerous domestic airports, including Beijing, Shanghai and Guangzhou,

Chengdu and Zhongdian. Travel agencies sell package deals including travel permits charged to your air ticket; the tour is nominal and members later go their own way. The best time to visit Tibet is from April to June and September to November.

PRACTICAL ADVICE

BARGAINING

Foreigners are often massively overcharged (especially in tourist areas), and bargaining is expected, unless prices are clearly marked. Top-end hotels sometimes sell local wares (such as oil paintings) that you can find for a tenth of the price if you investigate local markets. If the item is unmarked, the seller may quote a price from out of the air. Feel free to haggle, but don't be pushy.

COMMUNICATIONS

TELEPHONE

If you are going to use a public telephone, it's best to buy a phone card (*dianhuaka*). Pre-paid cards come in various denominations and can be used for international calls; card phones are increasingly plentiful. If you can't find one, try the nearest large hotel.

For mobile phone users, SIM cards can be bought from mobile phone shops, which will give you a phone number and Y50 worth of credit. When the credit runs out, you can top the number with a credit charging card. China's country code is 86.

Useful numbers in China:

International assistance	115
Local directory enquiries	114

POST OFFICES

Airmail letters to the U.S.A., Britain, and Australia should take between four days and a week to reach their destinations. Mark envelopes "airmail/par avion." Stamps are sold at the counter; there are no machines. Envelopes are often gumless; glue is available at the post office. Don't expect anyone to speak English.

As well as regular post offices, large top-end hotels have their own post offices; other hotels should have a mail service. Most cities and large towns have *poste restante* services and larger hotels should hold mail until you arrive.

E-MAIL, INTERNET, FAX

Internet cafés *(wangba)* are plentiful in large cities and towns. Avoid using Internet services in pricier hotels as they are overpriced. If using very cheap Internet cafés, check for escape routes in the event of fire. The Internet is a double-edged sword for the authorities, and they monitor and censor the medium obsessively. Politically sensitive websites and news organizations (e.g. The BBC Chinese Service) are jammed. Most hotels can provide fax service.

LANGUAGE

Don't expect people to understand English, but treat it as an enjoyable surprise when they do. Luxury hotels generally offer passable, but limited, standards of English. Cheaper hotels boast almost nonexistent English skills. Patience is an essential ingredient to communication success. Don't expect restaurant staff to understand you, and expect to do a lot of pointing.

You will quickly find yourself in a forest of Chinese signs with very few recognizable English words. A comprehensive phrase book is an essential companion. See the Chinese language section (pp. 360 & 389).

CULTURE

Face

Chinese pay close attention to face (*mianzi*), or lack of it (*diu mianzi*). The psychology of face is essentially pride in fragile form, and much maneuvering is employed to keep it intact. Try to be sensitive to the feelings of the Chinese. In this country especially, it is advisable to remain respectful, making any complaints with decorum, peppered with firmness.

Guanxi

Contacts *(guanxi)* remain all important in Communist China. The code of guanxi is mutual help and assistance in procuring what you want, and giving what others need. As a foreigner, you may have what many Chinese may want (a useful contact abroad) and their business card will signal a desire for guanxi.

Business cards

It's well worth getting business cards printed, with your name and company in both English and Chinese. The procedure of exchanging cards in China is like a handshake and is far more widespread than in the West. Chinese proffer their business cards with both hands in a respectful delivery; do the same if you wish.

Smoking

China is a tobacco company's paradise and the country is largely addicted to nicotine. The authorities have tried to limit smoking in certain places and the situation has much improved. Smokers on trains are now largely consigned to the carriage ends, but you will still see travelers light up on rural buses. If you dislike smoking, you may find China hard to stomach. If you smoke, most Chinese cigarettes are cheap and have a strong, dry flavor.

Taboos

Frank political discussions with Westerners are shunned by most Chinese people. The Chinese are not given to speaking openly about their concerns, and they may be sensitive to the implications of discussing such issues with you. It is tempting to proselytize when in China, but it leads nowhere.

Spitting

Posters exhort against spitting and fines are sporadically levied on offenders, but spitting carries on wholesale, even in crowded buses and trains. Apart from being very unpleasant, this is a main transmission route for air-borne diseases.

Karaoke
The Chinese take karaoke (*kala OK*) very seriously. If you are entertained by Chinese at a banquet, at some stage of the evening the karaoke equipment will be wheeled on and you will be exhorted to sing the one Western song on the menu (just pray it's not *Bohemian Rhapsody*).

If checking into one of the cheaper hotels, inquire where the karaoke lounge is and ask for the room farthest from that point if you want any sleep.

Settling the Bill
Meal bills are never divided up as is the Western custom and the honor will fall on one person (it is not uncommon to see a polite scramble for the bill at the conclusion of a meal). Don't attempt to pay for your share, but make an attempt to pay for the entire meal yourself (which will probably be politely refused, unless you are the host).

Banquets
If you are called upon to attend a Chinese banquet—enjoy it! In the middle of the dinner table is a small, circular table that is laden with all the dishes and rotated. If you are the guest of honor, the important dishes will be passed to you to sample. This can be a bit of a challenge, when specialties such as huge sea snails and snake sail into view, with all eyes upon your reaction.

The host will have made sure that there is plenty to drink on hand. The preferred tipple is *baijiu*, a clear and ferocious spirit that hits like a sledgehammer. Too much of this will have you rapidly talking nonsense.

If you smoke, it is essential that you offer your pack to everyone around the table. It's bad form to guard your cigarettes, and generosity is essential. If your host smokes, a carton (never just a pack) of Marlboro or Dunhill will make you friends for life.

Lining up
Standing in line is an alien concept that is slowly gaining ground in China, but be prepared to join a jostling mass with no beginning or end, all elbows and bellowing voices and no referee. Polite attempts at lining up are generally trampled.

Beggars
Chinese economic reforms have removed many safety nets for society's more impoverished. Rural hopefuls travel to the large cities in search of work; some end up penniless and hungry. Foreigners are natural targets for beggars. They will gravitate toward you if you give money to other vagrants, and they collect outside temples.

CUSTOMS

Cigarettes 400 if you stay less than six months; 600 if you stay more than six months.
Wine Two bottles each not exceeding 0.75 liter if you stay less than six months; four bottles if you stay more than six months.
Perfume Reasonable quantity for personal use.
Cultural relics Any items that are of antique value should be taken to the cultural administration department first for verification and issuing of an export license.
Electronic appliances One of each of the following is allowed: camera, portable tape recorder, portable cine camera, portable video camera, portable computer.

PROHIBITED ARTICLES
Travelers should be aware that "articles which are detrimental to the political, economic, cultural, and moral interest of China" (apart from the obvious arms, explosives, poisons, etc.) are subject to wide interpretation, but most things that are not inflammatory should be admitted. The Chinese do not treat drug traffickers leniently.

ELECTRICITY

China's electrical current is 220V, 50-cycle A/C. Plugs come in a variety of shapes (usually two or three flat or round pins), so a conversion plug is useful.

ENTRANCE TICKETS

Virtually all sights in China (museums, parks, temples, etc.) require that you buy a ticket. Prices are very acceptable, but for many sights these are going up way ahead of inflation and sometimes by as much as 100% per year. Small temples should cost around Y5–Y10, but drawcard temples can cost up to Y100. Large outdoor destinations such as Huangshan and Wutaishan can be very dear.

MEDIA

The main Chinese newspaper is the *People's Daily* (*renmin ribao*); it faces tough censorship, so reporting is one-sided. A clutch of similar papers exist, including the *People's Liberation Army Paper* (*jiefangjun bao*), and the *Worker's Paper* (*gongren bao*).

ENGLISH-LANGUAGE NEWSPAPERS
The *China Daily* is China's English-language paper, and like the Chinese-language papers, it strongly reflects the Communist Party line. The large five-star hotels generally have book-stores that sell the *International Herald Tribune*, *Newsweek*, *Time*, the *Far East Asian Economic Review*, and the *Wall Street Journal* (sometimes trimmed of unappetizing opinion). Some cities (Guangzhou, Kunming, Hong Kong, Shanghai, and Beijing) have enterprising local-events magazines that are worth picking up at expat bars. The two leading Hong Kong newspapers—the *Hong Kong Standard* and the *South China Morning Post*—are available in decent hotels throughout China.

TELEVISION
You will generally encounter Chinese television in your hotel room. Superior hotels will also provide CNN, MTV, and HBO (it is almost impossible to access CNN or BBC World outside of four/five star hotels). CCTV, the Chinese broadcaster, feeds the nation a diet of historical costume epics, glitzy game shows, and patriotic extravaganzas. CCTV 9 is the domestic English language channel, with censored news and flat content.

MONEY MATTERS

PEOPLE'S REPUBLIC OF CHINA
The currency of the People's Republic of China is the RMB *(renminbi),* also called the *yuan* (Y), or *kuai* in spoken Chinese. One yuan is divided into ten *jiao (mao).* One *jiao* is divided into ten *fen* (rarely used). Paper bills come in denominations of 1, 2, and 5 jiao, and 1, 2, 5, 10, 20, 50, and 100 yuan, but nickel and bronze equivalents exist for the smaller units.

Renminbi is not yet internationally convertible, so you will have to wait till you arrive in China to exchange your money; spend it all before you leave unless you are departing from Hong Kong, where you can change it to Hong Kong dollars. Be on your guard against the large number of forged bills in circulation and black-market moneychangers on the streets.

Credit cards can be used at most hotels above a three-star ranking; four- and five-star hotels should accept all major credit cards (Visa, MasterCard, Amex, Diners Club, JCB). Most cheap restaurants do not accept international credit cards and may only take cash.

You cannot rely on credit to see you through China, so carry a decent amount of cash with you at all times and wear a money belt to thwart pickpockets (especially prevalent on the crowded buses). ATMs accepting international cards have become increasingly common in China's large cities (typically the Bank of China). Carrying some US dollars around is a good idea.

Traveler's checks are the safest alternative to carrying large amounts of cash. They can be exchanged at banks and most large hotels and the exchange rate is better than that for cash.

HONG KONG & MACAU
In Hong Kong the Hong Kong dollar is used (pegged to the US$), and in Macau the currency is the *pataca.*

OPENING HOURS
Banks, businesses, and government offices are officially open weekdays, roughly from 8:30 a.m.–6 p.m., some with an hour or two lunch break. Temples, museums, zoos, and other tourist sites are generally open daily, from 8 or 9 a.m.–5 p.m.

PLACES OF WORSHIP
A number of active Christian churches are mentioned in the text, some holding regular services. If visiting Chinese temples, there is no strict dress code, but be quiet and respectful as you would when visiting any other place of worship.

TIME DIFFERENCES
China is eight hours ahead of Greenwich Mean Time (GMT). Despite China's size, Beijing time is followed by the whole land. Noon in Beijing is 11 p.m. in New York, 8 p.m. in Los Angeles, 5 a.m. in Paris, 4 a.m. in London, 2 p.m. in Melbourne, and 4 p.m. in Wellington. Time zone clocks in hotel foyers are often haywire, so don't rely on them.

TIPPING
The Chinese seem to be divided between those who refuse tips and those who expect them: It is simpler just to remind yourself that this is a communist country and that foreigners are sometimes overcharged, so don't tip.

REST ROOMS
Most hotels apart from those on the lowest rung will equip you with a Western toilet; beyond that, however, expect to acquaint yourself with the Chinese squat toilet. These vary, but as a rough guide, the further you stray from the large towns, the more gruesome they become. Often there is little privacy. Toilets in rural backwaters will leave an indelible impression of vivid horror. Bring your own toilet paper.

TOURIST OFFICES
China's tourist industry is still waking up to the fact that there's much money to be made from Western travelers. The Chinese are famed for their business sense, but when it comes to dealing with foreigners, they're still on the starting blocks.

There is no organization similar to the information office that you find in the West—replete with free maps, sound advice, and help. The China International Travel Service (CITS), a nationwide organization, deals unimaginatively with "foreign guests" and can be used as a last ditch measure to join a tour. CITS likes to work for tour groups, rather than the individual traveler, but can get hold of train, boat, or plane tickets, with a commission added on. It is often easier just to use the travel desk at your hotel, where you may find better English skills. Other organizations include CTS (China Travel Service), similar to CITS.

Western bars and cafés are often the best places to garner information.

TRAVELERS WITH DISABILITIES
Disabled travelers will find China inadequately equipped. Public transportation remains largely inaccessible, and only the best hotels and restaurants are prepared.

VEGETARIANS

Those on a vegetarian diet will find it hard-going in China. Although the Chinese do not eat large amounts of meat, vegetarianism hardly exists as a philosophy, except in the religious sense. Buddhist temples and restaurants are the best places for meat-free food. Otherwise, most restaurants offer a large, if unimaginative, range of vegetable dishes (*sucai*), many of which are prepared with meat-based cooking oils. Some vegetarian restaurant options are noted in the restaurant index.

WEIGHTS & MEASURES

The metric system is used in China, alongside its own system. The only Chinese measurement you are likely to see is the unit of weight: 1 *jin* (Cantonese: *gan*) weighs 0.5 kg (1.1 pounds). Both km (*gongli*) and miles (*yingli*) are used, as well as meters (*mi*).

EMERGENCIES

ACCIDENTS

Vehicle accidents are common in China. Minibus drivers pack passengers in till you can't move, and the law pays no attention. This, coupled with low driving standards and high-speed racing on terrible roads, frequently leads to disaster. There's not much you can do to avoid this, but be aware of the perils of traveling on China's roads and try to remain alert to danger. Gaping holes in sidewalks in cities are common; look where you are going (especially at night) to avoid breaking a leg.

CHINESE EMBASSIES & CONSULATES ABROAD

AUSTRALIA
Chinese Embassy
15 Coronation Dr., Yarralumla, ACT 2600, tel 02 6273-4783, fax 02 6273-4878

CANADA
Chinese Embassy 515 St. Patrick St., Ottawa, Ontario K1N 5H3, tel 613/789-3434, fax 613/789-1911, www.chinaembassycanada.org
Chinese Consulate 240 St. George St., Toronto, Ontario M5R 2P4, tel 416/964-7260, fax 416/324-6468 (further consulates in Vancouver and Calgary)

FRANCE
Chinese Embassy 9 Ave. V Cresson, 92130 Issy les Moulineaux, Paris, tel 1 47 36 02 58, www.amb-chine.fr

HONG KONG
Visa Office Ministry of Foreign Affairs of the PRC, 5th Floor, Low Block, China Resources Building, 26 Harbour Rd., Wan Chai, Hong Kong Island, tel 0852 3413-2300

ITALY
56 Via Bruxelles, 56-00198, Rome, tel 06 8413-458 or 06 8413-467

JAPAN
3-4-33 Moto-Azabu, Minato-ku, Tokyo, tel 03 3403-3389 or 03 3403-3065, www.china-embassy .or.jp

NETHERLANDS
Adriaan Goekooplaan 7, 2517 JX, The Hague, tel 070 355-1515

NEW ZEALAND
2–6 Glenmore St., Wellington, tel 04 4721-3821, www.china embassy.org.nz consulate in Auckland

U.K.
49-51 Portland Pl., London, tel 020 7299-4049, fax 020 7636-2981, www.chinese-embassy .org.uk; 43 Station Rd., Edinburgh EH12 7AF, tel 0131 337-3220

U.S.A.
Chinese Embassy 2201 Wisconsin Ave., N.W., Rm. 110 Washington, DC 20008,tel 202/ 338-6688, www.china-embassy .org
Chinese Consulate 100 West Erie St., Chicago, IL 60610, tel 312/803-0095, fax 312/803-0122
Chinese Consulate 443 Shatto Pl., Los Angeles, CA 90020, tel 213/380-2508, fax 213/380-1961
Chinese Consulate 520 12th Ave., New York, NY 10036, tel 212/330-7410, fax 212/502-0245
Chinese Consulate 1450 Laguna St., San Francisco, CA 94115, tel 415/563-9232, fax 415/563-0494

FOREIGN EMBASSIES & CONSULATES IN CHINA

AUSTRALIA
Embassy 21 Dongzhimenwai Dajie, Sanlitun, Beijing, tel 010 5140-4111
Consulate CITIC Square, 1168 Nanjing Xilu, 22nd fl., Shanghai, tel 021 5292-5500, www.aus-in-shanghai.com.cn
Consulate Room 1509, Main Tower, Guangdong International Hotel, 339 Huanshi Donglu, Guangzhou. tel 020 8335-5911, fax 020 8335-0718

CANADA
Embassy 19 Dongzhimenwai Dajie, Sanlitun, Beijing, tel 010 6532-3536
Consulate Room 604, Shanghai Center, 1376 Nanjing Xilu, Shanghai, tel 021 6279-8400
Consulate Room 801, China Hotel Office Tower, Liuhua Lu, Guangzhou, tel 020 8666-0569

FRANCE
Embassy 3 Dongsan Jie, Sanlitun, Beijing, tel 010 6532-1331
Consulate Room 1204, United Plaza, 1468 Nanjing Xilu, Shanghai, tel 021 6289-7414, www.consulfrance-shanghai.org
Consulate Room 803, Main Tower, Guangdong International Hotel, 339 Huanshi Donglu, Guangzhou, tel 020 8330-3405

GERMANY
Embassy 17 Dongzhimenwai Dajie, Sanlitun, Beijing, tel 010 6532-2161

Consulate 181 Yongfu Lu, Shanghai, tel 021 3401-0106
Consulate 19th floor, Main Tower, Guangdong International Hotel, 339 Huanshi Donglu, Guangzhou, tel 020 8330-6533, fax 020 8331-7033

JAPAN
Embassy 7 Ritan Lu, Beijing; tel 010 6532-2361
Consulate 8 Wanshan Lu, Hongqiao, Shanghai, tel 021 5257-4766; www.shanghai.cn.emb-japan.go.jp/cn

NEW ZEALAND
Embassy 1 Dong Erjie, Ritan Lu, Beijing, tel 010 6532-2731
Consulate 15a, Qihua Tower, 1375 Huaihai Zhonglu, Shanghai, tel 021 6471-1108

SOUTH KOREA
Embassy 3rd & 4th fl., China World Trade Center, 1 Jianguomenwai Dajie, Beijing, tel 010 6505-2608, fax 010 6505-3067

U.K.
Embassy 11 Guanghua Lu, Beijing, tel 010 5192-4000
Consulate Room 301, Shanghai Center, 1376 Nanjing Xilu, Shanghai, tel 021 6279-7650
Consulate 2nd Floor, Main Tower, Guangdong International Hotel, 339 Huanshi Donglu, Guangzhou, tel 020 8335-1354, fax 020 8332-7509

U.S.A.
Embassy 3 Xiushui Beijie, Beijing, tel 010 6532-3831
Consulate 1469 Huaihai Zhonglu, Shanghai, tel 021 6433-6880
Consulate 1 Shamian Nanjie, Shamian Island, Guangzhou, tel 020 8121-8428

VIETNAM
Embassy 32 Guanghua Lu, Beijing, tel 010 6532-1155

EMERGENCY PHONE NUMBERS

The following telephone numbers apply to the larger cities (Beijing, Shanghai, and Guangzhou):

Police 110
Fire 119
Ambulance 120

FEMALE TRAVELERS

China is generally a very safe travel destination for women, but, as with any other destination, individual travel has its own set of risks. Sexual harassment exists, but cases are rare.

HEALTH

In the large cities, you can generally find decent medical assistance in time of need. Medical services in rural or far-flung regions are usually far more basic.

IMMUNIZATIONS
First discuss what you may need in terms of immunizations with your doctor or nurse. Check that your immunizations for diphtheria, polio, and tetanus are up-to-date. Consult your doctor well in advance of when you plan to travel.

Hepatitis A
Immunization against Hepatitis A (*jia ganyan*) is recommended. In China this is often spread by consuming contaminated food and water and in areas of poor sanitation.

Hepatitis B
Immunization against Hepatitis B (*yi ganyan*) is also recommended because China is a high-risk country. It is spread through the same channels as HIV/AIDS (contaminated blood, sharing contaminated needles, or syringes). Preventive measures include avoiding high-risk activities and taking your own first-aid kit that has sterile syringe needles.

Typhoid
Immunization against typhoid (transmitted in areas with poor sanitation and contaminated food and water) is probably not necessary if you are staying in clean conditions. If you are unsure of your itinerary, err on the side of caution.

Yellow fever
Immunization against yellow fever is essential if traveling from an infected country.

OTHER DISEASES
Hepatitis C
There is no vaccine for Hepatitis C (*bing ganyan*). Transmission routes are the same as for Hepatitis B, so avoid associated high-risk activities.

Cholera
This intestinal infection caused by contaminated food is contracted mainly in areas of poor sanitation and is generally avoided if the procedures described in Food and water are followed (see opposite). Vaccine is available, but it offers little protection.

Diarrhea
Diarrhea (*la duzi*) is a common complaint with travelers and is a reaction to unfamiliar bacteria. It can be persistent and ruin a vacation; avoid eating meat and drink a lot of water to prevent dehydration. If problems persist for more than five days, or worsen, you may have dysentery.

Giardia
This parasite lurks in contaminated water. Symptoms are fever, nausea, rashes, and severe diarrhea. Treatable with drugs.

Bilharzia/schistosomiasis
This parasitic disease is caused by a worm living in contaminated water, found in South China and the Yangtze River basin. Worm larvae enter the skin, initially causing a rash and later fever, abdominal pain, diarrhea, and fatigue. Stick to the hotel swimming pool.

Malaria
A parasitic disease spread by the bite of the female mosquito, malaria (*nueji*) is potentially fatal, causing fever and possible organ damage. It is not a large threat

in China, but travelers to the tropical regions of Hainan Island and south Yunnan Province face a possible risk. Visitors to the rural regions of the south and southwest during summer might face exposure, but malaria mosquitoes have been virtually banished from cities.

If traveling to high-risk areas, discuss medications with your doctor. Otherwise, prevention is the best strategy. Using mosquito repellent (containing DEET), wearing long sleeves and pants, and using a mosquito net (preferably impregnated with insecticide), are all effective safeguards. Consult a doctor as quickly as possible if you suspect you have malaria.

Contact organizations

Centers for Disease Control and Prevention (CDC), tel 800 311-3435, www.cdc.gov

SARS

China was one of the nations hit with cases of Severe Acute Respiratory Syndrome (SARS) in 2003 and again in early 2004. There is still a great deal of mystery surrounding this disease; should you have any concerns about traveling to China, contact the CDC (see above) for specific warnings.

HIV

Precautions against HIV (*aisibing*) infection are the same as elsewhere in the world. Taking your own medical pack that includes needle/syringe is a good idea if traveling beyond the large cities. Take extra condoms if voyaging to rural regions of China as they can be difficult to buy. If you are HIV-positive, entry to China may prove difficult, and if you are planning to live or work in China for more than six months, you will require an HIV test.

Food and water

Thoroughly wash fruit and vegetables bought at markets (human manure is used in agriculture). Avoid eating shellfish and seafood unless you are by the sea. Very spicy food is safer than mild foods. Eat more vegetable than meat dishes if possible. Chew your rice softly—occasional stones can lead to costly dental repairs.

Avoid drinking water straight from the tap, even in Shanghai. All hotels either provide mineral water (*kuangquanshui*) or boiled water (*kaishui*) in thermos flasks. Always buy bottled mineral water, available all over China, and take water purification tablets for emergencies.

Environmental health

Air pollution is a serious problem in China, largely because of increasing industrial and vehicle emissions in the rapidly expanding economy. Large cities such as Beijing, Lanzhou, and Jilin suffer from dangerous levels, especially in winter (on bad days equivalent to smoking two packets of cigarettes a day). Those with respiratory problems such as asthma should speak to their doctors before traveling and make sure they take sufficient medication with them.

Heatstroke/sunburn

China's tropical South, Southwest, and arid Northwest can be extremely hot in summer; the rest of the country can also roast uncomfortably. Take sunscreen, sunglasses, wide-brimmed sun hat, and salt, and drink plenty of water. Prickly heat is caused by a blockage of the sweat pores. Heatstroke is caused by the body overheating, marked by headaches and a feeling of malaise, potentially leading to delirium and death.

Hypothermia and frostbite

Parts of China can be dangerously cold in winter, especially the far north and at high elevations. Wind chill or wet clothing can make the situation rapidly worse, and hypothermia may result. This sets in when the body's core temperature drops. Symptoms include numbness, slurred speech, lethargy, and poor coordination; death may follow.

Frostbite may occur in temperatures below freezing. If visiting Tibet and other cold regions in winter, it is imperative to take adequate warm, waterproof clothing, gloves, and shoes. Long bus rides can prove fatal if a breakdown coincides with a deterioration in the weather, so take extra clothing and gloves.

High elevation

High-elevation travel in China can be extremely cold, so take warm, waterproof clothing and shoes. Altitude sickness is also a risk, especially for travel to Tibet. Decreased oxygen levels and air pressure at elevations over 10,000 feet (3,000 m) can result in altitude sickness. Symptoms vary according to speed of ascent, age, fitness, and other factors. These can include headache, nausea, breathlessness, and mental impairment. If suffering from altitude sickness, it is imperative to reach a safer elevation quickly. When traveling to Lhasa and beyond, it is advisable to spend two days gently acclimatizing without exerting yourself. The risk of sunburn is also greater at high elevation.

Medical care

Chinese state hospitals are of a basic standard, but they will treat you for a fee. The larger cities (Hong Kong, Macau, Shanghai, Guangzhou, Beijing, etc.) have private foreign clinics where you can receive high levels of medical assistance (albeit costly). Taking out medical insurance before you travel to China is highly advisable.

Pharmacies are plentiful and can be identified by a green cross. Many Chinese pharmacies sell prescription drugs (such as sleeping pills) over the counter without prescription. Watson's is a reliably good Hong Kong chain of pharmacies with a number of branches in China's largest cities.

Health insurance

If you fall ill in China and expect

to receive a high standard of medical care, you will have to pay for it. Health insurance is essential if you wish to avoid such expenses and receive adequate medical care.

Dental care
It's a good idea to have your teeth checked over and have any work done before visiting China. Standards of dental care vary; expect only the most basic in remoter regions.

Medical conditions
Carry a record of any medical conditions you may have and the proper names (not just the trade names) of any prescribed medication you may be taking.

CRIME

Most travelers feel very safe when journeying through China. Most serious crime occurs between Chinese without the involvement of foreigners. Pick-pocketing is a problem: spread your money between a number of pockets and wear a money-belt. If changing money on the streets, caution is strongly advised. When traveling on buses between cities, keep a close eye on your bag.

Not a crime as such, but be on the alert for English language learners who befriend foreigners (especially in Guangzhou and Shanghai) and lead them to expensive restaurants where they are left to foot the bill for pricey meals and drinks. Also watch out for the fake art students that prey on tourists around sights such as Tiananmen Square in Beijing, shepherding them to overpriced art galleries.

RACISM

Despite being a multiethnic society, for the larger part, China's ethnic minorities are close to Han Chinese in appearance. This leaves the Chinese with little experience of other races and very conservative ideas about how to deal with them. Although white travelers from wealthy Western countries will be treated reasonably (sometimes surprisingly) well, Chinese prejudice often increases, the darker the skin color.

USEFUL ORGANIZATIONS

The Public Security Bureau (*gonganju*), more often called the PSB, is China's police force and an austere and bureaucratic organization par excellence. Every city has a main PSB office where you can report crime or extend your visa. You are unlikely to have a run in with the PSB, unless you have overstayed your visa. Below are some of the stations in the larger cities:
Beijing 2 Andingmen Dongdajie. tel 010 8402-0101
Shanghai 1500 Minsheng Lu; Pudong, tel 021 6854-1199
Guangzhou Jiefang Beilu, tel 0208 311-6688

LANGUAGE

Chinese is a tonal language, spoken as a mother tongue by approximately 1.2 billion people. The majority speak Mandarin, a dialect spread over much of North China and used nationwide as a lingua franca.

The most versatile Chinese dialect is Mandarin (*putonghua* or "common tongue"). You can use it in all parts of China (including Hong Kong and Macau), but as a very rough guide, you will find that the further away your are from Beijing, the more widespread the use of other dialects. It is not worth trying to learn other tongues for other dialect (*fangyan*) regions, for even in other dialect areas such as Cantonese and Shanghainese, Mandarin is readily understood.

Cantonese is a dialect spoken in south China, specifically in Hong Kong, Macau, Guangdong Province, and parts of Guangxi Province. Mandarin is not easy to learn, but it's worth trying to pick up as much as you can during your trip.

Written Chinese
This guide has used Chinese names in pinyin (in brackets) after places of note. Written Mandarin is the only major language in the world without an alphabet, using "pictures" or "characters" instead to describe the written word. Alphabets use letters to make up the sounds of words, while Mandarin (and other dialects of Chinese, such as Cantonese) essentially uses pictures.

Pronunciation
English speakers don't have a huge problem with Chinese vowels and consonants; below are some of the pinyin pronunciations you should pay more attention to:

Vowel sounds

a	as in father
ai	as in fight
ao	as in cow
ang	as in sung
e	as in duh
ei	as in weigh
eng	as in lung
i	"ee"; "er" sound after r, c, ch, s, sh, zh and z
ian	as in yen
ie	as in yellow
ou	as in oak
o	as in more
u	as in noodle
ui	as in way
uo	as in wart

Consonant sounds

c	as in cats
ch	as in catch
q	in between "ts" and "ch"
r	as in run
s	as in shine
x	"s" as in sing
z	"ds" as in duds
zh	"dge" as in dredge

For useful words and phrases see pp. 389 & 390.

HOTELS & RESTAURANTS

Accommodations in China, albeit quite uniform in appearance, come in a variety to suit all budgets. Facilities and standards, reflected in the price, have come a long way over the past two decades.
A major part of the China experience is the nation's cuisine, and you will find a vast number of restaurants with a blinding array of flavors and regional dishes.

ACCOMMODATIONS

Accommodations in China range from the cheap, low budget to five-star hotels of international quality. Cheaper hotels are called *binguan* (guest house); more expensive hotels are called *jiudian* (wineshop), *da jiudian* (large wine shop), or *fandian* (literally "restaurant").

China rates its hotels from one to five stars. Very cheap accommodations *(zhaodaisuo)* remain off limits to foreigners *(waiguoren)*, but a growing band of international youth hostels in large cities and tourist towns has rushed to fill the gap. See www.yhachina.com for a growing list of Hosteling International affiliated hostels. Otherwise, hotels of two stars and above should accept foreigners. Many of China's historical buildings failed to survive to the modern era, so the vast majority of hotels are of recent, unimaginative construction; this results in a very bland choice. Luxury hotels, while often tedious and dull on the exterior, encase splendid interiors. Outside of Hong Kong, Macau, Beijing, Shanghai, and Guangzhou, luxury hotels struggle to make the grade, but the Shangri-La chain is a dependable and reliably sophisticated choice, especially for the business traveler. You will encounter many hotels whose five-star ranking is undeserved, and four-star hotels that should be ranked lower.

In five-star hotels, expect to receive first-rate service, decent English-language skills, newspaper delivery, nightly turndown, free airport shuttle, limousine service, room safe, in-room movies, 24-hour business center, in-room tea- and coffee-making facilities, minibar, excellent restaurants and shopping facilities, a swimming pool, Wi-Fi zones, and more. Full Western breakfast will include bacon, eggs, sausage, toast, etc.

Four-star hotels may offer some, if not all, of the above, but they may lack the professionalism and excellence that is reserved for five-star status. Virtually all hotels in China have restaurants; four- and five-star hotels should have a Western as well as a Chinese restaurant.

Most three-star hotels should have in-room broadband Internet access, business centers, ticketing offices, and rooms should come with minibar, and perhaps tea and coffee-making facilities. Three-star hotels are, however, only modestly equipped to deal with foreigners.

Two-star hotels are simple and often unprofessional, so don't expect much more than a roof over your head. Some two-star hotels offer excellent quality within their league, and these have been listed below.

Some more remote parts of China are without four- or five-star hotels; in this case, the best alternatives have been listed. On every floor, most budget hotels have a female attendant (*xiaojie*) who will bring you boiled water (*kaishui*) and open the door to your room (unless you are given a key); she also acts as a security presence. Hotels from the budget class up sport karaoke lounges.

Single rooms are rare, and you will almost certainly find yourself in a double. When registering at a hotel, you will have to complete a form and hand over your passport for inspection; you generally have to pay a deposit. Breakfast is sometimes complimentary, but rarely in cheaper establishments.

PRICES

HOTELS

An indication of the cost of a double room without breakfast is given by **$** signs.

$	Under $40
$$	$40–$100
$$$	$100–$180
$$$$	$180–$350
$$$$$	Over $350

RESTAURANTS

An indication of the cost of a three-course dinner without drinks is given by $ signs.

$	Under $30
$$	$30–$50
$$$	$50–$75
$$$$	$75–$100
$$$$$	Over $100

International credit cards are not widely accepted at cheaper hotels (below three stars) so be prepared to pay cash. If a hotel takes credit cards in the list of recommended hotels following, this is indicated. Checkout (*tuifang*) is generally noon.

Most four-star hotels and above should have foreign-exchange counters. Apart from the major holiday periods (Chinese New Year, first week of May, and first week of October), hotels never charge the rack rate so ask for the discounted rate. Smarter hotels charge 10 to 15% service charge, but this is not levied at cheaper establishments.

The following list is a recommended selection of the most appealing hotels and restaurants within their class.

Grading system

✪✪ This standard is usually the cheapest type of hotel that takes foreign guests, although you may be accepted by those with no star ranking. Standard double rooms (*putong shuangren fang*) include separate bathroom (*weishengjian*), television (*dianshi*), and telephone (*dianhua*). Air-conditioning (*kongtiao*), is available at all hotels

in China except the very cheapest. A common Internet area may be available. English skills could be basic.
✪✪✪ Standard double rooms, larger and cleaner. You can expect an improved level of service and restaurant food. English skills are better and the hotel may offer Western movies. There should be a travel desk for procuring air and train tickets and a basic business center (*shangye zhongxin*). Suites should also be available at the hotel.
✪✪✪✪ Four-star hotels are five-star hotels in the making, replete with facilities including business and travel desks, stores, health clubs, and efficient amenities. They often appear much more tarnished than five-star hotels. Double rooms will be clean and spacious. Your stay will be comfortable, yet affordable.
✪✪✪✪✪ This category affords an internationally recognized level of luxury and a very high degree of service.

Red stars (✪), ranging from two to five, are awarded to hotels recognized for excellence within their own star rating for consistent, superior levels of hospitality, service, food, and comfort.

Please note: Unless otherwise stated, all rooms have telephone, television, and bathroom. Room prices are given only for guidance and do not take into account seasonal variations. Prices given are per double room.

RESTAURANTS

Better quality Chinese restaurants (*fandian/canguan*) generally have a large number of tables, with separate banquet/dining rooms at the wings (for private groups). Non-smoking sections are rare except in expensive, or hotel, restaurants, but the pricier banquet rooms (*danjian*) can be used for this purpose. English menus can be a rarity except in more expensive hotels, or those located along routes much traveled by Westerners. Food is not necessarily served in particular order, and you will probably have to remind the waitress for your rice (*baifan*). The Chinese eat many dishes at the same time, rather than courses. Many restaurants do not take credit cards, so check first or carry enough cash at all times. There is no need to tip at most restaurants, but smarter establishments may preempt you by adding a gratuity.

Not included in the list following are fast-food outlets that are plentiful. McDonald's and KFC (often the only English words taxi drivers recognize) can be found in large towns and cities throughout China. Other familiar names are T.G.I. Friday's, Häagen Dazs, and Starbucks.

Chopsticks

If you don't know how to use chopsticks, you might as well use your time in China learning the skill (once learned, you won't forget). They come in disposable bamboo, lacquer, or imitation ivory; occasionally you will see a silver pair. Practice with a pair of pencils, if you like. Hold them so that your middle finger acts as the fulcrum, with pressure from the thumb and second finger. The other two fingers are not used. When not using your chopsticks, do not thrust them upright into your bowl of rice, but place them across your plate or on the chopstick rest (provided in smarter restaurants).

Sichuan hotpot

Chongqing (see p. 146) is *the* place to sample a flaming Sichuan hotpot (*huoguo*). The hotpot is divided into two compartments, one hot and the other milder, or is just plain hot. Into the boiling furnace of each are liberally thrown skewers of sliced meat and vegetables. The experience guarantees a warm afterglow in winter. Chongqing is China's hotpot capital and restaurants can be found everywhere.

PRICES

HOTELS

An indication of the cost of a double room without breakfast is given by **$** signs.

$	Under $40
$$	$40–$100
$$$	$100–$180
$$$$	$180–$350
$$$$$	Over $350

RESTAURANTS

An indication of the cost of a three-course dinner without drinks is given by $ signs.

$	Under $30
$$	$30–$50
$$$	$50–$75
$$$$	$75–$100
$$$$$	Over $100

ORGANIZATION

The hotels and restaurants listed here have been grouped first according to their region, then listed alphabetically by price category.

BEIJING

PENINSULA BEIJING (WANGFU FANDIAN)

$$$$ ✪✪✪✪✪
8 GOLDFISH LANE
(JINYU HUTONG)
TEL 010 8516-2888
FAX 010 6510-6311
www.beijing.peninsula.com

Owned by the Peninsula group, the Peninsula Beijing is a sumptuous and well-polished hotel situated near the fashionable shopping experience of Wangfujing. Traditional-style Chinese exterior, shopping arcade, and a range of restaurants, from the *siheyua*-style Huang Ting, the celebrated Jing, and lobby lounge and bar. The Forbidden City is within walking distance. Mercedes/Rolls Royce limousine service.

530
All major cards

SOMETHING SPECIAL

ST REGIS

Centrally located, the St Regis is Beijing's most prestigious and elegant hotel and first choice for visiting dignitaries. The sumptuous foyer is a taster for the unbridled luxury throughout, which extends to a gamut of top-notch restaurants and bars, a profusion of five-star facilities and 24-hour butler service.

$$$$ ○○○○○
12 JIANGUOMENWAI DAJIE
TEL 010 6460-6688
FAX 010 6460-3299
www.stregis.com
273 All major cards

KERRY CENTRE HOTEL (JIALI ZHONGXIN FANDIAN)

$$$$ ○○○○
KERRY CENTRE,
1 GUANGHUA LU
TEL 010 6561-8833
www.shangrila.com/beijing/kerrycentre/en

Owned by the premier Shangri-La group, the modern Kerry Centre Hotel is a sophisticated and impressive business choice. Situated in east Beijing within reach of the embassy and commercial districts. Chinese restaurant and a hip 24-hour bar, Centro.

487 All major cards

NOVOTEL PEACE HOTEL (NUOFUTE HEPING BINGUAN)

$$$$ ○○○○
3 JINYU HUTONG
TEL 010 6512-8833
FAX 010 6512-6863
www.accorhotels.com

The crisp four-star Novotel has an excellent location just east off Wangfujing Dajie, with a decent range of facilities and the ever-popular international restaurant, The Square.

337 All major cards

LÜSONGYUAN HOTEL (LÜSONGYUAN BINGUAN)

$$ ○○
22 BANCHANG LANE, KUANJIE
TEL 010 6404-0436
FAX 010 6403-0418

The Lüsongyuan is an enterprising and historic *siheyuan* (walled courtyard) hotel lost down a charming alley in a *hutong*-riddled area of Beijing. The hotel boasts traditional Qing dynasty courtyard architecture, a garden, and offers bike rental and *hutong* tours. It's central location makes it very popular with travelers (there's a dorm as well), so reservations are recommended

60 All major cards

HAOYUAN HOTEL (HAOYUAN BINGUAN)

$
53 SHIJIA HUTONG
TEL 010 6512-5557
www.haoyuanhotel.com

Pleasant and quiet courtyard *(siheyuan)* hotel, enjoying an excellent location in a *hutong* not far east of Wangfujing, Beijing's main shopping haul. Very popular with foreigners. Clean rooms. Cable TV.

20 No credit cards accepted

HOME INN (RUJIA)

$ ○○
61 LIANGSHIDIAN JIE
DAZHALAN (WEST OFF QIANMEN DAJIE)
TEL 010 6317-3366
www.homeinns.com

With clean, smallish, and modern rooms a short stroll south of Tiananmen Square, this new branch of the reliable Home Inn chain is the most central in town. The immediate vicinity is grubby, but the surrounding area of Dazhalan has character and considering the location, the tariff offers value for the money.

81 All major cards

AJISEN (WEIQIAN LAMIAN)

$
3201 BLOCK S
SOHO NEW TOWN
TEL 010 8589-1475

Take the underground to the Dawanglu stop and it's a short stroll to this branch of the nationwide noodle chain, packed with diners unanimous in their adoration of their filling and tasty Japanese noodle and rice dishes (pay at the start of the meal).

107 No credit cards accepted

BAGUOBUYI

$
89-3 DIANMEN DONGDAJIE
TEL 010 6400-8888

It's a feat finding authentic Sichuan meals outside of its heartland in the west of China, but the dishes of Baguobuyi—with a branch in Chengdu—is a close second best, delivered up in a fun, garrulous, and centrally located restaurant to the east of the north gate of Beihai Park.

300+ Closed 2:15–5:15 p.m. No credit cards accepted

THE BOOKWORM CAFÉ

$
BLDG. 4, NAN SANLITUN LU
TEL 010 6586-9507
www.beijingbookworm.com

A haven for bibliophiles citywide, Bookworm has wormed its way into the expat consciousness as the heartiest place for a good cup of coffee, a bite to eat, and a book to read. Join the sedate hordes thumbing through hard-to-find fiction/non-fiction and take time out from Beijing's usual café seen.

100 No credit cards accepted

EJE BAR (ZHOUBA)

$
20 GUOXUE HUTONG
TEL 010 8404-4424
www.ejebar.com

Gorgeously secluded and almost impossible to find courtyard bar hidden away directly behind the Confucius Temple—well worth hunting down after visiting the Lama Temple (see p. 68). Opens at 2 p.m. until late.
30 Yonghegong subway No credit cards accepted

GONGDELIN VEGETARIAN RESTAURANT (GONGDELIN SUCAIGUAN)
$ ✪✪✪✪
158 QIANMEN NANDAJIE
TEL 010 6511-2542
The dishes here are fantastic for vegetarians and meat-eaters alike. Bursting with flavor, the Buddhist recipes ingeniously re-create meatlike textures and tastes from purely vegetable ingredients. The sweet and sour fish (*tangcuyu*), made from potato, is first-class. Gongdelin cuisine is an art, and to miss it is to miss some of the finest food in the capital. English menu.
250 No credit cards accepted

JOHN BULL PUB (ZUNBO YINGSHI JIUBA)
$
44 GUANGHUA LU
TEL 010 6532-5905
Located in the embassy quarter, the traditional pub-style pub is a quiet expat mainstay, serving up tasty meals and breakfasts; good value happy hour deals on beer. There's also pool, TV and Anglophone Chinese bar staff.
100 All major cards

LIQUN ROAST DUCK RESTAURANT (LIQUN KAOYADIAN)
$
11 BEIXIANGFENG HUTONG (SOUTH OF XIDAMOCHANG JIE, SOUTHEAST OF QIANMEN)
TEL 0106 705-5578
Much, much smaller and quieter than Quanjude, the unsophisticated Liqun is tricky to find (follow the signs in the surrounding tangle of hutong) but the duck has long won praise from Beijing's picky duck diners. Phoning ahead for a reservation is advised, otherwise you may have a long wait (but it's worth it).
80 No credit cards accepted

LIU JIA GUO
$
19 NANHEYAN DAJIE
TEL 010 6524-1487
Sandwiched between the Forbidden City and Wangfujing Dajie, this popular eatery serves up piquant delicacies (including vegetarian options) from Hunan, the provincial homeland of Mao Zedong. Sample the excellent "Mao Family Braised Pork" (Maoshi Hongshaorou). English menu.
200 No credit cards accepted

MAKYE AME (MAJI AMI)
$
A11 XIUSHUI NANJIE JIANGUOMENWAI
TEL 010 6506-9616
Dishes from the Land of Snows in a marvelous Tibetan setting at this upstairs restaurant behind the Friendship Store. English menu.
60 No credit cards accepted

PASSBY BAR (GUOKE)
$
108 NANLUOGU XIANG
TEL 010 8403-8004
Nanluogu Ziang—a lovely old north-south running *hutong* east of the lake of Qian Hai—is becoming increasingly impregnated with traveler-friendly watering holes and restaurants. This charming courtyard bar started it all off, and age has hardly dented its popularity.
60 Gulou No credit cards accepted

QIANMEN QUANJUDE ROAST DUCK (QIANMEN QUANJUDE KAOYADIAN)
$/$$ ✪✪✪
32 QIANMEN DAJIE
TEL 010 6511-2418
Along Qianmen Dajie south of Tiananmen Square, this is one of the ancestral homes of roast duck (kaoya), dating back to the 19th century and divided into sections for differing budgets. The place may be vast and a major stopping off point for tour groups, but you can't argue with the excellent duck value. Order your bird and the pancakes, onion and plum sauce will automatically arrive. There are further branches at: 143 Qianmen Xidajie (tel 010 6301-8833) and 9 Shuaifuyuan Hutong (off Wangfujing Dajie; tel 010 6525-3310).
1,000+ Qianmen subway Closed 1:30–4:30 p.m. daily AE

THE SICHUAN (SICHUAN FANDIAN)
$ ✪✪✪
14 LIUYIN JIE
TEL 0106 615-6924/6925
Located within Prince Gong's Residence, this is a useful pit stop to put fire in your belly if you are on the Beijing Bike Ride. The restaurant enjoys a well-deserved reputation. Specialties: *yuxiang daxia* (shrimps in hot fish oil) and *shuizhu roupian* (pork slices in chili).
300+ Closed 2–5 p.m. All major cards

THE NORTH

XI'AN

SOFITEL ON RENMIN SQUARE (SUOFEITE RENMIN DASHA)
$$$$$ ✪✪✪✪✪
319 DONG XIJIE
TEL 029 8792-8888

FAX 029 8792-8999
www.sofitel.com
Undoubtedly Xi'an's top choice, the Sofitel is a stunning top-league addition to Xi'an's growing galaxy of hotels, with eye-catching flair, exemplary service throughout, and elegant, modern rooms. Wi-fi zone, two bars, and four restaurants.
432 All major cards

HYATT REGENCY XI'AN (XIAN KAIYUE FANDIAN)
$$$ ✪✪✪✪✪
158 DONG DAJIE
TEL 029 8769-1234
www.xian.regency.hyatt.com
The uninspiring exterior conceals a grand and sophisticated center. Situated well within the city walls, this is the only five-star hotel in the thick of it. Bill Clinton made this his port of call when last in town. Service is crisp and efficient. Tennis court.
404 All major cards

CITY HOTEL X'IAN (XIAN CHENGSHI JIUDIAN)
$ ✪✪✪
70 NAN DAJIE
TEL 029 8721-9988
FAX 029 8721-6688
www.cityhotelxian.com
Centrally located hotel very close to the Bell Tower, the City Hotel is popular and inexpensive, with comfortable rooms and staff that are used to dealing with foreign guests. Business centers, Chinese and Western restaurant.
133 All major cards

PAVILION
$$$
HYATT REGENCY XI'AN
158 DONG DAJIE
TEL 029 723-1234 EXT 1148
Serving a choice of Cantonese Sichuan and Shaanxi delicacies, the elegantly designed Pavilion is one of Xi'an finest restaurants. Choice of set meals or à la carte dishes (including braised shark's fin and abalone). Private rooms available for more intimate gatherings. Traditional music performed nightly.
150 Closed 2:30–5:30 p.m. All major cards

HUASHAN

There are a number of hotels in Huashan Village (at the foot of the mountain) and along Yuquan Lu leading up to the Yuquan Temple. Hotels also dot the slopes and peaks of Huashan, but facilities and services are more basic. Food and water can be bought along the path up the mount.

WUTAISHAN/TAIHUAI

FRIENDSHIP HOTEL (YOUYI BINGUAN)
$ ✪✪✪
TEL 0350 654-2678
Cheaper hotels are in the village, but both of Wutaishan's more upscale tourist hotels lie in a cluster a few miles south of the Taihuai. The Friendship is a reasonably well-equipped place to put a pillow under your head. Chinese restaurant. Travel center.
120 No credit cards accepted

DATONG

GARDEN HOTEL (HUAYUAN DAFANDIAN)
$$$ ✪✪✪✪
59 DA NANJIE
TEL 0352 586-5888
FAX 0352 586-5894
www.huayuanhotel.com.cn
One of Datong's best hotels, the four-star Garden Hotel offers adequate comfort and a measure of elegance, albeit falling short of international standards. Rooms come with broadband Internet access and satellite TV channels. Chinese and Western restaurants.
108 All major cards

TIANJIN

HYATT REGENCY (KAIYUE FANDIAN)
$$$ ✪✪✪✪
219 JIEFANG BEILU
TEL 022 2330-1234
FAX 022 2331-1234
www.hyatt.com
The four-star Hyatt is an elegantly styled hotel benefiting from an excellent position on Tianjin's historic Jiefang Lu near the Hai River. This may not be Tianjin's most lavish hotel, but service is welcoming, the location convenient, and there's a fine choice of restaurants.
450 All major cards

ASTOR HOTEL (LISHUNDE DAFANDIAN)
$$ ✪✪✪✪
33 TAI'ERZHUANG LU
TEL 022 2331-1688
FAX 022 2331-6282
One of Tianjin's most historic hotels, the Astor was built in 1863. Henry Puyi (the last emperor), Sun Yat-sen, and Yuan Shikai have stayed here. Situated near the Hai River, it was the first to use electric lights in Tianjin during the Qing dynasty. Fragments of history remain inside: the original American Otis elevators are there, mid-19th-century furniture remains, and you can find the radio used by Puyi. A new building, constructed in 1987, was added to the existing hotel. If you can afford it, you can stay in the Sun Zhongshan (Yat-sen) Presidential Suite and eat in the vast Buckingham Palace banqueting hall (*baijinhangong guoyanting*).
223 All credit cards

GOUBULI
$
77 SHANDONG LU
TEL 022 2730-2540
The famous Goubuli, located just off the shopping drag of Binjiang Dadao, has been serving up its trademark specialty steamed buns *(baozi)* for over 100 years. The appetizing buns come in almost 100 varieties (pork, chicken, shrimp, vegetable, and more) and a selection of tasty and good value set meals is also available. There are further branches dotted around town, Beijing, and beyond.
300+ No credit cards accepted

LITTLE SHEEP (XIAOFEIYANG)
$
RONGYE DAJIE
TEL 022 2730-8318
Warm up cold Tianjin winter days with a steaming Mongolian lamb hotpot at this branch of the successful nationwide chain.
500 Cash only

XIANG WEI ZHAI
$/$$ ✪✪✪✪
HYATT HOTEL TIANJIN
219 JIEFANG BEILU
TEL 0222 2331-8888
This pleasantly designed dumpling restaurant is a joy. The name means Countryside Flavor, pointing to its emphasis on traditional simplicity. Try the crab and chive dumpling or the seafood and noodle soup, and wash it down with Chinese tea. Inexpensive and all very worthwhile. Service charge included. English menu.
44 All major cards

CHENGDE

MOUNTAIN VILLA HOTEL (SHANZHUANG BINGUAN)
$ ✪✪✪
127 LIZHENGMEN LU
TEL 0314 209-1188
www.hemvhotel.com
Excellent location south of the main entrance to the Bishu Shanzhuang resort in the north of town, this long-serving mid-range hotel has a decent variety of large and clean rooms, suiting a range of budgets, and a large spread of restaurants
340

LUOYANG

PEONY HOTEL (MUDAN DAJIUDIAN)
$$ ✪✪✪
15 ZHONGZHOU XILU
TEL 0379 6468-0000
FAX 0379 6468-0000
The Peony is a centrally located, inexpensive, mid-ranking hotel. All rooms are furnished with satellite TV.
196 All major cards

KAIFENG

DAJINTAI HOTEL (DAJINTAI BINGUAN)
$ ✪✪
23 GULOU JIE
TEL 0378 255-2999
FAX 0378 595-9932
Just around the corner from Kaifeng's lively night market, the Dajintai has a central location and perfectly adequate rooms. Breakfast is included.
120 No credit cards accepted

DONGJING HOTEL
$ ✪✪✪
14 YINGBIN LU
TEL 0378 398-9388
FAX 0378 595-6661
Kaifeng is sadly not blessed with great hotels, but the Dongjing at least offers a reasonably pleasant location (in the southwest within the city walls), a business center, and a complimentary breakfast. CITS north of the hotel. Chinese and Western cuisine. Also, there's a shopping center, post office, ticketing office.
300+ V

PRICES

HOTELS
An indication of the cost of a double room without breakfast is given by $ signs.

$	Under $40
$$	$40–$100
$$$	$100–$180
$$$$	$180–$350
$$$$$	Over $350

RESTAURANTS
An indication of the cost of a three-course dinner without drinks is given by $ signs.

$	Under $30
$$	$30–$50
$$$	$50–$75
$$$$	$75–$100
$$$$$	Over $100

THE SHAOLIN TEMPLE

It is possible to stay in accommodations near the temple, but the best strategy is to stay in Luoyang or Zhengzhou. If you are stuck here, try the Shaolin International Hotel in neighboring Dengfeng (16 Shaolin Lu, tel 0371 286-6188, www.shaolinhotel.com), the principle tourist hotel in the area with adequate facilities. Other cheaper hotels and restaurants can be found in Dengfeng.

ZHENGZHOU

HOLIDAY INN CROWNE PLAZA (HUANGGUAN JIARI FANDIAN)
$$$ ✪✪✪✪✪
115 JINSHUI LU
TEL 0371 6595-0055
www.crowneplaza.com
Finely serviced hotel, with facilities of international standards and decent restaurants. Nightclub, barber and beauty salons.
222 All major cards

QUFU

QUELI HOTEL (QUELI BINSHE)
$ ✪✪✪
1 QUELI STREET
TEL 0537 486-6401
FAX 0537 441-2022
Facing both the Confucius Temple and the Confucius Mansions, the Queli is admirably presented in architecture of traditional Chinese style. Nothing special, but reasonably pleasant and well situated.
160+ MC, V

TAISHAN

SHENQI GUESTHOUSE (SHENQI BINGUAN)
$$ ✪✪✪
10 TIAN JIE
TEL 0538 822-3866
FAX 0538 821-5399
Sun worshipers can snuggle up away from Taishan's chill in this two-story hotel, the best in the summit area. You will be awakened well before sunup. Suites available.
50+ No credit cards accepted

TAISHAN HOTEL (TAISHAN BINGUAN)
$$ ✪✪✪
26 HONGMEN LU
TEL 0538 822-4678
FAX 0538 822-1432
The most popular choice for those climbing Taishan, this hotel puts you at the start of the road up the mountain, just north of the most interesting part of town. Rooms are divided between newer, more expensive rooms and older, cheaper ones. Breakfast, shop and ticketing service.
100+ All major cards

QINGDAO

CROWNE PLAZA (YIZHONG HUANGUAN JIARI JIUDIAN)
$$$$ ✪✪✪✪✪
76 XIANGGANG ZHONGLU
TEL 0532 8571-8888
FAX 0532 8571-6666
www.sixcontinentshotels.com
The sparkling tower of the Crowne Plaza is a modern, hallmark hotel in the Qingdao's busy commercial district. Rooms are perfectly equipped for business travelers and there's a huge selection of fine restaurants. Breakfast included.
388 All major cards

SHANGRI-LA HOTEL QINGDAO (XIANG-GELILA JIUDIAN)
$$$ ✪✪✪✪✪
9 XIANGGANG ZHONGLU
TEL 0532 8388-3838
FAX 0532 8388-6868
www.shangri-la.com
The Shangri-La is a high-quality fixture among the charms of Qingdao. Excellent amenities, facilities, and standards of service. Executive floors offer an even higher level of service. Chinese restaurant, café, and pub. Tennis courts.
502 All major cards

ZHANQIAO HOTEL (ZHANQIAO BINGUAN)
$$ ✪✪✪
31 TAIPING LU
TEL 0532 8288-8666
FAX 0532 8287-0936
With excellent views over-looking Qingdao Bay, the three-story Zhanqiao Hotel is just up from its namesake pier.
98 V

AJISEN (WEIQIAN LAMIAN)
$
1ST FLOOR, CARREFOUR, 21 XIANGGANG ZHONGLU
TEL 0532 8580-6375
Bowls of spicy, searing noodles are the specialty here at this ever-busy Japanese hot spot. Excellent, filling food, served up at speed by attentive waitstaff.
150 No credit cards accepted

CHUNHE LOU
$
146 ZHONGSHAN LU
TEL 0532 8282-4346
The best way to sample Qingdao dishes is to visit one of its many seafood restaurants, but this old timer in the historic part of Qingdao remains one of the town's most famous established eateries.
400 No credit cards accepted

JINAN

CROWNE PLAZA JINAN (JINAN GUIHE HUANGGUAN JIARI JIUDIAN)
$$$$ ✪✪✪✪✪
3 TIANDITAN JIE
TEL 0531 8602-9999
FAX 0531 8602-3333
www.crowneplaza.com
Renovated in 2004 and bursting with fine restaurants and facilities, the Crowne Plaza is perfectly geared to travelers with its combination of elegance and excellence.
306 All major cards

YANGTZE REGION

CHONGQING

MARRIOTT HOTEL
$$$/$$$$ ✪✪✪✪✪
77 QINGNIAN LU
TEL 023 6388-8888
FAX 023 6388-8777
www.marriott.com
The glittering tower of the Marriott supplies five-star comfort and facilities in the heart of Chongqing. Adventurous travelers may be tempted away to visit one of the city's many hotpot *(huoguo)* restaurants, but the Marriott is equipped with splendid restaurants, including Chinese and Japanese.
498 All major cards

YICHANG

TAOHUALING HOTEL (TAOHUALING BINGUAN)

$ ✪✪✪✪
29 YUNJI LU
TEL 0717 623-6666
FAX 0717 623-8888

Built in 1957, the Taohualing is a renovated hotel in the center of town. Postal service, ticketing office, bowling, business center. Breakfast is included.

282 All major cards

WUHAN

SHANGRI-LA HOTEL (XIANGGELILA DAFANDIAN)

$$$$ ✪✪✪✪
700 JIANSHE DADAO, HANKOU
TEL 027 8580-6868
FAX 0278 8577-6868
www.shangri-la.com

This notable luxury hotel, Wuhan's first of an international standard, prides itself on a philosophy of cultured Oriental hospitality. The service is friendly and assured, unobtrusive yet caring, and the amenities are all first class. Chinese restaurant, Western café, and restaurant. Horizon Club (executive) floors. Excellent business facilities. Outdoor tennis court.

520 All major cards

JIANGHAN HOTEL (JIANGHAN FANDIAN)

$$ ✪✪✪✪
245 SHENGLI JIE
TEL 0278 281-1600
FAX 0278 281-4342

A colonial edifice in the heart of Hankou not far from the old Hankou train station. Built by the French early in the 19th century, the hotel is knee-deep in history. It's an excellent place from which to patrol the old concession architecture in riverside Hankou. Shops, restaurants (Cantonese/Chiu Chow, Northern Chinese).

110 All major cards

HUANGSHAN/TUNXI

XIHAI HOTEL (XIHAI FANDIAN)

$$/$$$ ✪✪✪
SUMMIT AREA
TEL 0559 558-8987/8888
FAX 0559 558-8988

The modern Xihai is not cheap, but it is one of the more comfortable entrées to watching the sunrise the next day. Nightclub, snooker.

150 All major cards

BEIHAI HOTEL (BEIHAI BINGUAN)

$$/$$$ ✪✪✪
TEL 0559 558-2555
FAX 0559 558-1996

Cheap, utilitarian, and poised within reach of Huangshan sunrise viewing area. 4-bed rooms available.

100+ No credit cards accepted

OLD STREET HOTEL (LAOJIEKOU KEZHAN)

$$ ✪✪✪✪
1 LAOJIEKOU, TUNXI
TEL 0559 253-4466
FAX 0559 253-1313
www.oldstreet-hotel.com

For those using Tunxi as a hopping-off point to Yixian and Shexian, and even nearby Huangshan, this pleasant hotel at the western tip of Old Street (Lao Jie) in Tunxi has traditional-style rooms with wooden floors. Breakfast included.

33 MC, V

JIUHUASHAN

As with all sacred mountain destinations in China, the quality of hotels is poor. There are a number of hotels in Jiuhua village, including the Julong Hotel (Julong Dajiudian), tel 0566 501-1368, fax 0566 501-1022, an unsurprising establishment (no credit cards). Pleasant accommodations can also be found at the homey Nanyuan Hotel (26 Furong Lu, tel 0566 501-1122) near the Tonghui Nunnery. Restaurants muster along the main street, Jiuhua Jie. Food and drink can also be found on the way up the mountain.

NANJING

JINLING HOTEL (JINLING FANDIAN)

$$$$ ✪✪✪✪✪
XINJIEKOU SQUARE
TEL 025 8471-1888
FAX 025 8471 1666

Centrally located, first-class hotel with excellent rooms. The executive suites are intelligently and thoughtfully designed. Standard rooms also of distinctive high quality. Boasts a legion of restaurants, both Eastern and Western (including revolving restaurant). Despite mainly catering to Chinese guests, the hotel is welcoming to Westerners.

All major cards

JINGLI HOTEL (JINGLI JIUDIAN)

$$ ✪✪✪
7 BEIJING XILU (WEST OF THE DRUM TOWER)
TEL 025 8331-0818
FAX 025 8663-6636

This clean three-star hotel offers good value and strives to be a cut above the rest. Put yourself in an executive suite for $130. Its attractive and central location puts you within striking distance of Nanjing's sights. Chinese restaurant, Internet access, and business center.

131 All major cards

NANSHAN HOTEL (NANJING SHIFAN DAXUE NANSHAN JIALOU)

$ ✪✪
NANJING NORMAL UNIVERSITY, 122 NINGHAI LU

TEL 025 371-6440
FAX 025 373-8174
The Nanshan Hotel is a province of backpacker-land, situated in the quiet heart of Nanjing Normal University, the grounds of which have a rare beauty. Amid the dry chorus of cicadas and gorgeous traditional Chinese rooftops, the hotel's rooms may have seen better days, but they offer some of the best value in town and as you set foot outside the door, you find yourself in the midst of students cycling to lectures. International phones in foyer.
200+ No credit cards accepted

YANGZHOU

YANGZHOU HOTEL
$$ ✪✪✪
5 FENGLE SHANGJIE
TEL 0514 734-2611
FAX 0514 734-3599
Situated near a canal in the center of town, and sporting a number of restaurants. Cable TV.
100+ All major cards

ZHENJIANG

INTERNATIONAL HOTEL (ZHENJIANG GUOJI FANDIAN)
$$ ✪✪✪✪
218 JIEFANG LU
TEL 0511 502-1888
FAX 0511 502-1777
Zhenjiang's best hotel, the four-star International is centrally located and has a revolving restaurant on the 29th floor.
430 All major cards

YANCHUN HOUSE (YANCHUN JIULOU)
$ ✪✪✪
17 RENMIN LU, OFF DAXI LU
TEL 0511 501-0478
This is Zhenjiang's most famous eatery, serving up dim sum and local specialties, not far from the museum in the north of town. Water is poured into your teacup—containing sugar, dried chamomile flowers, and berries—from an impressive distance by sharpshooter waiters. No English menu.
230 No credit cards accepted

SUZHOU

SHERATON SUZHOU & TOWERS
$$$$ ✪✪✪✪✪
388 XINSHI LU
TEL 0512 6510-3388
FAX 0512 6510-0888
www.sheraton-suzhou.com
Located north of the Panmen scenic area, the Sheraton Suzhou is the best in town, deftly embracing the local architectural vernacular with its upturned eaves, waterways, bridges, and gorgeous gardens. Tennis courts.
315 All major cards

BAMBOO GROVE
$$$ ✪✪✪✪
168 ZHUHUI LU
TEL 0512 6520-5601
FAX 0512 6520-8778
www.bg-hotel.com
One of Suzhou's few top-end hotels, the well-positioned Bamboo Grove, picturesquely surrounding a rock pool with ducks, deals with large numbers of Western travelers. The decor is beginning to look a bit threadbare, but the huge servings of bacon at breakfast are highly recommended. Evening live music in foyer bar.
405 All major cards

SONGHELOU (SONGHELOU)
$
18 TAIJIAN NONG, 141 GUANQIAN JIE
TEL 0512 6523-3270
The long-standing Songhelou dishes up standard Eastern Chinese seaboard fare, such as squirrel-shaped mandarin fish and *gu su* marinated duck, at tourist prices. The restaurant is near the Xuanmiao Temple. English menu.
220 AE, JCB

JIA YOU FANG
Not a restaurant but a street lined with restaurants just north of the Garden of Happiness. Popular with the locals (and that's where it counts), there is little to distinguish one eatery from another, so take your pick.

WUXI

NEW WORLD COURTYARD WUXI
$$$ ✪✪✪✪
335 ZHONGSHAN LU
TEL 0510 8276-3388
FAX 0510 8276-3388
www.marriott.com
Located in the center of town, the Marriott-run, 36-story New World Courtyard is the tallest tower in Wuxi. Guest rooms are supplied with daily newspapers, satellite TV, coffee, in-room safe and Internet access. Chinese and Japanese restaurants.
277 All major cards

MILIDO HOTEL
$$ ✪✪✪
2 LIANGXI LU
TEL 0510 586-5665
FAX 0510 580-1668
Situated near the Grand Canal, the Milido Hotel is one of the most upmarket places in town, with good service and inexpensive rooms making for an enjoyable stay. Business center. Bike rental.
188 All major cards

HANGZHOU

SHANGRI-LA HOTEL HANGZHOU (HANGZHOU XIANGGELILA FANDIAN)
$$$/$$$$ ✪✪✪✪✪
78 BEISHAN LU
TEL 0571 8707-7951

FAX 0571 8707 3545
www.shangri-la.com
Located on West Lake's northwest shore in 30 acres (12 ha) of landscaped gardens, the Shangri-La is one of the best hotels in town, bursting with fine dining opportunities and eager to please. Chinese and Italian restaurant, American bar and café. Snooker/billiards, bike rental.
387 All major cards

GRAND HYATT REGENCY (HANGZHOU KAIYUE JIUDIAN)
$$$$ ✪✪✪✪✪
28 HUBIN LU
TEL 0571 8779-1234
FAX 0571 8779-1818
www.hangzhou.regency.hyatt.com
The huge Hyatt comes replete with international standard five-star facilities and amenities, with fully-equipped rooms and a fine location on the east side of West Lake.
390 All major cards

LOUWAILOU (LOUWAILOU CAIGUAN)
$$ ✪✪✪
30 GUSHAN LU
TEL 0571 8796-9023
FAX 0571 8799-7264
Hangzhou's most famous eatery feeds everyone on immortal local recipes (Sudong po pork and beggar's chicken) and offers long views over West Lake from Solitary Hill Island. Specialties: West Lake vinegar fish (*xihu cuyu*) and Longjing shrimps (*longjing xiaren*). English menu.
1,400 All major cards

PEPPINO'S
$$
SHANGRI-LA HOTEL
TEL 0571 8707-7951
An impressive range of Italian flavors finds its way into the pizzas. English menu.
140 All major cards

SHAOXING

XIANHENG HOTEL (XIANHENG DAJIUDIAN)
$$$ ✪✪✪✪
680 JIEFANG NANJIE
TEL 0575 806-8688
FAX 0575 805-1028
Smart and not overly expensive choice located in the south of Shaoing. Tennis courts.
200+ All major cards

PUTUOSHAN

PUTUOSHAN HOTEL (PUTUOSHAN DAJIUDIAN)
$$ ✪✪✪✪
93 MEICEN LU
TEL 0580 609-2828
FAX 0580 609-1818
One of the most superior hotels to have arrived on the island, this four-star hotel offers comfort and a decent range of amenities.
160 MC, V, JCB

SANSHENGTANG (SANSHENGTANG FANDIAN)
$
121 MIAO ZHUANGYAN LU
TEL 0580 609-1277
FAX 0580 609-1140
This budget hotel was formerly a Buddhist nunnery in keeping with the island's sacred character. Diverse range of rooms, just a ten-minute walk from the ferry terminal, not far from Puji Temple. Ticketing service available.
100+ No credit cards accepted

RESTAURANTS IN PUTUOSHAN
Recommending a decent restaurant in Putuoshan is difficult because they are in short supply. Outside of hotel restaurants, decent small seafood eateries can be found not far from the ferry terminal and around the Puji Temple.

PRICES

HOTELS
An indication of the cost of a double room without breakfast is given by **$** signs.

$	Under $40
$$	$40–$100
$$$	$100–$180
$$$$	$180–$350
$$$$$	Over $350

RESTAURANTS
An indication of the cost of a three-course dinner without drinks is given by $ signs.

$	Under $30
$$	$30–$50
$$$	$50–$75
$$$$	$75–$100
$$$$$	Over $100

SHANGHAI

GRAND HYATT SHANGHAI
$$$$$ ✪✪✪✪✪
JINMAO DASHA (JINMAO TOWER), 88 SHIJI DADAO, PUDONG
TEL 021 5049-1234
FAX 021 5049-1111
www.hyatt.com
The highest hotel above ground level in the world may not suit those with vertigo, but the Hyatt—held aloft by the towering Jinmao Building in Pudong—is a landmark Shanghai hotel. Modern, slick, and affording magnificent views of the Bund, the hotel also boasts spacious guest rooms, an array of top-notch restaurants and excellent service.
555 All major cards

THE PORTMAN RITZ-CARLTON (BOTEMAN DAJIUDIAN)
$$$$$ ✪✪✪✪✪
SHANGHAI CENTER, 1376 NANJING XILU
TEL 021 6279-8888
FAX 021 6279-8800
www.ritzcarlton.com
After a $30 million renovation

in 1999, the Portman has reemerged with a fabulously opulent and sleek foyer (burning with polished chrome, softened by ebony and marble). The first-class standards that make this one of the very best business hotels in Shanghai have been preserved. Spacious guest rooms; Chinese, Japanese, and Western restaurants. Squash, racketball, and tennis courts. Restaurant/ service-equipped Shanghai Center on your doorstep.
564 All major cards

PEACE HOTEL (HEPING FANDIAN)
$$$$
20 NANJING DONGLU
TEL 021 6321-6888
www.shanghaipeacehotel.com
This famous hotel is rather scuffed and is wanting, but its sense of history remains intact and the location unparalleled. The international suites are superb, but prohibitively priced. Sparse range of facilities, although hunting down the stained glass is a worthwhile recreation.
279 Middle Henan Road subway All major cards

PUDONG SHANGRI-LA SHANGHAI (XIANGELILA JIUDIAN)
$$$
33 FUCHENG LU, LUJIAZUI, PUDONG
TEL 021 6882-8888
FAX 021 6882 6688
www.shangri-la.com
Facing the Bund from the riverside borders of Pudong, the Shangri-La enjoys a prestigious view over old Shanghai and provides excellent service. The premier rooms in the stunning Tower Two annex—finished in 2005—are Shanghai's roomiest at 581 square feet (54 sq. meters). Chinese and Japanese restaurants and coffee shop. Limousine service.
981 Lujiazui subway All major cards

PARK HOTEL (GUOJI FANDIAN)
$$
170 NANJING XILU
TEL 021 6327-5225
FAX 021 6327-6958
Excellently located grand old hotel overlooking Renmin Square (the old racecourse) and encasing a splendid art deco interior. Built in 1934, the Park is one of the old guard—not the most sophisticated of hotels, but distinguished nonetheless. Chinese and Western restaurants, nightclub, shopping arcade.
180 People's Square subway All major cards

OLD HOUSE INN
$$
NO. 18 LANE 351
OFF HUASHAN LU
TEL 021 6248-6118
FAX 021 6249-6869
After a meal or drink at neighboring bar/restaurant A Future Perfect, tuck yourself up for the night in this stylish boutique-size hotel with its handful of traditionally-styled rooms; there's no better way to experience mid-range comfort amid all the trappings of historic Shanghai.
12 MC, V

CAPTAIN HOSTEL (CHUANZHANG QINGNIAN JIUDIAN)
$
37 FUZHOU LU
TEL 021 6323-5053
FAX 021 6321-9331
www.captainhostel.com.cn
A chopstick's throw away from the Bund, the Captain comes up trumps with good-value dorm accommodations (but less value on double rooms) and a handy bar on the top floor.
Middle Henan Road subway No credit cards accepted

PACIFIC HOTEL (JINMEN DAJIUDIAN)
$
108 NANJING XILU
TEL 0216 327-6226
FAX 0216 372-3634
The Pacific is another slice of history with a fabulous foyer, but the rooms are affordable for those with an eye on their *yuan*. Not far from the Park Hotel, the Pacific, distinguished by its clock tower, overlooks Renmin Square.
170 Renmin Square subway All major cards

PUJIANG HOTEL (PUJIANG FANDIAN)
$/$$
15 HUANGPU LU
TEL 021 6324-6388
www.pujianghotel.com
Also called the Astor House Hotel, this noble relic sits north of Suzhou Creek near the Bund, overseen by staff putting a shine to its sense of history. This is one of the most rewarding addresses in the city (see the Bund walk, p. 182) for those with one eye on their wallet. Laundry facilities.
146 All major cards

T8
$$$
8 NORTH BLOCK
181 TAICANG LU
TEL 021 6355-8999
Serving up its signature international dishes from the stylish restaurant/shopping hub of Xintiandi, T8 easily ranks itself among the best of Shanghai's dining experiences in an increasingly competitive market of top chefs and hard-to-please diners. Lunchtime set menus.
150 2:30–6:30 p.m.; 2–6:30 p.m. Sat. & Sun. All major cards

M ON THE BUND (MISHI XICANTING)
$$
7TH FLOOR,
20 GUANGDONG LU
TEL 021 6350 9988
www.m-onthebund.com
If you are in the area of the Bund, you could do far worse than visit this international eatery. Fine view of the waterfront and fantastic, acclaimed dining.
130 All major cards

QUANJUDE (QUANJUDE KAOYADIAN)
$$
786 HUAIHAI ZHONGLU
TEL 0216 433-7286/6433-5799
Feverishly busy at weekends, Shanghai's Quanjude can't match its parent in Beijing, but this is still essential feasting for *kaoya* (Peking duck) enthusiasts. The waitresses are hectically efficient, and banquet rooms (one called the Forbidden City) wait on the wings. Wash it all down with sweet *babaocha* (eight-treasure tea). 60 tables. English menu.
All major cards

1221
$
1221 YAN'AN XILU
TEL 021 6213-2441
Despite a far-flung location in the city's west, this restaurant is much loved by both local and expat diners. The chefs have hit the nail on the head with some first rate and inventive Shanghai dishes. Try the onion cakes and wash them down with some sweet and refreshing *babao cha* (eight treasures tea).
100+ All major cards

GONGDELIN VEGETARIAN RESTAURANT (GONGDELIN SUSHI CHU)
$ ✪✪✪
445 NANJING XILU
TEL 021 6327-0218
Recently refitted and further improved, the stylish Gongdelin (look for the sign that says "Godly Restaurant"), serves tasty dishes resembling meat, but without a fiber of flesh. Examples include vegetable chicken *(suji)* and vegetable duck *(suya)*. 50 tables. English menu.
9:30–11 a.m.; 2–5 p.m.
No credit cards accepted

HUXINTING TEAHOUSE (HUXINTING CHALOU)
$
257 YUYUAN LU
TEL 021 6373-6950
Emerging from the pond in the heart of the Yuyan Bazaar, the old teahouse is a charming fragment of yesteryear and an excellent place to sample Chinese brews. Two floors. English menu.
180 No credit cards accepted

MALONE'S AMERICAN CAFÉ (MALONG MEISHI JIULOU)
$
257 TONGREN LU
TEL 021 6247-2400
Burgers, fish and chips, coffee, beer, live music, and a sporty theme. Good value, good atmosphere, just up the road from the Shanghai Center. English menu.
70 All major cards

WUYUE RENJIA MIANGUAN
$
10, ALLEY 706, HUAIHAI ZHONGLU
TEL 021 5306-5410
Perfect for a full-blown meal or a swift snack, this popular and traditionally-styled noodle house delivers bowl after bowl of delicious soup noodles and *hundun*. No English menu. Open 10:30 a.m.–9:30 p.m.
40 No credit cards accepted

NANXIANG STEAMED BREAD SHOP (NANXIANG MANTOUDIAN)
$ ✪✪✪
85 YUYUAN LU
TEL 021 6355-4206
Packed on weekends, Nanxiang offers gorgeous *prix fixe* meals of steamed buns (*xiaolongbao*), Shanghai's favorite dumpling. Try the delicious crabmeat variety (*xiefen xiaolong*), accompanied by a thin soup textured with strips of egg. Takeout.
33 All major cards

FACE BAR
$
BUILDING 1, RUIJIN GUESTHOUSE, 18 RUIJIN ERLU
TEL 021 6466-4328
To conjure up the mood of concession-era Shanghai, go no farther than the Face Bar, on the grounds of the historic Ruijin Guesthouse at the heart of the French Concession. It's an expat hangout for sure and prices are steep, but it's a relaxing and civilized point of entry to Shanghai's drinking world and miles from the hustle and bustle that make the city's streets such an effort to navigate. It also serves as a handy spot for sinking an aperitif en route to the excellent Thai restaurant Lan Na Thai upstairs or Hazara (Indian cuisine), also in the same block.
50 South Shaanxi Road subway All major cards

THE SOUTH

LUSHAN

LUSHAN VILLA HOTEL (LUSHAN BIESHU CUN BINGUAN)
$$$
182 ZHIHONG LU
TEL 0792 828-2927

KEY Hotel | Restaurant | No. of bedrooms | No. of seats | Subway | Parking | Closed | Elevator

FAX 0792 828-2927
The hotel has a number of villas and cottages tucked away in the forest and is one of the best ways to appreciate Lushan's charming character. Wide range of prices.
100+ No credit cards accepted

LUSHAN YUNTIAN VILLA (LUSHAN YUNTIAN BIESHU)
$$ ✪✪✪
GULING ZHENGJIE
TEL 0792 829-3555
Too many of Lushan's hotels are far too long in the tooth and slowly going to seed. This alternative—centrally located in Guling—brings a fresh approach to its original villa architecture.
30 Cash only

WULINGYUAN

DRAGON INTERNATIONAL (XIANGLONG GUOJI DAJIUDIAN)
$$ ✪✪✪✪
46 JIEFANG DONGLU, ZHANGJIAJIE CITY
TEL 0744 822-6888
FAX 0744 822-2935
This is the best choice if you want to stay in Zhang-jiajie City rather than the village. The hotel is decidedly a tour-group hotel but plusher than the more basic accommodations in Zhangjaijie Village. Tours of Wulingyuan, rafting, and cave trips can easily be arranged by the tourist center here.
200+ All major cards

PIPAXI HOTEL (PIPAXI BINGUAN)
$$
TEL 0744 571-8888
www.pipaxi-hotel.com
Quietly hidden away on the fringes of things, yet still only a short walk to the gates of Wulingyuan, the recently renovated Pipaxi Hotel offers pleasant and comfortable rooms and a measure of tranquility.
180 No credit cards accepted

XIAMEN

HOLIDAY INN CROWNE PLAZA HARBOUR VIEW (JIARI HUANGGUAN HAIJING DAJIUDIAN)
$$$ ✪✪✪✪
12-8 ZHENHAI LU
TEL 0592 202-3333
FAX 0592 203-6666
The Holiday Inn is reliably hospitable, and expert facilities are all within affordable reach. The hotel furthermore enjoys an excellent location in the heart of town, with towering views over to Gulangyu Island. Cable TV.
367 All major cards

BEAUTIFUL ISLAND HOTEL OF GULANGYU (LIZHIDAO JIUDIAN)
$
133 LONGTOU LU
TEL 0592 206-3309
FAX 0592 206-3311
Up from the pier, this charming and amenable small budget hotel has a fine selection of okay rooms. Come here if you just don't want to leave the island too soon. Ticketing service.
32 No credit cards accepted

GULANGYU VILLA HOTEL (GULANGYU BIESHU)
$$ ✪✪✪
14 GUSHENG LU
TEL 0592 206-3280
Ideal for eking out Xiamen's quietest pockets of tranquility, this lovely old villa hotel is ensconced away in the west of Gulangyu, with attractive sea views and a gorgeous garden and beachfront aspect.
66 MC, V, JCB

ZHAOQING

STAR LAKE HOTEL (XINGHU DAJIUDIAN)
$ ✪✪✪✪
37 DUANZHOU LU
TEL 0758 616-8888
FAX 0758 619-3333
Well-equipped hotel south of Seven Stars Lake. Business center, bank, travel center.
390 Domestic cards only

DINGHUSHAN

DINGHU SUMMER RESORT (DINGHU BISHU SHANZHUANG)
$ ✪✪
TEL 0758 262-1668
FAX 0758 262-1665
You may want to stay at Dinghushan for a while before the grind back to Guangzhou. The resort, not far from the bus stop, has a good range of amenities. Travel center, currency exchange.
47 No credit cards accepted

GUANGZHOU

CHINA HOTEL (ZHONGGUO DAJIUDIAN)
$$$/$$$$ ✪✪✪✪✪
LIUHUA LU
TEL 020 8666-6888
FAX 020 8667-7288
www.marriotthotels.com
Excellent and simply colossal Marriott-owned hotel situated west of Yuexiu Park with virtually every facility you could need, a first-class ambience, and a great crop of restaurants. Business center, fitness center, tennis courts.
889 All major cards

WHITE SWAN HOTEL (BAITIAN'E BINGUAN)
$$$ ✪✪✪✪✪
1 SHAMIAN NANJIE, SHAMIAN ISLAND
TEL 020 8188-6968
www.whiteswanhotel.com
The White Swan is not a new

hotel and it's lost some of its shine, but it sits commandingly on picturesque Shamian Island, replete with five-star amenities and service. The hotel is very popular with couples coming to China to adopt Chinese children. Impressive fountain in foyer and well-stocked shopping arcade. Pearl River night cruise. Nine restaurants. Limousine service. Tennis and squash courts.

834 All major cards

SHAMIAN HOTEL (SHAMIAN BINGUAN)

$ ✪✪

52 SHAMIAN NANJIE
TEL 020 8121-8288
FAX 020 8121-8628
www.gdshamianhotel.com

A budget hotel offering an extremely affordable and pleasant stay and a view over the Pearl River. The standards are rudimentary but serviceable, and with the rest of the island as your back garden, does it matter?

50 No credit cards accepted

BANXI (BANXI JIUJIA)

$$

151 LONGJIN XILU
TEL 0208 181-5718/8181-5955

This famous restaurant in west Guangzhou is the place to come for the full social event that surrounds the eating of Cantonese dim sum (especially on weekends). Beyond dim sum, the menu is a cavalcade of tasty regional Cantonese cuisine (*yuecai*).

1,500–2,000 No credit cards accepted

DONGBEIREN

$ ✪✪

2ND FLOOR
1 TAOJIN BEILU
TEL 020 8357-5276

The name means "Northeasterner," and this funky little chain of restaurants serves up fantastic dumplings (*jiaozi*) from China's Manchurian region. Nineteen different types of handmade dumplings are on offer. Professional service, gregarious, and fun. English menu. Also at 36 Garden Building, Tianhe Nanlu, tel 8750-1711; 668 Renmin Beilu, tel 020 8136-1466, 40–50 tables.

No credit cards accepted

GUANGZHOU (GUANGZHOU JIUJIA)

$

2 WENCHANG LU
TEL 020 8138-0388

The Guangzhou has been serving up Cantonese cuisine since 1936 and has spawned several branches. The restaurant is busy (perhaps phone for a reservation), the food authentic and well presented, the menu extensive, and the dim sum very popular. English menu.

500+ Closed 3–5:30 p.m. All major cards

HAINAN ISLAND

Winter season is the high season on Hainan Island. If you travel after March, hotel rooms will be up to 40 percent cheaper.

MERITUS MANDARIN HAIKOU

$$$ ✪✪✪✪✪

18 WENHUA LU
TEL 0898 6854-8888
FAX 0898 6851-1228
www.meritusmandarin.haikou.com

Located in the financial district of the provincial capital, Haikou's best hotel, the 23-story Meritus Mandarin supplies the full range of international standard facilities and services. Chinese and Italian restaurants. Tennis courts.

318 All major cards

SANYA

GLORIA RESORT SANYA (KALAI DUJIA JIUDIAN)

$$$/$$$$ ✪✪✪✪✪

YALONG BAY
TEL 0898 8856-8855
FAX 0898 8856-8533
www.gloriaresort.com

Enjoying an enviable location on Hainan's most pristine beach, the Gloria Resort is the perfect place to unwind. Rooms come with in-house movies, minibar and fabulous views. Restaurants and full range of resort facilities.

403 All major cards

HILTON SANYA RESORT & SPA (XIERDUN WENQUAN DUJIA JIUDIAN)

$$$$ ✪✪✪✪✪

WENLING LU NANDUAN
TEL 0898 8858-8888
FAX 0898 8858-8588
www.sanya.hilton.com

Bringing its brand of excellence to the beachfront of Yalong Bay, this new resort from Hilton has all you need for intensive comfort and relaxation.

501 All major cards

PRICES

HOTELS

An indication of the cost of a double room without breakfast is given by $ signs.

$	Under $40
$$	$40–$100
$$$	$100–$180
$$$$	$180–$350
$$$$$	Over $350

RESTAURANTS

An indication of the cost of a three-course dinner without drinks is given by $ signs.

$	Under $30
$$	$30–$50
$$$	$50–$75
$$$$	$75–$100
$$$$$	Over $100

HONG KONG & MACAU

HONG KONG

MANDARIN ORIENTAL
$$$$$ ○○○○○
5 CONNAUGHT RD., CENTRAL, HONG KONG ISLAND
TEL 0852 2522-0111
www.mandarinoriental.com
Thoroughly renovated in 2006, the Mandarin Oriental is a landmark in Hong Kong's dazzling hotel firmament. First-class service and facilities.
542 Central subway All major cards

SOMETHING SPECIAL

THE PENINSULA

The Peninsula enjoys an unrivaled reputation in Hong Kong. Highly sophisticated, grand, and elegant, this hotel makes your stay an event, with some of the territory's most distinguished restaurants (Gaddi's, Felix, see below) at hand for maximum indulgence. The corner suites are equipped with magnificently wide vistas, and the nocturnal harborside view over to Central is out of this world. Even if you feel you can't quite afford the cost, it's well worth throwing caution to the wind for gilt-edged memories. The Peninsula is a glamorous classic. First-class shopping arcade. Rolls Royce fleet. Helicopter service.
$$$$$ ○○○○○
SALISBURY RD., KOWLOON
TEL 0852 2920-2888
FAX 0852 2722-4170
www.hongkong.peninsula.com
300 Tsim Sha Tsui subway and spa All major cards

ISLAND SHANGRI-LA
$$$$ ○○○○○
PACIFIC PLACE, SUPREME COURT RD., CENTRAL, HONG KONG ISLAND
TEL 0852 2877-3838
www.shangri-la.com
Encased by one of the most attractive buildings on Hong Kong Island, the interior of the Shangri-La is equally breathtaking. The hotel is one of the jewels in the Shangri-La crown with panoramic views over to Kowloon. Chinese, Japanese, French, and seafood restaurants.
565 Admiralty subway All major cards

SOMETHING SPECIAL

JIA

It's never going to be everyone's cup of tea, but the Philippe Starck-designed Jia will be an instant hit with trendy young travelers in search of a super-chic boutique space to hang their hat in Honkers. While not spacious, the open-plan studios (with kitchen) are fine for short stays, and guests can avail themselves of the hotel's highlight restaurant—Opia (see p. 376)—one of Hong Kong's latest culinary sensations.
$$$
1–5 IRVING STREET CAUSEWAY BAY
TEL 00852 3196-9000
FAX 00852 3196-9001
www.jiahongkong.com
57 Causeway Bay subway All major cards

KOWLOON HOTEL
$$$ ○○○○
19–21 NATHAN RD., KOWLOON
TEL 00852 2929-2888
FAX 00852 2739-9811
www.thekowloonhotel.com
The Kowloon Hotel enjoys an excellent location on Nathan Road, Kowloon's "Golden Mile," within range of most sights of note and a short walk from the Star Ferry Pier. Convenient and inexpensive, standard rooms may not be spacious but are fine for short-stay travelers, coming computer-equipped (aim for rooms on upper floors if you want good views). Good choice of restaurants, shopping arcade.
736 Tsim Sha Tsui subway All major cards

SALISBURY YMCA
$$$
41 SALISBURY RD.
TEL 832 2268-7888
www.ymcahk.org.hk
The beds are very cheap here, and the location is excellent (just down from the Peninsula). It may not be upscale, but it's definitely one of the best mid-range options in town. Tennis court, business center.
380 Tsim Sha Tsui subway All major cards

JOCKEY CLUB MOUNT DAVIS HOSTEL
$
MOUNT DAVIS PATH
TEL/FAX 0852 2817-5715
Difficult to reach but very popular budget destination on Hong Kong Island. Dorm beds; shuttle bus connects with the hostel from the Sheung Wan Macau Ferry Terminal seven times a day (phone beforehand for times of bus and to check if there are vacancies).
112 No credit cards accepted

DYNASTY
$$$$ ○○○○○
4TH FLOOR., NEW WORLD HOTEL, 22 SALISBURY ROAD TSIM SHA TSUI
TEL 0852 2369-4111 EXT 6361
Cantonese dining in a traditional Chinese teahouse ambience. One of Hong Kong's finest Cantonese restaurants; specialties include baked silver cod and steamed sliced pork with preserved shrimp paste. Excellent wine list. No *prix fixe* meals.
88 Tsim Sha Tsui subway All major cards

FELIX
$$$$ ○○○○○
THE PENINSULA
TEL 852 2315-3188
Still eliciting gasps of approval, Felix takes dining to new heights on the 28th floor of the Peninsula. The work of French designer Philippe Starck, the restaurant is imaginatively theatrical and the views are as inspiring as the dishes. Felix has its own mood lighting-equipped elevator. International/Pan-Asian cuisine. Three bars (the Wine Bar, the Balcony, and the American Bar) and dance floor. Smart/casual dress code.
110 Tsim Sha Tsui subway All major cards

MAN WAH
$$$$ ○○○○
25TH FLOOR, MANDARIN ORIENTAL , 5 CONNAUGHT RD., CENTRAL
TEL 0852 2522-0111 EXT 4025
E-MAIL: manwah@mohg .com
With views over Victoria Harbour, the hallmark hotel's elegant Chinese restaurant offers a feast of Cantonese flavors in a refined, traditional Chinese setting. Signature dishes include fillet of sole in black bean sauce, beggar's chicken, and stuffed prawns, with dim sum served on weekends and public holidays.
130 Central All major cards

THE BAR
$$$ ○○○○○
1ST FLOOR
THE PENINSULA, SALISBURY RD., TSIM SHA TSUI
TEL 0852 2920-2888 EXT 3163
The Bar is expensive, but the highly civilized ambience and sterling service is almost peer-less. A hushed, seductive, and superlative tavern, but no formal restaurant. Smart/casual dress code.
46 Tsim Sha Tsui subway Open 5 p.m.–1 a.m. All major cards

HUNAN GARDEN
$$$ ○○○○
3RD FLOOR, THE FORUM, EXCHANGE SQUARE, CENTRAL
TEL 0852 2868-2880
This restaurant expertly re-creates the fiery aromas of Hunan cuisine. Spicy, strong, and hot; elegantly decorated ambience and fine presentation. The chicken in spicy sauce should set you in the right direction. Good wine list. *Prix fixe* meals.
300+ Central subway Closed 3–6 p.m. All major cards

JIMMY'S KITCHEN
$$$ ○○○○
BASEMENT, SOUTH CHINA BUILDING, 1 WYNDHAM ST., CENTRAL
TEL 0852 2526-5293
An old-timer that has seen a lot of restaurants close around it. Jimmy's plentiful European menu has a loyal fan base. Try the escargots in garlic butter or char-grilled king prawns, and round it all off with hot apple crumble. English menu.
120 Central subway 11 p.m All major cards

SOMETHING SPECIAL

OPIA

A culinary highlight of Jia (see p. 375), award-winning and lushly-styled Opia is a tempting piece of eye-candy whose inventive "Australian free style" menu has taken Hong Kong gastronomes into a seventh heaven. With its accent on sensual ambience, Opia has become one of the territory's most sought after dining experiences.
$$/$$$ ○○○○
1ST FLOOR, JIA
1–5 IRVING STREET
CAUSEWAY BAY
TEL 00852 3196-9100
70 Causeway Bay subway Closed Sun., & 3–6 p.m. Mon.–Sat. All major cards

PEAK LOOKOUT
$$$
121 PEAK ROAD, THE PEAK
HONG KONG ISLAND
TEL 0852 2849-1000
www.thepeaklookout.com.hk
Formerly the Peak Café, the relaxing colonial setting of the Lookout on Victoria Peak is splendid, with a respected menu celebrating Asian and International cuisine. The restaurant is notable for its seafood dishes and there's a much celebrated al fresco dining area on the terrace. Breakfast is served Saturday, Sunday and public holidays (8:30–11:30 a.m.).
250 Peak Tram Station MC, V

TOSCANA
$$$ ○○○○○
RITZ-CARLTON HOTEL, 3 CONNAUGHT RD., CENTRAL, HONG KONG ISLAND
TEL 0852 2532-2062
Highly accomplished Italian dishes (fine steaks) in sumptuous surroundings at this celebrated restaurant.
100+ Closed Sun. L, & 2:30–6 p.m. Mon.–Sat. All major cards

SAMPAN SEAFOOD RESTAURANT
$$
16 MAIN ST., YUNG SHUE WAN, LAMMA ISLAND
TEL 0852 2982-2388
A trip to Lamma Island should really include a sampling of seafood to accompany the splendid views. Go no farther than this restaurant in Yung Shue Wan's main street for Cantonese maritime fare and excellent vistas out to sea. Dim sum in mornings. English menu.
200+ All major cards

CLUB 71
$$
BASEMENT
67 HOLLYWOOD RD.

CENTRAL
TEL 0852 2858-7071
You'll be tripping over chic bars by the bundle in HK, but for the more no-frills, non-preening crowd, and devotees of its former Lan Kwai Fong incarnation Club 64 (which uprooted to relocate here), Club 71 is one of NoHo's (North of Hollywood Road) choice spots for intelligent discussions over alcohol.
50 Central or Sheungwan subway MC, V

TUTTO BENE
$$
7 KNUTSFORD TERRACE
TSIM SHA TSUI
TEL 0852 2316 2116
Quietly tucked away in an alley of restaurants and bars east off Nathan Road, Tutto Bene delivers quality, inexpensive Italian food and good service in an agreeable setting. There's an al fresco dining option around one of the tables parked on the pavement outside. Wi-Fi.
100 Tsim Sha Tsui Closed L All major cards

BOOKWORM CAFÉ
$
79 MAIN ST., YUNG SHUE WAN, LAMMA ISLAND
TEL 00852 2982-4838
The old-timer Lamma Island Wi-Fi–equipped Bookworm long ago won acclaim as a much-loved Yung Shue Wan second-hand bookshop and veggie café rolled into one.

LIFE ORGANIC HEALTH CAFÉ
$
10 SHELLY STREET
CENTRAL
TEL 00852 2810-9777
First stop for vegetarians and vegans alike or simply those aiming at a first-rate culinary detox.
50 Central subway All major cards

LUK YU TEAHOUSE & RESTAURANT
$
24–26 STANLEY ST.
TEL 0852 2523-5464
One of Hong Kong's most famous Cantonese teahouses, Luk Yu in Central is a very popular place to *yum cha* (drink tea, relax) and eat excellent dim sum. The service (cantankerous aged waiters) flags way behind, but everyone's used to it. Reservations recommended. Dim sum daily from 7 a.m.–6 p.m.
300 Central subway All major cards

OLIVER'S SUPER SANDWICHES (LIHUA CHAOJI SANWENZHI DIAN)
$
www.olivers-supersandwiches.com
SHOP 55, UG/F, CHINA HONG KONG CITY, 33 CANTON RD.
SUBWAY: TSIM SHA TSUI
TEL 0852 2376-2826
BASEMENT LEVEL ONE, CHEUNG KONG CENTER
2 QUEEN'S ROAD
SUBWAY: CENTRAL
TEL 0852 2185-7080
G006–010, G/F, WORLD TRADE CENTER, 280 GLOUCESTER RD
SUBWAY: CAUSEWAY BAY
TEL 0852 2895-0218
These are just three addresses of this ubiquitous and highly satisfying Hong Kong sandwich chain. Fine granola breakfasts, decent coffee, a freshly prepared and crisp range of sandwich fillers, baked potatoes, waffles, soup. Well run, efficient, and far healthier than McDonalds, Maxim's, or Hardee's (some of Hong Kong's other fast-food names).

STEAM AND STEW INN
$
21–23 TAI WONG ST. EAST, WAN CHAI, HONG KONG ISLAND
TEL 0852 2529-3913
The air heavy with steamy aromas and the boiled infusion of Cantonese herbs and spices, the emphasis here is not so much on elegance as on authentic, healthy dinner preparations. Highly popular. MSG-free dining. *Prix fixe* meals. No wine. English menu.
100+ Wan Chai subway Closed 2:30–5:30 p.m. MC, V

MACAU

Before heading to Macau on the jetfoil from Hong Kong, be aware that you can get a much cheaper room (up to 50 percent off) if you book your ticket and hotel room through one of the numerous outlets in the Shun Tak Centre at the Macau Ferry Terminal, Sheung Wan, Hong Kong Island. If you arrive in Macau without a room, a number of mid-range and up-scale hotels have counters at the jetfoil pier where you can negotiate a price much lower than the walk-in price. Hotel rooms are far cheaper during the slack weekday period, with large price hikes at the weekend (when large numbers of Hong Kong Chinese come to Macau). A number of shuttle buses run to hotels from the jetfoil pier.

POUSADA DE SAO TIAGO
$$$$$ ○○○○○
AVENIDA DE REPUBLICA
TEL 0853 378-111
FAX 0853 552-170
www.saotiago.com.mo
Perched on the southern tip of the Macau peninsula over looking the harbor, this hotel is delightfully incorporated into the 17th century Portuguese-built Fortaleza da Barra (Barra Fort), which also contains the Chapel of St James. Take a drink or an al fresco meal on the terrace and indulge in the peerless surroundings. The elegant hotel has a limited number of rooms, each equipped with its own balcony affording splendid views, so reservations are much recommended. Com-

plementary pier transfer and shuttle service.
24 All major cards

WESTIN RESORT MACAU
$$$$ ✪✪✪✪✪
1918 ESTRADA DE HAC SA COLOANE
TEL 00853 871-111
FAX 00853 871-122
www.westin.com/macau

Located on Hac Sa Beach on Coloane, the Westin is a popular resort with a plethora of five-star facilities, including a championship golf course, both indoor and outdoor pools, and tennis courts, while the Kids Club can lend a hand with children. Rooms all have terraces and sea views, and come with the trademark Westin Heavenly Bed.
208 (heated) All major cards

HOLIDAY INN
$$–$$$
82–86 RUA DE PEQUIM, MACAU PENINSULA
TEL 0853 783-333
www.macau.holiday-inn.com

A reliably decent hotel, equipped with an efficient range of amenities and services. Nightclub, cable TV, gym. Situated within easy reach of the jetfoil pier. Shuttle bus.
410 All major cards

EAST ASIA HOTEL
$ ✪✪✪
1A RUA DA MADEIRA, MACAU PENINSULA
TEL 0853 922-433

Attractively housed in a historic building just north of Avenida de Almeida Ribeiro near the Inner Harbour, the well-run East Asia offers good value and is clearly a few notches above Macau's parsimonious guesthouse options.
100+ MC, V

MEZZALUNA
$$$ ✪✪✪✪
MANDARIN ORIENTAL HOTEL, 956 AVENIDA DE AMIZADE, MACAU PENINSULA
TEL 0853 793-3861

Fine, upscale Italian restaurant in one of the territory's premier hotels. Nice setting, fresh pasta, very successful pizza. Dress code. Reservations recommended. English menu.
58 All major cards

CACAROLA
$$
8 RUA DOS GAIVOTAS, COLOANE
TEL 0853 882-226

Cacarola is popular for its excellent Portuguese cuisine. The regularly changing menu hangs on to some favorites: tasty salads, rabbit stew, turkey stroganoff, and delectable seafood including sardines and codfish. Good wine list. Weekend reservations recommended. English menu.
60 Closed Mon. AE, MC, V

SOMETHING SPECIAL

RESTAURANTE FERNANDO

An excellent wine list accompanies superb Portuguese dining at this noteworthy eatery on Coloane's eastern shore. Fernando conjures up some fine magic with lamb, clams, shrimps, prawns, and Portuguese recipes in a simple setting. The restaurant has a stunning reputation, so weekend reservations are necessary if not mandatory.

$$ ✪✪✪✪
9 HAC SA BEACH, COLOANE
TEL 0853 882-531
100+ No credit cards accepted

FLAMINGO
$$ ✪✪✪
HYATT REGENCY
2 ESTRADA ALMIRANTE MARQUES ESPARTEIRO, TAIPA ISLAND
TEL 0853 831-234

Fine, authentic selection of Portuguese/Macau dishes from this attractive hotel restaurant on Taipa Island. Recommended dishes include sautéed clams in tomato *(ameijoas na cataplana)*, African chicken *(galinha a Africana)*, Portuguese potato soup with spinach beets *(caldo verde)*, curry crab *(caril de carangueijo)*, and Portuguese deep-fried dough *(farturas)*. Try to get a seat outside if you can; the duck-filled lakeside setting is fantastic. Enterprising wine list.
138 All major cards

PINOCCHIO
$$
4 RUA DO SOL, TAIPA VILLAGE
TEL 0853 827-128

Huge Portuguese restaurant in picturesque Taipa Village, waylaying tourists with a mammoth menu including roast lamb, deep-fried sardines, curried crab, and grilled squid. Weekend reservations recommended. English menu. A choice of other restaurants

PRICES

HOTELS

An indication of the cost of a double room without breakfast is given by $ signs.

$	Under $40
$$	$40–$100
$$$	$100–$180
$$$$	$180–$350
$$$$$	Over $350

RESTAURANTS

An indication of the cost of a three-course dinner without drinks is given by $ signs.

$	Under $30
$$	$30–$50
$$$	$50–$75
$$$$	$75–$100
$$$$$	Over $100

peppers Rua da Cunha around the corner.
300+ All major cards

A LORCHA
$
289A RUA DO ALMIRANTE SERGIO, MACAU PENINSULA
TEL 0853 313-193
If you've done the walk south to the Maritime Museum/A-Ma Temple, treat yourself at A Lorcha. A feast of Portuguese flavors is conjured up by fine chefmanship; raw codfish salad, African chicken, pork knuckles, and other temptations. English menu. Weekend reservations recommended.
60 Tues. AE, MC, V

NGA TIM CAFÉ
$
8 RUA CAETANO, COLOANE VILLAGE
TEL 0853 882-086/880-021
Picturesquely situated opposite the Chapel of St. Francis Xavier, this little café is a feast of good-value Macau and Portuguese food, with a fine reputation for seafood.
64 MC, V

MARGARET'S CAFÉ E NATA
GUM LOI BUILDING, 17 RUA COMMANDANTE, MACAU PENINSULA
TEL 0853 710-032
Sit in the square outside and work your way through one of the breakfasts: egg tarts, sandwiches, cheesecake, and coffee. English menu. Also at Rua Almirante Costa Cabral (not far from the Lou Lim Ieoc Gardens, tel 527-791).
50 No credit cards accepted

THE SOUTHWEST

KUNMING

KUNMING HOTEL
$$ ○○○○
52 DONGFENG DONGLU
TEL 0871 316-2063/316-2172
www.kunminghotel.com.cn
For a four-star hotel, the lobby is a tad overblown, but the glitter, shine, and sparkling chandeliers are a presage of clean rooms along elegant corridors, especially on the executive floors. The exterior is certainly more stylish than the Holiday Inn opposite. Staying here puts you in the heart of the city, within striking distance of decent bars and restaurants. Tennis court.
236 All major cards

CAMELLIA HOTEL (CHAHUA BINGUAN)
$
96 DONGFENG DONGLU
TEL 0871 316-3000
FAX 0871 314-7033
Kunming's budget option, the Camellia dorms play host to most of the backpackers that drift into town. Very cheap and with no frills, this is the place to trade tales from the road with like-minded veterans on the Yunnan circuit. Bicycle rental.
279 No credit cards accepted

WHITE PAGODA DAI RESTAURANT (BAITA DAIWEITING)
$
127 SHANGYI JIE
TEL 0871 317-2932
For some of the flavors of Dai cooking, this simple and unpretentious restaurant is popular with travelers searching out authentic local food (much of it's spicy) or those simply aiming to get a further handle on Yunnan's ethnic culture and traditional diversity.
50 No credit cards accepted

WEI'S PIZZERIA (HAHA FANDIAN)
$
400 TUO DONGLU
TEL 0871 316-6189
This spot is popular with the Kunming expatriate crowd who congregate here. The decor may be unimaginative, but the pizzas are cartwheel size and surprisingly good. If you order soup, ask for it to arrive first, or it will come Chinese-style with everything else or at the end of the meal as you reach for your coffee. 30 tables.
No credit cards accepted

DALI

JIM'S GUESTHOUSE (HEPING ZHAODAISUO)
$
63 BOAI LU, DALI OLD TOWN
TEL 0872 267-1822
FAX 0872 267-0188
E-MAIL jimsguesthouse@hotmail.com
Clean, tidy, and ultra-cheap rooms along with snappy service. On top of this, there's excellent English from the half-Hui, half-Tibetan concierge Jim. His 40 percent proof No. 1 special, a stunning (literally) potion fermented from an exotic spray of herbs, turns your knees to rubber when you eventually stand up. Jim can also arrange a multitude of tours around the Dali area and beyond.
7 No credit cards accepted

JINHUA HOTEL (JINHUA DAJIUDIAN)
$ ○○
CORNER OF HUGUO LU AND FUXING JIE
TEL 0872 267-3343/267-3344/267-3845
FAX 0872 267-3846
Good-value rooms, though there are few concessions to local culture in the furnishings. Still, it's one of the plusher spots in Dali—if you can handle the menace of karaoke. Air-ticketing office, business center, massage parlor.
87 No credit cards accepted

MCA GUESTHOUSE (HUALANG JIUDIAN)
$ ✪✪
WENXIAN LU
TEL 0872 267-3666/267-1999
Farther south from the Dali Museum and 500 feet (150 m) south of Dali's south gate, the MCA House is a popular backpacker guesthouse. The hostel also functions as an art center, leaving an impression of cultivated simplicity. Bike rental, ticketing, Internet access.
48 No credit cards accepted

OLD DALI INN NO. 5 (DALI SIJI KEZHAN)
$
55 BOAI LU
TEL 0872 267-0382
Welcoming and popular place with an attractive courtyard and a restful ambience, with dorms, double and single rooms, bike rental, and free Internet access for guests; bus ticketing available at front desk.
50 No credit cards accepted

SUNSHINE CAFÉ (YANGGUANG KAFEI)
$
16 HUGUO LU
TEL 0872 266-0712
The charming staff at the Sunshine Café use the best of local ingredients, but don't expect miracles. The chicken sandwich is a door-stop filler, and don't drink the rich Yunnan coffee after 4 p.m. unless you plan to stay awake till dawn. If you eat al fresco, trinket sellers on the street will begin to move in on you. Traveler info, book exchange, and ticket service. English menu.
50 No credit cards accepted

TIBET CAFÉ (XIZANG KAFEI)
$
42 HUGUO LU
TEL 0872 266-2391
One of the most popular cafés that travelers gravitate to along Huguo Lu is this place with personality and a welcoming, crowd-pleasing menu from Tibet and beyond. A perfect place to soak up Dali's personable charms, get to meet fellow travelers, and sink a cup of thick, dark, and caffeine-rich Yunnan coffee.
180 No credit cards accepted

LIJIANG

GRAND LIJIANG (LIJIANG GELAN DAJIUDIAN)
$$ ✪✪✪
XINYI JIE, DAYAN TOWN
TEL 0888 512-8888
FAX 0888 512-7878
Sitting on the fringes of the old town of Lijiang, this Chinese-Thai joint venture hotel makes no concessions to the local architectural vernacular; it offers slightly more quality than the other mid-range hotels in town. Western and Oriental restaurants.
126 AE, MC, V

MOON INN (XINYUE KEZHAN)
$ ✪✪✪
34 XINGREN XIADUAN WUYI JIE
TEL 0888 518-0520/666-1073
E-MAIL mooninn@163.com
Lovingly put together by the Li family, this recommended inn creates just the right mood with polished bamboo floors, wooden furniture, traditional local cuisine, and charming old-town location. Rooms are comfy, the views are lovely, and the family-oriented feel is the perfect antidote to the impersonal style of many Chinese hotels.
14 No credit cards accepted

FIRST BEND INN (DIYI WAN JIUDIAN)
$
43 MISHI ALLEY, XINYI JIE
TEL 0888 518-1073
FAX 0888 518-1688
Atmospheric budget hotel in the heart of Lijiang's Old Town. Well kept, attractively appointed, and highly popular. Periodic hot water; travel information. Luggage storage, laundry. Bike rental available.
20 No credit cards accepted

BLUE PAGE VEGETARIAN (LANYE SUSHI CANGUAN)
$
69 MISHI ALLEY, XINYI JIE, OLD TOWN
TEL 0888 518-5206
Near the First Bend Inn (see above), the frugal 69 offers meat-free dishes. The Dali toasted cheese sandwich is scrumptious. Candles create a soothing mood.
20 No credit cards accepted

SAKURACAFÉ (YINGHUA WU)
$
123 CUIWENDUAN, XINHUA ST., OLD TOWN
TEL 0888 518-7619/312-6766
An engaging and comfortable mishmash of Italian, Korean, Japanese, and Naxi cuisine with travel advice thrown in, Sakuracafé is picturesquely sited next to the canal in Lijiang's Old Town. Internet .
50 section No credit cards accepted

JINGHONG

DAI BUILDING INN (DAIJIA HUAYUAN XIAOLOU)
$
57 MANTING LU
TEL 0691 216-2592
If you want your trip to Xishuangbanna to be fun come here. The bamboo huts on stilts, the moonlight poking through slits in the walls, the fans battling against the tide of heat, and the basic communality of it all make for a more authentic, and extremely cheap, stay. Range of rooms.

7 No credit cards accepted

TAI GARDEN HOTEL (DAIYUAN JIUDIAN)
$ ○○○○
8 NONGLIN NANLU
TEL 0691 212-3888
Jinghong's luxury option sports clean and attractive rooms and a marbled and bright interior. The hotel's restaurant and entertainment options are mainly Chinese (heavy on the karaoke), but the service is efficient and Jinghong's remorseless tacky character is kept at bay—a different world from the rest of Jinghong. The breakfast—coffee, pancakes, sausage, egg, and toast—is excellent.
172 All major cards

MEI MEI CAFÉ (MEIMEI KAFEIDIAN)
$
MANTING LU
TEL 0691 212-7324
The Mei Mei (pretty pretty) Café serves up pineapple shakes, burgers, and BLT sandwiches to enthusiastic backpackers. Settle into a rattan chair and reach for the gripping travelers' tales notebooks (with recommended sorties into the undergrowth around town). Book exchange and Internet.
20 No credit cards accepted

GUILIN

BRAVO HOTEL
$$$ ○○○○
14 RONGHUA NANLU
TEL 0773 282-3950
FAX 0773 282-2101
Among the best hotels in town, this former Holiday Inn offers good value for the money and a decent range of four-star amenities. Service is efficient, restaurants good, and some rooms overlook the river.
259 All major cards

SHERATON GUILIN (GUILIN DAYU DAFANDIAN)
$$ ○○○○○
15 BINJIANG NANLU
TEL 0773 282-5588
FAX 0773 282-5598
www.sheraton.com
Overlooking the Li River, the Sheraton has a majestic location, offers excellent facilities with very comfortable guest rooms. Restaurants include Chinese and Western fine dining options and a popular bar.
430 All major cards

GUILIN FUBO HOTEL (GUILIN FUBOSHAN ZHUANG)
$$ ○○○
121 BINJIANG LU
TEL 0773 282-9988
FAX 0773 282-2328
This clean three-star hotel is popular with Westerners. Spread over only a few floors like all hotels in Guilin (height restrictions protect the view), the Fubo is in a splendid location next to Fuboshan (Wave-subduing Hill) and the Li River. Chilled water delivered to your room.
150 All major cards

YANGSHUO

Xi Jie is full of restaurants and cafés serving up drinks, dishing up Western and local snacks, and dispensing travel advice. Among the best choices are the Red Star Express at No. 66, Minnie Mao's at No. 83, the Under the Moon Café, and Lisa's café, bar and guest house (see below).

PARADESA YANGSHUO RESORT
$$ ○○○
116 XI JIE
TEL 0773 882-2109
www.paradiseyangshuo.com
The resort hotel brings a measure of luxury to Yangshuo, distanced from Xi Jie within a landscaped setting of lakes and bridges. It doesn't capture the mood of Yangshuo, but it's comfortable. Satellite TV, business center.
145 All major cards

LISA'S
$
71 XI JIE
TEL/FAX 0773 882-0217
Lisa, the noisy and gregarious owner (motto: Got a problem? Lisa will sort), offers all those Yangshuo necessities: cheap food, beds, travel info, bike rental. Very popular establishment at the seasoned backpacker end of the market. Internet access. No limousine service.
20 V

BEIHAI

SHANGRI-LA HOTEL (XIANGGELILA FANDIAN)
$$ ○○○○
33 CHATING LU
TEL 0779 206-2288
FAX 0779 205-0085
www.shangri-la.com
This is by far Beihai's best hotel, facing the sea with spacious but affordable rooms. As with all Shangri-La hotels, executive floors provide a superior degree of comfort and service. Chinese and Western restaurants. Half an hour from the international airport. Horizon Club (executive) floors. Bike rental.
364 All major cards

SANJIANG

CHENGYANG BRIDGE HOSTEL (CHENGYANG QIAO ZHAODAISUO)
$ ○○
TEL 0772 861-2444
Dong-style hotel with riverside balconied restaurant near the bridge. Simple provisions, basic accommodations. Restaurant.

KEY: Non-smoking | Air-conditioning | Indoor/ Outdoor swimming pool | Health club | Credit cards

LONGSHENG

RIVERSIDE HOTEL (KAIKAI LÜSHE)
$ ✪✪
5 GUILONG LU
TEL 0773 751-1335
Spartan accommodations from a helpful and enterprising local English teacher. There's a choice of dorms and double rooms, and the guarantee of excellent local information. There are other options in town, but none quite so adept at dealing with foreign travelers.
10 No credit cards accepted

SICHUAN & THE TIBETAN PLATEAU

CHENGDU

HOLIDAY INN CROWNE PLAZA CHENGDU (ZONGFU HUANGGUAN JIARI JIUDIAN)
$$$ ✪✪✪✪✪
31 ZONGFU LU
TEL 028 8678-6666
FAX 028 8678-9789
Catering largely to the business set, this hotel won its five-star wings in 1999. The lobby, a cavernous expanse of orange marble buffed to a dizzying shine, says it all. One of Chengdu's best hotels.
433 All major cards

JINJIANG HOTEL (JINJIANG BINGUAN)
$$$ ✪✪✪✪✪
80 RENMIN NANLU
TEL 028 8550-6666
FAX 028 8550-6550
www.jjhotel.com
By the banks of the Jinjiang River, this is one of Chengdu's smartest hotels, despite its age and the more recent competition in town. Facilities are extensive and rooms decent. Bowling alley, medical clinic, airport shuttle bus. Tennis courts.
523 All major cards

TRAFFIC HOTEL (JIAOTONG FANDIAN)
$ ✪✪
77 LINJIANG LU
TEL 028 8545-1017
FAX 028 8544-0977
Well above average for the budget category, but the service can be perfunctory. The double rooms are spacious, dry, and reasonably clean, and a useful bulletin board puts you in touch with fellow travelers. The hotel's Travel Bureau speaks good English and can set you on your way to Tibet. Double rooms come with complimentary breakfast. Business center. Bike rental.
200 AE, MC, V

SOMETHING SPECIAL

BAGUOBUYI (BAGUOBUYI FENGWEI JIULOU)

The waitresses wear traditional short blouses and trousers, delivering the finest Sichuan food money can buy. The atmosphere is relaxed, but mildly exuberant, and the food is perfect. There's no English menu. Stick to the cheap plates, for the pricier ones are more exotic (like tortoise) and unnecessary. The delectably simple *suancai shaoniurou*, chunks of beef with crumbling potatoes settled in a wash of hot sauce, is pure heaven. The *dandan mian* (spicy noodles) are a sharp and fiery accompaniment.
$$ ✪✪✪✪✪
20 RENMIN NANLU SIDUAN
TEL 028 557-3839
400+ AE, MC, V

CHEN MAPO DOUFU (CHEN MAPO DOUFU DIAN)
$ ✪✪✪
197 XIYULONG JIE
TEL 028 8675-4512
The classic Sichuan dish, *mapo doufu*, must be sampled while in Chengdu. A number of restaurants claim a lineage to the original Chen Mapo Doufu restaurant as does this one. In the city center.
300+ No credit cards accepted

PRICES

HOTELS
An indication of the cost of a double room without breakfast is given by $ signs.

$	Under $40
$$	$40–$100
$$$	$100–$180
$$$$	$180–$350
$$$$$	Over $350

RESTAURANTS
An indication of the cost of a three-course dinner without drinks is given by $ signs.

$	Under $30
$$	$30–$50
$$$	$50–$75
$$$$	$75–$100
$$$$$	Over $100

EMEISHAN

The temples and monasteries on Emeishan all provide accommodations, although of a very basic standard; they are all roughly of the same quality. At the base of the mountain near the bus station, the Teddy Bear Hotel (tel 0833 559-0135) opposite the Teddy Bear Café (see below) is popular with travelers. The Hongzhushan Hotel ($ ✪✪✪; tel 0833 552-5888, fax 0833 333-788) is a three-star option south of Baoguo Monastery that takes major credit cards and has reasonable villa accommodations. The hotel is useful for procuring bus tickets through its travel agency.

TEDDY BEAR CAFÉ
$ ✪✪
On the main road leading to the Baoguo Monastery, the Teddy Bear Café is a magnet for Western travelers to Emeishan. This is the place to stock up on calories and

carbohydrates before your ascent: try the spicy Sichuan dishes, such as *suancai yu*, or sample the Western food. Very useful travel advice. Teddy Bear Hotel opposite.
100+ No credit cards accepted

DAZU

It's better to visit Dazu as a day trip from Chongqing, because accommodations are limited and poor in quality.

LHASA

LHASA HOTEL (LASA FANDIAN)

$$ ○○○
1 MINZU LU
TEL 0891 683-2221
FAX 0891 683-5796

This three-star hotel (formerly a Holiday Inn), north of the Norbu Lingka, is about as good as it gets in Lhasa. Five restaurants (Western, Tibetan and Nepalese, Chinese); business center; ticketing office.
450 All major cards

SNOWLANDS RESTAURANT (XUEYU CANTING)

$ ○○○
4 ZANGYIYUAN LU, NEXT TO SNOWLANDS HOTEL
TEL 0891 633-7323

Popular with travelers, this restaurant serves decent Chinese, Western, Indian and Tibetan dishes,and an English menu is available.
40 No credit cards accepted

INNER MONGOLIA & THE SILK ROAD

ÜRÜMQI

HOI TAK HOTEL (HAIDE JIUDIAN)

$$$$ ○○○○○
HOLIDAY INN
1 DONGFENG LU
TEL 0991 232-2828
FAX 0991 232-1818
www.hoitakhotel.com

The 33-story tower in the center of town offers reasonably equipped and acceptable rooms plus an okay selection of hotel facilities, including a bowling alley and a large range of dining options, from Muslim and Chinese to international cuisine. The hotel advertises itself as a five-star hotel, but you may find it wanting (remember this is Xinjiang and not Shanghai).
318 MC, V

SHERATON ÜRÜMQI HOTEL

$$$$ ○○○○○
9 YOUHAO BEILU
TEL 0991 699-9999
FAX 0991 699-9888
www.starwoodhotels.com

Not yet open at the time of writing, the Sheraton Ürümqi will without doubt be the best choice in the city, bringing its international standards of hospitality and service to the Xinjiang capital. With a choice of six fabulously designed restaurants and cafés, the hotel will also boast the full range of five-star facilities in up to the minute surrounds, including a stunning foyer.
398 All major cards

TURPAN

OASIS HOTEL (LÜZHOU BINGUAN)

$ ○○
41 QINGNIAN LU
TEL 0995 852-2491
FAX 0995 852-3348

One of Turpan's better hotels, attractively adorned with vines and flowers. Large, unkempt double rooms. CITS tour desk. Chinese restaurant.
167 No credit cards accepted

JOHN'S INFORMATION CAFÉ

$
OPPOSITE TURPAN HOTEL (TULUFAN BINGUAN), QINGNIAN NANLU
TEL 0995 852-4237

Chinese and Western food, chilled drinks, plus all the information you need for exploring the dry locality of Turpan. John Hu, the owner, is an intrepid entrepreneur who has other café outposts in Kashgar, Ürümqi, and Dunhuang. Internet access. English menu.
50+ No credit cards accepted

KASHGAR

QINIBAGH HOTEL (QINIWAKE BINGUAN)

$ ○○
93 SEMAN LU
TEL 0998 298-2103
FAX 0998 298-2299

You are at the edge of China here, so don't expect a Holiday Inn or a Shangri-La hotel. A couple of two-star hotels do battle for Kashgar's holiday market. The Qinibagh Hotel occupies the same site as the former British Consulate building, not far from Id Kah Square. Breakfast included. Business center. Internet access.
140 No credit cards accepted

JOHN'S INFORMATION CAFÉ (YUEHAN ZHONGXI CANTING)

$
SEMAN HOTEL, 170 SEMAN LU
TEL 0998 258-1186
E-MAIL johncafe@hotmail.com

This reliable outpost in the Seman Hotel, is a favorite backpacker meeting ground and a source of useful advice for traveling around the region. Coffee, pancakes, Chinese dishes. It can organize trips round Kashgar's sights and into the Taklimakan Desert and to Karakuri Lake. Internet access, bike rental,

English menu.
100+ No credit cards accepted

DUNHUANG

SILK ROAD DUNHUANG (DUNHUANG SHANZHUANG)
$$$ ○○○
DUNYUE LU
TEL 0937 888-2088
FAX 0937 888-2086
www.the-silk-road.com
Settled near the sand dunes of the Mingsha Hills south of Dunhuang City, this modern but traditionally designed hotel is artfully blended into the culture and topography of the region, and it is ideally located for trips to Crescent Moon Lake. Chinese and international restaurants. Business center. Camel-riding tours and live entertainment. Shuttle bus provided.
300 All major cards

JOHN'S INFORMATION CAFÉ
$
NEXT TO FEI TIAN HOTEL, 22 MINGSHAN LU
TEL 0937 882-7000
John's Information Cafés are a link in the Silk Road chain. Travelers come here for clues on exploring the area. Outdoor terrace; train and air tickets arranged. Chinese and Western food. Tours. Bike rental. Internet access.
50+ No credit cards accepted

JIAYUGUAN

GREAT WALL HOTEL (CHANGCHENG BINGUAN)
$ ○○○
6 JIANSHE XILU
TEL 0947 622-5213/622-5288
FAX 0947 622-6016
Jiayuguan is not well served by fine hotels. The Great Wall Hotel is a fortress-like, three-star hotel in the south of town. Good value and reasonably well equipped with amenities, although not plush. Bike rental, travel agency.
160 All major cards

XIAHE

LABRANG HOTEL (LABULENG BINGUAN)
$ ○○
TEL 0941 712-1849
FAX 0941 712-1328
Far out in the west of Xiahe, the Labrang Hotel is a quiet and rewarding retreat with rather scuffed rooms. Restaurant. Bike rental. Reservations recommended.
100+ No credit cards accepted

SNOWLANDS RESTAURANT (XUEYU CANTING)
$
NEXT TO LABRANG MONASTERY
TEL 0941 712-2856
Fine Tibetan, Western, and Chinese fare: apple pancakes, *tsampa* (barley flour dough), yogurt, and more. Friendly place attentive to Western travelers. English menu.
50+ No credit cards accepted

BAOTOU

TIANWAITIAN HOTEL (TIANWAITIAN DAJIUDIAN)
$ ○○○
50 HUDEMULIN DAJIE
TEL 0472 313-7766
FAX 0472 313-1771
This hotel in West Baotou is one of the plushest in town, but the foreigner's surcharge may make you wince. Breakfast included.
218 No credit cards accepted

HOHHOT

ZHAOJUN (ZHAOJUN DAJIUDIAN)
$/$$ ○○○
53 XINHUA DAJIE
TEL 0471 696-2211
FAX 0471 696-8825
Hohhot's hotels aren't the best in China. That said, the Zhaojun can offer a reliable and comfortable stay and although the hotel has little character, the central location is a considerable advantage.
200+ AE, D, V

QINGHAI

QINGHAI HOTEL (QINGHAI BINGUAN)
$ ○○○
152 HUANGHE LU
TEL 0971 614-4888
There's a sparce choice of hotels in Qinghai, so don't expect much. The Qinghai Hotel is about the best in town. There's a branch of CITS in the hotel.
395 No credit cards accepted

THE NORTHEAST

DALIAN

SHANGRI-LA HOTEL (XIANGGELILA DAJIUDIAN)
$$$$ ○○○○○
66 RENMIN LU
TEL 0411 8252-5000
FAX 0411 8252-5050
www.shangri-la.com
Just down Renmin Lu from Zhongshan Square, the superb Shangri-La (one of Dalian's various five-star hotels) puts you in the lap of luxury right in the heart of town. Chinese and Japanese restaurants. Horizon Club executive floor. American bar and café, delicatessen. 191 apartments. Limousine service. Tennis courts.
562 All major cards

DALIAN HOTEL (DALIAN BINGUAN)
$$ ✪✪✪
4 ZHONGSHAN SQUARE
TEL 0411 8263-3111
FAX 0411 8263-4363
Adorning Dalian's elegant hub on Zhongshan Square, the Dalian Hotel is a fine historic building, and inexpensive. Centrally located and stylish. Breakfast included.
220 All major cards

YIXIN RESTAURANT (YIXIN KAOROUDIAN)
$
24 TANGSHAN JIE
TEL 0411 8362-9230
Often heaving with customers, this chain of restaurants provides you with lumps of meat and large servings of vegetables, which you cast onto your own spitting griddle. Loners will feel crowded out, but those looking for gregarious feasting will be more than satisfied. The Yixin offers an alternative to Dalian's plethora of seafood restaurants. There is another branch at 56 Yan'an Lu (tel 0411 8265-5878).
100+ No credit cards accepted

SHENYANG

TRADERS (SHANGMAO FANDIAN)
$$$ ✪✪✪✪
68 ZHONGHUA LU
TEL 024 2341-2288
www.shangri-la.com
An elegant link in the Shangri-La chain of hotels, Traders is a fastidious, stylish port of call in downtown Shenyang. Chinese restaurant, bar, coffee shop. Traders club. Shopping center next door. Limousine service.
592 All major cards

HARBIN

HOLIDAY INN (WANDA JIARI JIUDIAN)
$$ ✪✪✪✪
90 JINGWEI JIE
TEL 0451 8422-6666
FAX 0451 8422-1661
Perched at the end of fashionable Zhongyang Dajie, the Holiday Inn is a reliable, if rather predictable and unexciting, welcoming sign. Clinic, snooker. Airport transportation.
157 All major cards

SHANGRI-LA HOTEL (XIANGGELILA DAJIUDIAN)
$$$ ✪✪✪✪
555 YOUYI LU, DAOLI DISTRICT
TEL 0451 8485-8888
FAX 0451 8462-1666
www.shangri-la.com
An 18-story, first-class hotel near the Songhua River in the Daoli District. The Shangri-La chain consistently steals a lead on the competition. Horizon Club (executive) floors feature free suit pressing, newspaper delivery, lounge facilities, free breakfast buffet, free drinks, and excellent business facilities. Limousine service. Chinese and Western restaurants. Tennis courts.
346 All major cards

HUAMEI WESTERN RESTAURANT (HUAMEI XICANTING)
$
112 ZHONGYANG DAJIE
ACROSS THE ROAD FROM THE MODERN HOTEL
TEL 0451 8467-5574
There are plenty of places around town steaming with Northeast Chinese *jiaozi* (dumplings), but this is the place to further capitalize on Harbin's Russian ingredients. English menu.
400–500 All major cards

CHANGCHUN

SHANGRI-LA CHANGCHUN (XIANGGELILA JIUDIAN)
$$$ ✪✪✪✪
569 XIAN DALU
TEL 0431 898-1818
FAX 0431 898-1919
www.shangri-la.com
The finest rooms in the city and superlative service. The Shangri-La chain has an exclusive formula that cuts no corners and offers the very best, from the impressive lobby to the clean-cut rooms. Two Chinese restaurants, coffee shop, nightclub, delicatessen. Horizon Club. Tennis courts. Limousine service.
458 All major cards

DANDONG

YALUJIANG MANSION (YALUJIANG DASHA)
$ ✪✪
87 JIUWEI LU
TEL 0415 2125-901
FAX 0415 2126-180
Dandong has a primitive hotel sector, appropriate considering its proximity to North Korea. If you have to stay in Dandong, this hotel is the best choice.
176 All major cards

JILIN

JIANGCHENG (JIANGCHENG BINGUAN)
$ ✪✪✪
4 JIANGWAN LU
TEL 0432 245-7721
FAX 0431 245-8973
One of the city's better hotels, but that's not saying much. The Jiangcheng is at least cheap and well situated for trips to the Catholic Church, the Confucian Temple, and the icicle shows along the Songhua River in winter. CITS can be found in the hotel. Free breakfast.
100 All major cards

SHOPPING IN CHINA

Tourist shops such as the Friendship Stores, present in most large cities, are mediocre but useful for souvenirs and presents (silk, cloisonné, ceramics, etc.). Objects of interest often surface in street markets, surrounded by fake antiques and litter from the Cultural Revolution. The most interesting items lie off the beaten track, away from the tourist routes, so dig far and deep. See Customs (p. 355) for export restrictions. Shopping in Hong Kong is more efficient and plentiful, with its international standards of retail and sheer choice.

BEIJING

Also see p. 92.

SHOPPING MALLS

Oriental Plaza
1 Dongchang'an Jie
Vast and glittering shopping complex at the foot of Wangfujing Dajie boasting top-of-the-line goods.

The Friendship Store (Youyi Shangdian)
17 Jianguomen Waijie
tel 0106 500-3311
In the old days, the huge Friendship Store had a monopoly on luxuries. Clothing, delicatessen, supermarket, books, souvenirs. Don't forget the nearby Silk Market.

SHANGHAI

BOOKSHOPS

Shanghai Museum Shop
Shanghai Museum, 201 Renmin Dadao
tel 021 6372-3500
Renmin Square subway
First-class range of books on Chinese arts and history, plus a fine array of gifts and postcards.

DEPARTMENT STORES

Nanjing Lu
Formerly in the English Concession, Nanjing Lu is a colossal shopping swell, partly pedestrianized, running west from the Peace Hotel and the Bund.

Nextage (Xinshiji Shangsha)
1111 Pudong Nanlu
Asia's largest department store boasts a huge range of shops.

Friendship Store (Youyi Shangdian)
40 Beijing Lu
Located just off the Bund, this store has large and worthwhile range of goods and souvenirs.

HONG KONG

North Hong Kong Island is carpeted with top-names. Including **Marks & Spencer** (Shop 120 & 229, The Mall, Pacific Place II, Queensway, tel 2921 8891; Basement—1st floor, Central Tower, 28 Queen's Rd. Central, Central, tel 2921-8059; Shop 102, 254, 355 & 356 Ocean Centre, Harbour City, 5 Canton Rd., Tsim Sha Shui) and **Sogo**, East Point Centre, 555 Hennessy Rd., Causeway Bay.

SHOPPING MALLS

The Mall
Pacific Place, 88 Queensway
Home to a movie theater, restaurants, and shops, and backed up by two five-star hotels, Pacific Place is an excellent shopping experience. Easily reached by tram from Central (5 minutes) or subway (Admiralty MTR).

Prince's Building
5 Ice House St., Central
Very elegant retail environment across the way from the Mandarin Oriental Hotel. Top names, top prices, and sophisticated design.

PHOTOGRAPHY

Color Six Laboratories Ltd.
18a Stanley St., Central
tel 0852 2526-0123
The best outlet for amateur and more experienced photographers. Professional film.

CHINESE MEDICINE

Eu Yan Sang Ltd.
Eu Yan Sang Tower, 11–15 Chatham Rd. South, Kowloon
tel 0852 2366-8321
Take a fantastic tour through the exotic world of Chinese medicine at this premier outlet.

BOOKSHOPS

Swindon Book Co. Ltd
Anson House, 13–15 Lock Rd., Tsim Sha Tsui
tel 0852 2366-8001
Varied collection and knowledgeable staff. English-language books.

SOUVENIRS/ARTS & CRAFTS/CHINESE EMPORIUMS

Yue Hwa Chinese Products Emporium Ltd.
301-309 Nathan Road
Tsim Sha Tsui
tel 0852 2384 0084
Chinese ceramics, cloisonné, clothes, and furniture in a large store. Also at 39 Queen's Road, Central, tel 0852 2522 2333.

MUSIC/CDS

HMV
Ground floor–5th floor, Sands Building, 12 Peking Rd., Tsim Sha Tsui
tel 0852 2302-0122
Tsim Sha Tsui subway
Magnificent range of CDs to stock up with before setting out. Low prices.

HMV
1st floor
Central Building, 1–3 Pedder St., Central
tel 0852 2739-0268
Central subway.

MACAU

Wandering the streets is the best way to shop in Macau. The region around Rua de Caldeira, near the Inner Harbour in the west of the peninsula, is an excellent place to find the dried, sugared meats popular in Macau.

ENTERTAINMENT

Most entertainment in the large towns and cities of China belongs to downtown bars and clubs. The growing number of expatriates and travelers to China has guaranteed an increasingly adventurous drink and dancing scene that didn't really exist 15 years ago. Excluding Hong Kong, cinemas are for Chinese audiences and the language puts them beyond comprehension (unless you speak Chinese). Beijing, Shanghai, Guangzhou, Hong Kong, Kunming, and a few other more entrepreneurial cities have entertainment magazines for expatriates, available at Western bars. Below is a selection of theaters, shows, and venues in China.

BEIJING

ACROBATS

Beijing Chaoyang Theater (Beijing Chaoyang Juchang)
36 Dongsanhuan Beilu
tel 0106 507-2421 or 0106 507-1818
Daily performances of rubber-jointed contortionists and fearless artists.

BEIJING OPERA

Liyuan Theater (Liyuan Juchang)
Qianmen Hotel, 175 Yongan Lu
tel 0106 301-6688 ext. 8860
Nightly performances of classic opera tales. Incomprehensible, but fun.

SUZHOU

Every evening a cultural performance is held at the **Master of the Nets Garden,** featuring musical compositions and Chinese opera. Performances take place between 7:30–10:00 p.m.; tickets cost Y60 and can be bought at the garden.

SHANGHAI

ACROBATS

Shanghai Acrobatics Theater
Shanghai Center Theatre, Shanghai Center, 1376 Nanjing Xilu
tel 021 6279-8663
One of the best venues in China for the legendary performances of Chinese acrobats.

JAZZ

Peace Bar Jazz Band
Peace Hotel, 20 Nanjing Donglu
tel 021 6321-6888 ext 6210
Vintage strummers, some members of the Peace Bar Jazz Band have amazingly struggled on longer than the Rolling Stones. The old-timers go through a succession of pre-Revolution jazz numbers that have been their staple since days long gone. Nightly, 8 p.m.–2 a.m.

HONG KONG

Hong Kong Dolphinwatch
1528a Star House
3 Salisbury Road
Tsim Sha Tsui
tel 0852 2984-1414
web:www.hkdolphinwatch.com
An ecological sideshow with waterborne tours to see Hong Kong's dwindling population of pink dolphins *(Sousa chinensis).*

MOVIE THEATERS

UA Queensway, Ground Floor, The Mall, Pacific Place 1, 88 Queensway, Admiralty
tel 0852 2869-0394
Admiralty subway.

UA Times Square, Ground and 2nd floor, Times Square, 1 Matheson St., Causeway Bay
tel 0852 2506-2904
Causeway Bay subway.

MACAU

Macau Cultural Centre (Omoon Manfa Zhongsam/ Centro Cultural de Macau)
Avenida Xian Xing Hai
tel 0853 797-418
fax 0853 751-401
E-MAIL: mccpm@macau.ctm.net
web:www.ccm.gov.mo
Cinema, theater, concerts of classical music, performances of Chinese opera, musicals, and more. The Cultural Centre consists of auditoria, conference halls, museum space (including the Macau Museum of Art), and a multimedia center. The building itself is a dynamic addition to the Macau skyline.

MACAU BARS

The stretch of shore on Avenida Dr. Sun Yat-sen, opposite the Guanyin statue, has attracted a host of new bars basking in the view. This is where Macau's young set comes to escape a rather barren bar scene. There's little to recommend one bar over the other, but they are mostly theme led. Oskar's Pub in the Holiday Inn, Rua de Pequim, has live music in the evenings. On Taipa there is a gaggle of pubs and bars across the way from the Macau Jockey Club to the west of Taipa Village.

GAMBLING

Gambling is illegal in Hong Kong, so half of Hong Kong's gamblers storm Macau at the weekends. Casinos include the **Lisboa** (the largest), the **Floating Casino** (literally), the **Mandarin Oriental Casino,** and the **Kingsway Casino.** On Taipa, there is a casino in the Hyatt Regency.

SHOWS

The **Crazy Paris Show** is a revue-style show performed nightly in the Lisboa Hotel (tel 0853 377-666).

MUSEUMS

Particularly notable museums are mentioned in the main text; this list is a further selection of museums of general interest throughout China. Telephone numbers are given, but we cannot guarantee an English reply.

BEIJING
Natural History Museum (Ziran Bowuguan)
$
126 Tianqiao Nandajie
tel 0106 702-4431
Huge and absorbing trawl through evolution and the natural world. Just west of the Temple of Heaven. Sporadic English translations. No tickets sold after 4 p.m.

China Art Gallery (Zhongguo Meishuguan)
$
1 Wusi Dajie
tel 010 6400-6326
Well-arranged museum east of Jingshan Park with exhibitions of contemporary Chinese art. Consult the *China Daily* for listings. No English captions. No tickets sold after 4 p.m.

Lu Xun Museum (Lu Xun Bowuguan)
$
19 Gongmenkou Ertiao
tel 010 6616-4168
Fuchengmen subway
Well-tended museum dedicated to China's famous novelist. No English captions. No tickets sold after 3:30 p.m.

TIANJIN
Tianjin Opera Museum (Tianjin Xiju Bowuguan)
$
31 Nanmennei Dajie
tel 022 2727-3443
Historical look at local opera with performances.

SUZHOU
Suzhou Museum (Suzhou Bowuguan)
$
204 Dongbei Jie
tel 0512 754-1534
Not far from the Humble Administrator's Garden, the museum is a jumbled glance back at Suzhou's cultural past.

Suzhou Silk Museum (Suzhou Sichou Bowuguan)
$
2001 Renmin Lu
Close to the North Pagoda, this excellent museum charts the history of silk production (sericulture), a process intimately tied to the prosperity of Suzhou.

SHANGHAI
First National Congress of the Chinese Communist Party (Zhonggong Yidahuizhi Jinianguan)
$
76 Xingye Lu (corner of Huangpi Nanlu)
South Huangpi Road subway
tel 021 6328-5266
The CCP was founded here in July 1921. English captions.

Former Residence of Sun Yat-sen (Sun Zhongshan Guju)
$
7 Xiangshan Lu
tel 021 6437-2954
The founder of Republican China, Sun Yat-sen, lived in this two-story Western-style house while in Shanghai.

LUSHAN
Lushan Museum (Lushan Bowuguan)
East of Lulin Lake, the museum traces the history of Lushan, dwelling on the later Communist infiltration of the society. Also exhibits of local natural history.

People's Hall (Renmin Juchang)
$
504 Hexi Lu
tel 0792 828-2584
Venue of a Communist conference in 1959 that shaped the turbulent Chinese political landscape of the 1960s.

CHANGSHA
Hunan Provincial Museum (Hunansheng Bowuguan)
$$
3 Dongfeng Lu
tel 0731 451-4629
Changsha isn't all about Mao Zedong. The museum contains fascinating Western Han excavations from Mawangdui, near Changsha, including the mummified remains of a Han woman. The site also yielded one of the earliest extant versions of the Taoist classic, the *Daode Jing*.

HONG KONG
University Museum & Art Gallery
Hong Kong University, 94 Bonham Rd., Kennedy Town, Hong Kong Island
tel 0852 2975-5600
Permanent exhibition of antique bronzes and ceramics displayed among the magnificent old Edwardian architecture of the university. Closed Sun. mornings.

Lei Cheng Uk Han Tomb Museum
41 Tonkin St., Sham Shui Po, Kowloon
tel 0852 2386-2863
Cheung Sha Wan subway
Housed in the museum is the earliest historical relic in Hong Kong, a 2,000-year-old Han dynasty tomb. Also displayed are associated funerary objects. Closed Thurs. and some public holidays; Sun. before 1 p.m.

KUNMING
Yunnan Provincial Museum (Yunnansheng Bowuguan)
2 Wuyi Lu
tel 0871 316-3694
Exhibits concentrate on the province's ethnic customs and lore, traced through a panoply of artifacts and mannequins.

CHENGDU
Sichuan Provincial Museum (Sichuansheng Bowuguan)
3 Renmin Nanlu
tel 028 522-2907
A large museum with an extensive collection of archaeological finds from Sichuan

LANGUAGE GUIDE

USEFUL WORDS AND PHRASES

Hello *ni hao*
Goodbye *zaijian*
Thank you *xiexie*
Pardon me *dui bu qi*
I *wo*
We, us *women*
You (sing.) *ni*
You (plur.) *nimen*
He, she *ta*
Them, they *tamen*
My name is… *wo jiao…*
What is your name? *ni gui xing?*
I want… *wo yao…*
Do you have…? *ni you mei you…?*
I do not have… *wo mei you…*
I understand *wo mingbai*
I don't understand *wo bu mingbai*
No problem *mei wenti*
I am American *wo shi meiguoren*
I am English *wo shi yingguoren*
I am Australian *wo shi aodaliyaren*
America *meiguo*
England *yingguo*
Australia *aodaliya*
Canada *jianada*
New Zealand *xinxilan*
China *zhongguo*
France *faguo*
Germany *deguo*
Toilet *cesuo*
Where is…? *zai nar…?*
Where is the toilet? *cesuo zai nar?*
How much is…? *duoshao qian…?*
Beer *pijiu*
Water *shui*
How much is the beer? *pijiu duoshao qian?*
Too expensive *tai gui le*
Vegetables *cai*
Fruit *shuiguo*
Money *qian*
I don't like… *wo bu xihuan…*

NUMBERS

one *yi*
two *er*
two (when followed by a noun) *liang*
three *san*
four *si*
five *wu*
six *liu*
seven *qi*
eight *ba*
nine *jiu*
ten *shi*
11 *shiyi*
20 *ershi*
21 *ershiyi*
30 *sanshi*
100 *yi bai*
200 *liang bai*
1,000 *yi qian*
10,000 *yi wan*
1,000,000 *yi bai wan*
0 *ling*

RESTAURANT

Beef *niurou*
Beer *pijiu*
Chicken *jirou*
Chopsticks *kuaizi*
Coffee *kafei*
Coke *kele*
Dumplings *jiaozi*
Fork *chazi*
Knife *daozi*
Lamb *yangrou*
Menu *caipu/caidan*
Plate *panzi*
Pork *zhurou*
Tea *cha*
Tofu *doufu*
Waitress *xiaojie!*
Water *shui*
Wine *putaojiu*
I am vegetarian *wo chisu*
Warm/hot *re*
Cold *leng*
The bill, please *qing jiezhang*

HOTEL

Do you have any rooms? *you mei you kong fangjian?*
Bed *chuangwei*
Check out *tuifang*
Deluxe room *haohuafang*
Double room *shuangrenfang*
Passport *huzhao*
Reception *zongfuwutai*
Standard room *biaozhunfang*
Suite *taofang*
Toilet paper *weishengzhi*

TIME

Today *jintian*
Tomorrow *mingtian*
Yesterday *zuotian*
What time is it? *ji dian zhong?*

GETTING AROUND

Airplane *feiji*
Airplane ticket *jipiao*
Airport *jichang*
Bicycle *zixingche*
Boarding card *dengjika*
Bus *gonggong qiche/bashi*
Car *qiche*
Map *ditu*
Medium-size bus *zhongba*
Seat *zuowei*
Small bus *xiaoba*
Subway *ditie*
Taxi *chuzu qiche*
Ticket *piao*
Train *huoche*
I want to go to… *wo xiang qu…*
How far is it? *duo yuan?*
Give me a receipt, OK? *gei wo yi ge shoutiao, hao bu hao?*

EMERGENCY

Ambulance *jiuhuche*
Antibiotics *kangjunsu*
Doctor *yisheng*
Fire! *zhao huo le!*
Help! *jiuming a!*
Hospital *yiyuan*
Police *jingcha*
Public Security Bureau (PSB) *gonganju*
I feel ill *wo bu shufu*

DIRECTIONS

North *bei*
South *nan*
East *dong*
West *xi*
Left *zuo*
Right *you*
Inside *limian*
Outside *waimian*

POST OFFICE

Envelope *xinfeng*
Letter *xin*
Post office *youju*
Telephone *dianhua*

SIGHTSEEING

Avenue *dadao*
Lake *hu*
Main street *dajie*
Mountain *shan*
River *he, jiang*
Road *lu*
Street *jie*
Temple *simiao/si/guan*

MENU READER

The following are recommended regional dishes.

BEIJING (PEKING), NORTH, & NORTHEASTERN DISHES IN BEIJING RESTAURANTS & EATERIES IN THE NORTH

Beijing duck	*Beijing kaoya*
Braised fish in soy sauce	*hongshao yu*
Braised spare ribs in soy sauce	*hongshao paigu*
Drunken crab	*zuixie*
Drunken shrimps	*zuixia*
Dumplings	*shuijiao*
Egg and tomato soup	*xihongshi jidan tang*
Hotpot	*huoguo*
Steamed crab	*qingzheng pangxie*
Stewed pork with rice noodles	*zhurou dun fentiao*
Stewed ribs with potatoes	*paigu dun tudou*

SHANGHAI/EASTERN CHINESE DISHES IN RESTAURANTS IN SHANGHAI, JIANGSU, & ZHEJIANG PROVINCE

Beggar's chicken	*fugui ji*
Cold spiced beef	*xuxiang niurou*
Drunken pigeon with wine sauce	*zuixiang ruge*
Fried crab with salty egg	*xiandan chaoxie*
Quick-fried freshwater shrimps	*qingchao xiaren*
Shanghai crab in wine	*zuixie*
Shanghai dumplings	*xiaolongbao*
Smoked fresh yellow fish	*xun xinxian huangyu*

CANTONESE/CHAOZHOU DISHES IN RESTAURANTS IN HONG KONG, MACAU, & THE SOUTH (CANTONESE IN BRACKETS)

Dim sum

Barbecued pork buns	*cha shao bao (cha siu bao)*
Deep-fried shrimps in bread crumbs	*suzha fengwei xia*
Fried dumplings	*guo tie (wok tit)*
Pork and shrimp dumplings	*shao mai (siu mai)*
Rice-flour rolls with shrimp or pork	*chang fen (cheung fan)*
Shrimp dumplings	*xia jiao (ha gau)*
Spare ribs	*paigu (paigwat)*
Spring rolls	*chun juan (chun guen)*

Other dishes

Barbecued pork	*chashao (chasiu)*
Deep-fried stuffed chicken wings	*cuipi niang jiyi*
Roast crispy pigeon with soya sauce	*shengchou huang cuipi ruge*
Shark's fin soup	*dayuchi tang (daiyuchee tong)*
Steamed crab	*zhengxie (jinghai)*

SICHUAN DISHES IN RESTAURANTS IN CHENGDU, CHONGQING, & AROUND CHINA

Chicken with chili	*lazi jiding*
Eggplant in hot fish sauce	*yuxiang qiezi*
Fish and cabbage in spicy soup	*suancai yu*
Hot-and-sour soup	*suanla tang*
Mapo tofu (tofu with pork in spicy sauce)	*mapo doufu*
Meat strips in hot fish sauce	*yuxiang rousi*
Pork slices in chili	*shuizhu roupian*
Spicy noodles	*dandan mian*

INDEX

Bold page numbers indicate illustrations

T

U

V

Founded in 1888, the National Geographic Society is one of the largest nonprofit scientific and educational organizations in the world. It reaches more than 285 million people worldwide each month through its official journal, NATIONAL GEOGRAPHIC, and its four other magazines; the National Geographic Channel; television documentaries; radio programs; films; books; videos and DVDs; maps; and interactive media. National Geographic has funded more than 8,000 scientific research projects and supports an education program combating geographic illiteracy.

For more information, please call 1-800-NGS LINE (647-5463) or write to the following address: National Geographic Society,1145 17th Street N.W.,Washington, D.C. 20036-4688 U.S.A.

Visit us online at: www.nationalgeographic .com/books

For information about special discounts for bulk purchases, please contact National Geographic Books Special Sales: ngspecsales@ngs.org

ILLUSTRATIONS CREDITS

Illustrations credits
Abbreviations for terms appearing below: (t) top; (b) bottom; (l) left; (r) right; (c) center

Cover, (l) Gettyone/Stone. (c) James Montgomery/Imagestate. (r) Gettyone/Stone. Spine, James Montgomery /Imagestate. Back cover inset, Ingrid Booz Morejohn/Picture Works. 1, Jeremy Horner/Corbis UK Ltd. 2/3, China Panorama. 4, Nigel Hicks. 9, Catherine Karnow. 10/11, Luo Xiaoguang/CORBIS. 12/13, Tibor Bognár/ CORBIS. 14/15, Yann Layma/Gettyone/Stone. 16/17, Lowe Paul/Magnum Photos. 19, Keren Su/Corbis UK Ltd. 20, Catherine Karnow. 23, O. Louis Mazzatenta/National Geographic Society. 24, Arthur M Sackler Museum, Harvard University Art Museums, USA/Bridgeman Art Library. 25, O. Louis Mazzatenta/National Geographic Society. 26/27, Nick Bonetti/Eye Ubiquitous. 29, Reza/National Geographic Society. 30, The ArtArchive. 31, The ArtArchive. 32/33, Maria Stenzel/National Geographic Society. 34, The ArtArchive. 35, AKG-images. 36, The ArtArchive. 37, Hulton Getty Picture Collection Ltd. 38, AKG-images.. 39, Hulton Getty Picture Collection Ltd. 40/41, Jodi Cobb/National Geographic Society. 43, Macduff Everton/National Geographic Society. 44, The Art Archive. 45, Freer Gallery, Smithsonian Institution, Washington, USA/Bridgeman Art Library. 46/47, Stuart Franklin/National Geographic Society. 48/49, China Panorama. 50, Kobal Collection. 51, Lou Linwei/ Alamy Ltd. 53, James Davis Worldwide. 56-57, Panorama Media (Beijing)/Alamy Ltd. 58/59, Catherine Karnow. 60(t), RF/CORBIS. 60(b), Robert Harding Picture Library. 61, Ingrid Booz Morejohn/Picture Works. 62, James Davis Worldwide. 63, Leon Schudeberg/Eye Ubiquitous. 64, Macduff Everton/National Geographic Society. 65, Catherine Karnow. 66, Paul Slattery. 67(t), Xie, Guang Hui/China Tourism Photo Library. 67(b), Thomas Hoepker/Magnum Photos. 68/69, 71, Ingrid Booz Morejohn/Picture Works. 72, Paddy Booz/Picture Works. 73(t), China Panorama. 73(b), Julia Waterlow/Eye Ubiquitous. 74, Paul Slattery. 75, James Davis Worldwide. 76/77, Gordon Clements/Axiom. 77, Robert Harding Picture Library. 78, Travel Ink/Alamy Ltd. 79, Travelchinaguide .com. 81, Ingrid Booz Morejohn/ Picture Works. 82, Travelchinaguide .com. 83, Ingrid Booz Morejohn/ Picture Works. 84/85, China Panorama. 85, China Panorama. 87, Ethel Davies/Imagestate. 88/89, Ingrid Booz Morejohn/ Picture Works. 90/91, James Davis Worldwide. 91, Ingrid Booz Morejohn/Picture Works. 93, Ingrid Booz Morejohn/Picture Works. 95, Liu Liqun/CORBIS. 96, Peter Adams/Alamy Ltd. 98, Julia Waterlow /Eye Ubiquitous. 99, Travelchinaguide .com. 100/101, O. Louis Mazzatenta/ National Geographic Society. 102(l), O. Louis Mazzatenta/National Geographic Society. 102(r), O. Louis Mazzatenta/National Geographic Society. 104, Ingrid Booz Morejohn/Picture Works. 105, Ingrid Booz Morejohn/ Picture Works. 106/107, Ingrid Booz Morejohn/Picture Works. 108/109, Ingrid Booz Morejohn/Picture Works. 110, Damian Harper. 111, Ingrid Booz Morejohn/Picture Works. 112, Archivo Iconografico, S. A./Corbis UK Ltd. 114/115, Ingrid Booz Morejohn/ Picture Works. 115, Ingrid Booz Morejohn/Picture Works. 117, Guy Marks/Axiom. 118/119, Paul Slattery. 120/121, Ingrid Booz Morejohn/ Picture Works. 121, Ingrid Booz Morejohn/Picture Works. 122, Ingrid Booz Morejohn/Picture Works. 123, Ingrid Booz Morejohn/Picture Works. 124, Ingrid Booz Morejohn/Picture Works. 126, Historical Picture Archive /Corbis UK Ltd. 127, Ingrid Booz Morejohn/Picture Works. 128, Ingrid Booz Morejohn/Picture Works. 129, Ingrid Booz Morejohn/Picture Works. 130, Ingrid Booz Morejohn/Picture Works. 131, Ingrid Booz Morejohn/ Picture Works. 132, China Panorama. 134, James Davis Worldwide. 135, Yiqing Wang. 136, Ingrid Booz Morejohn/Picture Works. 137, Ingrid Booz Morejohn/Picture Works. 139, Ingrid Booz Morejohn/Picture Works. 141, Travelchinaguide.com. 142, Paul Slattery. 144/45, Travelchinaguide.com. 146, View Stock/Alamy Ltd. 147, Travelchinaguide.com. 148, Damian Harper. 150/151, Stuart Franklin/ National Geographic Society. 153, Ingrid Booz Morejohn/Picture Works. 154, Ingrid Booz Morejohn/Picture Works. 156, Panorama Media (Beijing) /Alamy Ltd. 157, Damian Harper. 158/159, Mary Evans Picture Library. 159, Mary Evans Picture Library. 160, Ingrid Booz Morejohn/Picture Works. 161, Ingrid Booz Morejohn/Picture Works. 162/163, Alain le Garsmeur/ Gettyone/Stone. 164, Ingrid Booz Morejohn/Picture Works. 165, Ingrid Booz Morejohn/Picture Works. 166, Ingrid Booz Morejohn/Picture Works. 168, Ingrid Booz Morejohn/Picture Works. 169, Lang Lang/CORBIS. 171, Panorama Media (Beijing)/Alamy Ltd. 173, Keren Su/Corbis UK Ltd. 174/175, China Panorama. 176, Catherine Karnow. 177(t), Maria Stenzel/National Geographic Society. 177(b) China Panorama. 179, Dennis Cox/Alamy Ltd. 180, Liu Liqun/CORBIS. 182, Ingrid Booz Morejohn/Picture Works. 185(t), Ingrid Booz Morejohn/Picture Works. 185(b), Gueorgui Pinkhassov/ Magnum Photos. 186/87, Tibor Bognar/CORBIS. 187, Ingrid Booz Morejohn/Picture Works. 188, China Newsphoto/Reuters/CORBIS. 189, Ingrid Booz. Morejohn/Picture Works. 190, Nick Battersby/Travel Ink. 191, Eugene Hoshiko/AP/Wide World Photos. 193(t), Ingrid Booz Morejohn/ Picture Works. 193(b), Ingrid Booz Morejohn/Picture Works. 194, Ingrid Booz Morejohn/ Picture Works. 195, Visual Arts Library (London)/Alamy Ltd. 196/97, Jean Pierre Amet/Bel Ombra/CORBIS. 198, Ingrid Booz Morejohn/Picture Works. 199(tl), Simon Colmer and Abby Rex/Alamy Ltd. 199(tr), Catherine Karnow. 199(b), Damian Harper. 200/201, Ingrid Booz Morejohn/ Picture Works. 202, Asian Art and Archaeology, Inc./CORBIS. 203 (l), Visual Arts Library (London)/Alamy Ltd. 203 (r), Christie's Images/CORBIS. 204/205, Victoria and Albert Museum, London, UK/Bridgeman Art Library. 204(t), Percival David Foundation/Art Archive. 204(b), Trygve Bolstat/Panos Pictures. 205(bl), Royal Ontario Museum/Corbis UK Ltd. 205(br), Royal Ontario Museum/Corbis UK Ltd. 206, Damian Peters/Eye Ubiquitous. 207, Nigel Hicks. 208, Ingrid Booz Morejohn/Picture Works. 210, Nigel Hicks. 211, Nigel Hicks. 212, Peter Bengdahl/Alamy Ltd. 215, James L. Stanfield/National Geographic Society. 217, Damian Harper. 218, Ingrid Booz Morejohn/Picture Works. 219, Ingrid Booz Morejohn/ Picture Works. 221, Catherine Karnow. 224, Paul Yeung/Reuters /CORBIS. 225, Jodi Cobb/National Geographic Society. 226, David Henley/CPA Media. 228, Nigel Hicks. 229, Iain Masterton/ Alamy Ltd. 231, Ed Pritchard/Gettyone/Stone. 232, Catherine Karnow. 233, Rex Butcher /Gettyone/Stone. 234, Jodi Cobb/ National Geographic Society. 235, Catherine Karnow. 236, Roger Fletcher/Alamy Ltd. 237, AA Photo Library/A Kouprianoff. 239, Ace Stock Limited/Alamy Ltd. 240, Jon Bower/ Alamy Ltd. 241, Macduff Everton/ Corbis UK Ltd. 242, Nigel Hicks. 242/243, Nigel Hicks. 244, Nik Wheeler/Robert Harding Picture Library. 245, Catherine Karnow. 246/247, Catherine Karnow. 249, Yang Liu/CORBIS. 250, Adina Tovy Amsel/Eye Ubiquitous. 252, Ingrid Booz Morejohn/Picture Works. 253, Philip Jones Griffiths/Magnum Photos. 254, B. Barbey/Magnum Photos. 254/255, Catherine Karnow. 257, Keren Su/Corbis UK Ltd. 259, Tom Nebbia/Corbis UK Ltd. 260/261, Paul Slattery. 261, Ingrid Booz Morejohn/Picture Works. 262, Ingrid Booz

Morejohn/Picture Works. 263, Keren Su/CORBIS. 264, Paul Slattery. 264/265, Nick Bonetti/Eye Ubiquitous. 266, Nigel Hicks. 267, Ingrid Booz Morejohn/Picture Works. 268, China Panorama. 269, Nigel Hicks. 270, Ingrid Booz Morejohn/Picture Works. 270/271, Nick Bonetti/Eye Ubiquitous. 272/273, Paddy Booz/Picture Works. 273, Damian Harper. 274, Paddy Booz/Picture Works. 275, Ingrid Booz Morejohn/Picture Works. 277, James Davis Worldwide. 278, Guy Marks/Axiom. 280/281, Julia Waterlow/Eye Ubiquitous. 282, Ingrid Booz Morejohn/Picture Works. 283, Ingrid Booz Morejohn/ Picture Works. 285, Keren Su/Corbis UK Ltd. 287, Maria Stenzel/National Geographic Society. 288/289, Ian Cummings/Axiom. 290, Julia Waterlow/Eye Ubiquitous. 291, Damian Harper. 292, JTB Photo/Alamy Ltd. 293, China Panorama. 294/295, Ingrid Booz Morejohn/Picture Works. 295, Bruno Barbey/Magnum Photos. 296, Ingrid Booz Morejohn/Picture Works. 297, Ingrid Booz Morejohn/Picture Works. 298, Maria Stenzel/National Geographic Society. 299, Nigel Hicks. 300(t), Ingrid Booz Morejohn/Picture Works. 300(b), Bushnell/Soifer/Gettyone/Stone. 301, Ingrid Booz Morejohn/Picture Works. 302/303, Leon Schulberg/Eye Ubiquitous. 303, Nigel Hicks. 304/305, Ian Berry/Magnum Photos. 306, China Panorama. 307, Ingrid Booz Morejohn/Picture Works. 308, Nigel Hicks. 309, Keren Su/Corbis UK Ltd. 311, Julia Waterlow/Eye Ubiquitous. 312, Carl van der Shult/National Geographic Society. 313, Reza/National Geographic Society. 314/315, Nigel Hicks. 315, Nigel Hicks. 316, Paul Slattery. 317, Nigel Hicks. 318, Ingrid Booz Morejohn/Picture Works. 319, Robert Van Der Hils/Gettyone/Stone. 320, James Strachan/Gettyone/Stone. 322, Julia Waterlow/Eye Ubiquitous. 322/323, Ingrid Booz Morejohn/National Geographic Society. 324, G. Corrigan /Robert Harding Picture Library. 325, Carl van der Shult/National Geographic Society. 327, Paddy Booz/Picture Works. 328, Ingrid Booz Morejohn/Picture Works. 329, David Sanger/Alamy Ltd. 330, Ian Berry/Magnum Photos. 331, Julia Waterlow/Eye Ubiquitous. 332, Ingrid Booz Morejohn/Picture Works. 333, Julie Waterlow; Eye Ubiquitous/CORBIS. 335, Ingrid Booz Morejohn/Picture Works. 336, China Tourism Press/Getty Images. 338, Nigel Hicks. 339, Ingrid Booz Morejohn/Picture Works. 340/341, China Photo Library Ltd. 341, Travelchinaguide.com. 342/343, Keren Su/Gettyone/Stone. 344/345, Ingrid Booz Morejohn/Picture Works. 346/347, Bruce Dale/National Geographic Society. 349, Picture Works.

Published by the National Geographic Society
John M. Fahey, Jr., *President and Chief Executive Officer*
Gilbert M. Grosvenor, *Chairman of the Board*
Nina D. Hoffman, *Executive Vice President; President, Books Publishing Group*
Kevin Mulroy, *Senior Vice President and Publisher*
Leah Bendavid-Val, *Director of Photography Publishing and Illustrations*
Marianne R. Koszorus, *Director of Design*
Elizabeth L. Newhouse, *Director of Travel Publishing*
Barbara A. Noe, *Senior Editor and Project Manager*
Cinda Rose, *Art Director*
Carl Mehler, *Director of Maps*
Caroline Hickey, *Senior Researcher (Project Editor 2007 edition)*
Gary Colbert, *Production Director*
Richard S. Wain, *Production Project Manager*
Steven D. Gardner, Kay Hankins, Lynsey Jacob, Amy Jones, Marshall Kiker, Val Mattingley, Carol Stroud, Ruth Thompson, Maura Walsh, and Meredith Wilcox, *Contributors*

First Edition: Edited and designed by AA Publishing (a trading name of Automobile Association Developments Limited, whose registered office is Millstream, Maidenhead Road, Windsor, Berkshire, England SL4 5GD. Registered number: 1878835).
Rachel Alder, Marilynne Lanng, *Project Managers*
David Austin, *Senior Art Editor*
Allen Stidwill, *Editor*
Phillip Barfoot, *Designer*
Inna Nogeste, *Senior Cartographic Editor*
Cartography by AA Cartographic Production
Richard Firth, *Production Director*
Steve Gilchrist, *Prepress Production Controller*
Picture Research by Zooid Pictures Ltd.
River cruise maps drawn by Chris Orr Associates, Southampton, England
Cutaway illustrations drawn by Maltings Partnership, Derby, England

National Geographic Traveler: China , Second Edition (2007)
ISBN-13: 978-1-4262-0035-9

Library of Congress Cataloging-in- Publication Data (1st edition)
Harper, Damian.
The National Geographic traveler : China / Damian Harper.
p. cm.
Includes index.
ISBN 0-7922-7921-2
1. China--Description and travel. I. Title: China. II. Title.

DS712 .H365 2001
915.104'6--dc21 00-052682

Printed and bound by Cayfosa Quebecor, Barcelona, Spain.
Color separations by Leo Reprographic Ltd., Hong Kong
Cover separations by L.C. Repro, Aldermaston, U.K.